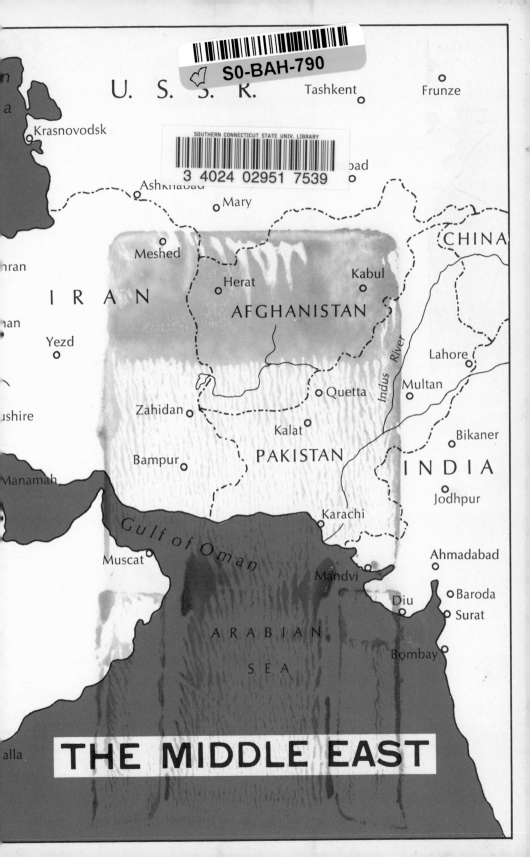

U. S. S. R.   Tashkent   Frunze

Krasnovodsk

Ashkhabad   Mary

Meshed   CHINA

IRAN   Herat   Kabul

AFGHANISTAN

Yezd

Indus River   Lahore

Zahidan   Quetta   Multan

Kalat   Bikaner

Bampur   PAKISTAN   INDIA

Manamah   Jodhpur

Karachi

Muscat   Gulf of Oman

Ahmadabad

Mandvi

Baroda
Diu   Surat

ARABIAN

SEA   Bombay

THE MIDDLE EAST

DAVID FELLMAN
Vilas Professor of Political Science
University of Wisconsin
ADVISORY EDITOR TO DODD, MEAD & COMPANY

POLITICAL SYSTEMS OF THE MIDDLE EAST IN THE 20TH CENTURY

W. F. ABBOUSHI

UNIVERSITY OF CINCINNATI

DODD, MEAD & COMPANY

NEW YORK   1970

POLITICAL
SYSTEMS
OF THE
MIDDLE EAST
IN THE
20TH CENTURY

To My Wife, Leah

EDITOR'S INTRODUCTION

THE MIDDLE EAST was the cradle of human civilization. While the great centers of power have shifted from time to time to various other parts of the world, it has always been an important center of population, culture, religion, commerce and government. For many centuries the home of vigorous independent nations, the Middle East has through its long history experienced all the vicissitudes which the human race has endured through the millennia of historic time. With the growth of the modern industrial systems in the West, the Middle East gradually slipped into various forms of subservience to the rising Western powers. The revolt against colonialism, however, has been, in both Asia and Africa, one of the leading developments of the contemporary world. Nowhere have the currents of this revolt been more powerful and more sustained than in the Middle East.

A group of new states has emerged from the ruins of an ancient past. They stand at the crossroads between Europe, Asia and Africa. They possess much of the world's oil reserves. They operate at the throat of a great deal of the world's commerce. They are experimenting with various forms of economic development and political organization. The festering, bitter conflict between Israel and the Arab states commands the attention of the entire world, since it could lead to world war.

Clearly this is a portion of the world which cannot be ignored. On the contrary, there is great need for more knowledge and more understanding of the area. Professor Abboushi, in writing this book, has made a significant contribution to this end. From its earliest days, American political science has been concerned with the description and analysis of comparative political institutions. Increasingly, as the countries of the Middle East, moving from static to dynamic conditions, grapple with the stubborn problems of economic development and state-building, they became important to scholars who are concerned with probing the foundations of man's political experience.

Professor Abboushi seeks in this book, which is addressed to college students, to describe and to explain the governmental and political systems of the states of the Middle East. His scholarship is wide-ranging, objective and dispassionate. A serious study of this book will add to the student's grasp of comparative political institutions. It will deepen his understanding of the world he lives in, and expand his intellectual horizons. The fulfillment of such purposes requires no further explication.

DAVID FELLMAN

PREFACE

AS A region, the Middle East covers more countries than I deal with in this book. I have selected for analysis those which in many respects represent the whole region, and I have made indirect references to the important events in the countries which are not included. If this arrangement does not seem very satisfactory to some scholars and teachers, it might be a consolation for them to remember that a more comprehensive coverage of the Middle East would increase the problem of limited classroom time or semester and quarter time. It is, therefore, better to concentrate on the few countries which seem to represent the whole region than to deal with all the political divisions of the Middle East without giving these divisions an adequate and fair treatment.

In writing the book I have made three important assumptions about the best method by which to help the reader understand Middle Eastern politics. First, I assumed that he has very little or no background in the history and politics of the area. Consequently, I attempted a simple and direct approach to the problems of the Middle East. I also attempted to explain foreign terminology, concepts, and institutions before proceeding to analyze problems, events, and circumstances.

The second assumption is that it is less difficult for the reader to understand the politics of the Middle East if he is able to deal with each country separately than if he is compelled to deal with the region as a whole. However, I have attempted to let the political picture of the whole region develop in the political laboratories of the separate countries, especially when reference is made to the foreign policies of these countries and their relations to each other.

The third assumption is that politics cannot be understood without the aid of history, economics, and cultural evaluation. I have, therefore, attempted to combine these elements in my analysis of Middle Eastern politics. In fact, the book should be of interest to both history and political science students. The economic and cultural factors mentioned in this book were limited to their relevance to history and politics and were designed to broaden the knowledge of the reader without requiring expert knowledge in these fields.

Many people have helped me in writing this book, and I am eternally indebted to them. For useful advice, I wish to thank Professor Harold M. Vinacke of the University of Cincinnati and Professor George Lenczowski of the University of California, Berkeley. For giving me my first lessons on Middle East politics, I wish to thank Professor Max Mark of Wayne State University. Mr. Robert Muir provided a greatly appreciated technical and editorial assistance. His contribution to the book was of immense value. Miss Barbara Henke, one of my graduate students, was very patient in typing the final draft of the manuscript, and she stimulated my thinking by bombarding me with questions.

Of course, I wish to thank those whose moral support has enabled me to survive the long hours of work. They are my parents, Fahmi and Nazlah Abboushi, who also contributed greatly to my education; my wife, Leah, who had more confidence in my ability to write than I; Samir Amin, Tom Kralian, Salim Sarafa, Faisal Arabo, Donald Kress, and Fuad Ghazali, who helped me pull through the darkest time of my undergraduate years; my good friend and colleague, Jay C. Heinlein, for his confidence in me and his encouragement; Dr. Charles Weichert and Dr. Robert Wessel also for their encouragement. Finally I wish to thank Wayne State University and the Taft Faculty Committee of the University of Cincinnati for their grants which made it possible for me to visit the Middle East four times since 1965.

W. F. ABBOUSHI

CONTENTS

THE MIDDLE EAST
AS A REGION

"MIDDLE East" is not a precise term; originally, it was used to describe the middle region of southern Asia, the other regions of this vast territory being the "Near" and the "Far" East. According to this traditional concept, the terms Near East, Middle East, and Far East are geographic designations, and each of the three designations assumes the existence of the other two. Historically, the term Near East applied to the territories along the coastline of the eastern Mediterranean. It has also been used to describe the territories which were under the Ottoman Empire until World War I. Although the terms Middle East and Near East are often used interchangeably, it is more correct to think of the Near East as a smaller area than the Middle East.

During World War II, the term Middle East became associated with the British military campaigns of Field Marshals Archibald Wavell, Harold Alexander, and Bernard Montgomery, and today the British public is accustomed to think of the Middle East in these terms. The confusion is even greater in the United States, where numerous definitions are given and no distinction is made between the Middle East and the Near East. In this book, the Middle East includes the Nile Valley, the Fertile Crescent, Arabia, Turkey, and Iran.

RELIGIOUS DIVERSITY

The Middle East gave the world the three great monotheistic religions: Judaism, Christianity, and Islam. This contribution alone makes the area the spiritual center of the world, and a great number of people from all over the world travel to worship in the Middle East every year. Zoroastrianism, Manicheism, Mithraism, and other religions also developed in the Middle East.

Judaism was instrumental in the development of modern civilization,

1

especially through its influence on Christianity and Islam. Judaism estab-lished the basis of Christian and Muslim ethics, and the Jewish concept of monotheism was inherited by the other two great religions. However, in its later development, Judaism was influenced by Christianity, the outcome of their interaction in the European environment.

The dispersion of the Jews after the Babylonian captivity in the sixth century B.C. resulted in the decline of Jewish influence on the nature and development of Middle Eastern life. With the passage of time, Judaism experienced a limited revival in the Western world. However, several cen-turies after the dispersion, Judaism divided into a number of sects. But the most outstanding development occurred at the end of the nineteenth cen-tury: Jewish nationalism began to assert itself, and the Zionist movement became the expression of its will. Zionist efforts to create a Jewish state in Palestine were crowned by the establishment of the State of Israel in 1948. This event gave Judaism a new identity: for the first time since the disper-sion of the Jews, Judaism became associated with a state.

In addition to Judaism, the Middle East produced Christianity. In the course of its development, Christianity also divided into sects, and today all the sects are represented in the Middle East. The most important of these sects are the Greeks (Orthodox), Latins (Roman Catholic), Copts (Egyp-tian), Abyssinians, Nestonians, Jacobites, Maronites, and Armenians. The rise of Islam in the seventh century forced some of these sects to affiliate with Rome and to accept the Pope's spiritual leadership. Among the sects so affiliated are the Copts and the Maronites. But most of the Christian sects remained unaffiliated. Today, more than twenty sects are represented in the Middle East, including the small minority of Protestants converted by Western missionaries during the nineteenth century.

In the Arab countries of the Middle East most of the Christians are Arabic-speaking and are thoroughly Arabized. Some of them have been active in twentieth-century Arab national movements. For example, the founder of the Baath party of Syria, Michael Aflaq, is a Christian, as is Faris al-Khouri, many times prime minister of Syria. However, in Lebanon some Christians oppose an Arab political union; they wish to maintain the independence of Lebanon, the only Arab country in which Christians are politically dominant.

The great majority of the people of the Middle East are Muslim. Islam originated in the Arabian peninsula in the seventh century and spread, mainly by conquest, to become the principal religion of the Middle East. Unlike Christianity, Islam was associated with the state from the begin-ning. This is why both the fortunes and the misfortunes of the Islamic reli-gion were dependent upon the state. The downfall of the Ottoman Em-pire during World War I brought an end to Islam as a state religion, and most of the Islamic countries of the Middle East became secular states in fact if not in theory.

Theoretically, Islam is more than a religion. It is also a state system and a system of law which is comprehensive and detailed. The law covers such areas as social welfare, taxation, marriage, divorce, inheritance, and the duties and obligations of individuals. Because of its political and legal prescriptions, Islam has become a controversial issue in modern Islamic society. The issue relates to the religion's compatibility with the requirements of twentieth-century life and its ability to lead the forces of progress and modernization in the Islamic world.

Although the controversy continues, it is largely a matter of intellectual discussion, and efforts to maintain Islam as a legal system are limited to political movements like the Muslim Brotherhood. However, most Islamic countries have ignored Islam as a political and legal system; only Saudi Arabia pays any attention to the legal and political doctrines of Islam. Other Middle Eastern countries either honor the religion by declaring in their constitutions that it is the state religion and proceed to ignore it or they ignore it altogether.

Like Christianity, Islam is divided into many sects. The majority of Muslims (perhaps 90 per cent) are Sunnites (orthodox). This sect makes the Koran and the prophet's teaching the most important sources of Islamic law. After the death of Mohammed in 632, the Sunnites took the position that the leadership of Islam should not be limited to the prophet's family and its descendants. This limitation was essentially instituted by the Shi'ites.

The Shi'ites supported Ali, Mohammed's son-in-law, as the prophet's successor. In time, the Shi'ites divided to subsects: the Isma'ilis, the followers of Agha Khan; the Zaidis, most of whom live in Yemen; and the Imamis, who constitute the majority of the Shi'ites. Today, the Shi'ites are the majority in Iran and Yemen, and they constitute a sizable minority of the population of southern Iraq.

In the eighteenth century, another Islamic sect was established by Muhammed Ibn Abdul Wahhab, an Arab reformer. Wahhab attempted to purify Islam from what he considered were unorthodox theories and practices; he wanted to restore the religion to its simpler form, the one which existed during the prophet's lifetime. Consequently, the Wahhabists became the puritans of Islam and in time a significant power in the Arabian peninsula. In the nineteenth century, they were in control of the peninsula's interior, and in the twentieth century they expanded, under the leadership of Ibn Saud, to include the greater part of the peninsula. In 1926, the state of Saudi Arabia was created, and it is today a Wahhabist state.

LINGUISTIC DIVERSITY

The predominant language of the Middle East is Arabic. This language developed in Arabia, and, with Ethiopic, it forms the southern branch of the Semitic languages. Northern Arabic, from which the classical Arabic of today derives, developed from Aramaic, the tongue spoken by Jesus.

The spread of the Arabic language outside Arabia was the result of the expansion of Islamic power. However, Islam traveled faster and farther than the Arabic language: more people converted to Islam than adopted the Arabic language, and in the world today there are more Muslims than there are Arabic-speaking people.

The Koran, the holy book of the Muslims, helped the Arabic language survive as one of the major languages of the world. This book is considered by the Arab intelligentsia to be the best book ever written in the Arabic language. It is appreciated for its literary qualities—its style and beauty—and many Arab Christians read the Koran for esthetic reasons. In fact, the Koran was an important source of Arabic literature for many of the Christian writers of the late nineteenth century, writers who later became known and respected for their contribution to the Arabic language.

The Arabic language exists in two forms: the classical and the colloquial. The classical is the written language and is used in formal communication. The classical language is used throughout the world in formal speeches, radio announcements, newspapers, and books. It is thus an important means of communication and one that serves as a unifying force in the Arab world. However, not all Arabs understand the classical language, since the colloquial form is the one used as the spoken language. Consequently, classical Arabic is the language of the elite; the colloquial is the language of the uneducated masses.

The colloquial Arabic consists of a great number of local and regional dialects. The syntax in many of these dialects is about the same, but there is a great deal of variation in the pronunciation. Thus, the Egyptian dialect is easily understood by the Arab Palestinian, but the North African dialects are not. Furthermore, in each country there are almost as many dialects as there are communities. Usually, however, the local dialects are not formidable obstacles of communication for the people of the same country.

Differences in the colloquial form ought not be exaggerated. They are not as pronounced as those between the Latin languages. An Arab from Palestine would have difficulty communicating with an Arab from Morocco, but if the two men have had some schooling they could always use classical words instead of colloquial words when necessary.

Another Middle Eastern language is Turkish, which is spoken in Turkey, of course, as the main and official language, and in Iran and the Soviet Union as a minority language. The Turkish language is of central Asiatic origin. Until 1928 it was written in Arabic characters, but afterward Latin characters were used instead.

Persian is the major language of Iran; it is an Indo-Aryan language written in Arabic characters. A fourth Middle Eastern language is Kurdish, the language of about one and a half million Kurds who live mainly in Turkey, Iraq, Syria, and Iran. The Kurds are Muslims belonging to the Sunnite sect of Islam. Finally, the Hebrew language is the official language of Israel. Because of the diversity of the background of the Israeli Jews, many of them do not speak Hebrew, and it is the major task of the Israeli government to make the Hebrew language the spoken language of all Israelis. There are other languages in the Middle East, such as the Armenian and Aramaic languages, but they are used by very small minorities.

WESTERN INFLUENCES

Because the Middle East has been a favorite target of invaders and conquerors throughout history, its social, economic, and political institutions have been unstable as well as continually transitional. Foreign influences on the Middle East have always been strong, and the area has reacted to these influences in a variety of ways ranging from acceptance and assimilation to resistance and rejection.

Resistance and total rejection have frequently been accompanied by the violence either of war or of internal turmoil. Assimilation had to be accomplished through alteration of indigenous institutions as well as through modification of the foreign elements themselves. At times, the result was a superior product which became salable in the world market. In other words, while the Middle East was the recipient of foreign influences it was also a great developer and exporter of varieties of cultural elements and institutions.

In the modern era, the Western world became the primary source of foreign influence in the Middle East. Beginning with the nineteenth century but mostly during the twentieth century, the Western institutions of constitutionalism, parliamentary democracy, capitalistic industrialism, and the national state made their way to the Middle East. In the period between the two world wars, these institutions and mechanisms were adopted, in varying forms and degrees, by all Middle Eastern countries. After World War II, when these countries became either semi-independent or independent, the situation began to change.

With the partial exception of Israel and Turkey, Middle Eastern constitutionalism became devoid of real substance. All Middle Eastern countries have constitutions of the Western type, but these constitutions exist more on paper than in reality. In the Middle East, constitutions are necessary for the legitimization of the political regime, but they are not relevant to the actual exercise of political power.

Like constitutionalism, the parliamentary democracy of the Middle East is more form than substance. Political parties, which in the Western world are instruments of power and are important in the electoral contest, are either proscribed in the Middle East or are permitted with stringent limitations upon their freedom. Some Middle Eastern countries, like Egypt, Syria, and Iraq, allow only one party to operate, and it is always the governmental party. Also, the electoral system favors the individual or individuals already in power. Although elections are occasionally held, they are usually controlled and manipulated by the governments. Even in Turkey and Israel, where elections are held with relative freedom, the electoral systems leave much to be desired. Furthermore, where parliaments exist, they do not have significant power except in Lebanon, Turkey, and Israel.

Capitalistic industrialism as imported from Britain and France is disappearing. Ironically, the countries responsible for its importation have themselves moved toward a socialistic industrial economy. Today, socialism characterizes the economies of Egypt, Syria, and Iraq. Countries like Turkey and Jordan have experimented with the mixed economy as a system of social welfare. Israel is socialistic. Saudi Arabia and Lebanon are capitalistic with a feudal element still embedded in their economic systems. In general, the Middle East is moving toward socialism. Part of the appeal of socialism is that it is anticolonial and antispecial-privilege. Socialism also appeals to political regimes that desire greater control over society and that are eager to plan their country's economic future.

The concept of the nation-state is the only Western influence which the Middle East has accepted with great enthusiasm. This is because the concept justifies people's demands for independence and argues for rights pertaining to national sovereignty. Also, anticolonialism, which in the Middle East often becomes anti-Westernism, is explained in terms of independence and sovereignty, which are the ingredients of the concept of the national state.

But this Western concept had to be modified to suit the Arab world. Arab nationalism, for instance, began as a cultural-revival movement, and it had very little consciousness of territorial boundaries. This latter element became relevant to the movements during World War I and the Arab revolt of 1916 but not in precise terms: territorial consciousness became important but there was no clear understanding of the exact boundaries of the anticipated or hoped-for Arab state. Furthermore, early Arab nationalism was characterized by its Islamic orientation. Generally, therefore, the Arab identity was largely Islamic.

After World War II, Arab nationalism acquired territorial conscious-ness. A major goal was the unification of all the Arab countries from the Atlantic Ocean to the Persian Gulf. At the same time, Arab nationalism became secular. Today, it no longer emphasizes the Islamic character of the future Arab state or the present identity of the Arab nation. Theoreti-cally, therefore, an Arab can be Christian or Jewish.

POLITICAL INSTITUTIONS

The rejection of Western institutions began in most areas after World War II. The fundamental change occurred in the power structures of Middle Eastern societies: in most countries, the army became an important instrument of power, and political parties were no longer aspects of demo-cratic developments. Instead, they became the organizations by which the ruling oligarchies or the dictators maintained themselves in power. Even in countries like Syria and Iraq, where the Baath party is in control of the governments, the armies are the backbone of the political regimes, and it is doubtful that the Baath party could have captured power without the army. In Egypt, the army took control of the government in 1952, and later the leaders of the regime organized a political party to continue them-selves in power. Of course, Nasser used both the army and the party to establish a military dictatorship, and the Egyptian regime is essentially a one-man rule.

Israel, Lebanon, and Turkey are exceptions. In Israel, the power struc-ture is oligarchic. The Mapai party has been in power since the establish-ment of the state, and it is controlled by a few politicians, although a degree of democracy exists in the party's organization and procedures. The Israeli ruling oligarchy is not unified, but it has been able to control the country by taking advantage of the insecure position of the Israeli state, which is threatened by the neighboring Arab countries.

Political rule in Lebanon is also oligarchic. Power is structured along sec-tarian lines. A delicate balance of power is maintained between the reli-gious groups, and it is the most important factor favoring the power posi-tion of the ruling oligarchy, which in turn perpetuates the *status quo*. But the ruling oligarchy allows a great deal of freedom. The Lebanese press, for instance, has more freedom than the press in other Middle Eastern coun-tries. Also, intellectual and cultural activities find full expression in the universities and social clubs. But Lebanon is politically and economically characterized by modern feudalism—a system in which the ownership is feudal but the product is modern and Western.

Turkey between 1923 and 1938 was ruled by one man, Mustafa Kamal, and between 1938 and 1950, it was ruled by one party, the Republican party. Between 1950 and 1960, it had a two-party system, but it was moving back to the one-party system before the military overthrew the government of the Democratic party in 1960. After a brief period of military rule, the country was once again in the hands of civilians, but the army still watches the civilians from the background, and since 1960 it has provided the individuals who assumed the presidency.

Jordan and Iran have monarchical regimes. In both countries, parliaments, political parties, and constitutions are manipulated to the advantage of the monarch. In Iran, the king has been able to introduce economic reforms, but his rule is essentially conservative. In Jordan, the position of the king has changed drastically since the 1967 Arab-Israeli war. Power has fallen into the hands of the Arab commandos, a group of guerrilla organizations dedicated to the destruction of the State of Israel and its replacement by a Palestinian state of Muslims, Christians, and Jews. The commando groups are largely nationalistic and nonideological.

The Arab-Israeli war of 1967 had an important impact upon the institutional life of the Arab world, and ideological interests and controversies, which were important after World War II, have assumed a very minor role. With the decline of the importance of ideology, there has been a corresponding decline in the significance of political parties. Nationalism has intensified, but it is less identified with political parties and leaders. In 1969, the Arab masses looked to the Arab commandos for leadership. Furthermore, the image of Nasser has changed. Although he is still preferred to the other Arab leaders, he is no longer the great hero he was.

Middle Eastern institutions are in the process of change, but no one can be certain what type of institutions will emerge. In the Arab Middle East and in Israel also, what the future institutions will be depends partly on the outcome of the Arab-Israeli conflict. If the Arabs win by military action, the military leaders will mold the institutions of the future. If the conflict is resolved in Arab favor diplomatically, one might expect a return to the situation that existed before the 1967 war. If Israel should win and obtain more territory, the result will have a negative impact on Arab governmental structures, and the institutions of Israel will also undergo fundamental changes. It is possible that the Israeli military organization and extremists will attain greater political power than they have now. In any case, no one should expect the Middle East to move in the direction of democracy, especially the Western type of democracy.

CHAPTER 1

TURKEY: FROM
EMPIRE TO REPUBLIC

THE origin of the Turkish people is largely unknown. Most probably, the first Turks lived in southern Siberia and in Turkestan before moving southward toward the general area now known as the Middle East. They were nomadic and pastoral people, and their movements were gradual and periodical.

In the tenth century, a branch of the Turkish tribes of Central Asia known as the Seljuks appeared in Iran, which was then under Arab rule. The Seljuk Turks embraced Islam but retained their military strength, and in time they turned against the Arab Abbassid dynasty (749–1258). In 1055, at a time when Abbassid rule was lax, they entered Baghdad, the Arab capital, upon the invitation of its ruler, who believed that the Seljuks would strengthen his position and protect him against his enemies. However, the Turks were able to dominate the Arab ruler, and, without destroying the Abbassids' nominal authority over their empire, the Turks ruled in fact. They were able to extend their control over Georgia, Armenia, and much of Asia Minor south of the Black Sea.

In western Asia Minor, the Byzantines were in command. The successor state to the Roman Empire, it became its eastern division after 395 and was later known as the East Roman Empire. The expansion of the Seljuks in the eleventh century became the immediate occasion for the First Crusade (1096–99), which was followed by others. However, the Crusades did not save the Byzantines, whose power was gradually crumbling.

The Seljuk Empire fell apart in the twelfth century, and another Turkish group, the Osmanlis, completed the destruction of the Byzantine Empire in 1453. The Osmanlis, the last of the invading Turks, had been consigned to an area bordering the Byzantine Empire by their Seljuk overlords. Sensitive to the Byzantine threat, they were to develop a highly disciplined organization, and this eventually gave them military superiority over the Byzantines, enabling them to build their own empire.

The first ruler of the Osmanlis was Othman (1281–1324), after whom the Ottoman Empire was named. He embraced the Islamic religion, an event which later made it possible for the Ottoman state to assume the leadership of the Islamic world. Othman's successors made widespread conquests. Selim I (1512–20) added Kurdistan to the Ottoman Empire in 1514 and defeated the Mamelukes in 1516 in Egypt and Syria, enabling him to annex their territories and thus became caliph, the religious leader of Islam (the temporal ruler was the sultan, but one man held both offices). From that time until the advent of the republican regime in Turkey in 1923, Ottoman rulers held the title of caliph.

Suleiman I (1520–66), son of Selim I and known as Suleiman the Magnificent, led the Ottoman Empire to the height of its power and prestige. In 1521 Suleiman conquered Belgrade, and in 1526 he defeated the Hungarians and annexed their territory. His siege of Vienna, in 1529, was unsuccessful, but his European activity nevertheless made him an important figure in the continental power structure. His contemporary, Holy Roman Emperor Charles V (1516–56), was compelled to recognize Ottoman conquests in Hungary; and Ferdinand of Hapsburg, brother of the Emperor, agreed to pay tribute to Suleiman in return for part of Hungary. And in Africa, the Ottomans for many years thwarted Charles V's efforts to dominate the northern part of that continent.

The sixteenth century, then, marked the peak of Turkish expansion. At its greatest, the Ottoman Empire extended from the gates of Vienna to the Indian Ocean and from Tunis to the Caucasus. After Suleiman, however, the Empire began to decline, mainly as a result of the deterioration of both military standards and civil values of the Turks. In 1918, as an outcome of World War I, the Empire was disbanded according to the provisions of the Treaty of Lausanne, which we shall discuss later.

OTTOMAN LAWS AND INSTITUTIONS

The laws of the Empire came from several sources. The Shariah, the sacred law of the Koran, was inviolable and supreme over all other laws. It could not be ignored even by the sultan himself. Secondly, there were the kanuns, the decrees issued by the sultan for administrative purposes or to implement or supplement the Shariah. Kanuns dealt with such matters as policing, the military, and finance. They were next in importance to the Shariah, and they could invalidate both of the two lower sources of law, the Urf and Adet. The Urf was the will of the sultan, and it could invalidate the Adet, which was the source of the customary laws of the various communities. The Adet differed from one community to another.[1]

1. Sydney N. Fisher, *The Middle East: A History* (New York: Alfred A. Knopf, 1959), p. 208.

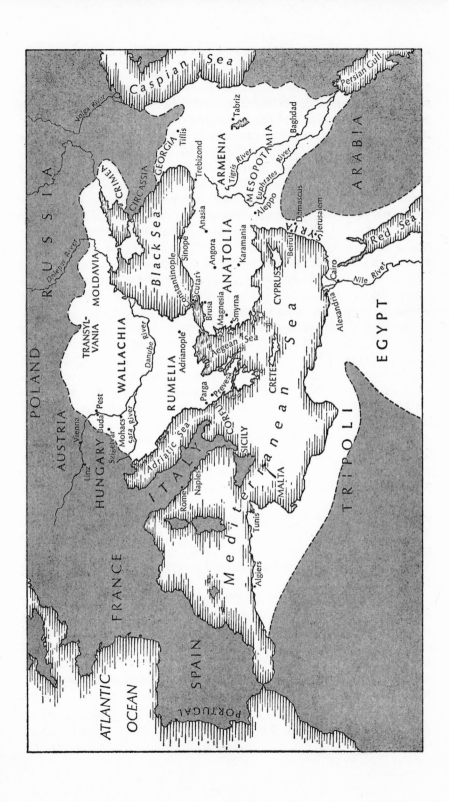

Governmental functions were vested in two institutions: the Ruling Institution and the Muslim Institution. The Ruling Institution included the sultan, his officers, the standing army, and public servants. It dealt with all governmental affairs except the administration of justice in cases involving the Shariah. Matters which affected the non-Muslim population were also excluded.

The sultan was the head of the state. But since the Ottoman Empire based its law and its theory of state on Islamic principles, there was no separation of state and religion, and the sultan was also the religious leader, the caliph. Accordingly, the authority of the caliph was held to be derived directly from God, and he was charged with the dual responsibility of protecting the Islamic faith and enforcing religious laws. The sultan's council of advisers was the *Divan,* comparable to the cabinet or the council of ministers of modern European systems. Members of the Divan were called *vizirs;* one of them was usually designated as first vizir, who, again, was similar to the prime minister in modern systems.

The Muslim Institution drew its membership from educators, ministers of religion, judges, and Islamic monks, the *dervishes.* The function of this group was to provide "the whole substance and structure of Muslim learning, religion, and law." [2] Whereas the Ruling Institutions's membership came mostly from Muslim individuals born of Christian parents, that of the Muslim Institution came almost exclusively from Muslim individuals born of Muslim parents.

Related to the Muslin Institution were the *ulema,* who were trained in the Shariah and exercised the important function of invalidating all laws and official acts that conflicted with it. Thus, although the caliph was theoretically the religious head, the ulema wielded much power, so much that they sometimes weakened the sultan politically and hence the Empire itself. The ulema were composed of the grand mufti, who was appointed by the caliph and served as the official head of the ulema; the cadis (judges); and the muftis, who were selected to interpret religious principles and to determine the conformity of private and public acts with the Islamic religion.

There were three other special categories of institution. First there was the millet system, which was developed to insure Muslim control of non-Muslim groups within the Empire. Under this system, non-Muslims, primarily Christians and Jews, enjoyed limited autonomy under their ecclesiastical leaders, who were responsible to the sultan for all matters pertaining to their communities. Islamic laws required only that these religious groups pay a poll tax and conduct themselves in accordance with customs and

2. William Stearns Davis, *A Short History of the Middle East* (New York: The Macmillan Company, 1924), p. 236.

mores in return for full protection and safety under Ottoman authority.

A second institution was designed to define the status of foreigners residing in the Empire. This was the famous institution known as the capitulations, according to which alien groups were exempt from Turkish law and from the payment of taxes. Foreigners involved in judicial proceedings were tried in consular courts according to the law and legal practices of the defendant's country. Ordinarily, the sultan signed a treaty with the country of the foreign group which described the foreign group's rights and duties. Non-Muslim Turkish subjects who were employed by foreigners could obtain the privileges of foreigners if they secured the approval of a consular authority.[3] The capitulation, adopted from Arab and Byzantine practices at a time when it was believed the institution would serve the interests of the state, later became an instrument of foreign exploitation and, consequently, a controversial issue in Ottoman politics.

The third institution was the Janissaries (young soldiers). This organization developed out of the old Ottoman practice of recruiting captured prisoners as mercenaries. Membership in the Janissaries was restricted to young men whose parents were Christian, but who were reared as Muslims and trained to be dedicated to the service and protection of the sultan. These individuals usually became fanatic in their devotion both to the Muslim faith and to the person of the sultan, and owing to their extreme loyalty and severe discipline they were highly dependable in times of crisis. The efficiency of this fighting guard was out of all proportion to its number, even in an age when all Western powers depended on small professional armies.[4]

IMPERIAL DECLINE AND ATTEMPTS AT REFORM

For several centuries Ottoman institutions and laws exhibited a high degree of flexibility and adaptability. As far as the Muslim majority of the Empire's subjects were concerned, the institutions of the Empire allowed them to live, at least in theory, under the laws of God. They gave the system their loyalty, and the system gave them the spiritual satisfaction they needed. The non-Muslim subjects were moderately satisfied with the arrangements of the millet system, for they were able to preserve their religious identities under a political system which did not reflect their cultures. The foreign groups in the Empire were relatively free from rigid political controls, and the capitulations afforded them the economic opportunities they wanted. In fact, foreigners had a monopoly over much of the com-

3. Geoffrey Lewis, *Turkey* (New York: Frederick A. Praeger, 1955), p. 23.
4. Davis, *A Short History of the Middle East*, p. 245.

merce of the Empire, a monopoly made safe by the desire of the Muslim population to specialize in agriculture rather than in trade.

But there were problems, many of which had existed throughout much of Ottoman history. During the eighteenth and nineteenth centuries they began to contribute seriously to the weakening of the Empire. There was the major problem of defending a long frontier threatened by the expansion (1683–1791) of Austria and Russia. Until 1683, when the Ottomans were forced to abandon Vienna during its second siege, European nations were busy fighting among themselves. After 1683, however, Western countries were free to look elsewhere. Moreover, some nations had found that their constant strife had so developed the science of war that they were militarily superior to the Ottoman state. Although European arms did not actually destroy the Ottoman state until World War I, continental military prowess enabled Europe to develop interest in the internal affairs of the Ottoman Empire and influence these affairs by an occasional show of force.

By the seventeenth century, the system of feudal cavalry, which awarded fiefs to military commanders, had contributed to the decline of the Ottoman armies. As holders of military fiefs became more interested in their fiefs, which contributed to their economic well-being and increased their political influence, the armed forces began to suffer from lack of discipline and from evasion of responsibility by high-ranking officers.

During the same century, the Janissaries contributed to the decline of the Empire. Their political influence had grown to the point of acquiring effective control over the sultan and his advisers. Furthermore, their source of recruits was altered to allow admission of children of Muslims; and discipline, in which their greatest strength lay, was no longer emphasized. Children of Muslims had been excluded from this military organization because, it was assumed, they would inherit the political loyalties of their parents and thus become embroiled in politics, weakening their devotion to the sultan. This is exactly what happened during the seventeenth century.

Still another problem was the development, in the nineteenth century, of separatist movements and uprisings among many nationality groups. The Serbs, for example, achieved autonomy as a result of their struggle against the Ottomans (1804–17); the Greeks aimed at independence and got it (1815–29); there was trouble in Rumania beginning in 1861; and the efforts of the Bulgarians culminated in their independence in 1908. In addition, the Empire's Arab population became increasingly nationalistic and restless during the nineteenth century, bringing about the Arab revolt in 1916.

Other factors besides military weakness contributed to the decline of the

Ottoman Empire. Some of the most important were: "(1) Failure to keep pace with the West in technology; (2) weakness of national loyalties above and beyond regional, religious, and ethnic ties; (3) continued identity of church and state; (4) popular disinterest in economic pursuits other than agriculture; and (5) administrative and political corruption." [5]

Several attempts at reforming the Ottoman system were made during the nineteenth century. Although they were unsuccessful in saving the Empire from gradual disintegration, these reforms were significant because they were part of the heritage of later reform movements, especially that of Mustafa Kemal, who was to become the first president of the Turkish Republic. The reform efforts failed because they were limited to certain areas of political life, such as the legal administration, and because they were unable to penetrate to the grass-roots level of cultural life. The reforms did not affect the rural-agricultural people, who were the majority of the Empire's population, nor did they affect some of the institutions (mainly the economy and local administration) which in the nineteenth century were becoming obsolete.

In 1839, Sultan Abdul Majid (1839–61) introduced the first Tanzimat (reform), known as the Charter of Liberties and designed to give equal rights to all Ottoman subjects who, until then, retained their separate political statuses with their own systems of obligations and duties. Legal reforms were also part of the charter. These included civil and criminal codes modeled on European law but modified to conform with Muslim law. The second Tanzimat was declared in 1856; it reiterated some of the provisions of the 1839 Tanzimat, especially with regard to the equality of all Ottoman subjects and the definition of minority rights.

In 1876, Sultan Abdul Hamid II (1876–1909) granted his subjects a liberal constitution which established a Parliament composed of two houses: a Senate and a House of Deputies. The Constitution granted certain rights to citizens, rights familiar to modern Western constitutions, but failed to limit the powers of the sultan, who could appoint and dismiss executive officials and convene or dismiss Parliament. Abdul Hamid ignored the Constitution soon after he declared it, returned to autocratic practices, and ruled despotically. Parliament was suspended after its first session and was not reconvened until 1908. Although the Constitution failed, its restoration became the slogan of revolutionary and liberal movements which pressed for democracy and reform.

---

5. Richard D. Robinson, *The First Turkish Republic* (Cambridge: Harvard University Press, 1963), p. 3.

THE DEVELOPMENT OF SECRET
OPPOSITION MOVEMENTS

The despotic rule of Sultan Abdul Hamid and the failure of reform contributed heavily to the appearance of secret organizations which opposed the prevailing conditions in the Empire. When they first emerged, these groups were merely reform movements seriously concerned with the welfare and preservation of the Empire and its monarchy. The most important of them were the "Young Turk" associations which originated in the 1860's and 1870's.[6] One of these, the New Ottoman Society, was established in 1865 by the Turkish poet Namik Kemal, the first Turkish intellectual to advance the Western concepts of fatherland, freedom, and constitutional government. Pan-Ottomanism was the basic philosophy of Namik Kemal, a philosophy that attempted to create through a constitution a national identity for the multiracial, multireligious population of the Empire. As suggested earlier, the traditional Ottoman system had failed to establish a common identity for all its subjects and recognized instead many categories of groups with different national, racial, and religious identities. The millet system was essentially a system of categorization, and so were the capitulations.

Abdul Hamid's failure to enforce the 1876 Constitution resulted in the establishment of another young Turk organization, the Ottoman Union and Progress Committee in Istanbul in 1889. Although this organization advocated nonviolent change, it had to hold its first congress (1902) in Paris, owing to the unfriendly attitude of the Ottoman government. In 1906 a faction of the committee united with the Ottoman Freedom Association, primarily a secret military organization established in Salonica, and formed the Committee of Union and Progress. Soon the new organization began to conspire to overthrow Abdul Hamid. By this time Mustafa Kemal was actively participating in the movements of the young Turks through his military organization known as the Fatherland and Freedom Society, but he was not the most important man in these movements.

The Committee of Union and Progress was gradually getting additional support from the armed forces, and many officers were members. During 1906 and 1907, mutinies among officers occurred so frequently that they alarmed the sultan. To counteract these revolts the sultan withheld authority from commanders he no longer trusted and planted spies in the armed forces. But all of this did not stop the growth of secret organizations; on

6. For more details on the Young Turks, see Ernest Ramsaur, Jr., *The Young Turks: Prelude to the Revolution of 1908* (Princeton: Princeton University Press, 1957).

the contrary, the young Turks found followers among Muslims as well as non-Muslims.

Although the young Turks had organization and support, they lacked ideological unity. They all wanted to save the Empire but disagreed about the methods. The Ottomanists believed in the establishment of an Ottoman nationality. The Islamists believed in the establishment of the Islamic state on a more solid basis and proposed complete adherence to the often-ignored religious laws and teachings. Still others believed in Pan-Turkism, the union of all people who possessed a Turkish culture or were of the Turkish "race." Finally, there were those who believed in Turkish nationalism, and it was this group that won the struggle for power and was able to overthrow, in 1923, the Ottoman regime with its sultanate and caliphate. Turkish nationalism, however, unlike Pan-Turkism, would unite Turks living in ethnic Turkey only.

Most of the people of the Empire were confused about which ideology to support. The Ottomanist theory foundered because it came into being at a time when the ethnic and national groups were feeling the impact of their own cultural and national identities; instead of uniting in an Ottoman identity, they desired autonomy and independence. The major weakness of the Islamist ideology was that it appealed neither to the non-Muslims nor to the non-Turkish Muslims who by now had no confidence in the intentions of the Turkish Muslims. Pan-Turkism and Turkish nationalism were opposed by non-Turks because it was obvious that they favored the supremacy of Turks over non-Turks, both Muslim and non-Muslim.

But in spite of the ideological confusion, the work of the secret organizations did produce some changes in the political picture. In 1908 a young Turk group successfully revolted in Salonica, forcing the sultan to reinstate the 1876 Constitution. But this success was only partial from the standpoint of the Committee of Union and Progress, which had hoped to gain the control of the government. The repressive measures taken by the sultan during the few years before the 1908 revolution had weakened the committee's organizational work in Istanbul, the capital.

The people of the Empire reacted favorably to the reinstitution of the 1876 Constitution. The Committee of Union and Progress, however, had no confidence in Abdul Hamid, for it knew he would soon ignore his own promises. Therefore, they were determined to bring about his downfall. This came more quickly and more suddenly than was anticipated. On April 13, 1909, the Istanbul garrison mutinied; a Macedonian military force marched on the capital and took control of it. Immediately, the new Parliament, which had been reconvened upon the reinstitution of the 1876 Constitution, voted unanimously to depose Abdul Hamid, who was then replaced by his brother, Mohammed V.

WORLD WAR I AND THE END
OF THE EMPIRE

The victors in the 1909 revolution were the young Turk groups. With the exception of the 1912–13 period, they were in power until 1918. But the reforms they promised were never realized. The religious laws, the millet system, and other institutions which dominated the Ottoman system continued; most important, the idea of empire persisted in spite of the rise of nationalism among the non-Turkish peoples. Because nothing was done to accommodate the changes of the nineteenth century, such as the rise of nationalism, many of the institutions became ineffective and unrealistic.

World War I brought the Empire to a crisis. Perhaps the most important decision made by the government of the young Turks was the declaration of war against the Allies in 1914. The strain of war brought about the destruction of the Empire. At the end of the war the Allied forces had occupied Turkey, and the sultan's government came under the influence of the British.

In Paris and at San Remo the Western Allies met to negotiate the fate of the defeated Ottoman Empire. The result was the humiliating Treaty of Sèvres, which the puppet Turkish government grudgingly signed on August 10, 1920.[7] By the terms of the treaty, the Empire was to be divided in the following manner: (1) Syria, Mesopotamia, and Palestine were to be placed under the mandates of France and Great Britain, with France taking charge of Syria and Britain the other two countries; (2) the Hejaz was granted independence; (3) Smyrna was to be put under a Greek administration for as long as five years, after which the territory would decide whether it wanted to belong to Greece; (4) the islands of Imbros and Tenedos would be granted to Greece; (5) Armenia was to become independent; (6) Egypt, the Sudan, and Cyprus were to be under British control; (7) the Straits, including the Dardanelles, Marmara, and Bosporus, were to be controlled by an international committee representing England, France, Italy, Japan, Russia, Greece, Rumania, Bulgaria, Turkey, and the United States.

While the Ottoman Empire was being liquidated internal developments were taking a shape which was to give Turkey a new life. These

7. The text is in Jacob C. Hurewitz, ed., *Diplomacy in the Near and Middle East, A Documentary Record: 1914–1956* (Princeton: Van Nostrand, 1956), vol. II, Doc. 31, pp. 81–87.

developments were centered around the career of one man, Mustafa Kemal. Kemal had had a brilliant military career and during the war which lost Turkey her Empire had demonstrated his military genius. Desiring reform and progress, Kemal had previously been part of the young Turk movements, but he had become disenchanted with the government of the young Turks, and he believed that a new outlook and a new order were the only hope for Turkey.

Kemal's efforts to create that new outlook and order began in 1919. Early that year the sultan commissioned Kemal to effect the demobilization of the Turkish forces in northeast Turkey, which the Allied authorities had insisted upon under the terms of the Mudros Armistice (October 30, 1918). It is not clear why the sultan selected Kemal for this mission; but, in any case, once in that area Kemal began to organize a national resistance movement to eliminate foreign rule and to safeguard Turkish national interests.

Two historic conferences took place at this time that were to give the Kemalist movement organization as well as popular support. The first, in Erzurum during July 1919, declared a "National Pact" in which the participants agreed on the following policies: (1) safeguarding the national frontiers (i.e., Asia Minor and Istanbul) at any cost; (2) the creation of a provisional government for Turkey in the event the Istanbul government was unable to protect the country's independence; (3) consolidating the national forces and establishing the will of the nation as a sovereign power; (4) resisting all attempts by foreign powers to occupy territory or to establish mandates over any segment of it.[8]

The Erzurum Conference was of a regional nature and represented mainly northeastern Turkey. The second conference, however, which met at Sivas on September 4, 1919, was to include three representatives from each provincial subdivision, giving the meeting a national character. However, what it did for the most part was simply to elaborate on the Erzurum resolutions. It did, however, select a committee known as the Representative Committee of the Sivas Congress, with Kemal as its president. The committee was the nucleus of a provisional government.

Kemalist activity in the northeast region forced the sultan to agree to hold elections. The National Assembly which met after the elections (January 20, 1920) was dominated by nationalist deputies; it voted to proclaim the National Pact whose aims we have outlined previously in reference to the Erzurum Conference. This, of course, angered the Allies, who decided to place Istanbul under formal military occupation and arrest the nation-

8. The text is in Helen Miller Davis, ed., *Constitutions, Electoral Laws, Treaties of States in the Near and Middle East* (Durham, N.C.: Duke University Press, 1953), pp. 465–66.

alist leaders. Many of the nationalist deputies made their way to Ankara, however, where Mustafa Kemal had established his headquarters. And there, on April 23, 1920, they met in a newly constituted Grand National Assembly of Turkey and elected Mustafa Kemal as their president and head of the government. The Assembly, according to the new arrangements, was to select members of the government and to possess all executive and legislative powers, although the fate of the sultanate and the caliphate was not determined.

Mustafa Kemal's main concern was to establish Turkish sovereignty over the territories inhabited by ethnic Turks. To do so, his army, composed of volunteers and former soldiers, had to confront five enemies: the French, Italians, Greeks, Armenians, and British. By the spring of 1920, he succeeded in driving the French out of ethnic Turkish areas, and he concluded a treaty with them in May 1920. After military victories against the Armenians, the nationalists were able to capture Kars and to conclude a treaty with the Communist government in Erivan. On March 13, 1921, the Italians agreed to leave Anatolia in return for economic privileges. The Greeks were more difficult; but in August 1922, the Turks began a major offensive which resulted in the final expulsion of Greek troops from Turkish soil. The British too had to negotiate peace.

The nationalist government under Kemal had never recognized the disgraceful Treaty of Sèvres. Now it was in a position to request a new peace treaty. Accordingly, negotiations between the Allies and Turkey were commenced, with the Soviet Union as a participant. The result of these negotiations was the Treaty of Lausanne, July 24, 1923.[9]

According to this treaty, Turkey was to renounce all claims to the non-Turkish territories of the Empire, but its sovereignty over Istanbul, Eastern Thrace, and Anatolia was to be unlimited. Non-Muslim nationals of Turkey were to enjoy "the same civil and political rights as Muslims." Equality before the law was guaranteed for all inhabitants. On the subject of the Straits, the treaty compromised, providing for their control by an international supervisory commission under the permanent presidency of Turkey. The term "straits" in the treaty referred to the Strait of the Dardanelles, the Sea of Marmara, and the Bosporus. The capitulations were abolished.

A separate agreement between Turkey and Greece provided for the transfer to Greece of the Greek population in Turkey and to Turkey of the Turkish population in Greece. Exceptions were made regarding the Greeks of Istanbul and the Turks of Western Thrace, who were to remain where they were. The Franklin-Bouillon Agreement of October 20, 1921, fixed the Turkish boundary with Syria, and the Treaty of Lausanne recog-

9. Text in Hurewitz, ed., *Diplomacy*, vol. II, Doc. 41, pp. 119–27.

nized this boundary as valid. The Treaty of Lausanne advised that a separate agreement fixing the Turkish boundary with Iraq be made between Turkey and Great Britain within a year; if no agreement was reached, the League of Nations was to arbitrate the issue.

The Treaty of Lausanne was the climax of the Kemalist struggle to assert Turkish sovereignty over the territories of ethnic Turkey. Thus the Kemalist regime was successful in both the art of diplomacy and the art of war, and although the Turks lost their empire, they did not lose their country.

THE FOUNDATION OF THE REPUBLIC

The years between January 21, 1921, when an interim constitutional act was proclaimed, and April 20, 1924, when the first all-new republican constitution was proclaimed, were turbulent. They saw a number of significant changes in the legal framework of the Turkish state. During that time the country was governed by the Grand National Assembly, under a constitutional act recognizing those provisions of the 1876 and 1918 constitutions that were not in conflict with it. Such an arrangement, however, was not adequate to the problems facing the Kemalist regime, and new measures were periodically introduced.

On November 1, 1922, the Assembly abolished the sultanate and deposed the reigning sultan. The caliphate, the office of religious leadership, was retained, however, and Abdul Majid, a cousin of the deposed Sultan Mohammed VI, was chosen as the new caliph. To replace the sultanate, the Grand National Assembly added, on October 29, 1923, a constitutional provision that gave Turkey a republican form of government. Naturally, Mustafa Kemal was elected to the office of president.

Then on March 3, 1924, the Assembly abolished the caliphate, and on April 8 the religious courts which enforced the Shariah were also abolished, and the enforcement power was vested in civil courts. Finally, the new constitutional law was proclaimed taking into account the changes which were already introduced and adding new provisions designed to complete the structure of the republican state.

The new Constitution retained elements from the past.[10] For instance, it stated that the religion of the Turkish state was Islam and thus did not recognize the principle of separation of church and state. However, in April 1928, the provision dealing with the religion of the state and the provision empowering the Assembly to enforce the Shariah were abolished. Also, the oath of the presidency and the oath taken by the deputies of the

10. The text is in Donald E. Webster, *The Turkey of Ataturk* (Philadelphia: The American Academy of Political and Social Science, 1939), pp. 297–306.

Assembly were modified so that the formula, "I affirm upon my honor" would replace the old formula, "I swear by God." [11]

New changes occurred in statutory law following Western models. In 1926, the Grand National Assembly adopted a new civil code, based on the Swiss civil code; a new penal code, based on the Italian; and a new commercial code, based on the German. These codes were examined by special commissions with the objective of adapting them to the Turkish situation. The University of Ankara was to train Turkish jurists in the secular law.

KEMALIST IDEOLOGY AND ACHIEVEMENTS

In addition to constitutional and statutory changes, there were new political developments. Most important was the establishment of the People's party (later the Republican People's party). Founded officially on September 9, 1923, the People's party was an instrument whereby Kemal could reach the people, organize their political activity, and control that activity. According to Kemal, it was to be more than a merely political organization. In Kemal's view, it had the important functions of educating the citizenry and providing them with an ideology—it was to be a school of civic education for the Turks. This was evident in the party's program, which defined such concepts as "fatherland" and "nation" and explained such matters as the public rights of citizens, constitutionalism, finance, education, health, and defense.

Article 5 of the party's program explained the basic characteristics of the party which were republicanism, nationalism, populism, etatism, secularism, and revolutionism.[12] These six elements, now referred to as the six principles of Kemalism, were supposedly the ideological basis of the new republic. Before considering these principles, however, it should be noted that Kemalism was a complex of separate policies rather than a comprehensive ideology or body of principles and doctrines on which to base the formulation of policy. Had it been a preconceived theory, it most certainly would have run into more difficulties than did the separate policies that ultimately came under the label.

Republicanism. Although it is difficult to describe the type of republicanism Turkey acquired in the years following the establishment of the new state, changes in the forms of government substantially influenced the power structure.[13] The old ruling class, for example, was replaced by a new

11. Alfred Bonne, *State and Economics in the Middle East* (London: Routledge and Kegan Paul Ltd., 1960), p. 71.

12. For the text of the party's program, see Webster, *The Turkey of Ataturk*, Appendix E, pp. 307–18.

13. Bonne, *State and Economics*, p. 72.

official class. Republicanism created the conditions necessary for a new society. The Turks were to become "state-minded." They were to acquire a new concept of state, one altogether different from the one they experienced under the Islamic and imperial Ottoman state.

Nationalism. The concept of common citizenship and attachment to the national ideal was to replace identification by race or religion. The principle of territoriality was closely linked with the Kemalist concept of nation, and it meant that the sense of nationality of the population within the territory was to be based on national origin, language, and national spirit.

Prior to the Kemalist revolution, Turkish political philosophy had lacked a clear concept of nationalism. Consequently, the Turks were unable to make progress in many aspects of social and economic life. Ziya Gokalp, an outstanding Turkish sociologist, makes this point clear: "As the non-existence of the ideal of nationalism among the Turks resulted in the lack of any national economy, so the same factor has been an obstacle to the development of a national language and to the appearance of national patterns in fine arts. And, again, because the ideal of nationalism was not present, Turkish morality remained only a personal and family morality. The notions of solidarity, patriotism, and heroism did not transcend the confines of the family, the village, and the town." [14]

Populism. The emphasis of this principle was on equality and a classless society. It declared the end of privileges based on family membership, occupation, or economic status and the beginning of progress on the basis of merit. Populism also meant democracy. According to Mustafa Kemal himself, it meant "the passing of government into the hands of the people." [15] Whether the Kemalists really desired democracy, however, remains a crucial and undecided issue in modern Turkish history. There are three points of view. One holds that Kemal was sincere in his attempt to create a multiparty democracy in Turkey but that he had to abandon the idea because the country was not ready for it; reactionary violence proved that the idea was premature. A second believes that Kemal wanted to create an opposition party "to release tension during a time of economic crisis" but wanted to crush it when it became a serious threat.[16] Another view is that he desired an opposition party in order to prevent his premier, Ismet, from becoming too powerful.

Regardless of which view is correct, Mustafa Kemal did permit opposition on two occasions. In 1924–25, an opposition party developed out of a group of Kemal's former supporters who feared the threat of his personal

14. Niyazi Berkes, ed., *Turkish Nationalism and Western Civilization: Selected Essays of Ziya Gokalp* (New York: Columbia University Press, 1959), p. 73.

15. Kemal was quoted in Bernard Lewis, *The Emergence of Modern Turkey* (London: Oxford University Press, 1961), p. 251.

16. Bernard Lewis, *The Emergence of Modern Turkey*, p. 275.

power. This was the Progressive Republican party. The Kurdish revolt, however, convinced Kemal that an opposition during such a crisis would be dangerous, and the progressives were prohibited from being politically active. The second occasion was in 1930, when Fethi Bey, a former prime minister, criticized the economic policies of the government and declared in a letter to the president the need for an opposition party and free criticism in the Assembly. On August 12, he submitted the constitution of the Free Republican party to the government for the issuance of a license. His program promised greater freedom, lower taxes, and less government.[17] This experiment, although authorized and partly guided by Kemal himself, also failed. Its failure was caused by the decision of its leaders to dissolve their party; they claimed that Kemal failed to take a neutral policy between the Free Republicans and his own, the Republican People's party.

The Republican People's party dominated the political scene. Within the organization of the party, a degree of democracy existed in the form of free discussion and majority rule. But important political decisions were made by the party organization before the Grand National Assembly had a chance to consider the issues involved. Since the party was always sure of a majority in the Assembly, it did not fear elections, and after the adoption of the new constitution in April 1924, elections were held in 1927, 1931, and 1935. The party, which had the power to approve or disapprove candidates, allowed a small number of independents to stand for election in 1931, perhaps to answer the charges that the Republican party had a complete monopoly of power.[18] But their impact was nil, and in the election of 1935 the government party won 386 seats while the "independent" group won only 13. Women voted for the first time in 1935, winning 17 seats.[19]

Etatism. This principle meant that the state had the right to intervene in the economic affairs whenever the general welfare of Turkish society required such intervention. The program of the Republican People's party explained the position of the state in regard to the economic activity as follows: "Although considering private work and activity a basic idea, it is one of our main principles to interest the state actively in matters where the general and vital interests of the nation are in question, especially in the economic field, in order to lead the nation and the country to prosperity in as short a time as possible." [20]

The assumption of etatism is that private ownership and private enterprise may exist as long as they function effectively. The state has primary

17. Lewis, *The Emergence of Modern Turkey*, p. 274.
18. Webster, *The Turkey of Ataturk*, p. 110.
19. Webster, *The Turkey of Ataturk*, p. 111.
20. Webster, *The Turkey of Ataturk*, p. 167.

responsibility of sound economic policy, however, and state intervention is exercised when private enterprise is unable to serve the public interest in a particular economic area. Etatism and socialism, therefore, are not the same, a point which Mustafa Kemal tried to explain: "The system of etatism in Turkey is not a system copied and translated from the idea that socialist theoreticians have been putting forward since the 19th century; our etatism takes as its basis the private initiative and personal aptitudes of individuals, but at the same time, taking account of all the needs of a great nation and a broad land, and of the fact that so much still remains to be done, it rests on the principle that the state must take charge of the national economy." [21]

There are today different views as to whether etatism was a good, effective policy or not. Max Thornburg, whose 1949 economic report on Turkey is often cited, accuses the etatists of having deliberately discouraged private enterprise and declares: "There is reason to believe that the succession of five-year plans in Turkey has not in fact constituted the guiding and activating force in the economic development which has taken place but rather has reflected and summarized, for publicity purposes, projects which originated in political, military, or particularistic sources." [22] On the other hand, the report of the International Bank for Reconstruction and Development admits that substantial progress was made under etatism and doubts whether comparable success could have been made under private enterprise.[23] Regardless of which view is espoused, there can be no doubt that economic development was the most difficult area of responsibility confronting the Kemalist government.

Secularism. Changing the way of life of a people is extremely difficult. Time, energy, and a willingness to take risks are needed to accomplish a substantial degree of change in the culture of a nation, especially when such a nation has been steeped for centuries in religious traditions considered by many as incompatible with new—in this case Western—methods and goals.[24] The Kemalist policy of secularization was aimed at modernization and the creation of a national state. These goals could not be realized without facing the traditions and principles of Islam.

We have already mentioned some of the reforms which directly or indirectly affected the status of religion in Turkish society. The abolition of the caliphate and the religious courts in 1924, the institution of secular judicial

21. Kemal was quoted in Lewis, *The Emergence of Modern Turkey,* p. 281.
22. M. W. Thornburg, G. Spry, and G. Soule, *Turkey: An Economic Appraisal* (New York: The Twentieth Century Fund, 1949), p. 39.
23. International Bank for Reconstruction and Development, *The Economy of Turkey* (Baltimore: The Johns Hopkins Press, 1951), p. 9.
24. Kemal H. Karpat, *Turkey's Politics* (Princeton: Princeton University Press, 1959), p. 59.

reform in 1926, and the amendment in 1928 of the Constitution which repealed the article affirming Islam as the state religion were all important steps in the long and arduous process of secularization. Other religious symbols were also abolished. On November 25, 1925, a new law was passed forbidding the fez, the traditional Turkish headdress. On December 26, 1925, the Turkish calendar was abolished, and the Georgian calendar was adopted. In 1935 the weekly holiday became Sunday instead of the traditional Friday. In 1926, polygamy was abolished. Finally, Ankara became the new capital instead of Istanbul, which until 1923 was the seat of the caliphs and was symbolic of past traditions. The building of mosques in certain parts of the new capital was prohibited.

Perhaps the most important symbol binding Turkey to the Muslim culture was the Arabic script. The idea of replacing the Arabic script with the Latin alphabet was first considered in 1923 and 1924, but was abandoned. It may be that the Kemalist regime felt it was not strong enough to introduce such a radical change at the time; but by 1927, the situation had changed. The regime was in complete control, and a precedent had been set by the Soviet Union when it decided to substitute the Latin alphabet for the Arabic in her Turkish-speaking areas. On November 3, 1928, the Latin alphabet was officially introduced in Turkey, and virtually every Turk was required to pass an examination or attend school to learn it: "The entire country became a school to teach the new alphabet. Evening classes were compulsory for men up to sixty and women up to fifty years old. Ataturk (Mustafa Kemal) was one of the teachers. From partly Arabic and partly Latin, the newspapers went, in a few months to entirely Latin characters. Circulation fell; the government had to subsidize some papers, and then circulation began to rise and soon passed the old sales limits of papers in Arabic letters." [25]

Thus, Turkey became a secular state. We should bear in mind, however, that the new republic did not intend to subvert Islam, but only to limit its influence in those areas of public life which were considered vital in the realization of a modern and progressive way of life. Without secularization of political life, the energies of the state and the people could not have been released. Social change would have been extremely difficult.

Revolutionism. This sixth, and last, principle of Kemalism declared "the determination to depart from tradition and precedent if they did not serve national interests." [26] The new republic did not have sufficient time to wait for the results of evolutionary change which, in any case, would have been difficult in a defeated country.

25. Ahmed Amin Yalman, *Turkey in My Time* (Norman: University of Oklahoma Press, 1956), p. 176.
26. George Lenczowski, *The Middle East in World Affairs* (Ithaca: Cornell University Press, 1961), p. 120.

Revolutionism meant organized effort directed and controlled by a central authority, a new spirit created by the evaluation of future destiny, and the creation of new goals. It meant a constant need for reform and continuous change in all aspects of Turkish life. Such reform and such change, Kemalism assumed, could not take place unless the old institutions were destroyed.

THE KEMALIST REGIME: AN EVALUATION

While it is easy to belittle the contributions of Mustafa Kemal to Turkish life, especially when they are judged by Western standards, it is also difficult to imagine what Turkey would be today if Kemal had never existed. The Turkish nation owes him much for providing effective leadership for the nationalist movement, which he helped to create at a time when the Allies had already agreed on how to divide the Ottoman Empire of which Turkey was a part. The Treaty of Sèvres, as we have seen, would have eliminated every possibility of creating a sovereign nation of Turkey. The Treaty of Lausanne, which Kemal's government negotiated, was a more dignified peace agreement. Unlike the Treaty of Sèvres, which Kemal ignored, the Lausanne agreement enabled the Turks to unite under a distinct national identity. It is, therefore, no exaggeration of the Turkish people who today refer to Kemal as "Ataturk" (Father of the Turks). He is the man who prevented the destruction of his people's identity and their sovereign existence.

Of course, Kemal could not have done it alone. Part of the credit must go to the thousands of Turkish soldiers who, while their sultan had already submitted to foreign influence, fought against great odds to preserve their country from being occupied and ruled by foreign powers. They fought Greeks, French, Italians, Armenians, and the British and won, all in a short time and under severe political and military handicaps.

Kemal's second contribution was the founding of a republican state. This was something other than the creation of a nation. It was no small contribution to be able to establish a republican form of government in a country that had no experience in it and whose past was wholly imperial. Furthermore, republicanism survived Kemal's death, an indication that the institutions of Kemal's regime had enduring capacities. After Kemal's death, Ismet Inonu was elected president without the serious trouble that sometimes follows the death of a great leader. This is another indication that the Kemalist system succeeded in building a permanent political order.

There was a third contribution of great significance. Kemal's insistence upon a new social order in Turkey, encompassing new attitudes as well as new institutions, made it possible for Turkey to take a place among the progressive countries of the world. It was not, therefore, only a political revolution which took place in Turkey, but rather a revolution which had influenced the whole culture. Turkish attitudes toward their state, community, economy, and life in general were either modified or reconstructed, and the archaic Muslim system of values was also changed. It is true that some of these attitudes were modified only slightly, particularly in rural areas, but by and large the social forces which moved Turkey in the direction of modernization were new. It is also true that Turkey has not yet achieved a standard of living comparable to that of Western nations but it has made more progress than most countries of the Middle East and that progress was due to Kemalist indoctrination and the goals Kemal helped fix during the 1920's and 1930's.

Finally, the foreign policy of the Kemalist regime was a source of strength for Turkey. It was consistent and logical. Kemal foresaw that Turkey's only hope after the defeat of the Ottoman state was to concentrate on securing recognition of its territorial rights. To do so it must abandon the idea of empire and negotiate with the victorious states on the assumption that it was the Empire which was defeated and not Turkey, the country, which if left alone would pose no threat to the world. To accomplish his great task, he avoided antagonizing the European powers. His position was neutralist, and neutralism continued to be the guiding principle of foreign policy throughout his life.

CHAPTER 2

TURKEY'S EXPERIMENT
IN DEMOCRACY

U N D E R Kemal Ataturk, Turkey had a dictatorship. We should distinguish, however, between Ataturk's dictatorship and the kind represented by Fascist Italy and Nazi Germany. Ataturk's rule was paternalistic. His regime resorted to violence only when faced with violent opposition, and it did not practice such methods of repression as concentration camps, assassination, and mass extermination. It was less restrictive than the dictatorships of Hitler and Mussolini and allowed criticism in speech and in books, although it did not tolerate newspaper criticism. Officials who criticized the regime, however, were banished to remote, unimportant posts.[1] Ataturk's, then, might be called a benevolent dictatorship. He believed that Turkey was not ready for democracy and that certain reforms were desperately needed before the regime could turn the government over to the people.

DEVELOPMENT OF OPPOSITION

A basic policy of Ataturk's dictatorship was the political monopoly of the Republican party. While he was alive, no other party was allowed to exist for any significant length of time. After his death more overt expression of a desire for democracy appeared, but World War II made its realization impossible. After the war, however, opposition became so strong that the Republicans could not maintain their monopoly. Three factors, particularly, compelled a gradual transition to a multiparty system: First, the implication of the Republican party's philosophy that the dictatorship should remain only until Turkey was ready for democracy. After nearly a quarter of a century of one-party rule, the question of readiness became prominent, not only in the minds of the masses of the Turkish people, but within the

1. Bernard Lewis, "Recent Developments in Turkey," *International Affairs,* XXVII (July, 1951), 321.

Republican party itself. The liberal wing of the party maintained that the time had come to relax political restrictions and that an organized opposition party should now be tolerated. President Ismet Inonu, who succeeded Ataturk to the presidency, was of such an opinion, and although he did not wish to lead an opposition, he is credited with encouraging the growth of opposition parties.

Second, the defeat of Germany and Italy aided democratic forces because it demonstrated that democratic governments could be strong governments. Since its inception, the Republican party had sought the modernization and Westernization of Turkey's political institutions as well as its culture, and the Republic was especially sensitive to trends associated with the outcome of the war: the triumph of the democracies had an immense impact.

Third, the Turkish government realized that, in the postwar period, it would need help from the West both for economic development and for defense against possible Soviet aggression. To obtain this assistance—and the "proper moral recognition"—Turkish leaders believed that democratization of the political system would be necessary.[2]

The most significant pressure for democratization came from within the Republican party when, on August 15, 1945, the Charter of the United Nations was being discussed for ratification in the Grand National Assembly. The issue of one-party rule was brought up by Adnan Menderes (after the 1950 election, Menderes would become the prime minister). He maintained that the charter would be meaningless unless the government respected the sovereignty of the people. Other issues, too, provided occasions for voicing opposition to the government; finally, in June 1945, four outstanding members of Parliament—Celal Bayar, Adnan Menderes, Faud Koprulu, and Refik Koraltan—submitted a proposal to the Republican party's membership in Parliament. The Proposal of the Four, as it was known, contained three demands, which were designed to achieve democratic political life in Turkey: (1) The Grand National Assembly should be allowed to exercise some control over the government; (2) the constitutional rights of Turkish citizens should be respected; (3) political parties should be permitted to exist, and political activity should be encouraged.[3]

The Republican party's Parliamentary Group rejected these demands, and as a result, open opposition rapidly developed in the party organization and among the masses of the people. Subsequently, Menderes, Koprulu, and Koraltan were expelled from the Republican party; and Bayar, who

2. Kemal H. Karpat, *Turkey's Politics* (Princeton: Princeton University Press, 1959), pp. 137–43.
3. Karpat, *Turkey's Politics,* p. 145.

would become the Republic's president in 1950, resigned from the Assembly. These four men became the nucleus of the new, opposition Democratic party, formally established in January, 1946.

The leaders of the new party realized that unless the laws pertaining to freedom of the press, to freedom of association, and to the electoral system were amended, their chances of winning an election or even of the party's staying in existence were extremely slight. Therefore, they boycotted the nationwide municipal elections held in May 1946 and continued to press for reform of the electoral system; thus, the Republican party again ran unopposed.

But although the elections gave no immediate strength to the Democratic party, they were important to the development of democracy. Pressure from the new opposition freed the nomination process from interference. Previously, nomination of candidates was controlled by the Republican party. In addition, as a result of these municipal elections, for the first time the Republican party began to realize that the Turkish voter was concerned about the extent of influence he should have on government. Consequently, the Republican party became aware of the importance of election campaigns and of the fact that political power was, in the final analysis, based on popular support.

The municipal elections also made the issue of electoral reform so important on the national scale that the government could no longer ignore it and decided to introduce certain reforms prior to the next general elections, which had been scheduled for 1947. Legislation regulating the press was modified so that the power to close newspapers was transferred from the executive branch of the government to the courts. Newspapermen were allowed to form their own professional societies without governmental interference. Legislation regulating freedom of association was amended so that only the courts could limit such freedom. Some changes were made in the election law, but the Democratic party remained dissatisfied in this area, for the government retained the power to regulate election procedure instead of giving the courts the responsibility for determining the validity of elections and the legality of electoral practices. The Democrats had also strongly advocated proportional representation, but this was unacceptable to the government.

The government advanced the national elections from 1947 to July 21, 1946, ignoring Democratic protests that this was a tactical move designed to allow the opposition party insufficient time to strengthen its organization in the provinces. Because of this tactic, the Democratic party had no chance to gain control of the government, but the outcome of the 1946 elections did guarantee an opposition in the Assembly, for out of a total of

465 seats, the Democrats won 64 and the Republicans 395, with Independents holding the remaining 6.

After the election the Democratic party was subjected to pressures from factions that hoped to dominate the new party and to inject its philosophy into the party's official program. There were those who wanted the new party to support the theory of the corporate state and hence to present itself to the people as the party of change; others wanted it to adhere to the Ataturk tradition by claiming the Republicans had betrayed that tradition. When it emerged, however, the Democratic party's program was very similar to that of the Republicans. The Democrats adopted the six Kemalist principles embodied in the philosophy of the Republican party and in the Constitution of the Republic. Thus, the Democratic party's principles reflected no real ideological differences from the Republican; they arose merely because of the government's failure to put into effect the basic principles of the Turkish Constitution.[4] The similarity of the parties' programs meant that the Turkish voter's choice was between two parties which differed only in their interpretation of Kemalism, and, of course, between personalities.

Perhaps the most important disagreement between the parties was in their interpretation of etatism. Etatism had originally meant that the state could enter only those economic areas which private enterprise could not develop. The Democratic party accused the government of having corrupted etatism by giving the state too much economic power, which destroyed private initiative. It promised to encourage private enterprise and to withdraw the government from economic activities which could be better handled by private enterprise. The state would regulate only such key activities as transportation, electric power production, and water power and mining.[5]

The Democratic party also declared that it would restore citizens' rights as they had been guaranteed by the Constitution of 1924—rights which it claimed the Republicans had abrogated. Moreover, it guaranteed full employment and promised insurance protection for the aged, the sick, and the disabled.[6] Further, it promised such electoral reforms as direct and secret ballot and freedom of action for all political parties and organizations except those dominated by foreign powers.

4. Ahmed Amin Yalman, "The Struggle for Multi-Party Government in Turkey," *The Middle East Journal* (1947), p. 55.

5. Yalman, *The Middle East Journal*, p. 55.

6. A. C. Edwards, "The Impact of the War on Turkey," *International Affairs*, XXXI (July, 1946), 394.

THE LIBERALIZATION OF THE
REPUBLICAN PARTY

The establishment of the Democratic party affected the political character of the Republican party. For the first time, the old party was faced with opposition that had popular support and that was determined to win control of the government. This challenge divided the Republican party into two factions: an extremist, led by Prime Minister Recep Peker; and a moderate, led by Professor Nihat Erim. The extremists wanted to limit the political activity of the opposition and to use the government's power to prevent its growth. They feared that political freedom would reduce their influence and finally destroy them politically. The second group was liberal enough to concede that the opposition had as much right to free political action as the party in power. President Inonu gave moral support to the moderates when he declared, on July 12, 1947, that "an opposition party which uses legal methods and not revolutionary ones must enjoy the same privileges as the party in power." [7]

Both factions realized that the Democratic party could benefit from these rivalries, especially if they brought about the separation of Inonu from his party. And both factions were determined to resolve their differences without a split, which would most certainly bring the Democrats closer to power. Although the extremists were in the majority, they lost the battle against the moderates. The extremists had to yield; if they did not, they would have run the risk of severing the party's relations with the president, who supported the moderates. Prime Minister Peker resigned, and it seemed as if a new, democratic era was about to begin. The new premier, Hasan Saka, was a liberal Republican whose program was designed to make the two-party system a reality. He was determined to enforce the reform policies President Inonu had proclaimed on various occasions.

The liberal trend within the Republican party necessitated certain changes in the party's philosophy and structure, and the Seventh Republican Convention, which met in Ankara on November 17, 1947, considered the question of reform and made recommendations to liberalize the party's philosophy. Although these recommendations were not of a fundamental nature, they did lessen governmental control in the social and cultural areas (family affairs, education, etc.).

Also, the Convention's recommendations brought about a somewhat more democratic party structure, making it possible for the rank and file of the party to participate in policy-making and in selection of officials. The party chairman and vice-chairman were to be elected for two years and in

7. Quoted by Karpat, *Turkey's Politics*, p. 191.

case the chairman was elected to the national presidency, the vice-chairman was to perform his duties in the party organization; the convention was to become the most powerful organ of the party; and 70 per cent of the party's candidates to the Grand National Assembly were to be nominated by the local organization.[8] This liberalization deprived the Democratic party of its most effective weapon: the accusation that the Republicans did not want any serious opposition and, therefore, did not desire democratic government in Turkey. Thus, the Republican party was able to regain some of its popularity.

Additional reforms were introduced in the period preceding the 1950 elections. Most notable among these were: (1) The abolition of legislation allowing the police to arrest citizens without warrants; (2) the adoption of a liberal policy toward religion whereby religious instruction was reintroduced into the public schools, and a faculty of theology was created at the University of Ankara; (3) the encouragement of free enterprise and the reduction of taxes; (4) the passage of a new electoral law (February 1950) which provided for secret ballot, public counting of votes, equal distribution of radio time among political parties, and most important, the supervision of elections by the courts.[9]

MINOR PARTIES

From 1945 to 1950, minor parties were organized in addition to the Democratic party. On July 20, 1948, the Millet Partisi (National party) was organized by those who, believing that the Democrats were actually conspiring with the Republicans to share power, were dissatisfied with the Democratic party as the party of opposition. Marshal Fevzi Cakmak, a man with great prestige, supported the new party and soon assumed its chairmanship. The party's principles were vague, and it did not offer a concrete program. Nevertheless, the party promised to subordinate the state to the individual rather than the opposite, as was the case under the Republicans; to lower taxes; to hold honest elections; to raise the standard of living; and to safeguard the moral standards of the Turks by strengthening the institutions of family and religion.[10]

Many Turks criticized the Millet Partisi for dividing the opposition at a time when the country desperately needed a strong, united opposition party. However, although the program of the party was vague, its leaders were more vigorous than the Democrats in their opposition to and criti-

8. Karpat, *Turkey's Politics*, pp. 207–8.
9. Geoffrey Lewis, *Turkey* (New York: Frederick A. Praeger, 1955), p. 127.
10. Siegbert J. Weinberger, "Political Upset in Turkey," *Middle East Affairs* (May, 1950), p. 139.

cism of the government, so much so that the Republicans became less sensitive to Democratic opposition and, therefore, more tolerant of the Democratic party. On the other hand, the type of opposition the Millet Partisi launched forced the Democrats to define their program more carefully in hopes of convincing the Turkish voter that theirs was truly an opposition party. Thus, the net impact of the Millet Partisi strengthened rather than weakened the two-party system in Turkey.

The assumption of power by the Democratic party in 1950 saw the creation of a number of minor parties, most of them small protest movements aimed at the prevailing political conditions, such as the lack of political freedom, and at the policies of the Democratic party. Some favored a return to Republican policies; others were disappointed that the Democratic party had not lived up to all its promises.

Disappointment with the Democrats brought about the organization of the Freedom party in 1955. This party included erstwhile Democrats and numerous influential individuals, many of whom were deputies and former ministers. Its program comprised a series of specific proposals to amend the Constitution in order to prevent the party in power from destroying democratic government. Among these proposals were a system of checks and balances, an independent judiciary with a supreme court possessing the power of judicial review, additional constitutional provisions for the protection of political parties, and a bicameral legislature.

We shall consider other parties when we discuss the politics of elections and the political developments after the military coup of 1960. The important point is that, for a number of reasons, minor parties in the years 1946–60 did not play any really important role in Turkish political life. They were, as we mentioned, protest movements, and as such they objected to one or another of the political conditions but did not present concrete programs of action. Furthermore, they were not very different from the two major parties except, perhaps, in that they seemed determined to fulfill the promises which the major parties made but did not keep. Their dissatisfaction was mainly with the leadership of the two major parties. Thus, they acted on the assumption that the political system suffered mainly because of the incompetence of its leadership and, above all, by a lack of sincerity and honesty. Finally, they did not know how to organize on the grassroots level and therefore did not amass the popular support necessary to win power.

Nevertheless, these parties served some purpose. They warned the two major parties of the danger that might result from excessive use of power; they kept the issue of democracy alive in Turkish politics; and finally, their generally moderate positions demonstrated that there was in Turkey a consensus regarding political philosophies and goals.

THE POLITICS OF ELECTIONS 1950-60

The liberal policies of the Republican party and the electoral reforms it introduced made possible the first truly free elections in Turkey. And with these elections, held May 14, 1950, the Republican regime fell at last. The platforms of the two parties were very similar in the 1950 campaign. They were in complete agreement on foreign policy and on major domestic goals. Both promised to lower taxes, encourage private enterprise, and strengthen the economy. The Democrats made an issue of economic difficulties, blaming them on lack of investment and productions,[11] poor political organization, government monopolies, an unbalanced budget, and the government's inability to use foreign capital effectively. The economic argument, although it could not be considered an ideological difference, was the strongest, since economic conditions in Turkey were not good.[12] Taxes were high and so were most prices.

The results of the elections were totally unexpected. The new Democratic party won 408 seats in the National Assembly; the Republicans won only 69; the Independents, 9; and the National party, 1. This overwhelming Democratic victory marked the end of one-party rule in Turkey. Democracy had been brought to Turkey through peaceful methods; both the defeated Republicans and the victorious Democrats displayed dignity and restraint in the transfer of power.[13]

How had it happened? The most likely explanation is simply that the Turks were tired of the political monopoly of the Republicans and wanted a different group of representatives in the government. No one was looking for radical changes in domestic or foreign policies, although the new government was expected to improve economic conditions. Another reason for the Democratic victory was that the Turks were anxious to know whether anyone who was not a member of the Republican party could be trusted with the future of the country. Then, too, many Turks felt that an actual transfer of power through the means of free election was an essential test of democratic institutions in Turkey.[14]

In addition, powerful social groups and religious leaders were eager to see the Republican party out of power. The landowning class, which had enjoyed privileged status under the Ottoman regime, had been deprived of its privileges by local Republican organizations. And many of the social

11. Excerpts from the Democratic Party Election Manifesto can be found in *Middle Eastern Affairs*, I, 149.
12. Sarah P. McCally, "Party Government in Turkey," *Journal of Politics*, XVIII (May, 1956), 316.
13. Bernard Lewis, *International Affairs*, XXVII, 326.
14. Malcolm Burr, "Change in Turkey," *The Fortnightly*, CLXVIII (1950), 151.

and economic functions once performed by the rural landowners had been appropriated by local party organizations.[15] Although the Democratic party also had local organizations similar in some respects to the Republican groups, they functioned chiefly as an instrument of party propaganda rather than as governmental agencies. Therefore, discontent in the rural areas fell on the Republicans. Many religious leaders also did not support the Republican party because of its anticlerical policy while in power, and these groups were influential among the peasants. Although the Republicans had shown more tolerance toward religion after 1945, they had not satisfied these leaders who apparently wished to even old scores. Most clericalists voted for the Democrats, although the more extreme elements among them voted for the Millet Partisi. Non-Muslim minorities also contributed to the defeat of the Republicans. The Republicans had reduced the commercial influence and activity of these minorities by its policy of state ownership and supervision of the economy. And the minorities also wanted a change of personalities.

The next elections were to be held in 1954. The events preceding them are important, since they reveal the accomplishments of the new party during its first four years in power. Immediately after the 1950 election, the Democratic party made several changes in existing governmental policies. Prices of basic commodities were lowered; a general amnesty for political criminals was declared; free movement, which had long been curtailed by cumbersome formalities, was allowed; the recitation of the call to prayer in Arabic was also permitted; and the Turkish radio was permitted to broadcast readings from the Koran.[16]

The Democrats were most successful in their economic policies. The peasant, for example, benefited substantially from the Democrats' agricultural policy. Arable land used for growing cereal rose from 8,244,000 hectares [17] in 1950 to 10,832,000 in 1953. Turkey became a wheat-exporting country, ranking fourth in the world. Cotton production rose also from 118,000 metric tons in 1950 to 140,000 tons in 1953, and tobacco production rose from 93,000 metric tons to 122,000 during the same period. The increase in agricultural production was caused by the use of modern agricultural machinery. For example, in 1949 there were 6,500 tractors in use on Turkish farms; in 1953 there were 42,000. Industrial production also expanded. Coal output increased from 4.4 million tons to 5.7 million tons; steel production rose from 90,786 tons to 162,641 tons; cement production increased from 396,000 tons to 517,200 tons. This

15. Bernard Lewis, *International Affairs*, XXVII, 327.
16. Bernard Lewis, *International Affairs*, XXVII, 325.
17. A hectare (ha.) is a metric unit of area equal to 10,000 square meters or 2.471 acres.

economic-improvement program required imported capital equipment the cost of which affected the foreign-trade balance by bringing about a rise in the deficit from 62 million Turkish liras [18] in 1950 to 382 million in 1953. Thus, the government of the Democratic party had to rely heavily on credit. Without United States assistance, the Turkish government could not possibly have made such rapid economic progress, nor could it long afford the trade deficit which had been a problem in the past. By the end of 1953, Turkey had received $284 million in economic aid from the United States; it had also received loans amounting to $60 million from the International Bank for Reconstruction and Development.[19] The modification of etatism and the encouragement of free enterprise seem to have contributed to these improvements in the economy. Agricultural successes were such that when there was a substantial drop in agricultural production in 1954, the Office of Soil Products was able to provide needed goods from the stored surplus of the years 1951–53.

The economic boom of the first three years following the 1950 elections enabled the Democratic party to win 503 seats in the National Assembly in 1954. The Republicans won only 31 seats, while the Independents won 2 seats, and the National party increased its membership from 1 to 5.

The new government's policies in regard to personal freedom were a great disappointment, however.[20] In 1954, the Grand National Assembly empowered the government to dismiss civil servants without allowing them the right to appeal. In these categories of employees were judges with less than ten years of service and university professors. A press law made it a crime to insult government officials and members of Parliament or to publish false information which would discredit the state. The election laws were modified to enable the National Assembly, and therefore the party with the majority, to certify the validity of the credentials of its members. "Mixed lists" and "electoral coalitions" were declared illegal. Finally, political parties were not permitted to use radio facilities for propaganda or election campaigns. This, of course, gave the government an advantage, since it did not prevent government officials from reporting on their activities.

Election campaigns displayed interest in particular social classes.[21] The support of the peasant, who accounted for over 80 per cent of the electorate [22] and whose defection from the Republican party brought the Demo-

18. U.S. $1.00 equals TL. 2.825.
19. Figures on economic developments in Turkey were taken from K. M. Smogorzewski, "Democracy in Turkey," *The Contemporary Review,* CXXCVI (August, 1954), 81–82.
20. McCally, *Journal of Politics,* XVIII, 322.
21. McCally, *Journal of Politics,* XVIII, 322.
22. See "Turkey Votes," *New Statesman* (October, 1957), pp. 519–20.

cratic party to power, was sought by all parties. The Democratic party's agricultural policy benefited the large landowners, who managed for some time to provide the support of the rural areas to the Democrats. But there were dangerous signs of restlessness among the small landowners and the peasantry.

To a lesser degree, organized labor was influencing political life. The Turkish Confederation of Labor Unions had been established in September 1952 with government approval. Collective bargaining and the right to strike were among the demands of the union, and before the Democrats came to power they promised to grant labor the right to strike. However, the Democratic party was reluctant to fulfill its promises, and labor became a potential enemy of the government.

Gradually the Democratic party became aware of dangerous trends in the political situation. We have already mentioned the establishment of the Freedom party in 1955, an outgrowth of internal dissension that threatened the party's future. Inflation was becoming a serious problem after 1954, and government policy on the issue of civil liberties brought criticism from opposition parties and from other sources. For fear that its political position might become still worse, the government announced that the elections would be held in 1957 instead of May 1958, the regularly scheduled time. This strategy, plus a well-organized campaign that used government resources such as radio and transport facilities, saved the Democrats from defeat: they won 421 seats in the National Assembly as against 173 for the Republicans; the Millet Partisi was able to capture 4 seats, and the Freedom party another 4.

But the Democratic party's success at the polls did not obscure the fact that many people were becoming disenchanted with its policies. Furthermore, popular strength could not be measured by the number of seats a party obtained in a previous election. Because of the use of the single-member district in elections, it was possible for a political party with a small majority of the popular vote to win a large majority of seats in the National Assembly.[23] Nevertheless, the Democratic party had, after the 1957 election, a sufficient majority to work with in order to improve its chances in the next elections, which were to come in 1961.

THE 1960 COUP AND ITS PROBLEMS

Following the elections of 1957, the Democrats continued the policies that had been eroding their popularity. The policy of deficit spending continued. There was no rational planning of the economy, and for political reasons factories were often built in unsuitable areas. Sugar refineries, for

23. "Amber for Mr. Menderes," *The Economist*, CXXCV (November, 1957), 388.

example, were built where peasants did not grow sugar beets.[24] Also, Turkey's commercial debt increased, and by 1958 it had reached $420 million. The budget for 1959–60 showed an increase in expenditures of 22 per cent, while there was no change in the amount of revenue. It was obvious that the Menderes government wanted to spend but did not want to tax. Such a policy, calculated to cultivate political support, had to be dangerous economically. And the worse the economic picture looked, the greater became the opposition to the government responsible for it.

Menderes began to suppress the opposition with more vigor than previously. The climax to the government's oppressive policies was the establishment of a special court to try members of Parliament who dared to criticize the government. Students began to demonstrate against the government, and opposition parties became more outspoken. Finally, when word came that Menderes was about to order the arrest of several high-ranking army officers, the army decided to strike first. In a very short time, all government offices were occupied and many important government officials were arrested.[25]

The coup took place on May 27, 1960 under the leadership of General Cemal Gursel. A national Unity Committee composed of the military was set up to rule the country until arrangements for a civilian government could be worked out. The committee was to assume the powers of the Grand National Assembly. Immediately after the coup the ruling junta promised the elimination of corruption, a return to civilian government, and, above all, the reinstitution of democratic government. The need for social and economic reforms, long neglected by the ousted regime, was stressed.

Menderes and his colleagues were tried on October 14, 1960. The trials lasted eleven months, and the new government did its best to insure fair trials for the 592 defendants. However, in an attempt to justify the coup, the government encouraged sensational news and publicity, and unfortunate incidents took place in which the government appeared too anxious to discredit the old regime. But all this did not jeopardize the rights of the defendants in the proceedings of the trials; in fact, the trials were held on the island of Yassiada, partly for security reasons, but also to remove the judges from the influence of the publicity in the press, promoted by the government. On September 15, 1961, the court sentenced to death President Bayar, Menderes, Foreign Minister Zorlu, and Finance Minister Polatkin.

The military group, inexperienced in politics, found that governing and

24. M. Philips Price, "Turkey Since the May Revolution," *The Contemporary Review*, CXCIX (1961), 18.
25. Price, *The Contemporary Review*, CXCIX (1961), 18.

reforming were not easy tasks. For one thing, just prior to the coup Turkey had begun to experience a social transformation that required a new political approach—an acceptance of the fact that the new social structure required modification in government policy and party strategy. Industrialization and state sponsorship of economic planning made possible the interplay of economics and politics, and economic problems became political issues. New social groups were emerging and, as they increased in size, were beginning to influence politics. The urban proletariat, the new entrepreneur class, and the now power-conscious peasantry were no longer satisfied with the political philosophies of either the Democrats or the Republicans. The intelligentsia in Turkey did not favor democracy at all, for they felt it was conservative and uninteresting. They distrusted the economically privileged classes as well as the masses of the Turkish people, suspecting the first group of being too selfish to want real democracy and the second of being ignorant. Democracy, therefore, would either result in a system of exploitation or in no system at all, with resulting chaos. The best form of government, these intellectuals believed, would be a government composed of their own kind. The moderate intellectuals were opposed to universal suffrage and favored instead a system which would rigidly limit democracy. They wanted a political scene that would be dominated by intellectuals, but they did not wish the destruction of the democratic system. The extremists, however, wanted to do away with the multiparty system in favor of an enlightened dictatorship.[26]

In addition to tensions among classes, there were conflicts between civilians and military within the ruling group. Not accustomed to the political process which demands flexibility, the military began to resent and to lose patience with civilian officials in government, and they began making decisions without consulting them. For instance, when the military planned a national health service and a land-reform program, they did not discuss either matter with the civilian ministers in charge. One cannot say that the lack of communication between the civilian and the military was the result of civilian involvement in politics, for these officials were selected largely because they were "above party." Nevertheless, the problem of communication between the two groups was real,[27] and on August 25, 1960, General Gursel, the prime minister, dismissed ten of the fifteen civilian ministers. For fear that he would be accused of creating a military dictatorship, he declared that he intended to replace the ousted ministers by other civilians with whom he could cooperate.

26. For social developments before the 1960 coup see Kemal H. Karpat, "Recent Political Developments in Turkey and Their Social Background," *International Affairs*, XXXVIII, 3 (1961), 304–23.

27. Geoffrey Lewis, "Turkey: The Thorny Road to Democracy," *The World Today*, XVIII, 5 (1961), 182.

There was also the problem of factions within the military group. One faction believed that the military should establish itself permanently in power. Only if this were done, this faction believed, could Turkey advance into a new progressive era—into the twentieth century. To return to civilian government and democracy would mean to surrender the country to another political party as corrupt as the Democratic party, which, this faction argued, had, after all, come to power democratically through the elections of 1950.

THE CONSTITUTION AND THE RESTORATION OF POLITICAL PARTIES

The first step toward return to civilian government was the establishment of a Constituent Assembly on January 6, 1961, to draft a new constitution. The Assembly was composed of an upper house, the Committee, and a lower house, which represented the provinces, political parties, and professional groups. Of course, the Democratic party was not represented, having been officially disbanded by court order in September 1960. The Republican party had nearly 80 per cent of the vote in the Assembly.[28] In July 1961, the new Constitution was submitted to the electorate for approval: 6.3 million voted for the Constitution, 3.9 million voted against it, and 2.4 million did not vote.

On January 13, 1961, political parties were permitted to organize, and eleven new parties were officially founded. Only four of these had any chance of becoming politically important: the Republican party, the Justice party, the New Turkey party, and the Peasant National party.

In the mind of the average Turkish citizen, the Republican party was identified with the ruling military group. The majority of the members of the constituent assembly which drafted the Constitution either belonged to the Republican party or sympathized with it; therefore, the party was responsible for establishing the institutional forms of the new civilian regime. The party was not wholly identified with the military group, for on a few occasions it checked the power of the military. Generally speaking, however, the Republicans refrained from showing signs of opposition to the military group, for two important reasons. First, they were afraid that even limited opposition might induce the military to outlaw political parties and even to establish a military dictatorship. Second, they believed that open opposition to the military group would validate the accusation that the Republican party's "obstructive" policies prior to the coup were responsible

28. Geoffrey Lewis, *The World Today*, XVIII, 186.

for Turkey's political and economic situation. In other words, the Republicans feared that the public might blame them along with the Democrats for all the ills of Turkey.[29]

Naturally, political developments after the coup necessitated a reassessment of the policies of the Republican party. The new Republican party was dominated by the progressives, an indication that the party would be a forward-looking political organization. Ismet Inonu continued to lead the Republicans, but this time he was assisted by a young and progressive group. On the local level, however, the old conservative element was in full control of the party organization. These conservatives believed in the economic policy of etatism as it was interpreted during their one-party rule, before the Democrats had gained control of the government. The result of the election of October 15, 1961 showed that the party suffered because the unpopular conservative group controlled the local organizations.[30]

The Justice party was led by General Ragib Gumuspala, who, prior to the coup, was commander of the Third Army. After the coup, Gumuspala became chief of the general staff, but was among five thousand officers who were retired when the government decided to "rejuvenate" the armed forces. His party hoped to attract the support of these officers and also of the followers of the outlawed Democratic party. The Justice party promised to strengthen local government by transferring many of national governmental functions to local authorities. This, the party believed, would establish better democracy in Turkey.[31] It also promised to exempt from taxes real estate and agricultural produce, and to tax only earnings. In addition, the party proposed to turn over many state monopolies to private enterprise and to reduce prices on many commodities such as gasoline and oil. General Gumuspala was outspoken in criticizing the military group, and it is possible that only the intervention of Ismet Inonu saved his party from being outlawed by the military.

The New Turkey party also relied on former Democrats for political support; and its leadership was new as was that of the Justice party. On the local level both parties were controlled by former Democrats. The program of the New Turkey party was extremely vague. It made reference to liberal economic policies and expressed opposition to the etatism of the Republican party. It warned against concentration of wealth and unfair distribution of income. On the other hand, the party promised to use the power of the state to aid private enterprise in every way possible. Some principles of the

29. Karpat, *International Affairs*, XXXVIII, 316.
30. Karpat, *International Affairs*, XXXVIII, 317.
31. Walter F. Weiker, *The Turkish Revolution 1960–1961* (Washington, D.C.: The Brooklings Institution, 1963), p. 95.

New Turkey party were similar to those of Ataturk. For instance, there was emphasis upon secularism which was one of the basic principles of Kemalism.

Finally, there was the Peasant National party, the most conservative of the four important parties. It was an offshoot of General Cakmak's National party, established in 1948. Although a national party, its strength was mainly in the thirteen provinces east of Ankara, the capital. Like the New Turkey party, the Peasant National party had no concrete program to speak of. In the election of 1961, it campaigned against the Republican party by pointing out its weaknesses but did not really offer solutions or plans. Thus, its appeal was based largely upon its conservative attitude and the few attractive personalities in its ranks.

THE 1961 ELECTIONS AND FORMATION OF A NEW GOVERNMENT

On October 15, 1961, Turkey went to the polls to elect its representatives to the new, bicameral Grand National Assembly. In the Senate, the upper house in the Assembly, the Republican party gained 36 seats, the Justice party, 70; the New Turkey party, 28; and the Peasant National party, 16. In the National Assembly, the lower house, the Republicans obtained 173 seats, the Justice party, 158; the New Turkey party, 65; and the Peasant National party, 54.

These election results meant that the electorate did not give any party a clear mandate, although the Republican party controlled the largest number of seats in the lower house; that if the three parties united in opposition to the Republican party, they could obstruct the policies of a government formed by the Republicans; and that a coalition government, usually unstable and ineffective, would possibly be the only alternative to having no government at all.

The outcome of the elections was a great disappointment to the military, which believed that the Republican party would protect the dignity of the military and would refrain from doing anything which would weaken its traditional status.

Nevertheless, a government had to be organized. Thus on October 26, the two houses elected General Gursel to the presidency by a vote of 434 to 173. The only one candidate opposing the general was Professor Ali Fuad Bashgil, who was intimidated into leaving Ankara.[32] Professor Bashgil had defended Menderes, maintaining that the former prime minister had not violated the Constitution. The new president appointed Inonu prime minister. It was clear that a new government could be formed only if

32. Geoffrey Lewis, *The World Today,* XVIII, 188.

the new prime minister could persuade the other parties to participate in a coalition. The Justice party refused to be part of such a coalition unless the imprisoned Democrats were given amnesty and unless the prime minister resigned from his party so that both the president and the prime minister would be "above party." The army then threatened to take repressive measures against the Justice party to force it to cooperate; and a coalition government was formed composed of the Republican and Justice parties, each providing eleven ministers.

THE GOVERNMENT OF THE JUSTICE PARTY

The issue of amnesty for the convicted followers of Menderes and differences over economic policies broke up the first coalition government on May 31, 1962. Opposition groups in the Assembly, being heirs to the outlawed Democratic party, demanded the release of political prisoners. They were not disposed to support a government that did not respond to their demands. Consequently, Inonu had to agree on the amnesty, which was to be granted within six months, before he was able to form his second coalition government. This new government consisted of twelve Republicans, six members of the New Turkey party, four members of the Peasant National party, and one independent. One of the government's first acts was an amnesty bill which freed those serving prison sentences under six years.

Inonu's second coalition government collapsed under the impact of the local elections held in November 1963. These elections were the first of their kind since 1954. Of course, the government did not have to resign except for the fact that Inonu's junior partners in the coalition, who lost heavily in these local elections, had decided not to continue the partnership. Since it became impossible for Inonu to form another coalition government and the military establishment was not yet ready to cooperate with the Justice party, the second largest party in the Assembly, a one-party government under Inonu was the only possible alternative.

In spite of the fact that the new government received a vote of confidence from the Assembly, it was nevertheless a minority government, and its future was therefore very uncertain. Toward the end of 1964 circumstances were such that a major change in the governmental leadership was forthcoming. In the Senate election of June 1964, the Republican party was overshadowed by the Justice party, which won 31 out of 51 seats contested. In February 1965, the Assembly voted down the government on a budgetary issue. It was the first time that a Turkish government was compelled to resign in this manner, and it meant the end of Inonu as prime minister.

There was concern that the army might prevent the opposition parties from forming a government in the Assembly. These parties had not been able to gain the confidence of the army, which naturally suspected their loyalty to the Menderes tradition. A compromise was worked out according to which opposition parties were able to form a government under the leadership of an independent, Senator Suat Urguplu, who became the prime minister. The coalition consisted of the Justice party, the New Turkish party, the Peasant National party, and the National party.

The Justice party, which so far has been gaining influence but has not been able to control governments, became the predominant party in the Assembly after the elections which were held in October 1965. The party captured 240 out of 450 seats, while the Republican party dropped to 134. The National party gained 3 seats; the New Turkish party, 19; the Peasant National party, 11; and the Turkish Workers' party, 15. This last party was the big surprise of the elections. It was established in 1964 as a leftist group with a Marxist ideology—an innovation in Turkish politics. Nevertheless, the fact that it was allowed to exist and participate in the election signifies that those who staged the military coup of 1960 were sincere in their promises to give Turkey a democratic system of government.

The government that was formed after the elections was led by Suleiman Demirel, who had become the leader of the Justice party in November 1964. Before taking office, Demirel and his party gave ample proof that they would respect the principles of the 1960 "revolution." The conflict between the army and the new party appeared to have been resolved. Part of the credit should go to the former president of the Republic, General Gursel, who died in February 1966, and to his successor, General Cevdet Sunay. These two men tried their best to give Turkey a stable and moderate political posture.

The most significant fact about Turkish political life since 1965 is the lack of military interference in the affairs of state. The cabinet crisis of February 1965, the release of political prisoners, including former President Bayar, and the elections of 1965 all demonstrate the military's restraint. There are signs that Turkey may have succeeded in returning to civilian rule.

CHAPTER 3

TURKEY: THE POLITICAL SYSTEM AND PUBLIC POLICY

FOR institutions to take form, mature, and function properly, time and experience are necessary. The Turkish Second Republic is still in its formative years. Consequently, a study of its political institutions must emphasize the formal governmental organization, procedures, and relationships. In this chapter we shall concern ourselves with the constitutional framework of the Turkish state and with two aspects of public policy; economics and foreign relations.

THE CONSTITUTIONAL FRAMEWORK

The Constitution of 1961 is composed of 168 articles.[1] It was not designed to bring about a radical change in the institutional life of Turkish society. Rather, it was aimed at creating a political system that would profit by the experiences of the First Republic by avoiding past mistakes and preserving past contributions.

In drawing on previous experience, the 1961 Constitution has shown itself to be both practical and conservative. These characteristics may stem from the fact that the Republican party, which dominated the First Republic, was also the dominant force in the Constituent Assembly which drafted the new Constitution. In other aspects, the Constitution is idealistic and philosophical. For instance, in the area of fundamental rights it is concerned more with what ought to be than with what can be under present conditions in Turkey—with regard to both political and social institutions. Thus, it has made the Turkish citizen promises that could not be kept; whether or not this failure will yet cause trouble remains to be seen. It is evident that Turks were eager to institute a regime that would allow democratic participation in the political process. Such idealism, however, has the disadvantage of making judicial interpretation and application of constitu-

1. See text of Constitution in *The Middle East Journal*, XVI (1962), 215.

tional provisions very difficult; legal documents, to be applicable, must be practical.[2]

The outstanding feature of the 1961 Constitution pertains to the judiciary, which is independent and is given certain checks on the legislature and executive. The Constitution assumes that a powerful independent judiciary is the best safeguard against the development of a legislative-executive monopoly of power in a parliamentary regime which might wish to perpetuate itself by disregarding constitutional limitations. Judicial independence is assured in two ways. First, no single branch of the government controls judicial appointments or matters affecting the status of judges; second, disciplinary powers over the judiciary are given to the courts themselves. More will be said about these points when we explain the constitutional provisions pertaining to courts.

THE LEGISLATURE

The new Constitution has given Turkey a bicameral legislature. The two houses, together known as the Grand National Assembly, have the power "to enact and repeal laws, to debate and adopt the bills on the state budget and final accounts, to pass resolutions in regard to minting currency, proclaiming pardons and amnesties, and to the carrying out of definitive death sentences passed by the courts" (Art. 64). The Grand National Assembly also has the power to confirm treaties, declare war, and permit foreign troops to be stationed in Turkey. Confirmation by the Grand National Assembly is not necessary, however, for economic, commercial, and technical treaties which (1) are not valid after one year, (2) do not commit the state's finances, and (3) do not change existing law.

The lower house is the National Assembly, which is composed of 450 deputies elected directly by the people. The Constitution does not prescribe the method of election, although the Constituent Assembly which drafted it did specify, in a separate electoral law, that members of the National Assembly should be elected on the basis of a system of proportional representation and that senators must be elected by a plurality of votes.[3]

Each house elects its chairman, who serves in that capacity for two years. The chairman is not permitted to participate in debate except when his official role as chairman requires it. He cannot vote (Art. 84).

To qualify for election, a candidate for the lower house must be thirty years old; a candidate for the senate, forty. Ineligible for candidacy are:

2. Examples of this idealism are the constitutional guarantees of the right to rest (Art. 44), equity in wages (Art. 45), social security (Art. 48), and the right to medical care (Art. 49). These guarantees are possible only in financially sound political systems and well-rounded economies.

3. Ismet Giritli, "Some Aspects of the New Turkish Constitution," *The Middle East Journal*, XVI (1962), 8.

illiterates; those who illegally avoid conscription into the armed forces; anyone imprisoned for five years or more; or anyone convicted of a serious crime such as embezzlement, forgery, or bribery. Membership in the Grand National Assembly is incompatible with positions in the judiciary and the military. Higher education, something the Constitution leaves undefined, is a requirement for candidacy for the Senate.

The Senate is composed of 150 elected members and 15 members appointed by the president. Members of the National Unity Committee and former presidents are ex officio members of the Senate provided they do not join a political party after they become senators. No age limit applies to ex officio membership; and ex officio members, who serve for life, have the same duties and powers as elected senators.

Elections to the lower house are held every four years, although this house has the right to decide to hold an election before a current four-year term has expired. The Constitution provides that both houses may postpone elections for a period of one year in time of war. A senator's term of office is six years, but terms are staggered, so that one-third of the Senate comes up for re-election every two years. In making his fifteen allotted Senate appointments, the president is required to select individuals "distinguished for their services in various fields." At least ten appointees shall not be members of any political party.

The control and supervision of elections is the responsibility of the judiciary. To receive and review cases of irregularities in elections, a Supreme Election Board is set up composed of seven regular members and four alternates chosen by the Court of Cassation, the highest regular court, and the Council of State, the highest administrative court, in accordance with a specific formula.

Turkish legislators have immunities which exceed those accorded their American and British counterparts and which are more like those granted French legislators. They are not legally liable for the opinions they express or the votes they cast in the exercise of their duties (Art. 79). Authorization of the house to which they belong is required before they can be arrested or brought to trial in connection with any crime they have allegedly committed. A legislator may be arrested in the act of committing a crime; but even then, the arresting officer must inform the house of which the accused is a member. If the legislator is found guilty and sentenced to a prison term, the sentence is not enforced until after his term of office expires.

The legislative session begins each year on the first day of November, and the legislature may not be in recess for more than five months. While in recess, it may be reconvened in extraordinary session by the president or by the chairman of either house. It may also be reconvened at the request of the cabinet or of one-fifth of the membership of either house (Art. 83). An extraordinary session must give priority to the matters for which it has been called.

The Constitution recognizes the importance of political parties in the legislative process. The bylaws and procedures of each house are required to enable a political party group to participate in legislative activity "in proportion to its size." A political party group is recognized if it has at least ten members; members of smaller party groups have only the rights and privileges of ordinary members of the legislature.

LEGISLATIVE PROCEDURE

The Council of Ministers and members of either house may propose legislation. Whatever their origin, proposals must be considered by the lower house first. After the Assembly [4] has voted a bill, the Senate considers it; if accepted by the Senate, the bill becomes a draft law. If the Senate amends the bill, it goes back to the Assembly, where the amendments must be approved for the bill to become a draft law. If the Assembly rejects the Senate amendments, a conference committee is established to work on the bill.[5] The conference committee reports its revised bill to the National Assembly (the lower house) which can now accept without change the Senate amendments, accept without change the bill as reported by the conference committee, or adopt the bill in its original form. Whichever of the alternatives the Assembly chooses becomes a draft law. There are, however, two limitations on the Assembly's powers: (1) It needs an absolute majority of its total membership to adopt the bill in its original form if the Senate amendments were adopted by a similar majority of the Senate; and (2) it needs an absolute majority or a two-thirds vote of its total membership to approve a bill which was rejected in toto by a corresponding majority in the Senate.

Although all bills are introduced in the lower house, the upper house may act even if the lower house does not produce a draft bill. If a proposal is rejected in the lower house, it still requires Senate rejection to be void. If the Senate adopts the proposal after rejection by the lower house, with or without amendments, the Senate bill returns to the lower house to be reviewed. Should the Assembly approve the Senate bill, it becomes a draft law; otherwise it is declared void.

A draft law enacted by the Grand National Assembly requires the ap-

---

4. The reader should be careful to distinguish between the National Assembly which is the lower house of the legislature and the Grand National Assembly which refers to the two houses. To help the reader we sometimes refer to the National Assembly as "the Assembly" or, specifically, "the lower house."

5. Conference committees are "Composed of an equal number of members from among the relevant committees of both legislative bodies" (Art. 92).

proval of the president to become law. The president has ten days to approve or reject a bill. The Grand National Assembly may override a presidential veto simply by re-enacting the draft in the same manner as it did before the veto.

Budget bills and budget estimates follow a different procedure. They are submitted to the Council of Ministers at least three months prior to the beginning of the fiscal year (Art. 94), and a conference committee [6] is set up to work on them. The committee has eight weeks to act upon the bill, and the text the committee approves is sent to the Senate, which must review and vote on it within ten days. The bill is then returned to the conference committee which reviews it for a second time, for a period of one week. The final draft is then forwarded to the lower house for consideration, and the lower house must act before the beginning of the new fiscal year.

LEGISLATIVE CONTROLS OVER THE EXECUTIVE

In addition to making laws, the Grand National Assembly has powers of control over the government. Either house may inquire, investigate, or question the government as long as inquiries and investigations are conducted for the purpose of obtaining information on a specific subject (Art. 88). Only the lower house has the power of interpellation. Procedurally, a motion of interpellation is introduced by a member of a political party group in the Assembly. During debate on this motion, only the member who introduces it or a representative of the political party group sponsoring it can speak. The Council of Ministers is represented by either the prime minister or one of the ministers, who also may speak in regard to the motion made. If the motion is approved, the question of the interpellation is put on the agenda; but the interpellation itself is not discussed until at least two days after it is put on the agenda. A motion of nonconfidence may be introduced by a deputy during the discussion of the interpellation, and the Council of Ministers may also ask for a vote of confidence. However, such a motion or request may not be voted upon until after an interim of one full day, and an absolute majority of the Assembly is required to overthrow the government (Art. 89).

The prime minister can ask for a vote of confidence from the Assembly at any time. If such a request is denied by an absolute majority of the Assembly, the government is considered to have resigned (Art. 104). However, if within a period of eighteen months the Assembly forces three gov-

6. This type of conference committee is composed of thirty-five members from the lower house and fifteen from the upper house. At least thirty of the fifty seats in that committee should be assigned to the party or parties in power. The remaining seats are distributed proportionately among the remaining political parties and the independents.

ernments to resign, the prime minister may ask the president to call for new elections. The president may make such a decision after consulting the chairmen of the two legislative bodies (Art. 108).

The Constitution requires that before elections to the lower house are held, changes in the organization of the Council of Ministers must take place. If the elections are to be held before the legislative session expires, the ministers of Justice, Interior, and Communications must resign, and the prime minister must appoint in their places three independent members of the Grand National Assembly. If, on the other hand, the election is to be held after the dissolution of the Assembly by the president, all members of the Council of Ministers must resign. In this event, the prime minister forms a provisional Council of Ministers, which must represent proportionately the various political party groups in the lower house, and must have independents in the positions of minister of justice, minister of interior, and minister of communications.

THE EXECUTIVE

Executive power is shared by the president and the Council of Ministers (Art. 6). The president is elected by the Grand National Assembly from among its members for a term of seven years. A two-thirds majority of the total membership of the Grand National Assembly is necessary for the election of a president. However, if no candidate receives a two-thirds majority on the first two ballots, on the third ballot an absolute majority is sufficient. The president must be forty years of age or older and must meet the requirements for "higher education." Upon election, he must disassociate himself from his political party and surrender his membership in the Grand National Assembly. The president is not eligible for re-election.

The Grand National Assembly can impeach a president only for high treason. Any proposal to impeach must be approved by one-third of the total membership of the Grand National Assembly. This step constitutes an indictment, but for conviction a two-thirds majority of the total membership of the same body is required. In regard to offenses connected with his duties, the president is tried by the Constitutional Court (Art. 147).

If a president dies or his office otherwise becomes vacant, a new election must be held "immediately" (a term undefined by the Constitution). Meanwhile, the chairman of the Senate assumes the presidential duties, as he does if the president is temporarily incapacitated. Also, the Constitution stipulates that the Grand National Assembly must elect a new president fifteen days before the term of the incumbent president expires.

The president is the head of the state, and in this role he represents the Turkish people. He receives foreign representatives and dispatches representatives to foreign countries. He holds the power of veto over legislation, the power to ratify and promulgate treaties, and the power to pardon "on grounds of chronic illness, infirmity, or old age." He also presides over the Council of Ministers.

Perhaps the president's most important power is his authority to appoint the prime minister and the Council of Ministers. However, these appointments are subject to the approval of the lower house, which takes the form of a vote of confidence in the government's program. Failing to win the approval of the absolute majority of the National Assembly, the government is not formed, and the president must then nominate a new prime minister.

The prime minister is chosen from the membership of the Grand National Assembly. He nominates members for the Council of Ministers, also from the membership of the Grand National Assembly, by submitting their names to the president for his approval. The Council of Ministers is collectively and individually responsible for the implementation of the government's general policy and for the actions of their subordinates. Article 125 of the Constitution stipulates that if a public servant considers the orders of his superior illegal, he may refuse to obey the orders unless his superior reiterates them in writing, in which case the lower-ranking official is not held responsible. The ministers are granted the same immunities and are subject to the same liabilities as members of the Grand National Assembly.

The Council of Ministers may make all the necessary auxiliary regulations for the enforcement of law, provided that they are not in conflict with existing legislation. Such regulations are reviewed by the Council of Ministers and are signed by the president of the Republic. Individual ministers and corporate bodies may issue additional bylaws for the enforcement of laws and regulations, but here again, the bylaws must not be in conflict with existing legislation or regulations. These administrative acts and procedures are subject to judicial review, and the government is held responsible for any damages resulting from its operation.

NATIONAL DEFENSE

The Constitution makes specific provisions for national defense. Article 110 makes the president the commander-in-chief of the armed forces, representing the Grand National Assembly. The chief of the General Staff is appointed by the president on the recommendation of the Council of Ministers. The peculiarity of Article 110 is that it makes the chief of the General Staff responsible to the Council of Ministers and that body in turn responsible to the Grand National Assembly "for ensuring national security and preparing the armed forces for war." Consequently, it would appear that the president is only a nominal commander-in-chief.

There is a National Security Council composed of a number of ministers (to be determined by a special law), the chief of the General Staff, and representatives of the armed forces. The president presides over the council, and in his absence the prime minister takes his place. The council makes recommendations to the Council of Ministers on matters of national security.

In case of a state or threat of war, revolt, or uprising, the Council of Ministers may declare martial law for a period of one month, provided such a declaration receives the approval of the Grand National Assembly. At its discretion, the Grand National Assembly may shorten the period of martial law or abolish it. Only approval by the combined houses may extend martial law beyond the one-month limit, and extension periods may not exceed two months. The Constitution requires specific legislative definition of the manner in which areas under martial law are administered and of the limitations placed upon personal freedoms.

THE JUDICIARY

As we mentioned before, the Constitution provides for an independent judiciary, and this independence is ensured in part by the fact that disciplinary action against judges is left to the judiciary itself. With a few exceptions, disciplinary action may be taken only by the Supreme Council of Judges, which while not a court, is the agency that has the power to decide on all personnel matters pertaining to judges. The council has eighteen regular and five alternate members. Six regular members are elected by the Court of Cassation, Turkey's highest court of appeal; six regular members are chosen by judges of the first rank (a term the Constitution leaves undefined); and three are elected by each of the houses of the Grand National Assembly. Two of the five alternate members are chosen by the Court of Cassation, and one each by judges of the first rank and the houses of the legislature.

An absolute majority vote of the Supreme Council is required for the dismissal of a judge. The approval of the council is necessary to abolish a court or a staff position, or even to make changes in the jurisdiction of a court. The Constitution does, however, permit the minister of justice to ask the council to take disciplinary action against a judge. To ensure that the Supreme Council of Judges does not come under the influence of other agencies, the Constitution limits the term of office of its members to four years and requires that half of the members be elected every two years.

It is to be remembered that the Turkish Constitution creates only the higher courts. Lower courts are established by the legislature. Higher courts are of three types: regular, administrative, and military.

The highest regular court is the Court of Cassation, which reviews decisions of the lower courts. Although the Constitution makes this court primarily one of appeal, the Grand National Assembly may, by specific legislation, give the court original jurisdiction over certain cases. Members of the Court of Cassation are elected by the Supreme Council of Judges. The Court of Cassation elects its own chairman and vice-chairman as well as the chief prosecutor of the republic, by an absolute majority and by secret ballot.

The highest administrative court is the Council of State. This council is also primarily a court of appeal set up to review decisions of lower administrative courts. Cases which the legislature does not, by law, refer to other administrative courts, are heard by the council on original jurisdiction. The Constitution assigns other responsibilities to the Council of State, including the expression of opinion on draft laws submitted by the Council of Ministers and the examination of regulations made by the Council of Ministers for the purpose of implementing laws.

Members of the Constitutional Court, which determines the constitutionality of laws, elect the chairman, chief attorney, and other members of the Council of State by means of secret ballot. A two-thirds majority is sought, but if this majority cannot be obtained on the first two ballots, an absolute majority is then sufficient. The Constitution specifies that the nomination of candidates to the Council of State is the prerogative of the Council of Ministers and the Council of State itself, and each proposes a number of candidates equal to the number of vacancies.

The highest military court is the Military Court of Cassation, which has appellate jurisdiction, although the legislature may define areas of original jurisdiction. The president appoints judges to the Military Court of Cassation. Judges who serve on this court must meet the ordinary qualifications of other judges and in addition must be at least forty years of age, have at least ten years of experience as military judges and prosecutors, and must be recommended by an absolute majority of the Military Court of Cassation.

Outside the three types of court systems mentioned above, a Court of Jurisdictional Disputes was created by the Constitution to decide disagreements over the proper and legal jurisdiction of the various courts. However, the Constitution leaves matters pertaining to the organization and functions of this court to the legislature.

The establishment of a Constitutional Court is perhaps the unique feature of the judicial system of Turkey. Article 147 says: "the Constitutional Court shall review the constitutionality of laws and the by-laws of the

Turkish Grand National Assembly." Thus, the Turkish judicial system differs from that of the United States in the way it separates court functions and court jurisdictions: one has the power to review the constitutionality of laws (the Constitutional Court); the other is primarily designed to receive cases on final appeal (the Court of Cassation). The Supreme Court of the United States exercises the power of judicial review and is also a final court of appeal. Also, unlike the Supreme Court of the United States, which cannot determine the constitutionality of a law unless it receives a specific case involving such a law, the Constitutional Court of Turkey can declare a law unconstitutional upon request and without actually receiving a specific case. However, the right to contest the constitutionality of laws is granted by the Constitution only to specific governmental and corporate bodies. Among these are: the president; political parties which have received at least 10 per cent of the total valid votes cast in the previous general election; political parties (or their parliamentary groups) represented in the legislature; and one-sixth of the total membership of the legislature. In addition, but only insofar as "their duties and welfare" are concerned, the following agencies may contest the constitutionality of laws: the Supreme Council of Judges, the Court of Cassation, the Council of State, the Military Court of Cassation, and the universities. The right to contest laws directly to the Constitutional Court is revoked "after ninety days beginning with the promulgation of the contested law or by-laws in the *Official Gazette*" (Art. 150). The constitutionality of laws may also be challenged through the lower courts. If, while deciding a particular case, a lower court finds the relevant law unconstitutional, that court may postpone the case until the Constitutional Court has resolved the matter. A similar step may be taken by a lower court if one of the parties to a case contests, and the court is convinced of the validity of such contention, the constitutionality of the relevant law. If, however, the court is not convinced of the seriousness of the party's argument, the question of constitutionality along with the case itself are decided by a higher court of review or by the Court of Cassation. Thus, Turkish citizens involved in judicial proceedings are able to contest the validity of their laws as are citizens of the United States.

Annulments of laws made by the Constitutional Court are final, but cannot be retroactive. The court may set the date by which its decision is to be implemented provided that the date is no later than six months from the time of the decision. It can also restrict the application of its decisions to the particular case involved.

The fifteen regular and five alternate members of the Constitutional Court are elected according to an extremely complicated formula. The important point about the entire procedure is that no one agency or group of related agencies can control appointments to the Constitutional Court.

ECONOMIC POLICY

Some reference to the economic problems of Turkey has been made in the two previous chapters. We have explained the meaning of etatism as the economic principle upon which economic planning was based during the First Republic. We have also seen how the government of the Democratic party, after the election of 1950, attempted to give etatism a different meaning, and how the economy improved between the years 1950 and 1953.

In the years following the 1950–53 boom economic difficulties became apparent. These were due to several factors: the government's inflationary policies; foreign-exchange imbalances; and initial shortages of goods, both producer's and consumer's.[7] By 1958, the economic situation of Turkey was very bad. Western powers friendly to Turkey expressed their concern by pressing Prime Minister Menderes to agree to a joint stabilization plan which would "make possible a return to realistic prices at home and in foreign trade." The plan provided for the devaluation of the Turkish pound, uniform rates of exchange, the abolition of price controls, and aid to Turkey in the amount of $359 million to be used for payments for necessary imports.[8]

As a result of the stabilization plan, the value of imports increased from $315 million in 1958 to $443 million in 1959. The value of exports also rose during the same period, from $247 million to $355 million. The rise in exports was due to a good harvest and to the elimination of difficulties in the foreign-exchange system.

Although production recovered slightly after it had fallen in 1958, a return to the old policies and economic methods in 1960 offset the gains made from the joint stabilization plan of 1959. Expenditures as shown in the budget of 1960/61 were increased, and credit expansion was renewed —the deficit-spending policy which was characteristic of the government's economic policy between 1954 and 1958.

MEASURES TAKEN BY THE NEW REGIME

When the revolution took place in May 1961, the Menderes regime had accumulated a foreign debt totaling $1.3 billion. A 1961 amortization plan estimated that in 1962 the servicing of debts would require $115 million; in 1963, $179 million; and $100 million each year thereafter.[9] Agricul-

7. James A. Morris, "Recent Problems of Economic Development in Turkey," *The Middle East Journal,* XIV (1960), 2.
8. Erwin Marki, "Turkey's Struggle for Stability and Prosperity," *Swiss Review of World Affairs,* April, 1962, pp. 9–10.
9. Marki, *Swiss Review of World Affairs,* p. 10.

ture, which accounted for nearly half of the national income and for three-fourths of Turkey's employment, had to be reinvigorated so as to increase production to keep up with the growth of the rural population, which between 1950 and 1960 had increased from 15.7 to 19 million. During the same period, the area under cultivation had increased by only one-half of one per cent. More land, therefore, had to be put under cultivation, and additional capital was needed so that scientific farming practices, including irrigation systems, could be instituted. Of course, in addition to its domestic importance, agriculture was also extremely important to Turkey's balance-of-payment problem, since agricultural products accounted for four-fifths of all exports.

The new regime also attempted to renew the people's confidence in their currency. It established new sources of government revenue, so that although the budget for the fiscal year 1961/62 showed an increase in expenditure, revenue was also increased. For political reasons the Menderes government had not imposed taxes on the farmer, but the new regime realized that it must extend taxation to agriculture if enough revenue was to be accumulated. Income-tax rates were also increased, and the government instituted a forced-savings plan under which all recipients of income were "required to place three per cent of their income in ten year government savings bond, interest on them being fixed at between 4 and 7 per cent annually." [10]

The Constitution of 1961 committed all future governments of Turkey to the promotion of economic development, and the Turkish people have become conscious of their economic well-being. In a country where the population increases at the rate of 3 per cent annually, and the average per capita income is less than $200, economic development is a difficult task. Turkey's long-range economic planning is aimed at meeting the needs of the steadily increasing population as well as at approaching the economic levels of technologically advanced countries. To oversee economic planning, the Constitution established a special agency, the Planning Council, comprising the prime minister and three members of the Council of Ministers (Art. 129).

The Planning Council has established an economic development program based on five-year plans.[11] The first of these covered the period 1963–68 and was aimed at increasing the gross national product 7 per cent. It was estimated that an increase of one per cent in the national income would require the investment of 2.58 per cent; thus, a 7 per cent growth would require 18 per cent of the national income for investment.

10. Marki, *Swiss Review of World Affairs*, p. 13.
11. See the second part of Marki's article in *Swiss Review of World Affairs*, May 1, 1962, p. 11.

The council assumed that it would be possible to achieve a rate of savings sufficient for a large part of that investment by tax reforms, increased productivity, reorganization of government enterprises, and putting hoarded funds to use. It was also assumed that 4 per cent of the necessary investment would come from foreign sources.

TURKISH FOREIGN POLICY

Ever since the establishment of the Republic in 1923, Turkish foreign policy has had as one of its aims the realization of a viable national state in Turkey. Under Mustafa Kemal the emphasis was on achieving territorial integrity, an understandable goal, in view of the fact that Turkey, defeated in World War I, stood a chance of losing not only territories which were part of the Ottoman Empire but also territory within the peninsula, her ethnic and historic domain. We mentioned the conditions of the Treaty of Sèvres in Chapter One. These would have lost Turkey a large portion of Anatolia. The efforts of the Kemalist regime resulted in the conclusion of the more dignifying Treaty of Lausanne (1923) which established Turkish sovereignty over Constantinople, Eastern Thrace, and Anatolia. Boundary disputes with Iraq and Syria were later settled through negotiations with Britain and France, who were at the time in control of the two neighboring countries. With the settlement of the problem of the Straits, and the conclusion in 1939 of a nonaggression pact with France, giving Turkey possession of the Sanjak of Alexandretta, Turkey was in complete control of its ethnic territory.

TURKEY AND THE MIDDLE EAST

Turkey is a Middle Eastern country with a European outlook, a fact which has strongly influenced its international position. Geographic and military considerations required that Turkey seek alliance with neighboring Middle Eastern countries for protection against possible Soviet aggression. Logically, this meant that Turkey should develop friendly relations with the Arab countries and perhaps participate in political developments within the Middle East.

However, Turkey found herself in semi-isolation from regional political developments until the middle of the 1950's, and even today remains in an extremely difficult position. The country's European outlook is an important factor contributing to Turkey's difficulties in the region. Other factors are: (1) Westernization meant to Turkey the severing of cultural ties with the past, of which the region had been a part; (2) Communist infiltration of certain countries in the Middle East, especially Syria, in 1957, intensified Turkish fear of Soviet domination of the region; (3) the anti-Western attitude of Arab nationalism was contrary to Turkey's pro-Western policy; (4) Syria resented Turkey's control of the Sanjak of Alexandretta, which strained Turkish-Syrian relations; and (5) the Arab-Israeli conflict and United States support of Israel made the possibility of regional cooperation more difficult, since such cooperation would most certainly exclude Israel.

Turkey did what it could under the circumstances, and a degree of regional cooperation was accomplished in 1955. The most outstanding feature of this cooperation was the Baghdad Pact, a regional alliance which included the "northern tier" states. The pact was the product of a treaty between Turkey and Iraq which declared that the two parties would cooperate for their security and defense in accordance with measures to be determined by special agreement.[12] The two parties promised that they would not interfere in each other's internal affairs and that they would settle disputes between themselves peacefully and in accordance with the Charter of the United Nations. Members of the Arab League could become parties to the treaty upon their accession to its terms. The treaty was also open to other states which were "actively concerned" with the security of the region as long as both Iraq and Turkey recognized such states. This, of course, was designed to exclude Israel from the collective-security agreement. Upon the accession to the treaty of four states, a Permanent Council was to be organized to fulfill the purposes of the pact. The treaty was to be renewed every five years. Any member could withdraw from the pact but was required to notify the other parties of its intention six months prior to the date the withdrawal was to become effective.

Accession to the pact by Britain, Pakistan, and Iran was effected on April 5, September 23, and October 2, 1955, respectively. In 1958 a revolution took place in Iraq and the new government of Iraq withdrew from the pact. The pact, although it remained in existence, became less effective. To offset the loss of Iraq and to assure the remaining pact members of the importance and necessity of their alliance, the United States offered to conclude bilateral treaties with them to guarantee their security and safety. Consequently, on March 5, 1959, Turkey and the United States signed a mutual-defense treaty.

Turkey exercised great restraint in not taking part in major political developments in the region, especially those within the Arab Middle East. It did, however, show great concern for what was happening in Syria in 1957, when Syria became a Communist-infiltrated regime. As a warning to the Syrian government, Turkey concentrated troops along the Syrian border. In this instance, Turkey would probably have intervened in the Syrian situation had the United States been willing to participate.

12. For text of treaty see J. C. Hurewitz, ed., *Diplomacy in the Near and Middle East, A Documentary Record: 1914–1956* (Princeton: Van Nostrand, 1956), vol. II, Doc. 107.

On March 28, 1949, Turkey came out of semi-isolation and recognized the State of Israel, an act which the Arab countries considered a betrayal of Islam and "a stab in the back." Turkey was more sympathetic with the Arabs after their defeat by the Israelis in June 1967, and she warned the United States and Britain that their policies toward the Arab Middle East were reaching the danger point, because many Arab countries were falling under Soviet influence and control.

It should be mentioned that the Arab countries had always regarded Turkey with mistrust, because of Turkey's domination prior to World War I, and later because of her renunciation of the Islamic tradition of which the Arabs are a part. It might be that Turkey was wise in not taking an active part in regional politics, since this would have embroiled her in the confusion of Arab political life.

On the other hand, Turkey's position in the Middle East could not be strengthened as long as she refused to identify with the other countries in the region. Her European outlook should not have deterred her from this identification, even if she wanted to stay out of regional politics. Perhaps it would have been to the advantage of the West if Turkey had been closer to its neighboring countries, for Turkey could be trusted to safeguard Western interests throughout the region, especially with regard to security and defense.

TURKEY'S RELATIONS WITH NON-MIDDLE EASTERN COUNTRIES

Ataturk's main interest, as we have seen, was in preserving Turkey's territorial rights and giving her a modern culture of the Western type. By Westernization, Ataturk did not mean pursuing a pro-Western policy. As far as he was concerned, Turkey's interest lay in staying out of international conflicts and rivalries and securing recognition of its territorial rights. However, in the early years of his regime he was more friendly to Soviet Russia than to the Western world. As early as 1920, his provisional government was exchanging diplomatic representation with the Soviet Union, and the following year a treaty of friendship was ratified by the two governments.[13] The treaty mentioned "the common struggle against imperialism," the obvious reference being to Western imperialism. Viewed from a historical perspective, it is possible to conclude that Ataturk's friendship with Soviet Russia was necessary to effect the withdrawal of French and Italian troops which were in occupation of a large part of Anatolia, and to induce Britain not to support the Greek invasion of Turkey. Once these objectives were accomplished, Ataturk gradually sought the friendship of the West. In a number of treaties with Western countries, he was able to

13. Text of treaty in Hurewitz, vol. II, Doc. 34.

reach an understanding on most of their differences with Turkey. At the same time, he maintained Turkey's position with Russia and concluded a new Treaty of Friendship and Neutrality on December 17, 1925.[14]

Turkish foreign policy continued along the same lines after the death of Ataturk in 1938. But the advent of World War II placed great stress upon Turkey's neutrality, and as the war years went by she became increasingly pressed to take sides. She had already signed, on October 19, 1939, a tripartite treaty of "mutual alliance" with Britain and France, committing her to come to the assistance of the two countries "in the event of war in the Mediterranean area in which France and the United Kingdom are involved." [15] But she continued to pursue a foreign policy which would keep her out of the war and at the same time safeguard her territory.

Germany, fearing that Turkey might enter the war on the side of the Allies, attempted to persuade Turkey to stay neutral. On June 18, 1941, a treaty of nonaggression was concluded in which both Germany and Turkey promised "to respect mutually the inviolability and integrity of their territories, and to abstain from all action aimed directly or indirectly against one another." [16] But the treaty stipulated that its provisions would be "subject to the already existing agreements of each party," thus allowing Turkey to keep its previous commitments to Britain, France, and the Soviet Union. Turkey remained neutral until it became obvious that Germany would lose the war. Then, in order to gain admission to the San Francisco Conference and to benefit from being on the side of the victor, she declared war on Germany, on February 23, 1945.

World War II brought an end to the policy of neutrality Turkey had been following not only in the war but in world affairs in general. The Soviet Union, which after World War II stood in opposition to the West, became Turkey's main concern and a source of danger to her. On March 19, 1945, the Soviet government denounced the 1925 Soviet-Turkish Treaty of Friendship and Neutrality and notified Turkey of the necessity of revising the Montreux Straits Convention of 1936. The Soviet government rejected proposals by the United States aimed at a solution to the problem, although these proposals were accepted by Turkey and the United Kingdom.[17] The Soviet government insisted upon the establishment of a new regime for the Straits, which would include the "Black Sea Powers" and which would make the Soviet Union jointly responsible with Turkey for the organization

14. Text in Hurewitz, vol. II, Doc. 45.
15. Text in Hurewitz, vol. II, Doc. 66.
16. Text in Hurewitz, vol. II, Doc. 68.
17. See U.S. Department of State *Bulletin* (Washington, D.C.: Government Printing Office, 1951), p. 811.

of the defense of the Straits. Turkey flatly refused these demands and so did the United States.

President Truman declared in a statement before Congress on March 12, 1947, that if the United States failed to help Turkey and Greece in their struggle against communism, "the effect will be far-reaching to the West as well as the East." [18] To counteract the Soviet threat, on July 30, 1947, following the signing of a Turko-American Aid Agreement, Congress appropriated $400 million for military and economic assistance to Turkey and Greece. The Truman Doctrine, as this policy became known, deeply committed the United States to the Middle East; it meant that the United States would no longer be content with the position of observer, but would become actively involved in regional developments.

Today, the United States considers Turkey important because politically Turkey "serves as an example to other lands of an underdeveloped country which has achieved progress without resorting to a totalitarian organization of society," and militarily it is a "strong Western defense partner." [19] Turkey became a member of the North Atlantic Treaty Organization (NATO) in 1952. It also participated in the Korean War on the side of the West, and Turkish troops "fought with exceptional bravery" and "won the respect and admiration of all the United Nations troops." [20]

The Soviet menace to Turkey lost some of its vigor as a result of Khrushchev's policy of coexistence and the easing of the cold war. The emergence of Communist China as a rival power has also had an important effect on Soviet policy. On June 28, 1960, Khrushchev wrote General Gursel saying that his government had no intention of "disrupting Turkey's relations with the West"; however, he indicated that a neutral Turkish foreign policy similar to that of Ataturk would improve Soviet-Turkish relations.[21] General Gursel replied that he saw no reason why Turkey's purely defensive commitments should prevent the two countries from enjoying good relations. Thus, between 1960 and 1965 Soviet-Turkish relations seemed to be tied to Soviet-Western relations. However, after the Turkish election of 1965 and the coming of the Justice party to power, Turkish-Soviet relations began to improve. The Turkish government seemed determined to appease the Soviet Union and pursue a more friendly policy toward that state than was previously possible. For instance, Prime Minister Demirel selected the Turkish ambassador to Moscow as his

18. Quoted in *ibid*. (November, 1951), p. 812.
19. U.S. Department of State, *Mutual Security in Action: Turkey*, U.S. Government Printing Office, publication 7208 (October, 1961), p. 6.
20. U.S. Department of State, Office of Public Affairs, *Turkey: Frontier of Freedom*, June, 1952, p. 12.
21. *The Economist*, September 10, 1960, p. 12.

foreign minister. In the West, this was interpreted as the signal for closer Soviet-Turkish ties. And during 1967, there were significant high-level official visits between both countries, which resulted in increased economic cooperation. After 1965, Turkish fear of the Soviet Union was reduced, and the future of relations between the two countries became more encouraging.

GREEK-TURKISH RELATIONS

Historically, there have been animosities between Greece and Turkey, but the threat of communism after World War II and the need for economic and military assistance from the West forced the two countries to forget their past grievances and to establish good relations. Both countries received economic and military aid from the United States, and both are members of NATO. Thus the two countries have become important partners in the defense arrangements of Europe. The United States, also a member of NATO, has demonstrated its interest in keeping the Western alliance strong, and it has, accordingly, encouraged Greece and Turkey to continue their new and friendly relations.

The disruption of Greek-Turkish friendship has been threatened by recent developments on Cyprus. In order to understand the political and international implication of the Cyprus problem, we must go back a little in the history of the Cyprus situation.

The Cyprus Problem. Cyprus, the third largest island in the Mediterranean, has at various times been under the political control of Phoenicians, Greeks, Assyrians, Macedonians, Egyptians, Persians, Romans, Byzantines, Saracens, Franks, Venetians, Genoese, Turks, and British. The Turks ruled it from 1571 until 1878, when they were replaced by the British who, in 1914, made the island a crown colony and continued to govern it as such until it became independent on August 16, 1960.

The predominant culture of Cyprus is Greek; about 80 per cent of the Cypriots are of Greek origin, and 18 per cent are of Turkish origin. The Greek Cypriots have desired *enosis* (unity) with Greece; the Turkish Cypriots have feared that such a union would mean their loss of freedom and outright persecution or even annihilation. The historical animosities between Greece and Turkey have been reflected in the attitudes of Cyprus' Turkish and Greek populations. In 1954 Greece supported the claim of the Greek Cypriots for self-determination before the General Assembly of the United Nations, and Turkey declared that the interest of the Turkish Cypriots required either Turkish control or the partitioning of the island. In the following year, the Greek Cypriot underground movement called EUKA resorted to violence in its demand for *enosis*. The Turks also took part in the civil unrest which ripped up the island during the next four years. Friction among Britain, Greece, and Turkey was inevitable since all three countries were interested in the future of the island.[22]

Cyprus Becomes Independent. In the 1950's, various solutions to the problem of Cyprus were explored, all of which failed because of the extreme positions of the two Cypriot communities. Finally, Archbishop Makarios, the leader of the Greek Cypriots, proposed, late in 1958, an acceptable compromise. Cyprus was to become independent with guarantees against both partition and union. On the basis of the Makarios compromise, negotiation between Greece, Turkey, Britain, and the Cypriot leaders resulted in the London-Zurich Agreements of February 19, 1959. One of these agreements, the Treaty of Guarantee, provided for safeguarding the island's independence by Britain, Greece, and Turkey, and prohibited either the partition of the island or its unification with any other state. It also permitted each of the three guaranteeing powers to intervene unilaterally if such intervention was thought necessary. A second agreement, the Treaty of Alliance, provided for the stationing of Greek and Turkish military contingents in Cyprus and for cooperation between these two countries and the Republic of Cyprus in common defense. The third agreement, the Treaty of Establishment, provided, among other things, for the retention and sovereignty of British bases.[23]

Whereas Greece and Turkey have interests in Cyprus because of the composition of the island's population, Britain's interest is wholly strategic. Britain claims that its military bases in Cyprus are necessary for maintaining strong NATO and CENTO alliances.[24] The United States welcomed the establishment of the Republic and made known its desire "to see Cyprus remain an example of close British-Greek-Turkish cooperation." [25] The United States' position was made clear to President Makarios by President Kennedy during Makarios' visit to the United States in June 1962.

Although Cyprus had become sovereign and independent, her future remained uncertain. The Cyprus problem involved the question of how to reconcile the rights of the Greek majority with those of the Turkish minority. In other words, the Greek majority had the right to rule, and the Turkish minority had the rights of citizenship which included participation in the political process.

22. For events leading up to the Zurich and London agreements, see "Cyprus: Conflict and Reconciliation," *The World Today,* April, 1954.

23. Text of the three treaties in "Cyprus," *Command,* 1093, July, 1960.

24. Anthony Verrier, "Cyprus: Britain's Security Role," *The World Today,* March, 1964, p. 137.

25. U.S. Department of State, *The Newly Independent Nations: Cyprus,* publication 7503 (April, 1963).

In an environment comprised of two antagonistic cultures, the balance between the principles of majority rule and minority rights is difficult to establish. Consequently, the island was to experience more crises of unrest even after its independence. Such crises occurred in 1964 and 1967. In the latter case, Greece and Turkey verged on a major war. Had it not been for the efforts of the United States, which became concerned about the future of the Western alliance, such a war could have become a dangerous reality.

CHAPTER 4

IRANIAN POLITICS

THE HISTORICAL BACKGROUND

SO M E thirty dynasties have ruled Iran in the past twenty-five hundred years.[1] During most of this time the structure of Iranian society was feudal, and the political system was a monarchy limited by feudal lords. The power of the lords was great, and the strength of the monarch's position depended largely upon his ability to control and obtain the support of the nobility. Monarchs have usually ruled by bestowing high honors and patronage upon certain lords; those who could not control the lords were controlled by them. The periods of history in which the lords were dominant reveal the ruthlessness and extreme selfishness of the Iranian nobility.

The population of Iran's agricultural society was of course made up largely of peasants. Oppressed by the aristocratic few who possessed all the wealth of the country, the only hope of peasants lay in a strong monarch who somehow managed to control the nobility. But though there were times when the peasants found some justice under strong monarchs, by and large they remained impoverished and oppressed.[2]

The rich landowner, who cared little for the public interest and whose loyalty to the monarch was often precarious, was an obstacle to progress and political stability. He ruled the lives of the peasants, whose whole status was dependent upon his will. With the passage of time, the peasants became politically passive and submissive.

However, at the beginning of the twentieth century, when commerce and industry were being developed, an urban class began to become important and arose to defy the feudal system and threatened its continuity. Unlike the peasant, the city dweller was dynamic, sensitive to economic change, and politically active. A government dominated by landowners was not the

---

1. The traditional name of Iran is Persia.
2. Donald N. Wilbur, *Iran: Past and Present* (Princeton: Princeton University Press, 1958), p. 86.

government he wanted, and he was suspicious of the central government and the class interests of those in power. Today, the resigned attitude of the peasant and the suspicious attitude of the urban class are characteristic of Iran's political culture and are at the foundation of the country's political problems.

In 1906, the frustrated urban elements revolted and demanded a constitutional document that would give them a share of power. Shah Muzaffar ed-Din (1896–1907) reluctantly granted a constitution, but was succeeded a year later by his son, Muhammed Ali, who ignored the document. Ali relied on the Russians to maintain him in power, and he used the Cossack Brigade, a military unit originally organized by the Russians, against rebellious urban groups. However, this military unit was unable to suppress the 1909 revolution which resulted in the forced abdication of Ali and the succession to the throne of his son, Ahmad.

Ahmad was twelve years old when he ascended the Iranian throne, and real power passed into the hands of politicians in the cabinet and the legislature. Until the end of his rule in 1925, which also ended the rule of the Qajar dynasty, the royal palace became primarily a place of intrigue among urban politicians and feudal lords.[3] The new leaders were confronted with economic problems and problems of maintaining peace and order, both largely the product of the civil war of 1909. Deficit spending coupled with excessive borrowing from foreign governments during the reign of Ahmad and his father added to the financial problem of the central government. Furthermore, the Bakhtiari tribes,[4] which played a decisive part in the 1909 civil war, demanded greater influence in the government and threatened to start another civil war. Religious groups, which also took part in the civil war because of the monarch's consistent violation of Islamic law, wanted a share of power. Thus, there were uncertainties about the ability of the new government to deal with Iran's pressing problems.

To help solve its economic difficulties, the government employed a group of American advisers under the leadership of Morgan Shuster, formerly a United States Treasury Department official. Russia, always interested in the internal affairs of Iran, was suspicious and, fearing that Shuster's economic reform might lead to economic stability and the employment of other Western advisers, she demanded his expulsion. The Majlis (legislature) rejected the demand, but soon it appeared that Russian troops were moving toward Teheran, the capital, and the government had to yield.

Iran's economic problems, therefore, remained unsolved. Moreover, the

3. Amin Banani, *The Modernization of Iran 1921–1941* (Stanford: Stanford University Press, 1961), p. 31.
4. A nomadic mountain people who live in the Southwest region of Iran. They live primarily by pastoral pursuits and are known to have a warlike behavior.

advent of World War I confused the internal picture as never before. More so, perhaps, than those of most other countries of the Middle East, Iran's domestic developments have always been heavily influenced by external factors. During World War I, Iran became a battlefield for the armed forces of Russia, Turkey, and Britain, while Germany was busy trying to organize Iranian tribes in the southeast for guerrilla warfare against the Allies. Of course, Iranian oil was the major factor in all this.

From the outset of the war, the Iranian government wanted neutrality. But a weak government commanding a highly disorganized army could not possibly hope to have its policy respected by powers that viewed its territory and oil of immense importance to the conduct of the war. Consequently, Iran's proclaimed neutrality did not have the slightest significance.

The 1909 revolution, which succeeded in ousting the monarch (but not the monarchy), failed to produce a strong leader. Ahmad reigned but did not rule. The government was under the control of an oligarchy which represented private interests and had little experience in the art of ruling. All this, plus Iran's precarious international position, created in the first few years following World War I a popular dissatisfaction with the ruling oligarchy, and there were widespread demands for stronger leadership and for reform.

Agitation for change and reform was led by Sayed Ziya, a journalist, who called for the support of the only well-disciplined, well-trained army unit, the Cossack Brigade. (The army was the most neglected of Iranian institutions, although the Cossack Brigade, by now free of Russian control, remained in fairly good condition.) In February 1921, Reza Khan, who was the commander of the Cossacks, responded to Ziya's appeal for reform and seized the Teheran government. A new cabinet was formed with Ziya as prime minister and Reza as minister of war.

REZA SHAH PAHLAVI (1926-1941)

The 1921 coup d'état was successful, but it did not immediately bring to the front the man who was to become the strong leader of Iran. This man, Reza Khan, first began to move into a position of power by ousting Ziya from the office of prime minister; later, in October 1923, he assumed this office himself. The young King Ahmad left the country permanently, leaving Reza Khan in full control of the government. The final act in this political drama came in the spring of 1926, when Reza Khan was crowned as Reza Shah Pahlavi,[5] the first ruler of the new Pahlavi dynasty.

5. The word "shah" which comes in the names of Iranian monarchs means "king." Sometimes the word "shahanshah" is used in reference to Iranian monarchs. It means "king of kings."

Reza Shah is regarded as the monarch who introduced Western reforms into Iranian social and political life. Some students of Iranian history like to compare his achievements with those of Mustafa Kemal who, during the same period, presided over the reform movement in Turkey. But it is really not fair to compare the achievements of the two men, because conditions in each country were quite different.

First, Turkey's population was, after the fall of the Ottoman Empire, more homogeneous than Iran's, and thus Kemalist reforms had fewer obstacles to overcome than did those of Reza Shah, who had to use more forceful means to induce acceptance of his reforms. Iran's population included a number of racially diverse and politically powerful tribal groups. These tribes constituted a strong tribal subculture which required a special kind of political approach and stubbornly resisted all aspects of cultural change.

Secondly, the Turks were a disciplined society capable of accepting fundamental changes in their culture, whereas the Iranians were both more individualistic and more traditional. Some historians believe that the Shi'ite faith of the Iranians is more fanatic than the Sunnite branch of Islam to which the Turks adhere. If this is true, the religious factor might have been important in Iranian resistance to the cultural changes introduced by Reza Shah. Finally, it is important to remember that the backgrounds of Kemal and Reza were different. Mustafa Kemal had had more experience with Western culture than Reza Shah.[6] Westernization in Turkey, therefore, had a better chance of succeeding than in Iran.

In spite of Iran's severely limited ability to Westernize and modernize, Reza Shah attempted serious reform measures. The army was enlarged and was given more attention than it previously received. With a better army, the problems of law and order that plagued previous governments were no longer serious. The power and prestige of the Muslim clergy were destroyed. Civil and criminal codes were adopted and were given precedence over religious laws, and civil proceedings for marriage and divorce were established. Large sums of money were spent on education, including the establishment of new schools. Higher education was encouraged, and in 1935 Reza Shah established the University of Teheran. Reforms affecting the status of women were also introduced, such as the prohibition of the wearing of veils and measures to encourage their education.

All these reforms were important, but when we evaluate them we must remember that they were designed to produce changes in Iranian culture without destroying or radically departing from Iranian heritage. In this respect, Westernization in Iran differed from that in Turkey, which attempted to divorce itself from its cultural past.

6. William S. Haas, *Iran* (New York: Columbia University Press, 1946), pp. 143–45.

In some aspects, the rule of Reza Shah was not successful; in others it was. On the credit side, he was able to give Iran political stability for about fifteen years. During this period, he was able to curb the powers and selfish interests of the feudal lords; and the tribes, which threatened political stability and modernization, were controlled. Although these attempts to modernize and reform did not bring Iran into the ranks of modern nations, they were a significant step in that direction.

On the debit side, the governmental system under Reza Shah did not develop the institutions capable of maintaining stability. The stability of Reza Shah's Iran was the product of his strong rule and personal determination; it depended on personal qualities rather than on modes of conduct which, if established, would have guaranteed continuing stability.

The forms of constitutional government were, to be sure, preserved under Reza Shah; but in reality the government was essentially a military dictatorship, or perhaps something like a totalitarian regime.[7] Although the Majlis remained in existence and elections were held during Reza Shah's reign, there were virtually no limits to his power, and the outward forms of constitutional government did not deter him from enforcing his own policies and using his own political methods. Political parties were proscribed, the Majlis was reduced to the status of a rubber stamp, the press was suppressed, and trade unions were abolished. Furthermore, the concentration of so much power in the hands of the shah destroyed all hope of the development of mature democratic institutions.[8] As a result, Reza Shah left a political vacuum which was difficult to fill in the years following his abdication in 1941.

WORLD WAR II AND ITS AFTERMATH

World War II brought the rule of Reza Shah to an end on September 16, 1941. Shortly after Germany attacked Russia, British and Soviet troops invaded Iran, claiming that the Iranian government had failed to curb the subversive activities of Axis nationals. The Soviet Union and Britain viewed these activities as threatening their security and in conflict with Iran's announced neutrality. The real reason behind the Anglo-Russian invasion, of course, was to gain access to Iranian territory, which was "the only feasible road for the shipment of war supplies to Russia." [9] Iranian military resistance was suspended by the shah who realized that his army, although rejuvenated and reformed, could not possibly challenge the military might of Britain and Russia.

7. A. K. S. Lambton, "Some of the Problems Facing Persia," *International Affairs*, XXII (1946), 266.

8. R. M. Savory, "Persia Since the Constitution," *University of Toronto Quarterly*, XXIX (Oct.–July, 1959/60), 246.

9. Richard N. Frye, *Iran* (New York: Henry Holt and Company, 1953), p. 80.

Apparently, the Allied governments were suspicious of Reza Shah and wanted to have more control of Iranian policies. Under pressure from them, the shah abdicated in favor of his son, Mohammed Reza, who was then young and inexperienced. Until the end of the war, Iran was under foreign domination and the young shah was cautious not to antagonize the occupation powers to the point that they would interfere more directly in his country's internal affairs. He was aware of the rivalries between the army officers and the Majlis, and, perhaps wisely, he avoided a showdown between the two groups. He was also aware of the influence of private interest groups and of their extreme selfishness. In order to gain popular support, he declared that the wealth his father had accumulated and which he had inherited would be put to public use. Only in the years following World War II did the young shah assume additional powers and responsibilities. During the war years, he presented himself as a constitutional monarch who was concerned about democratic government in Iran.

The war years, however, left their impact upon the socioeconomic structure of Iranian society.[10] By 1946, Iran faced a number of crucial problems, some of which persist. Socially, there was a conflict between rural and urban values; and there was a great need to achieve a balance between the two that would insure social stability and continuity. While the majority of Iranians were rural and the wealth of the country was mostly agricultural, the predominant social values were urban. This situation produced a conflict between urban and rural interests as well as confusion in the objectives and goals of public policy.

The impact of the war upon the economy was severe. Inflation developed rapidly, and the lower and middle classes suffered considerably. Government employees, being salaried people, suffered most, a fact which helps account for the graft and corruption in government.

In addition, there was the problem of reducing the great gap between the rich and the poor. Two distinct classes existed in Iran: a small class of rich landowners and merchants, and the mass of people who lived in extreme poverty. Of course, the development of a middle class large enough to moderate the extremes of wealth and poverty and reduce the antagonism between the two was one solution to this crucial problem. In the postwar period, the government formulated a policy designed to relieve the poor by the redistribution of wealth and the adjustment of income.

Politically, Iran needed to find ways and means of stabilizing its political system on firm constitutional bases. The people had had more experience with dictatorial government than democratic government. Their brief experience in parliamentary democracy after the 1909 civil war proved to be a failure.

10. See Lambton, *International Affairs,* XXII, pp. 269-72.

We shall see later in this chapter how these problems and others influenced the Iranian political picture and how, in turn, governmental policies dealt with them.

THE CONSTITUTIONAL SYSTEM

The constitutional movement which began in Iran in 1905 expressed itself in a revolution led by the merchants and religious groups. The ruling shah at the time of the revolution had misused his powers. He was weak and corrupt and had irresponsibly accepted foreign loans in return for concessions which were contrary to the national interest. The constitutional movement wanted to clarify the position of the monarch and limit his powers in certain areas, especially those involving foreign interests in Iran. Britain, who did not desire radical change in the internal political picture of Iran, played the role of mediator and succeeded in persuading the shah to declare his willingness to create a constitutional instrument allowing public participation in the political process. In August 1906, the shah issued a royal proclamation authorizing the establishment of a Constitutional Assembly to draft a national constitution.[11]

The shah ratified the Assembly's constitutional document on December 30, 1906. The new law dealt exclusively with the organization of a bicameral legislature and consisted of fifty-one articles, the construction of which was weak and often vague.[12] On October 7, 1907, a second part, the Supplementary Fundamental Law, was added.[13] This consisted of 107 articles and dealt with more subjects, such as the powers of the monarch and individual rights. Much was borrowed from the Belgian constitution, but an attempt was made to clarify some of the ambiguous provisions of the 1906 law.

These two parts—the Fundamental Laws of December 30, 1906, and the Supplementary Fundamental Laws of October 7, 1907—make up the Constitution of Iran. A few changes made by constitutional amendments were later added, and we will mention them in this chapter at the appropriate point.

Two features of the Iranian Constitution are foreign to Western concepts of constitutionalism. The first is that an official religion is recognized—Islam. The monarch must "profess and promote" the Shi'ite sect of Islam, which believes in the return of the twelfth *imam* (caliph), who was supposed to have disappeared around the year 873. Furthermore, the Consti-

11. See text in Helen Miller Davis, ed., *Constitutions, Electoral Laws, Treaties in the Near and Middle East* (Durham, N.C.: Duke University Press, 1953), pp. 104–5.
12. Text in Davis, *Constitutions*, pp. 106–16.
13. Text in Davis, *Constitutions*, pp. 117–28.

tution prohibits the enactment of laws which are in conflict with ecclesiastical laws. To insure compatibility between the laws of the state and the laws of God, the Constitution established an ecclesiastical committee composed of at least five *mujtahids* [14] and theologians. The committee has the power to declare void all laws in conflict with Islam.

Other provisions of the Constitution also relate to religion: Article 18 permits the study of all sciences, arts, and crafts as long as they are not in conflict with the Islamic religion; Article 20 prohibits the publication of any material conflicting with religious teaching; Article 22 prohibits the establishment of societies and associations which are "productive of mischief to religion"; Article 58 requires that ministers of the Iranian government must be Muslims. All of these provisions reinforce the legal position and the social status of religion.

The second non-Western feature of Iranian constitutionalism is the acceptance of social class as part of the political system. The original Assembly created by the Royal Proclamation of August 5, 1906 represented seven classes: the Princes, the Doctors of Divinity, the Qajar family (which was in power at the time), the nobles and notables, the landowners, the merchants, and the guilds. The class concept is also injected into Article 30 of the Fundamental Law, which requires that direct communication between Parliament and the monarch be made through a committee consisting of the president of the Assembly and six other members to be selected to represent the social classes. Iran no longer adheres to constitutional provisions relating to social class, since these provisions have been made obsolete by the impact of Western influence on the country. However, they remain, in the statute books; moreover, class still informally dominates the politics of Iran and plays an important role in Iranian social life.

Does the Constitution have any significance in the life of the Iranians? In Iran, constitutionalism has become synonymous with parliamentarianism.[15] This does not mean that Parliament is the most powerful political institution, for by and large, it is subservient to the government. All that Parliament can do is delay legislation or make minor changes in law to support the private interests of its members.[16] However, constitutionalism and parliamentarianism are related in the sense that government policies are usually justified by the claim that they have received the approval of

14. The *mujtahids* in Islam are those who apply independent reason in the interpretation of religious principles and the solution of problems related to religion. If no precedent is found in such matters, the *mujtahids* have jurisdiction.

15. See the excellent work of Leonard Binder, *Iran* (Berkeley: University of California Press, 1962), p. 83.

16. Binder, *Iran*, p. 84.

Parliament.[17] Since generally Parliament does not lead, but follows, it is not the constitutional details that are important in Iran but only the symbolic role of Parliament and the delicate power structure in which it is involved.

The Legislature. The constitutional movement of 1905 was seriously concerned with the monarch's excessive control over the finances of the state. Consequently, the Fundamental Laws instituted limitations. Article 18, for instance, requires the approval of the Assembly in all matters pertaining to the public treasury, the budget, and expenditures. Article 19 empowers the legislature to demand from the heads of government departments the implementation of all financial reforms required by law. More important, the monarch and his government can no longer dispose of public property or natural resources without the consent of the Assembly. Likewise, specific legislative authorization is required to establish public corporations; for granting special advantages to them; and, as a matter of fact, for granting special concessions regardless of whether such concessions are to be given to citizens or foreigners. Loans contracted by the state must be approved by the legislature. Even the construction of railroads whether by the state or by private companies needs legislative approval.

In theory at least, the Assembly seems to possess sufficient powers to enable it to control the executive branch if it so wishes. But the so-called power of the purse, which historically gave the British Parliament control of the government, is, we shall see, simply not exercised in Iran, which has little experience with democracy and even less experience in the development of legal attitudes similar to those which exist in Britain.

The Constitution gives Parliament more than financial powers. Legally, it can hold the executive branch of the government accountable for its policies and public acts. Ministers are required to report to the Assembly all important matters affecting their departments, and they are also required to explain any neglect in the implementation of laws. The Assembly has the constitutional right to demand from the king the dismissal of the minister or ministers charged with negligence. Ministers can, however, explain why they are unable to implement policy if national security is at stake.

Ministers are individually and collectively responsible to the two chambers of Parliament. They cannot avoid these responsibilities "by pleading verbal or written orders from the King." Furthermore, either of the houses of Parliament can, by an absolute majority of votes, compel the resignation of individual ministers as well as the cabinet. This, of course, would be equivalent to the "no confidence" vote in other parliamentary systems.

Here again we should not conclude that the Iranian Parliament actually

17. Binder, *Iran,* p. 84.

controls the government. To a large extent, legislative controls over the executive are theoretical. Nevertheless, they are important in the sense that under proper circumstances they can be used. Executive supremacy in Iran is the product of the passiveness of the legislature rather than the aggressiveness of the government. The legislature seems willing to leave matters of public policy to the government, which cannot, therefore, be accused of usurping legislative prerogatives.

Thus the Constitution has become an instrument which defines relations between the branches of government. Over the years it has established something like an "informal equilibrium" between Parliament and the government. This equilibrium, although at times difficult to maintain, has made possible the functioning of government in a country where the political climate is filled with uncertainties and doubt.[18]

Structurally, Parliament consists of two houses: the Majlis and the Senate. The Majlis is elected on the basis of population and consists, since the adoption of a constitutional amendment in 1957, of two hundred deputies. The term of office is four years. Elections are staggered instead of being held on the same day throughout the country—a practice which can lead to manipulation of election results and interference in the electoral process by local and national authorities. Any citizen over twenty-one is entitled to vote, except convicted criminals and members of the armed forces.

Neither the Constitution nor the electoral laws requires members of the Majlis to reside in their districts. Since many deputies own land in the rural districts but reside permanently in the capital, it is not unusual for the capital to have more *de facto* representation than it deserves on the basis of population. However, the Constitution requires the deputies to represent the interests of the whole nation rather than the special interests of the constituency which elected them. Although this would seem to reduce the impact of residence upon representation, sectional and private interests are still predominant.

The landowners weigh heavily in the membership of the Majlis. But recently there has been a tendency toward broadening membership to include more intellectuals and members of the middle class. Whether this tendency will eventually bring about substantial changes in the goals of public policy or the modification of the political system remains to be seen.

The upper house of the legislature is the Senate, which is composed of sixty members, half of whom are elected directly by the people and half of whom are appointed by the shah. Half of those elected and half of those appointed must come from the capital. Thus the composition of the Senate also favors Teheran and the position of the shah in regard to legislation.

18. Herbert H. Vreeland, ed., *Iran* (New Haven: Human Relations Files, 1957), p. 61.

The shah's influence over legislation, however, is partly counterbalanced by the fact that the Senate plays only a secondary role in the law-making process.[19]

For many years, the Majlis was the only legislative chamber in existence; the Senate was not convened until 1950, even though it had been created by the 1906 Constitution. This did not violate the Constitution, since Article 47 provided that, so long as the Senate was not organized, the acts of the Majlis would have the force of law.

The Iranian legislature enjoys freedom of discussion, and such discussions are vigorous and at times violent. Most legislative proposals are introduced by cabinet ministers. An individual member of the legislature may also introduce a measure provided it is signed by fifteen other members. Ministers of the government are allowed to attend meetings of Parliament; ordinarily the minister or his assistant is present at the time Parliament is discussing a proposal pertaining to his department.

The Executive. According to Article 27 of the Supplementary Fundamental Laws, executive power belongs to the shah, and in his name the ministers and state officials carry out all laws and ordinances. Sovereignty resides with the king in the form of "a trust confided (as a Divine gift) by the people" to his person.

Succession to the throne takes place in the following manner: if the shah dies, his eldest son becomes the new shah provided he is born of a Persian mother. If the eldest son has not attained the age of twenty at the time of the shah's death, the Majlis appoints a regent who will rule until the crown prince comes of age. (In 1967, the Constitution was amended to qualify the queen for the regency.) Only males may succeed, and if the shah has no son, he designates, with the approval of the Majlis, an heir to the throne. No member of the Qajar family, which preceded the present royal family, can succeed to the throne or be designated regent.

As chief executive, the shah has the power to appoint and remove ministers of the government. This is an important power, since it puts him in a position to control the government and, to a large extent, its policies. The Constitution, however, places the ministers in a difficult situation since, as we have seen, they are also responsible to Parliament. Ministers are responsible for the consequences of royal decrees if they sign them, but the shah is absolved from responsibility by the Constitution. This means that ministers should not sign royal decrees unless they are willing to take full responsibility for the political consequences.

19. "For example, the Senate may not initiate or pass on fiscal legislation. In case of disagreement on legislation, the joint committee procedure prescribed by the constitution is heavily weighted in favor of the Majlis. In fact the Majlis may force dissolution of the entire Legislature rather than accept the Senate's views." Vreeland, *Iran*, p. 75.

In case of serious disagreement between Parliament and the shah, the ministers are usually in trouble. If they side with Parliament, the shah has the power to remove them; if they side with the shah, Parliament can also remove them. Under these conditions, governmental stability is possible only if Parliament and the shah are generally on good terms, or if one is dominated by the other. In reality, however, it is Parliament which usually has inferior status; the government is ordinarily on the side of the shah.

Of course, the day-to-day conduct of policy is the responsibility of the cabinet, which is headed by the prime minister. Professor Leonard Binder in his book on Iran points to the development of two recent tendencies in governmental operations: [20] one is the gradual acceptance of the prime minister as the focal point of authority in the cabinet; the other is the impersonalization and professionalization of the civil service. These arise from increasing government interest in recent years in social welfare and economic planning. Government activity has expanded to the point where coordination of policy by the prime minister and a professional governmental staff has become necessary.

However, cabinet influence on the affairs of government depends largely on the willingness of the shah to direct the policy-making process and assume authority. The shah's involvement in policy and administration naturally restricts the authority of the prime minister and the cabinet.[21] In this regard, we must bear in mind that developing a parliamentary government in which the monarch becomes perhaps a little more than a figurehead is not an easy matter. In addition to an electoral system which, as we have seen, seems to favor the conservative elements over the more liberal urban elements, the army is also a conservative institution that can be relied on to support the shah. Consequently, any effort to reduce the powers of the monarch can be frustrated by a powerful coalition—the army and the conservative elements in Parliament.

Furthermore, the king is always in a position to exercise leadership in the legislative process. Not only are the king's ministers able to introduce legislation and attend the meetings of Parliament, but the king is empowered by the Constitution to dissolve the two chambers of Parliament separately or together, although he cannot use this power twice for the same reason, and new elections must be held within one month from the date Parliament is ordered dissolved. The Constitution also gives the shah the power to veto financial measures and to call the legislature into an extraordinary session.

The Legal System. Although the Constitution provides for a separation of political powers, the judicial branch of the government is not indepen-

20. Binder, *Iran*, p. 98.
21. Binder, *Iran*, pp. 97–98.

dent from the executive. Organizationally, the courts are under the Ministry of Justice, and they are politically controlled by the Ministry. This control is clearly established through the Ministry's power to appoint, promote, transfer, and remove judges. In the exercise of such powers, the executive frequently ignores the principle of judicial independence, an important characteristic of the judicial systems of the advanced countries of the West.

Perhaps because the courts are ordinarily under the influence of the political men in the government, the reputation of these courts has suffered over the years—and the confidence of Iranians in their courts does not exceed their confidence in their government.[22]

Regardless of the status and prestige of the legal system, Iran's greatest achievements have nevertheless been in the modernization of its jurisprudence.[23] Until the advent of Reza Shah, Iran was subject to the dictates of the Shariah (the religious law) and the old system of ecclesiastical courts. The religious laws were unable to cope with the demands and needs of a changing society. In many instances, they were obstacles to progress. More important, they gave the clerics important political influence, and these men opposed modernization and Westernization. But in 1925, a new commercial code was adopted, and in 1926 and 1928 new criminal and civil codes were established. The new judicial system followed European patterns, particularly those of France and Switzerland.[24] Thus, Iran was able to modernize its legal system, although it may take a long time before the reputation of her courts improves.

Modernization of the court system did not result in the abolition of the ecclesiastical courts; but these courts have been limited to advisory roles in matrimonial cases and are allowed to function in other areas only with the specific authorization of the civil courts. Interest in the Shariah continues, and the University of Teheran still offers courses in Islamic law.

Another aspect of law affected by the reform measures of the 1920's and 1930's pertains to the registration of certain legal documents such as marriage certificates, property titles, and birth certificates. The new system made registration compulsory, and hence the definition of property rights became much easier than under the old system, in which landholdings were frequently undiscernible. Today the Department of Justice enforces birth, marriage, and title registration, although the system of registration itself is in desperate need of reorganization. Nevertheless, property ownership is more secure since the compulsory requirement of registration was instituted.

22. Wilber, *Iran,* p. 153.
23. Vreeland, *Iran,* p. 77.
24. Vreeland, *Iran,* p. 76.

The consular courts, which under the capitulations had jurisdiction in cases involving foreign nationals, were abolished. Today, foreign nationals, unless they have diplomatic immunity, are tried in Iranian courts.

Structurally, the Iranian judicial system begins with the justices of the peace in the rural areas and the towns. These courts handle minor offenses. In the larger towns, the district courts have original jurisdiction in all but minor offenses. The courts of appeal, which exercise only appellate jurisdiction, are found in the major cities only. At the apex of the judicial pyramid is the Court of Cassation in Teheran, which is the final court of appeal. This court exercises original jurisdiction only in cases involving the impeachment of ministers.

POLITICAL BEHAVIOR AND PARTICIPATION

It is sometimes difficult for Westerners to understand Iranian political behavior. For example, anyone in Iran who is not involved in a political "cause" is considered to be a nobody and without honor. Yet Iranians do not have political parties in the Western sense of the term [25] (except for the Tudeh [Masses] party which we will discuss later). Iranian parties are basically nondoctrinal, transitional, based on personal loyalty to a leader, and noninstitutional—that is, they are not an integral part of the political system. Thus, while Iranians tend to follow a cause of some kind, they have not developed a national political ideology or established permanent party organizations.

The reasons for this failure are not entirely cultural, although the cultural factor is significant. The suppression of political freedom by Reza Shah, and later (although to a much lesser degree) by his son, the present ruler of Iran, made it difficult for Iranians to acquire experience in democracy. In a political environment characterized by personal politics and dominated by selfish interest, it is difficult for party institutions to become part of the political process. Furthermore, despite the shah's insistence upon being the sponsor of a "guided democracy," no genuine party system has developed in Iran. In part, this is due to the shah's confusion about the meaning of opposition and the meaning of loyalty. When does opposition become disloyalty? The shah does not seem to be sure, and neither are the people or the politicians. In Iran, therefore, the limits of legitimate opposition and the requirements of loyalty are unknown elements. This problem is further complicated by the fact that the limits of the shah's powers are also unknown, since the constitutional regulations are neither obeyed nor respected.

25. Vreeland, *Iran*, p. 82.

Elections in Iran do not reflect a choice of the people; they are usually government-controlled. Nor does the legislature represent the divergent views of the populace. The deputies in the Majlis have no loyalty to political parties, since parties never last long enough to become important instruments of legislation. Instead, deputies divide informally into factions depending on the issues which confront the legislature.[26] The factions are as shifty as the issues themselves, and they never persist long enough to become anything like political parties. If deputies are motivated by anything, it is their class interest.

Political Groupings. Although there are no real parties, three political groups usually influence political trends in Iran.[27] The "center" group is the most moderate and consists of the shah and his court, the high-ranking military officers, the big landowners, and the merchants. It would be a mistake, of course, to assume that all these elements in the center group agree on all issues and are continually united. During Mohammed Mosaddeq's rise to power, for example, they were not. Normally, however, they strive to maintain a common front in the political struggle. When they fail to do so, Iran's internal political stability suffers.

The center group believes in the gradual transformation of the socio-economic structure of Iran. But the changes it aspires to bring about cannot be far-reaching since such changes would ultimately work against its vested interest as the dominant social group. (This is why the reforms it introduces never satisfy the liberals in the country.) The landlords are especially fearful of drastic changes in the social picture. They opposed the shah's land reforms of the 1950's and the 1960's because they viewed such reform as a threat to their privileged economic status. Some of them went as far as supporting Mosaddeq against the shah. In any case, the landlords and the merchants believe in the inviolability of the private enterprise system and look with great alarm at the extension of state control over the economy, especially when such control involves the redistribution of land or the establishment of state economic enterprises.

The shah is more liberal than the landlords and the merchants. He considers Iranian poverty and the inequitable distribution of wealth a threat to his position as the country's ruler. His position, therefore, is a very difficult one. If he alienates the traditional social groups, he then must be able to balance their loss by acquiring the support of new groups: the industrial workers, the freed peasants, and the middle-class intellectuals. But the new groups are in a transitional period, and until they become more secure and prosperous, their support cannot be substantial.

26. James M. Upton, *The History of Modern Iran, an Interpretation* (Cambridge: Harvard University Press, 1960), p. 92.

27. John Marlowe, *Iran: A Short Political Guide* (New York: Frederick A. Praeger, 1963), p. 86.

The shah's position within the center group is further complicated by the fact that the new groups could give their loyalties to either the right or the left. If either happened, he would have lost the support of the traditional classes before finding new support. This possibility has already caused the shah to procrastinate in carrying economic reforms to their logical ends. For the time being, and probably indefinitely, therefore, the shah will remain identified with the center group.

The second political group influencing Iranian political trends is the political right. Of course, what characterizes this group is its conservative, nationalistic, anti-imperialistic outlook. It is most conscious of the history of foreign intervention in Iranian affairs and desires to give the country a greater measure of independence. Mosaddeq was the leader of this group.

The right has displayed three main weaknesses: inexperience in the art of politics, lack of interest in economics, and lack of unity as a group. After the downfall of Mosaddeq the movement became leaderless. Under Mosaddeq, there was a minority of the landlords in the right group. Some of them were willing to sacrifice their personal economic interest and status for the sake of their nationalistic aims. Mosaddeq himself was wealthy, and he was among those who were willing to sacrifice. Most of the landlords, however, pursued their own selfish interests.

The third political group, the left, consists mainly of the Tudeh (Masses) party, whose leaders come mainly from the middle class. The Tudeh party originated in the Iranian Communist movement of the 1920's and 1930's, but was not officially organized until 1942, when the Red Army, which was then in occupation of Iran, helped organize it. It is probably the only party in Iran that deserves to be called a party. In 1945, for instance, its members in the Majlis voted in unity, a practice rare among the other political groups. Outside the Majlis, it was also well organized and disciplined.

The Tudeh party refrains from openly advocating the establishment of a Communist system in Iran; instead, it proposes sweeping social and economic reforms and attempts to build the image of a nationalistic group whose interest is in the salvation of Iran. And in this the Tudeh party finds many adherents among those to whom present conditions in Iran are very distasteful. The party proposes to destroy the power of the landlords, to nationalize industry, and to end Western economic and political influence.

During the early 1950's, the Tudeh party and the conservatives agreed on the question of nationalizing the oil industry. The two groups also found themselves agreeing on the necessity of ending Western influence in Iran, although for different reasons. Thus after Mosaddeq nationalized the oil industry in May 1951, the Tudeh party supported him but tried to exploit the political situation. However, the failure of Mosaddeq was followed by the arrest of the Tudeh leaders and members. The party was then outlawed, but it still operates underground and might under the proper circumstances experience a revival.

As mentioned earlier, political parties other than the Tudeh party are transitional. They usually belong to the political right or to the political center. The Iran party is an example of a rightist group. It was established during World War II and included many of the young intellectuals who were educated in Europe and the United States. This intellectual element was rarely affiliated with the center and expressed its dissatisfaction with the prevailing social and economic conditions through the Iran party or the Tudeh party. Some of the intelligentsia, of course, did cooperate with the government, and therefore with the political center; but by and large they have aligned to the right or the left in the political spectrum.

The Iran party accepted Mosaddeq's leadership, but Mosaddeq did not appreciate the advantages of having the support of a political party, nor did he understand how to use such a political organization to maintain himself in power. Mosaddeq's leadership was moral rather than political, and he expected every patriotic Iranian to follow him because he was trying to save the country from foreign domination. Many groups followed him, some because they thought they could exploit him, and others because they were truly patriotic. The multitude of factions and political groups which supported him were known as the National Front, of which the Iran party was the most important. The coalition collapsed when the Mosaddeq regime was overthrown in August 1953. The Iran party suffered a similar fate, although in 1963 some of its members regrouped under the name of the New Iran party. This 1963 group supports the shah's reform program, and it is doubtful that it is the true successor to the old Iran party.

After the downfall of Mosaddeq and the disintegration of the National Front, the formation of political parties merely reflected the shah's desire to institute what he considered "responsible democracy," one which evolves gradually within the limits of the monarchical system. Thus the shah ordered the formation of two parliamentary parties in 1955. He wished to create a two-party system similar to that in Great Britain, in which one party ruled and the other opposed. The shah wanted "a loyal opposition" party, but one that would not go beyond the limits of his guided democracy. In other words, the opposition must be manageable to be accepted.

The opposition party was called the People's party and was headed by Mr. Assadollah Alam, a close friend of the shah. The government party was called the Nationalist party and was headed by Dr. Manoutchehr Igbal, a devoted servant of the shah. The experiment in the two-party system failed because the opposition party took its responsibility too seriously, and the shah became fearful of the consequences. Also, and perhaps more important, the new arrangement had no relationship with the realities of political life in Iran, since it was imposed by the shah and not instituted by the people themselves.

The shah's interference in the governmental process and his domination of the political situation increased in the 1960's. He suspended the constitution in May 1961; and the Maljis, which was dissolved at that time, was not replaced until September 1963. Consequently, both left and right groups became determined to oppose the shah's unconstitutional act. In spite of the fact that the shah's reform program had attracted some of their followers, these groups were able to threaten the security of the regime. In January 1965, the prime minister, Hassan Mansour, was assassinated, and in April an attempt was made on the shah's life by a member of the Imperial Guard, who was said to have been corrupted by the Communists.

As long as the political system does not allow for the participation of the left and the right, it is probable that violence and plots will continue to threaten the shah's leadership. Assassination will probably be the most important method of political change available to the radical groups.

THE STRUGGLE FOR POWER DURING THE OIL CRISIS, 1949–1954

Since World War II it has been impossible to talk about Iranian politics without talking about oil. The events surrounding the nationalization of the Iranian oil in 1951, taken together, constitute the most important episode in the country's recent history. Consequently, we will cover the "oil crisis" in detail.

The oil crisis was caused not only by economic factors, but by political factors as well. If the difficulties had been purely economic, they would have been resolved with less difficulty, and the Iranian government would not have had to nationalize the industry. The nationalists under Mosaddeq were unshakable in their belief that the country's sovereignty had been undermined by the foreign interest in oil. It was this conviction which brought about the dangerous situation existing in 1951, when the oil industry was nationalized—a situation that led to a direct conflict between the shah and the nationalists under Mosaddeq.

However, the nationalists did not capture political power until after the moderates had already decided that the existing 1933 Oil Agreement was no longer satisfactory.[28] The agreement gave Iran only a small share of the oil revenue, and its terms were, by the standards of the late 1940's,

28. Text in J. C. Hurewitz, ed., *Diplomacy in the Near and Middle East, A Documentary Record: 1914–1956* (Princeton: Van Nostrand, 1956), vol. II, pp. 188–95.

generally unfavorable. The moderates' demand for the revision of the agreement, however, was primarily motivated by economics, including the need to increase government revenues to revive an economy devastated by the war and inflation.

But once the moderates made up their minds to press the British-owned Anglo-Iranian Oil Company (A.I.O.C.) for a revision of the 1933 Agreement, the nationalists began to agitate for the end of foreign interference in Iranian affairs. The issue of oil became an issue of foreign interference. As far as the nationalists were concerned, the sovereignty of Iran was at stake.

The surge of Iranian nationalism was not the only factor in the development of the oil crisis. There was also the rivalry between the landlords, who were in control of the Majlis, and the shah, who was trying to improve his image in the country.

The shah, as mentioned earlier, was installed as king after the forced abdication of his father in 1941. Young and inexperienced, he could not play an important role in the political life of his country and presented himself as a constitutional monarch very much like his British counterpart. He showed inclinations of favoring the development of strong representative institutions in Iran. Toward the end of the 1940's, however, he decided that the time was opportune for him to assume a greater political role, and he began to move toward the political center. This, of course, irritated the landlords, who had gotten used to the freedom they had acquired while the young shah was not exercising the traditional authority of his office.

In February 1949 the shah was shot and wounded by a member of a leftist group while on a visit to the University of Teheran, and the shah made up his mind to gain control of the political situation by enhancing his position in the governmental system. In March 1949, he succeeded in having the Constitution amended to give him the right to dissolve the two houses of the legislature provided he called for elections within three months from the time of dissolution. The Senate, which was established under the Constitution but had not met since 1906, he ordered to convene. Obviously, the shah intended to use the Senate as a rival body to the Majlis. Constitutionally, he could appoint thirty members of the sixty Senate members; the remaining thirty were to be elected.

But to attain power it was not enough to win the political battle against the Majlis and the landlords. The shah also had to improve his image with the population. He did this by instituting major economic reforms. The shah had already begun distributing some of his land to extremely poor peasants. And in 1949, he had the Majlis agree—reluctantly—to establish an imperial foundation to dispense with some of his personal property for the benefit of the poor. Much publicity was given to this reform. Of course, the landlords had no choice but to vote for the reform measure, since if they did not, their own image would have suffered. They were afraid, however, that a reform spirit might eventually force them to distribute their own land, and the rivalry between landlords and king was thus sharpened.

In the meantime, the oil issue was assuming greater significance. Negotiations between the Iranian government and the A.I.O.C. began in spite of the deterioration of the political situation in Iran. And in July 1949, the two parties reached an agreement, known as the Supplementary Oil Agreement, which offered Iran considerable financial gains.[29] However, in November 1950, the Oil Commission in the Majlis recommended the rejection of the agreement in spite of the fact the government supported it.

While the government was renegotiating an agreement with A.I.O.C., the Oil Commission of the Majlis was considering the possibility of nationalizing the oil industry. Mosaddeq, chairman of the commission, was the leader of the nationalist group in the Majlis, and he was determined to get the nationalization bill through. In February, his commission decided in favor of nationalization, and in March the Majlis confirmed the commission's decision. A wave of enthusiasm swept the country; about the only segments of Iranian society that did not share this enthusiasm were the shah, the army, and the government—none of which dared to oppose the measure. Violence had already shown the readiness of extremists to punish dissenters on March 7, 1951, when Razm-Ara, the prime minister, was assassinated by a member of a religious organization. He was the second prime minister to be murdered in two years.

On April 27, 1951, Mosaddeq became prime minister by vote of the legislature, and the shah had no choice but to accept. Mosaddeq was already a popular national hero, and he was supported by a peculiar assortment of political groups. The National Front, which we mentioned earlier, was the organization which attempted to unite these groups. On May 1, a law was passed to implement the nationalization program. The A.I.O.C. was required to leave the country, and an Iranian board was created to administer the details of the program.

Although Mosaddeq guaranteed the company's technicians and experts that they would have the same working conditions they had had with the British company, the technicians preferred to leave with the company. Thus the Iranian government was seriously threatened by the fact that it did not have the knowledge to run the industry. Perhaps this situation was the most important factor in the downfall of Mosaddeq. The economic situation was deteriorating rapidly, and many of the people who had supported Mosaddeq at the beginning were having second thoughts.

The nationalization decision had significant international implications.

29. Text in Hurewitz, pp. 305–8.

The Labour government of Great Britain accepted it; after all, being itself a Socialist government it could hardly take a contrary position. However, it rejected the proposed financial arrangements because, although the A.I.O.C. was a private concern, the British government owned shares in it. The crisis which developed out of the nationalization of the Iranian oil brought the United States into the picture. W. Averell Harriman was sent by the American government to Teheran to explore possible solutions. He was not successful. Later, both President Truman and the new British Prime Minister, Winston Churchill, proposed solutions, but they were also unsuccessful. The conditions which Mosaddeq proposed as bases for new negotiations were not acceptable to the British, and an impasse was reached.

In May, the British government and the A.I.O.C. filed separate petitions with the International Court of Justice. The company requested the court to declare Iran bound by the 1933 Agreement to accept its request for arbitration. The British government asked the court to nominate an arbitrator. The Iranian government, however, declared that it would not accept the court's jurisdiction. In September, the British government referred the dispute to the Security Council of the United Nations, which decided, the following month, to wait for the decision of the International Court. This court, in turn, decided on July 22, 1952, that it had no jurisdiction over the matter.

While Britain was exploring these possibilities for the settlement of the oil issue, she was relying on economic sanctions to bring about a change in the position of Mosaddeq's government. Sanctions included trade restrictions, the freezing of Iran's sterling balances, and discouraging other nations from buying Iran's disputed oil. Diplomatic relations between the two countries were broken in October 1952.

In the meantime, the Iranian domestic situation was worsening. Serious opposition to Mosaddeq developed within the Majlis, and relations between the government and the shah were gradually deteriorating. During the oil crisis, the shah was overshadowed by Mosaddeq. In February 1953, he declared his intention to leave the country, although he did not actually leave until a few months later. And as the gaps between Mosaddeq and the Majlis on the one hand and Mosaddeq and the shah on the other were widening, the leftist groups were intensifying their anti-shah activities and were becoming less interested in Mosaddeq. As Mosaddeq weakened, the leftists began to make their own plans for Iran, which included neither the shah nor Mosaddeq.

The economic situation was even worse. Oil production had stopped. Furthermore, President Eisenhower announced in June that unless Iran would cooperate in finding a solution to the oil problem she would not receive any more United States aid. Thus, the Iranian government was left with no significant sources of revenue.

Many members of the Majlis resigned in protest against Mosaddeq's uncompromising policies. Mosaddeq first retaliated by intimidation and tried to use protest demonstrations as a weapon against them. Finally, however, he took a more drastic step. In August 1953, he held a referendum, after which he claimed a great majority of the Iranian people voted for the dissolution of the Majlis. This was a strong indication that Mosaddeq was determined to eliminate all opposition, including that of the Majlis.

In August, the shah left the country after he had appointed Fozlollah Zahedi, a former minister of the interior, as prime minister, and dismissed Mosaddeq. Of course, Mosaddeq did not obey the dismissal order. At this point, Iran was at the crossroad between the monarchical and republican systems. The monarchy had only one hope of survival—the army.

The army was built by Reza Shah, the father of the present ruler, and was loyal to the monarchy. This was true in spite of the fact that Mosaddeq, as minister of defense, had purged the high military command, which was loyal to the shah, and in 1952 had appointed instead officers loyal to himself. However, his changes did not win him the loyalty of the whole army: some remained loyal to the shah, and although others stayed neutral, they were willing to swing to the shah's side if the opportunity came.

One of the military units which remained loyal to the shah was the Imperial Guard, which attempted a coup against Mosaddeq on August 15, 1953. Although the coup failed, it enabled the pro-shah elements to come into the open. At this critical moment, Mosaddeq was betrayed by many of his supporters, and on August 19 pro-shah demonstrators appeared in the streets of Teheran. Joined by policemen and soldiers, the demonstrators took over the government radio station, ransacked government buildings and newspaper offices, and created so much confusion that by the end of the day Zahedi was able to tell the people that he was the new prime minister of Iran by order of the shah. Mosaddeq was arrested and later tried for crimes against the Constitution. Because of his advanced age he received a sentence of three years in prison.

In October 1954, the Iranian Majlis approved a new oil agreement which granted a concession to a consortium of eight companies. The agreement recognized the fact of nationalization but granted the consortium the right to operate under a forty-year lease. The National Iranian Oil Company, a government enterprise, was to own the oil properties and take charge of the distribution of petroleum products within Iran, while the consortium of foreign organizations took charge of matters such as exploration, production, refining, and marketing of oil. Under the agreement, the Iranian government was to receive 50 per cent of the net profit of all oil sold outside Iran.[30] In 1955, the year after the agreement was signed, Iran received £30 million in oil revenues. This amount increased to about £100 million in 1960 and £158.8 million in 1964.

THE ECONOMY

In Iran, the principal economic activity is agriculture; about 75 per cent of the people derive their livelihood from farming. However, productivity is very low, and until the shah's land reforms of the 1960's were introduced, the peasant who worked the land did not own it. In fact, only 5 per cent of Iranian land was owned by the peasants, and tenant farmers constituted 90 per cent of those engaged in farming. These tenants lived at a subsistence level.

In industry as well as in agriculture, work relations and work attitudes followed traditional patterns characterized by paternalistic owners and totally dependent employees. These traditional patterns have been and remain obstacles to modernization and economic progress. For although government-sponsored industrialization programs are changing some of the traditional patterns of work relations, these older patterns are still the predominant features of the Iranian economic system. It will be some time before they can be replaced by new and more efficient work arrangements. Industry is largely government-sponsored. In the past, private individuals had very little interest in the development of industry; thus the state took the initiative of developing industrial projects. Private entrepreneurs lacked initiative; there was little technical knowhow; communications were poor; and the populace had little buying power. Consequently, governments had to subsidize private enterprises, but such enterprises were rarely stable because of their interest in "quick profits." [31]

Today, the government considers industrialization the key to Iran's economic future. Its decision to embark on a program of industrialization was made immediately after World War II, but the lack of capital and later the oil controversy made the execution of the program impossible. Thus, Iran's effort to industrialize did not actually begin until the late 1950's and early 1960's.

Agriculture and the Shah's Land Reforms. Some of the obstacles which retard the industrial progress of Iran also retard her agricultural development. Lack of capital and knowhow are only two of these. In recent years,

30. Marlowe, *Iran*, p. 106.
31. Vreeland, *Iran*, p. 204.

however, American aid and government subsidies have been used to establish agricultural institutions, research centers, and extension programs, all in an effort to improve farm technology.

The problem of poor transportation, another obstacle to economic progress, has received some attention under the economic plans, especially the five-year plan which was started in 1963. An improved transportation system may someday ease the agricultural marketing problem. Because transportation is costly, the farmer usually cannot afford to send his products to distant markets where he can get a higher price and is compelled to sell his products in the local market where he must compete with producers of similar crops, who bid down prices. Furthermore, he is forced to sell immediately, both because of his indebtedness and because—even if he had the money—storage facilities are not available, particularly for perishable products. A solution to this problem of marketing requires not only a good and inexpensive transportation system but the elimination of the peasant's heavy debt.

Agricultural reform programs were needed not only to increase output but also to improve the standards of living of most Iranians. In 1965, the average annual income of the Iranian peasant was estimated at $168; if this amount were divided among the members of his family, the resulting per capita income would be less than $56.[32]

The shah led the way for improvements in the economic and social status of the peasants, in the face of the obstruction by the landlords, who owned so much and cared so little. The absentee landlords were politically powerful and dominated the Majlis. While they would normally support the shah against his political enemies, they would oppose him in his efforts to redistribute land; and if the shah were to carry his reforms too far, they were prepared to turn against him.

But in spite of opposition, Prime Minister Ali Amini introduced in 1962 a strong land-reform law—at a time when the Majlis had been dissolved and the government was ruling by decree. The program limited landholdings to one village only and turned over the freed land to the peasants. In view of the fact that 10,000 villages out of a total of 45,000 belonged to landlords who owned five or more villages each, the law was an economic as well as a social necessity. The new decree also organized the peasants into cooperatives to help them work their land more efficiently. The first phase of the program was to affect 20 per cent of all villages; it was completed in 1964.

The second phase of the program had a still greater impact. The maximum size of landholdings was to be determined according to soil fertility,

32. *The Middle East and North Africa, 1965–66* (London: Europa Publications, 1965), p. 196.

reducing the size of holdings to 300 acres in some instances, and in others to 75. The government was fearful, however, that the second phase of the program would run into more difficulties than the first and, therefore, provided that the maximum landholding would be increased to 1,250 acres if the farmer cultivated the land by mechanized means. The government decree also provided certain incentives in the program for the benefit of the landlords. For instance, it would pay the landlord in cash one-third of the price of the land he sold to the peasant, who was required to pay the same amount to the government over the short period of fourteen months.

The government has been pushing its reform program through, in spite of landlord opposition, and by 1963–64 agricultural production was already showing a substantial increase. By March 1967, three-fourths of the Iranian farmers owned land.[33] This, of course, is an outstanding governmental improvement. However, Iran is still a long way from being the modern state it desires to be.

Economic Planning. Between 1949 and 1968, three economic plans were launched in Iran. The first (1949–56) was a failure; the second (1956–63) had serious difficulties; and the third (1963–68) was fairly successful. Today, the government is committed to the sponsorship of economic development.

The first seven-year plan was supposed to spend £160 million on economic development. Agriculture was to receive 25 per cent of this amount, communication another 25 per cent, and the remaining 50 per cent was to go to industry and social services. The plan was to be financed in equal shares from oil revenue, the national budget, and the International Bank. However, for many reasons the plan failed to materialize. The International Bank did not come through with its expected share because it did not think the plan was economically sound. The nationalization of the oil stopped oil production, thereby making it impossible for the government to obtain the revenue necessary for the plan. And finally, the conflict between the shah and Mosaddeq distracted attention from the plan. Thus only £50 million was invested under the first plan.

The second seven-year plan, launched in 1956, was to spend £400 million. Most of this amount was to come from oil revenues. Thirty-three per cent of this money was to go for communication; 26 per cent for agriculture, another 26 per cent for social services; and the remaining 15 per cent for industry.[34]

This second plan, too, was largely a failure. One set of causes was basically economic. A severe drought and a rise in the cost of living of about 10 per cent over the period of the plan reduced money available for invest-

33. *Time,* March 31, 1967, p. 28.
34. *The Middle East and North Africa, 1965–66, op. cit.,* p. 199.

ment. In addition, there was a drop in the price of oil over these years that was only partly offset by increases in oil sales.

Other causes lay in unsound fiscal policy. Increases in domestic expenditures diverted oil revenues that were earmarked for financing the second plan. In addition, tax revenues were low because the tax system favored landlords and merchants, who were the best prospective sources of tax moneys. Thus, the plan did not have adequate financial support.

Had it not been for United States aid, Iran's economic situation would have been worse. Between 1951 and 1961, this aid amounted to about $200 million in the form of loans, and $850 million in the form of grants for economic and military purposes. However, when the United States government began to realize that the Iranian government's financial policy was not sound, it warned that aid would be cut off unless it adopted a stabilization plan that would introduce a sounder fiscal policy. In 1960, such a plan was announced by the Iranian government and approved by the International Monetary Fund.

Under the stabilization plan the government was committed to create a surplus in the budget, to increase taxes for revenue, to impose import restrictions, and to restrict bank credit in the private sector.[35] At the time the stabilization plan was adopted, Iran's total debt, private and public, was $800 million, and her annual debt payment was $100 million. Inflation was a problem. In 1959, the previous year, the official cost of living index rose 9 per cent. Thus, there was reason for alarm. Nevertheless, the adoption of the stabilization plan made it possible for the Iranian government to obtain more money from foreign sources.

Unfortunately, the government ignored its own stabilization plan shortly after it was adopted. As a result, the International Bank decided to freeze Iran's unpaid credit. In 1962, Prime Minister Amini took charge of the economic situation and followed a conservative financial policy that halted the inflationary trend. The foreign-exchange problem was alleviated by import restrictions. Amini failed to balance the budget, however, but his successor, Mr. Alam, was more successful in this matter. By the end of 1964, it was clear that the stabilization plan had succeeded, and the economic situation had improved.

The third economic plan (1963–68) was realistic. It emphasized agriculture, which had not had priority in the previous plans. Thus, it gave priority to Iran's traditional and principal occupation, and this was in line with the 1947 recommendations of the American consultants, Morrison and Knudsen, recommendations which had been ignored by the Iranian government at the time they were originally made. Also, the plan preferred small projects to the big ones that characterized the old plans, and a real

35. *Middle East Affairs,* 1961, Vol. XII, p. 69.

effort was made to establish a definite and logical relationship between projects and natural resources—an important relationship that had been ignored under the previous plans.

The plan was divided into two parts so that the essential projects would be completed before unforeseen obstacles (such as difficulty in obtaining the necessary additional funds to finance the plan) could develop. The first part represented 60 per cent of the plan and included most of the agricultural projects. The remaining 40 per cent included projects considered only desirable, which could be abandoned easily without hurting the essential projects. Furthermore, the plan paid attention to the private sector of the economy, also neglected by the old plans. Under it, 55 per cent was to be spent in the public sector and 45 per cent in the private sector.

The plan was to be financed mostly from the oil revenues and the domestic budget. Only a small percentage of the required capital was to come from foreign sources. Ironically, the success of the plan resulted in offers by foreign sources to aid the Iranian economy. Such aid, which was in the form of loans, came from countries such as Russia, Poland, Hungary, Japan, West Germany, the United Kingdom, the United States, the World Bank, and other countries and organizations. As a result of successful and realistic planning, Iran now had access to a number of financial sources. In 1967, it was estimated that the industrial sector had grown 17 per cent over 1966. Foreign investment increased to $186 million a year. Exports increased four times from 1957 to 1967, to $1.3 billion; and the gross national product doubled during the same period, to $6.5 billion per year.[36]

FOREIGN POLICY

In modern times, Iran has been the victim of the international power struggle. At one time or another, Russia, France, Germany, Turkey, and Great Britain wanted to dominate Iran. Peter the Great desired the control of Persia to gain access to India. Napoleon had hoped to conquer Persia for the same reason. And during the nineteenth century, Great Britain's policy toward Persia was enforced by her India Office. Thus in the eighteenth and nineteenth centuries, the interest of the big powers in Iran was based upon their interest in India, to which Iran was considered the gateway.

In 1907, Russia and Great Britain became concerned about the rising power of Germany. Consequently, they agreed to divide Persia into "spheres of influence," the northern part to become the Russian sphere and the southern part the British sphere. The Anglo-Russian Treaty of 1907 also

36. *Time*, March 31, 1967, p. 28.

recognized central Persia as a buffer zone to be controlled by the Persians themselves.

During World War I, Persia became the battleground for the armed forces of Britain and Turkey. At the end of the war, Russia attempted to establish a Communist regime in the northern part of the country, while the British were attempting to force an agreement upon the Persian government which would have given them control over Persia's financial and military affairs.[37] But the coming of Reza Shah to power in the early 1920's saved Iran; he was able to free his country from Russian and British domination.

Germany became interested in Iran between the two world wars. Unlike the British and the Russians, who forced themselves upon the country, the Germans used the technique of infiltration rather than outright military occupation to gain influence. Thus, while Iranians considered the British and the Russians as aggressors, they did not consider the Germans in the same way. When World War II broke out, Iran and Germany were on fairly good terms, and in spite of Allied pressure, Iran's official policy at the beginning of the war was neutral.

However, Iran's neutrality was a source of discomfort for Britain and Russia. The two countries were fully aware of Iran's important strategic location and of the importance of her oil to both themselves and the Germans. Consequently, they invaded Iran under the pretext that Reza Shah did not adhere to his own policy of neutrality and that he had allowed the country to be infiltrated by Germans whose objective was to gain political control. Although these charges were partly true, they did not justify the intervention of the two powers which could have accomplished strict adherence to neutrality by other means. At any rate, the two invading countries promised Iran in the Tripartite Treaty of 1942 to evacuate her territory within a period of six months after the end of the war.

Iran and the Soviet Union in the Postwar Period. Toward the end of the war, it appeared that the Soviet Union had planned to gain a permanent foothold in Iran, while Britain was preparing for the withdrawal of her troops as she had promised. In the northern province of Azerbaijan, the Tudeh party, under the name of the Democratic party, engineered a coup with the assistance of Soviet troops. In December 1945, it proclaimed the Autonomous Republic of Azerbaijan and designated a new government under the premiership of Ja'afar Pishevar, "a veteran commintern agent." [38]

About the same time the Azerbaijan Autonomous Republic was pro-

37. Donald N. Wilber, *Iran: Oasis of Stability in the Middle East?* (New York: Foreign Policy Association, 1959), p. 34.

38. George Lenczowski, *Russia and the West in Iran, 1918–1948* (Ithaca: Cornell University Press, 1948), p. 289.

claimed a Kurdish uprising took place in western Azerbaijan, where a Kurdish People's Republic was also proclaimed. Consequently, the whole of the Azerbaijan area was separated from Iran. Soviet troops were used to prevent the Iranian army from entering the area to enforce Iranian law.

The Iranian government complained to the Security Council of the United Nations, but results could hardly be expected from the newly created international organization. After deadline for the withdrawal of foreign troops from Iran (March 2, 1946), Soviet troops were still in the country. The United States and Britain complied with the deadline requirement in the Tripartite Treaty, and their troops were withdrawn.

The Iranian government received enormous publicity for its case when the question of Soviet occupation was brought to the United Nations for the second time, soon after the deadline had passed. The United States expressed its pro-Iran position in the most emphatic terms and warned the Soviet government of serious consequences if it continued its policy. Furthermore, world opinion in support of Iran made it difficult for the Soviet Union to continue its occupation. Finally, on April 4, 1946, the two feuding countries concluded an agreement in which (1) the Soviet Union agreed to withdraw its forces from Iran within six weeks; (2) a joint oil company was to be established and ratified by the Iranian Majlis within seven months; and (3) the Azerbaijan problem was to be solved by direct negotiation between the Azerbaijan authorities and the Iranian government. On this last point, an agreement was worked out giving the Iranian government control over Azerbaijan. As to the establishment of the joint oil company, the Iranian Majlis refused to approve its establishment. Thus, Iran was once again free from Soviet domination.

This freedom, however, was strained by the continuance of Soviet interest in Iran. Russia has always shown excessive concern about the security of her borders, whether under the tsars or under communism. After the war, the Soviet Union was able to dominate eastern Europe and thereby safeguard its western borders. Its failure to achieve similar success with regard to its southern borders was a major weakness in its foreign policy and a source of tension between her and Iran. Again, the existence of oil in Iran was another reason for that country's extreme importance to the Soviet Union. The control of Iran by Soviet Russia or by an Iranian Communist regime would serve the dual purpose of securing the southern borders of the Soviet Union while depriving western Europe of a great portion of its oil supply.

After Azerbaijan, Soviet policy in Iran shifted from occupation to subversion in a new effort to establish control. But this new strategy was proven ineffective in the early 1950's when the Tudeh party failed to subvert the Mosaddeq regime and gain control of political power in Iran. It was, therefore, necessary for the Soviet Union to lessen its reliance upon subversion and to attempt instead to restate its political objectives in Iran. The Soviet policy after 1954 aimed at pushing Iran into a neutral position [39] in world affairs. This, however, would have meant the abandonment of her pro-Western policy, and this the Iranian government did not wish to do, for two main reasons. First, she benefited more by selling her oil where it was needed most, that is, to western Europe; second, she felt safer with the democratic regimes of the West than with the totalitarian regime of the Soviet Union. There was, of course, the belief derived from the past experience of Iran and many other countries that it is more difficult to free oneself from Soviet dominance than from Western dominance. And if it were to be a choice between the two evils, Western imperialism was the lesser. Furthermore, an important consideration was the fact that the empires of the Western powers were being dissolved while the empire of the Soviet Union was being formed. Iran felt safer with the powers whose empires were dying. Thus, Iran did not hesitate to join the Baghdad Pact in 1955 in spite of Soviet warnings and threats.

Present Soviet policy in Iran continues to demand that Iran should be neutral. To accomplish this goal, the Soviet Union had to appear at times lenient and friendly with Iran, and at other times tough and belligerent. In 1956, for instance, the shah, during his visit to the Soviet Union, listened to Soviet apologies for the mistakes of the past, including the Azerbaijan affair. In 1957, several economic agreements were concluded between the two countries, and they were beneficial to both countries.

Soviet flirtation with Iran was not free from pressure. When, for instance, the United States offered the members of the Baghdad Pact bilateral treaties guaranteeing their security, the Soviet Union warned Iran not to conclude such an agreement with the United States. Iran told the Soviet government that such security arrangements with the United States were merely defensive and did not in any way threaten the position of the Soviet Union. In 1959, Iran offered to negotiate a nonaggression pact with the Soviet Union, which refused unless Iran promised not to accept the United States treaty offer. The Soviet condition was rejected by Iran, and the bilateral treaty with the United States was concluded during the same year. Thereafter, and until 1962, the Soviet Union conducted intense propaganda against the shah's government and called for the overthrow of the imperial regime in Iran. However, the propaganda accomplished nothing, and the Soviet Union returned to a policy of conciliation at the end of 1962. This time, the Soviet government tried its best to eliminate the fear of the Iranian government of the consequences of close relations with the

39. Donald N. Wilber, *Contemporary Iran* (New York: Frederick A. Praeger, 1963), p. 195.

Soviet Union. It tried to show how Afghanistan, a neighboring country, benefited from friendly relations with the Soviet Union and that such relations did not minimize or compromise Afghanistan's independence and sovereignty.

Early in 1967, there were signs that the Soviet strategy was beginning to pay off. In February 1967, the Iranian government announced the purchase on credit of $110 million worth of Soviet arms. The amount was to be repaid over a period of eight years at an interest of 2.5 per cent.[40] Of course, the arms deal is no proof that Iran has decided to abandon her pro-Western policy or that she has been fully persuaded of the rightness of a neutral course in foreign affairs. But the event does mark the beginning of a trend toward the proliferation of Iran's partnerships in international relations. Iran no longer sees her national interest exclusively dependent on her relations with the West, and there is no doubt that Iran has been influenced by the benefits gained by neutral policies in other countries. While Iran has not adopted neutrality as an official policy, she is attempting to receive the benefits of such a policy by dealing with countries other than the United States and Great Britain.

Iran and the Western World. Before World War II, American activity in Iran was primarily missionary and educational; it was, that is to say, the same interest she had throughout the Middle East. Of course, the United States was also interested in Iran's oil, as well as in the oil of other Middle Eastern countries; but this interest was indirect in that the United States government was involved only to the extent of helping American companies secure oil concessions in Iran. Politically speaking, therefore, United States involvement in Iran—and the Middle East in general—was extremely limited, suggesting no desire to dominate. Such an ambition was, however, characteristic of British policy toward Iran.

On a few occasions, American financial experts visited Iran to assist her government in developing sound economic and financial policies. Morgan Shuster who, as an independent, was employed in 1911 by the Iranian Majlis, attempted to reorganize Iran's financial policy, but was dismissed before he could accomplish his task. Russian pressure upon the government of Iran was too great to allow the American expert a free hand. In 1922, A. C. Millspaugh headed an American financial group which was organized to advise the Iranian government on how to reconstruct Iran's ailing economy. He too was unsuccessful, and in 1927 his mission left Iran under controversial circumstances. In 1943, Millspaugh returned to Iran for the same purpose, but two years later he resigned under heavy criticism from the wealthy groups who opposed his plan for fiscal centralization. Thus, the activities of the American advisers in Iran did not directly involve the gov-

40. *The New York Times,* February 20, 1967.

ernment of the United States, and although American individuals acquired positions of power in Iran, their positions were the outcome of their economic activities.

During the war, American troops were stationed in Iran upon the invitation of Britain and the Soviet Union. They were employed to safeguard the supply route between the Persian Gulf and the Soviet Union. It was during the war years and specifically after the Teheran Conference of November 1943 that the general outline of American policy toward Iran was worked out by President Roosevelt. According to this outline, the objective of United States Iranian policy was twofold: the preservation of Iran's independence, and the promotion of American economic interest in the area.

Immediately after the war, the preservation of Iran's independence meant simply keeping the Soviet Union out. Thus, the United States was instrumental in bringing about the withdrawal of Soviet troops, through intense diplomatic efforts both inside and outside the United Nations. From that time on, the United States became the most important Western power in Iranian affairs—a position previously occupied by Great Britain, which, somewhat reluctantly, accepted the new power relation.

But the role of the United States in Iran became very different from that of Great Britain before the end of the war. Although the objectives of American policy in Iran were clear, its methods and means were often ambiguous and uncertain. Hesitation and procrastination were characteristic of American policy in the first few years following the withdrawal of Soviet troops—a situation primarily caused by indecision about how much and what kind of involvement was needed to fulfill American objectives. The answers to such questions were not provided by the policy-makers in Washington. Fundamentally, the United States accepts the principle of nonintervention in the internal affairs of other countries. Very often, however, the internal affairs of a country directly influence its international relations, which includes the power position of the United States. Iran is such a country, and United States policy toward Iran has thus experienced great difficulties; a dangerous point has usually been reached before the United States could decide to intervene to support the objectives of her own policy. In other words, American policy reacts more than it acts, and American interests are often jeopardized in the process of reaction.

This dilemma of American policy exists not only in Iran but in many other parts of the world. The British, on the other hand, have had no such problem. In Iran, once they knew what they wanted they took the necessary steps to get it. They had no guilt feelings about intervention in the affairs of other countries because they once had a great empire which they took for granted. With the United States, the contrary is true, although the results have often been confusing. United States intervention does take place, but it comes a little late and, because of that, is often less than enlightened.

Thus, the rise of Mosaddeq in Iran was preceded by an ineffectual and hesitant American policy which provided very little assistance to the shah's government. The shah visited the United States in 1949 and asked for a more generous assistance, but he returned to his country extremely disappointed.[41] Obviously, the United States was not yet certain of the means it should use to accomplish the objectives of her policy in Iran. And when Mosaddeq became the prime minister, the uncertainty of American policy continued to characterize the relations between the two countries. Mosaddeq attempted to obtain American aid and support for his regime on condition, of course, that the United States would sympathize with his cause. There was some hope that a sympathetic American policy would strengthen the Mosaddeq regime. To be effective, however, such an American policy would have had to be based on an understanding and sympathy with revolutionary regimes like that of Mosaddeq, which it did not, generally speaking, possess. Furthermore, the United States felt obligated to render at least partial support to her old ally, Great Britain. Consequently, the Mosaddeq regime drifted to an uncompromising and unreasonable posture, and a political crisis of international dimensions ensued.

The partial and limited aid which Iran received from the United States in the few years preceding the downfall of Mosaddeq consisted mainly of programs initiated under the 1950 Point Four Agreement and under the International Cooperation Administration Mission. In 1951, the I.C.A.'s Iranian budget was limited to a modest $1.6 million. It is true that such aid was increased while Mosaddeq was still in power, to $22 million in 1953, but its impact was offset by the disappearance of oil revenues. Obviously, Mosaddeq was hoping that he could continue his oil policy while expecting American aid to solve his financial and economic problems. This expectation was proved erroneous when in October 1953 Eisenhower made clear his intention to discontinue American aid unless Mosaddeq found a solution to the oil crisis.

The Mosaddeq episode reminded the American foreign-policy makers of the danger of uncertainty about the exact means by which the objectives of policy were to be accomplished. In the following years, therefore, American-Iranian relations became more intimate and more cordial. During the fiscal year 1954, for instance, Iran received $84 million in American aid, and by the end of 1957 the total amount of American aid amounted to $322.7 million.[42] It is to be remembered, however, that most

41. See the shah's autobiography, *Mission for My Country* (New York: McGraw-Hill Book Company, 1961), p. 88.
42. Figures on American aid to Iran are taken from Wilber's *Contemporary Iran*, pp. 189–95.

of this aid went to support the government's budget, which was seriously unbalanced by the oil crisis. Nevertheless, American aid continued to increase until it reached a total of $880 million by the end of fiscal year 1959. And although the annual amounts of American aid began to decrease after 1958, the aid total reached $1.3 billion by the end of fiscal year 1961.

Early in 1962, American aid programs to foreign countries underwent changes in their emphases and over-all objectives. Some of these changes have already affected Iran. Upon the suggestion of President Kennedy, the new emphasis was to be on loans rather than grants, on economic assistance rather than military assistance, and on putting an end to grants for the purpose of balancing the government budgets of recipient countries.[43] The new American aid policy was not welcome in the Iranian official circles. Iran preferred to have more freedom in the allocation of American financial resources. She also wanted to build her armed forces, perhaps in the way similar to that of Turkey; Iran government officials felt that she, like Turkey, was in a vulnerable position vis-à-vis the Soviet Union. They could not understand why the United States had different standards for Turkey and Iran, when these two countries were in similar geographic and strategic situations, and were also active members of CENTO, the defense organization formerly known as the Baghdad Pact. Furthermore, for the shah, the army is a significant instrument of domestic power, which he uses to maintain his control over his country.

The Soviet-Iranian arms deal made early in 1967 was a manifestation of Iran's frustration with America's reluctance "to go all the way" for Iran. It is also an indication that Soviet policy of inducing Iran to move toward a neutral position in world affairs was successful. But Iran's inclination to deal with the Soviet Union has not been a source of friction with the United States, which has shown no alarm at the prospect of a two-sided Iranian foreign policy or even an Iranian neutralism.[44] It is, therefore, quite possible that the present policy of Iran, friendly to the Soviet Union but basically pro-Western, will continue in the coming years and prove to be very beneficial to Iran.

CONCLUSION

The establishment of constitutional government in Iran requires fundamental changes in the attitudes of the Iranians and their political leaders. One serious problem which needs to be solved soon is the people's lack of

43. Wilber, *Contemporary Iran,* p. 192.
44. Leonard Binder, *The Middle East Crisis: Background and Issues* (Chicago: The University of Chicago Center for Policy Study, 1967), p. 14.

understanding of their fundamental laws and their apathy toward legalism. In addition, adherence to constitutional provisions requires a change in the attitude of the shah toward the political system and its legal framework. At the present time, the shah pays little or no attention to the Constitution. His political role is not clear, and there is need to provide a clearer definition of his legal powers.

The future of the monarchy is uncertain. However, in recent years the shah has sponsored social reform, and this has strengthened his position. There is, therefore, no immediate danger to the Iranian monarchy. But in the long run, the monarchy is not so secure. Throughout the Middle East, monarchical regimes are either being seriously challenged, as in Jordan and Saudi Arabia, or have already disappeared, as in Turkey, Iraq, and Egypt. The example of these countries must have some impact upon certain elements of the Iranian political society. Furthermore, with the exception of the few countries who managed to restrict the roles of their monarchs, most countries view monarchies as reactionary regimes incapable of bringing their countries into the twentieth century. This notion has many adherents in Iran, although it is not held by a majority of the population.

The economic conditions of Iran have improved, but we must remember that Iran has a long way to go to achieve general prosperity and a high standard of living. While we can credit the shah for the many projects he initiated, we must not forget that these projects are only of recent history and have had only limited effect. Iran is an extremely backward country, and time, patience, and good planning are required if Iran is to be able to reach reasonable levels of economic and social development. One thing is certain, however: economic and social change will have profound impact upon Iran's political picture.

Finally, in international relations, no dramatic change is expected. However, it is important to note that the foreign policy of Iran is related to her political system. So long as Iran continues to have a monarchy, her foreign policy will continue to be basically pro-Western. If the monarchy were to disappear, the country's foreign policy might undergo important and perhaps fundamental changes; what kind of changes would depend upon the type of regime which replaced the monarchy.

CHAPTER 5

EGYPT UNDER FOREIGN RULE

THE control of Egypt by foreign powers (almost continuous from 525 B.C. to 1922) has had profound effects on the country's attitudes and political institutions. It has been, perhaps, one of the most important influences in modern Egyptian political developments, affecting the thinking of Egyptian political leaders, the nation's foreign policy, and the character of Egyptian nationalism. To understand Egyptian politics, then, we must know something of this long history of foreign domination. In this chapter, we shall deal with it first historically; then we shall evaluate its impact upon Egyptian political life.

THE EARLY CONQUERORS (525 B.C. TO A.D. 642)

The year 525 B.C. marked the end of a four-thousand-year civilization ruled primarily by the Egyptian Pharaohs—one which had contributed immensely to the larger culture of man. From that time until the coming of the Arabs, the country was ruled successively for almost a thousand years by four great ancient empires—Persia, Greece, Rome, and Byzantium.

Both the Persians, who ruled from 525 to 332 B.C., and the Greeks who conquered under Alexander the Great and ruled from 332 to 30 B.C., governed Egypt as absolute monarchies—continuing the tradition of the Pharaohs and making little change in fundamental Egyptian institutions. Under the Persians, Egypt was politically oriented toward the Fertile Crescent, but under the Greeks it faced, for the first time, the European continent. Both Europe and Asia benefited from the new orientation. From the time of Alexander, Egypt was involved in cultural exchanges with Europe; these exchanges were to influence the character of Egypt's later political position.

In 30 B.C. the Romans became Egypt's new masters. To a much larger degree than their predecessors, their political control and management of Egyptian affairs affected the lower levels of Egyptian society. Roman insti-

102

tutions were established, although cultural adaptation affected both the ruler and the ruled. The Egyptian priesthood was brought under Roman control, and divine qualities were given to the Roman Emperor in the Egyptian religion.

During the Roman period, Christianity was brought to Egypt. Legend has it that St. Mark was the one responsible for its introduction in A.D. 37, and tradition relates that the Church of Alexandria was established three years later.[1] In spite of the fact that Christianity in Egypt was undermined by the disintegration of the Western division of the Roman Empire in the fifth century A.D., the Coptic Christian Church survived and continues until the present time.

When at the end of the fourth century the Roman Empire split into Western and Eastern divisions, Egypt became part of the latter which came ultimately to be known as the Byzantine Empire. The Byzantines ruled from 395 to 642, except for the brief period between 616 and 628 when Egypt was once again under Persian rule. In 642, Egypt became part of the Arab Muslim empire and remained under Arab domination until 1517, almost another thousand years.

THE ARAB PERIOD (642-1517)

Of all the foreign powers that ruled Egypt after 525 B.C., only the Arabs transformed Egyptian culture so profoundly as to make it resemble their own. Their rule was the longest, and their influence was permanent.

Why were the Arabs so successful? There is no simple answer. But in large measure their success came from the effective use of two important instruments of cultural change: a new religion, Islam; and a new language, Arabic. Both became integral parts of Egyptian culture, and they are the same elements which have today created an identity common to almost all the Arabic-speaking countries of the Middle East and North Africa. They are also the common features of Arab nationalism.

As a religious doctrine, Islam was simple, and it was this simplicity which enabled it to gain widespread acceptance in the area more rapidly than did Christianity. The new religion contained a code of law which became fully integrated in the institutional life of Egypt. Matters pertaining to family, marriage, and inheritance were subject to the legal controls of the Islamic religion.

The power of Islam was the product of the fusion of faith and law.[2] The religion was directly connected with the social and political order of society

1. Georgiana G. Stevens, *Egypt: Yesterday and Today* (New York: Holt, Rinehart & Winston, 1963), p. 48.
2. Stevens, *Egypt*, p. 54.

and was therefore an effective method of political and social control; it was this effectiveness that enabled the Islamic state to survive in Egypt longer than any other foreign system.

Arabic was imposed upon the Egyptians and other peoples because it was the language of the Koran, the Bible of the Muslims, which was not allowed to be translated into other languages. Although the adoption of Islam by the Egyptians was faster than their adoption of the Arabic language, in time this language was able to replace the old Coptic Egyptian and become the official language of Egypt.

Language, being the main carrier of culture, contributed immensely to the transformation of Egyptian life. Reinforced by the new system of belief and the standards of morals of the Islamic religion, Arabic became more than a language; it was, at least to some Egyptians, the basis of a new identity.

The identity, however, was not a national identity; it was regional, extending beyond Egyptian borders. The national identity, although no longer distinguished by a language and a religion of its own, remained Egyptian, for the process of Arabization did leave certain parts of the Egyptian traditional life intact. Most important among these were the cultural patterns and social behavior shaped by the economic system and the physical environment. Farming, for instance, continued to be the principal occupation for most Egyptians. Methods of irrigation did not change, nor did the system of agriculture as a whole. Certain psychic traits remained the same also. The Egyptian never lost a feeling of insecurity which was the result of his awareness of economic scarcity and of the harshness of his physical environment. Also remaining was the Egyptian's tendency to rely on the state in many aspects of his daily life, a result of the same economic and physical conditions that produced his feeling of insecurity.

Under Arab rule, Egypt was part of a vast empire whose political center changed from time to time. During periods of Arab disunity, Egypt was able to maintain a certain autonomy, although she was never wholly free of foreign rule. Thus after 1252, Egypt was controlled by the Mameluke [3] governors until she was incorporated into the Ottoman Empire by Selim I in 1517.

OTTOMAN RULE 1517–1882

Islam continued to be the religion of the Egyptians under the Ottoman rule since it was the religion of the new ruler also; the religious culture,

---

3. The Mamelukes were originally slaves brought to Egypt by the Fatimite caliphs in the tenth century. Many of them were later freed, and they rose to positions of great power. Their rule was part of the history of the Arab empire.

therefore, did not change. As for language differences, although the Ottoman ruler spoke Turkish, no attempt was made to replace Arabic among
the Egyptians. The new ruler was content to claim authority over Egypt
without attempting to Turkify the country.[4]

The Ottomans ruled Egypt as a province through a governor. Called *vali*
by the Ottomans and *pasha* by the Egyptians, the governor was the sultan's
representative in the province. His administrative, military, and financial
authority was limited only by that of the sultan and by his own willingness
to use his powers.

To help him in the performance of his duties, the governor was assisted
by the Imperial Council of Cairo, which had advisory functions only and
was convoked and dismissed at the pleasure of the governor. Administratively, twelve provincial officials were appointed to carry out his decrees
within twelve units known as Sanjaks. Until 1798, however, the Sanjak
administrators were Mamelukes, the former masters of Egypt. As long as
the Mamelukes remained loyal and exploited the nation's wealth for the
Turkish rulers, the Turks were content. They were not interested in introducing political change or reform into Egypt.

The administrative structure of Egypt under the Ottomans established a
system of social stratification which was to influence the country's later
social developments and attitudes. There were two distinct classes then in
existence: the ruling class of Ottomans who were called "Egyptians," and
the vast majority of subjects who were known as the *rayas*. The duty of the
first class was "to defend and exploit the wealth of the Sultan"; the function of the second class was "to produce by trade, industry and agriculture
for the benefit of the Sultan and his ruling class."[5] Although Egypt before
the Ottoman period did have privileged classes with political influence, the
new master went much further in pairing social class with political privilege, and in institutionalizing such arrangements. Until the military coup of
1952, Egypt suffered immensely from the rigidity of this social system.

It was characteristic of Ottoman rule that economic and political exploitation were encouraged with little regard for the public interest. The exploitation was carried out under a system of taxation in which tax collec-
tors at every level derived their incomes from what they collected over and
above those due their superiors. Consequently, exploitation came to characterize the attitudes of many Egyptian officials toward their own country-
men, a social and economic problem that, once imbedded, was hard to
eliminate. Under the Ottoman system, the governor was required to pay the
central treasury in Istanbul a fixed annual amount of money taken from the
surplus in the Egyptian treasury of revenues over expenditures. To be able

---

4. Stevens, *Egypt*, p. 50.
5. Stanford J. Show, trans., *Ottoman Egypt in the Age of the French Revolution*
(Cambridge: Harvard University Press, 1964), p. 3.

to do this and still have enough for his own expenses as governor, he relied on a tax-farm system, according to which a tax was imposed over each source, or combination of sources, of wealth. This tax was called farm tax, and the collector of the tax was known as the tax farmer. The Treasury would make sure that the tax farmer had collected his taxes and delivered them. The tax farmer was allowed to keep a portion of the taxes he had collected, since the government did not pay him a salary. Thus, the income of the governor and the income of the tax official depended on profits made from the collection of taxes.[6]

Because Egypt was neglected by her Turkish masters, economic and cultural decadence set in. Thus by the end of the eighteenth century, the city of Alexandria, which was once a great commercial and cultural center, declined in importance and her population decreased tremendously.[7] The country itself was experiencing similar effects of Turkish rule. More important, however, was the fact that the people of Egypt were denied the opportunity to participate in the government of their country. At the end of the eighteenth century, therefore, Egypt was in desperate need of change.

THE FRENCH OCCUPATION 1798-1801

In July 1798, the French under Napoleon occupied Egypt. Their main purpose was to revive their Eastern trade by the disruption of British trade and ultimately by overthrowing British rule in India. To achieve this purpose, the French considered the colonization of Egypt to be essential.

If the occupation of Egypt by the French had lasted longer, Egypt might have acquired a partial modification of her cultural identity. The French occupation, however, lasted for only three years, during which time the French were involved in a vicious struggle for power with the Ottomans and their ally, the British. It ended with the reassertion of Ottoman rule.

Nevertheless, the period of French occupation was of great significance for Egypt. Minor aspects of her culture were changed, and certain reforms were introduced by the French. French, for example, became a fashionable language for the Egyptian middle class. A strong attraction to French culture was felt among the Egyptians of that time as well as by the Egyptians of today. Furthermore, the French were able to stimulate European scholarly interest in Egyptian archeology and history. Napoleon Bonaparte (1769–1821) had brought with him in 1798 a group of French scholars who were instructed by him to study Egypt and reveal its past accomplishments. Some of these scholars stayed in Egypt and continued their studies

6. Show, *Ottoman Egypt*, p. 6.
7. John Marlowe, *Anglo-Egyptian Relations 1800–1953* (London: The Cresset Press, 1954), p. 7.

after the withdrawal of French troops in 1801. Today, the results of their effort are among the important sources of our knowledge about Egypt.

Of far more significance to Egypt, however, was the fact that the country became an area of interest for European diplomacy and power politics as Europe became more aware of Egypt's strategic position as a bridge linking the European continent with India and the Far East. This political interest was ultimately to make Westernization—associated with progress and industrialization—a cultural factor in Egypt. Thus, although politically the whole history of the relationship between the two areas was to be viewed by future Egyptians as imperialistic and colonial, Egypt benefited by French success in exposing her to further influences by the European powers. This exposure can be viewed as the major French contribution to early Egyptian-European relations.

Insofar as the internal social structure of Egypt was concerned, several important changes took place during the three years of French occupation. The old ruling class was replaced by Muslims. The Coptic population was given special status and became an important participant in the political process. The Egyptian *ulema* (religious leaders) gained additional powers such as becoming the most represented group in local councils. The Mamelukes, whom we have mentioned in connection with the provincial administration of Egypt, lost their power: their wealth was confiscated and their influence was destroyed. Furthermore, the tax system was modified, although this came toward the end of the French occupation. The system was centralized, and a single land tax was introduced replacing the old tax-farm system, which had been decentralized.

Finally, Egyptians were given important positions in the government. This came about, perhaps, because after the French were cut off from France by British naval operations in the Mediterranean, they did not have a sufficient number of trained personnel to staff their occupation government. It may also be that the French policy of respect for the customs of Egypt—a policy formulated by Napoleon himself—had an influence. In any case, the Egyptian people had a greater share in the government of their country under the French than under the Ottomans.

THE RULE OF MOHAMMED ALI 1805-1849: A PERIOD OF SEMI-INDEPENDENCE

Even a brief historical account of Egypt cannot be complete without mentioning the rule of Mohammed Ali. Historians agree that he was the founder of modern Egypt, although the Turks retained legal sovereignty over the country throughout the nineteenth century and until the outbreak of World War I, when Egypt became a British protectorate.

An Albanian soldier in the Ottoman army, Ali rose to power in 1805 after his participation in the Turkish military effort to force the French out of Egypt. In that year, the Ottoman sultan appointed him governor of Egypt, with the title of pasha, in recognition of his capacity for strong leadership and the support he received from the religious leaders of Egypt.

The new governor was ambitious, and in time he built Egyptian military power to the point where he could threaten the position of his overlord, the sultan. He hoped not only to make Egypt secure and independent, but to create, many historians believe, an Arab empire at the expense of the Ottomans—with Egypt as its political center. In 1820, for instance, he sent a military force to the Sudan, south of Egypt; and in 1883, in an actual confrontation with the Ottoman army, he attempted to assert his authority over Syria and Palestine. Both efforts failed, however, because of European intervention. Had it not been for the European powers, who feared Ali's expansionist policy and preferred also to deal with the weak Turkish government, the Egyptian ruler might have succeeded in realizing his dream.

The failure of Ali's foreign activity did not prevent him from pursuing a dynamic policy domestically: he launched and vigorously pursued numerous internal reforms intended to modernize Egypt and give her a European cultural appearance. In these efforts, he relied heavily upon the expert knowledge of Frenchmen. To support his future plans for building a mighty Egyptian army and for industrializing Egypt, he sent a large number of Egyptians to France to study various technical specialties, especially in military science and engineering. Naturally, his educational programs were to produce an Egyptian elite, which was destined to play later an important role in the country's political developments, especially in the growth of nationalism.

The economic organization which Ali used to enforce his economic policies was based on state monopoly. In agriculture, for instance, he expropriated all land and urged farmers to increase production for the benefit of the state. Furthermore, land revenues were directly taken by the state, and cultivable land was increased.

Although Ali's agricultural policy had difficulties, it was more successful than his industrialization efforts, which were severely handicapped by lack of technical knowhow, both foreign and Egyptian. Moreover, Ali's interest in industrialization was primarily political; he considered it necessary for building Egypt's military supremacy in the region and also for securing his own political power. Consequently, many of his industrial projects, which might have been important politically, proved to be too costly and were therefore self-defeating.

The period of Ali's rule established three major precedents that influenced the thinking of later rulers of modern Egypt. The first was the importance of the Sudan for Egypt; the second was a revitalized, though vague, notion of an Arab empire dominated by Egypt; and the third established the importance of modernization and industrialization in improving Egypt's regional and wider international stature. We shall see later how these ideas affected Egyptian affairs throughout the twentieth century.

THE SUEZ CANAL PROJECT—REASSERTION OF FOREIGN DOMINATION

The Ottoman sultan, long before the death of Mohammed Ali in 1849, had decreed that the office of governor of Egypt would be hereditary. Consequently, Ali's family ruled Egypt until the beginning of the republican regime in 1953. Events after 1849, however, succeeded in destroying the semi-independent status built up by Ali.

The building of the Suez Canal was the most decisive of these events. It was a major cause of an expanding European intervention in Egyptian affairs that culminated, in 1882, in a British occupation of the country. In considering this period in Egypt's history, therefore, it is necessary to understand the international politics surrounding the construction of the canal as well as its impact on the political status of Egypt.

The immense political and commercial value of a waterway between the Mediterranean and Red seas had long been recognized. Indeed, an indirect route had existed as far back as 2000 B.C., when a canal connected the Red Sea and the Nile River. Maintenance of the canal had been too much for the ancient governments, however, and reconstruction was considered too costly.

But the appeal of the idea persisted, and it gathered momentum during the Anglo-French trade rivalry of the nineteenth century. British trade around the Cape of Good Hope to the Far East was hurting the French seaports on the Mediterranean.[8] It was the French, then, who revived the idea of the canal and who were its most strenuous advocates, and it was a Frenchman who ultimately directed the construction of the hundred-mile waterway between Port Said and Port Tawfik, near Suez—perhaps one of the greatest engineering enterprises ever devised by man.

Frenchmen made many attempts to secure from Turkish and Egyptian authorities concessions for the construction of the canal, but none was successful during the first half of the nineteenth century. Mohammed Ali believed, and events proved him correct, that the canal project could not benefit Egypt politically and that Egypt would become susceptible to foreign political influence as well as outright domination by the European powers.

8. Hugh J. Schonfield, *The Suez Canal in World Affairs* (New York: Philosophical Library, 1953), p. 6.

Ali's successor, Abbas I (1849–54), also resisted similar attempts. Additional obstacles were raised by the British, who were naturally fearful that a French canal in Egypt would result in political advantages for France and the decrease of British influence in the area. They used their influence over the Ottoman sultan to prevent the realization of the project. In addition to the British policy and the resistance of Egyptian governors, there was another important obstacle: the widespread belief that the Red Sea and the Mediterranean were not at the same level and therefore could not be joined without flooding Egypt. The construction of the canal was thus considered an impossibility by most people.

But the succession of Said to the governorship of Egypt and the findings of an international committee, which showed the physical practicability of the canal project, disposed of two of the main obstacles. The succession of Said brought favorable political conditions in Egypt, a result of the personal friendship between the new Egyptian ruler and a Frenchman, Ferdinand de Lesseps, a friendship developed during Said's earlier years, when de Lesseps was serving as a French diplomat.

De Lesseps had devoted most of his life to realizing the idea of the canal, and it was his friendship with Said that finally achieved the concession, in 1854. The concession, however, could not be made valid without ratification by the sultan, Said's overlord. Ironically, France was not yet ready to use her influence on behalf of de Lesseps to persuade either Britain or the sultan for a more favorable policy. France and Britain were allies in the Crimean War against Russia (1854–56), and France did not wish to antagonize Britain. Mainly for this reason, the project was postponed for nearly another decade.

The year 1864, however, was a fortunate one for de Lesseps. Britain had a Liberal government that showed little interest in the whole Suez affair, and it was possible for the Ottoman sultan to ratify the concession which Said granted to de Lesseps. Thus, the Suez Canal project became legally possible and construction could begin.

The financial arrangements had already been worked out by de Lesseps.[9] (Indeed, shares had been sold six years before the concession was ratified.) The Egyptian government was entitled to 15 per cent of the net profit: the promoters were to receive 10 per cent; and the shareholders the remaining 75 per cent. When, in 1858, the shares of the Suez Canal Company, which was chartered in France, were put up for sale, the French bought the majority of them, and the Egyptian government became the second largest owner. But within a short time Egypt's share began to diminish.

9. Marlowe, *Anglo-Egyptian Relations*, p. 65.

In 1874, Ismail (1863–79),[10] Said's successor, sold to the British part of his shares, and shortly after his deposition by the Turkish sultan in 1879, the Anglo-French comptrollers of the Egyptian treasury sold the remaining part, leaving Egypt with no shares whatsoever. Thus Egypt lost some 44 per cent of the Suez Canal Company's shareholding. Great Britain became the second largest owner of the company's shares.

When the construction of the canal was completed in 1869 the total cost of the operation was approximately £16,000,000.[11] Of this the Egyptian government paid about £11,500,000 in return for 15 per cent of the company's net profits. These figures clearly indicate that Egypt had paid by far the largest portion of the bill for the construction of the canal while being entitled to only a small part of the profit. The promoters and the shareholders, who paid a little over 25 per cent of the cost of construction, were entitled to the remaining 85 per cent of the profit.

Nevertheless, the political aftermath of the construction of the canal was more detrimental to the future of Egypt than were the unfair financial arrangements that had made possible the completion of this monumental project. Beginning in 1876, Egypt began to lose its semi-independent status, and in 1882 it was occupied by the British. But it was not until 1914 that the legal status of Egypt was changed. In the meantime, Egypt continued to be part of the Ottoman Empire, with the British in actual control of her domestic and international affairs.

THE BRITISH IN EGYPT

As mentioned earlier, Ismail borrowed too much money to finance his ambitious projects, including the building of the Suez Canal. His predecessor, Said, had also incurred heavy debts in the name of Egypt. The creditors were European businessmen who were interested in business adventures in Africa. They charged exorbitant interest rates on their loans, and when their Egyptian debtors were unable to make their payments on time, they attempted to use their governments' political influence to bring about Egyptian compliance. Finally, the Egyptian financial situation became worse in the mid-1870's, and Ismail had to accept the Anglo-French super-

10. Ismail was a very ambitious man. He attempted to obtain credits to finance his grandiose schemes, including irrigation projects, the building of schools, and the construction of the Suez Canal. Much of the money which he borrowed was wasted and his country was seriously involved in debt. Finally in 1876, he was forced to accept dual French and British management of the Egyptian treasury. In 1878, he attempted to throw off foreign control, but failed. The sultan deposed him the following year.

11. Marlowe, *Anglo-Egyptian Relations,* p. 71.

vision of the Egyptian treasury as being necessary for insuring the payment of the Egyptian debt to the European creditors.

Of course, the Suez Canal project was only one reason for the accumulation of the Egyptian debt; there were numerous other projects, such as the building of schools and palaces, that were very costly and that had not been tailored to Egypt's financial abilities. Ismail in particular was too ambitious and knew very little about public finance. He appears to have wanted to build personal power at any cost; and, like his grandfather, Mohammed Ali, he wanted to make Egypt into a strong and modern state. But he seems not to have realized that these goals required a careful assessment of the financial resources of his country. At any rate, the financial problems of Egypt were the most important cause of her coming under European control. (Again, we must remember that while Britain and France were in control of the Egyptian treasury and, more or less, of political power in Egypt, the official legal status of the country did not change. It continued to be part of the Ottoman Empire.)

The Capitulations. Perhaps the most controversial aspect of European hegemony in Egypt was the distortion there of the Ottoman institution for dealing with foreigners—the capitulations—to the point where it became the basis of European economic power in Egypt and an important instrument of European political control.

Originally, as mentioned in Chapter One, the capitulations were extraterritorial privileges given to European nationals residing in the Ottoman Empire on the basis of treaties concluded between the sultan and the nationals' countries of origin. The first treaty of this kind came into existence in 1535. The general object of the capitulations was to allow European Christians of the empire to live under the laws of their former countries, independent, to some extent, of Muslim legal control. In Egypt, however, the capitulations went much further. For the first time they were buttressed by foreign pressure and foreign intervention, and they were actively employed to promote the interests of foreign governments. The status of European minorities was no longer determined by the terms of the capitulation treaties themselves, but rather by the amount of pressure put on the Egyptian government by a foreign power in favor of its own nationals or other Europeans. Consequently, their status became political in nature, dependent on the continuing involvement of their home governments in Egyptian affairs—and not on negotiated agreements that, once made, required no further involvement by foreign governments.

Until the 1870's there had been no serious problems associated with the capitulations, perhaps because the European minorities were not interested in the possession of land and because their contacts with the native people were very few. Also, they were rarely involved in civil judicial proceedings.

But by the end of the nineteenth century, the number of Europeans in Egypt increased, and they became interested in owning land. As a result, their status became more complicated, especially with regard to the payments of certain taxes which were not mentioned in the capitulation agreements.

In 1873 a solution was worked out between a number of European countries and the Egyptian government, accepted by Egypt perhaps because its position vis-à-vis the European powers was weaker. By this solution, a system of Mixed Courts was established to adjudicate civil cases between Egyptians and foreigners and between foreigners of different nationalities. The law applied by the Mixed Courts was to be based on the French civil code, and the panels of judges on these courts were to have foreign majorities.

The most humiliating aspect of the new arrangement to Egypt was a provision giving the Mixed Courts power over civil controversies between foreigners and the Egyptian state. Even the Egyptian royal family was subject to their jurisdiction, a contradiction of prevailing European judicial theories, where the state was given sovereign rights and could not be sued against its will. In time, therefore, the Mixed Courts became a thorny problem in Egyptian-European relations. Egyptian nationalists, for instance, took issue with the system of Mixed Courts during the last part of the nineteenth century and also during the twentieth century. They complained that, in addition to limiting the powers of the Egyptian state and giving the Europeans legal superiority over Egyptians, the Mixed Courts gave the foreigners numerous economic advantages that enabled them to exploit the country for their own selfish interests.

The British Occupation. Many Egyptians believed that the capitulation and all other aspects of European exploitation would disappear soon after the end of the Anglo-French control of Egypt. As time went on, however, it became clear that the presence in Egypt of the Anglo-French administrators would continue. After Ismail was deposed in 1879 by the two European powers and replaced by his son Tewfik (1879–92) the political situation of the country continued to deteriorate. Nationalist sentiments ran high, and army officers conspired against foreign influence. The 1881 Arabi rebellion succeeded in putting nationalist officers in positions of power. Its leader, Colonel Ahmed Arabi, became minister of war in a government that looked with favor upon the cause of the nationalists. Naturally, the rebellion threatened the continuation of the Anglo-French dominance in Egypt thereby giving these two countries a pretext for direct military intervention. There were possibilities of reconciliation between the aims of the rebellion and the financial interests of France and Britain, but France had already decided in favor of military intervention. The British, at the beginning, were not receptive to the French idea of intervention, but later they changed their minds. Ironically, when intervention did finally take place in the summer of 1882, a change of government in Paris prevented French participation.

The period of British occupation of Egypt thus began in 1882. At the time, Britain believed that her occupation would last only until a program of financial reform could bring Egypt out of debt. Consequently, she left the existing governmental institutions almost unchanged. The Egyptian khedive (the title held by Egyptian governors since 1867) continued to issue his customary decrees and preside over an Egyptian ministry; but the British held real power and controlled the actual formulation of policy. The Organic Law of May 1, 1883 was established to give legal authority to Egyptian political forms and a democratic appearance to the political institutions. For example, an elected General Assembly was formed, having advisory functions and limited financial responsibilities.

Since the British had no intention of remaining indefinitely, the economic reforms they undertook were temporary. They were not motivated to attempt rehabilitation of the entire economy on the basis of long-range economic planning but preferred limited reforms that could produce sufficient surplus in state revenues to pay the Egyptian debt and balance the budget. These policies emphasized agriculture at the expense of industry, whose successful development, Britain feared, would hurt its own export industries. Britain also needed food products to feed its population and cotton for its textile industry, and consequently Egyptian agricultural products were compatible with the British economy.

Perhaps the greatest British project that had the distinction of being of long-term benefit to Egypt was the Aswan Dam. Completed around the turn of this century, this dam considerably increased the area of cultivable land. After World War II, the dam became the basis of a much larger project, known by the same name, which would become the hope of millions of Egyptians who believed it would solve many of the country's economic problems.

Although agricultural improvements were able to increase the revenues of the state, they failed, because of population increases, to raise the standard of living of the Egyptian *fellahin* (peasants). Nevertheless, the peasant's social and political existence improved under British rule, and many of the severe restrictions of previous regimes were lifted. In other words, the peasant remained poor but was treated with more dignity and consideration.

When it became clear by the end of the 1880's that the British economic policies in Egypt were relatively successful and that state finances were improved to the point where it was possible to pay the larger portion of the

Egyptian debt, the question of moral justification of British presence in Egypt arose. Since the Egyptian treasury was in good shape and was able to handle the financial responsibilities of the country, why should the British stay on? This question troubled not only the Egyptians but also the British.

In the late 1880's, political developments in the Sudan provided the British with a temporary argument in favor of continued occupation. Later they could say that they must remain in Egypt to quell a Sudanese revolution that broke out in 1881 and was, according to the British, a serious threat to the security of the Suez Canal and, therefore, to British trade interests in the East. A second argument arose from pre-World War I political conditions. Britain pointed to the strategic importance of Egypt to her military operations in the Middle East and to the necessity of controlling Egypt for that reason.

British Involvement in the Sudan. The British became interested in the Sudan as a result of rebellions against Egyptian control in the 1880's, which threatened the Suez Canal and the British role in Egypt. Egyptian interest begins with Mohammed Ali who, in 1820, sent an Egyptian expedition to establish authority in that country. Originally, Ali was interested in the possibility of finding new recruits for his armies. But he was also interested in dominating the Sudan trade, which included such important export items as gold, ivory, and slaves. In 1842, the Ottoman sultan officially recognized the fact that the Sudan had become part of Ali's domain.

After Ali's death Egyptian interest in the Sudan diminished for a time; but beginning in 1865, Ismail became interested in controlling the sources of the Nile to guarantee the continuous flow of water to Egypt. To strengthen as well as perpetuate his control over the Sudan, Ismail attempted to get the British to share his interest in that country by announcing his intention to put an end to the slave trade there, something about which Britain had shown concern. He also appointed, in 1869, a British citizen to the governorship of Equatoria, a Sudanese province under Egyptian control. The British, however, were not interested in the Sudan, and this was their position when they occupied Egypt in 1882.

In 1881, however, a rebellion in the Sudan led by the Mahdi (the guide), a Muslim Sudanese, broke out against the Egyptian rulers, and the revolt ultimately caused the British to question their neutral policy in the Sudan. The rebellion continued for several years, becoming more violent and intense after the death of the Mahdi in 1885 and the assumption of its leadership by a more determined fanatic known as the Khalifa (the successor). Finally, when the Khalifa made known his intentions to invade Egypt, the rebellion threatened Britain's interests in that country and in the Suez Canal.

A second factor affecting British neutrality in the Sudan was the fierce struggle at this time among many European countries, mainly France, England, and Italy, for control of Africa. At one point there was a danger of a military showdown between Britain and France over spheres of influence in the area. Finally, late in 1896, the British government decided to occupy the Sudan and suppress the rebellion. An expedition largely composed of Egyptians was sent to the Sudan under Sir Herbert Kitchener. After a series of battles with the rebels, culminating in the famous Battle of Omdurman (September 1898), Kitchener was able to destroy and disperse the rebel forces almost completely. The Khalifa was killed in a minor battle shortly after Omdurman, and the Sudan was finally brought under a new foreign rule.

What type of governmental arrangements in the Sudan would be acceptable to the British? To leave Egypt in sole control of the Sudan would be illogical since the British were in control of Egypt itself, and also, the Egyptian administration which existed in the Sudan before the Mahdi rebellion was unpopular and had the reputation of being irresponsible and exploitative. The new arrangement Britain worked out was unusual in terms of colonial administrative theory but was, nevertheless, a logical compromise between Egypt's legal rights in the Sudan and Britain's new interests in that country. The condominium, as this arrangement was called, established a dual control or a joint rule by Britain and Egypt. However, in view of the fact that Egypt was already under British control, the condominium was in practice nothing more than British rule over the Sudan.

The Sudan Convention of 1899 was the legal instrument upon which the condominium was based.[12] Ratified by both Egypt and Britain on January 19, 1899, the convention basically required: (1) That the flags of the two countries be raised over public buildings in the Sudan; (2) that a governor-general, appointed by the khedive (Egypt's ruler) upon the recommendation of the British government, should possess all military and civil powers in the Sudan; (3) that no import duties could be levied on goods entering the Sudan from Egypt; (4) that Europeans could have no special privileges in the Sudan; and (5) that the slave trade be abolished once and for all.

World War I. Political developments within the Sudan—which was only important in relation to the security of the Suez Canal—were only one reason why Britain did not leave Egypt sooner. The second reason was World War I.

When Turkey entered the war on the side of Germany, thereby becoming Britain's enemy, a crucial issue developed concerning the legal status of

12. The text is in Jacob C. Hurewitz, ed., *Diplomacy in the Near and Middle East, A Documentary Record: 1835–1914* (Princeton: Van Nostrand, 1956), vol. I, Doc. 99, p. 210.

Egypt, which was still part of the Ottoman (Turkish) Empire. The British, although militarily occupying and politically controlling Egypt, recognized this legal status. But now, since Britain could no longer recognize Turkey's suzerainty in Egypt, it had only two alternatives: it could either grant Egypt independence or bring it into the British Empire.

The first alternative would have been impractical in view of the military necessities, which included, once more, the defense of the canal and also the need for a military base from which Britain could launch an offensive against Turkish forces in the Fertile Crescent. The second alternative, therefore, was the only practical solution, and it was this alternative which was adopted by the British policy-makers. Thus, British control of Egypt was to continue indefinitely. The new legal status conferred on Egypt was that of a British protectorate.

What is a protectorate? Usually one country becomes a protectorate of another country upon the request of the first and acceptance by the second. No such procedure preceded the new Egyptian status; Egypt became a British protectorate by the unilateral act of Great Britain.

The new Egyptian status did not fundamentally change the political realities of the earlier relationship between the two countries, except, of course, of the new conditions imposed upon Egypt by the facts of World War I. Among these was the declaration of martial law in December 1914 and the consequent enlargements in the responsibilities of the British military to include many of the functions of the civilian administrations. The Egyptian population, of course, suffered numerous hardships, but most of these were the product of the exigencies of war.

FOREIGN RULE: IMPLICATIONS

An understanding of the impact of foreign rule upon Egyptian life is essential to an understanding of the forces underlying some of the more recent events in Egypt, such as the military takeover in 1952 and the Suez Canal crisis of 1956.

Foreign rule, directly or indirectly, has had an impact on both social and political aspects of Egyptian life. The two are closely related, since social attitudes are often the result of a persistent political situation, and political problems are often produced by social attitudes. The history of Egypt shows clearly the relationship of the two.

THE SOCIAL IMPACT OF FOREIGN RULE

The long period of foreign control of Egypt resulted in the creation of a negative Egyptian attitude toward authority. Egyptians, as we have seen, had little opportunity to rule themselves: the British, known for their democratic ideals at home, failed to give them adequate experience in self-government, although part of their failure was due to the fact that they believed their stay in Egypt would be temporary. Consequently, the state—the most encompassing institution in any society—became alien to most Egyptians. This attitude toward the state and government lies behind nearly all Egyptian political problems.

The Egyptian mistrusted not only the foreign ruler but also his own upper class. Egyptian aristocracy was, until the introduction of socialism by the Nasser regime, one of the oldest aristocracies in the world. The majority of Egyptians believed that the foreign rulers were responsible for the entrenchment of the Egyptian aristocracy in its privileged position. Although there is no proof that this is true, there is ample evidence to support a slightly different assertion—that the foreign rulers did very little to balance the relative positions of the Egyptian upper class and the populace.

The negativism of the Egyptian turned to bitter frustration when, after the end of the British rule, the country gradually developed an oligarchic form of government in which the Egyptian aristocracy was the dominant force. The masses of Egyptian poor continued to be exploited by the privileged classes. This situation reinforced the Egyptian's belief that his own aristocracy was just as bad as the foreign ruler.

In the Egyptian's mind the monarch was still directly associated with the evils of foreign rule. Of course, the founder of the last ruling dynasty, Mohammed Ali, was himself foreign. But many Egyptians would have been willing to forget this fact and to consider Ali's descendants to be Egyptians had it not been for the failure of these descendants to govern Egypt responsibly. The monarchy, like the aristocracy, showed little interest in the welfare of the people.

Lack of confidence in the state influenced the people's sense of civic responsibility. They saw the governmental apparatus as no more than a place of work for thousands of Egyptians, who received low salaries and produced very little. Government was not an institutional structure created to serve the citizens; it was primarily an agency of exploitation.

Yet the Egyptian was fully aware of the importance of the state in an environment where no more than 3.5 per cent of the land was cultivable. He knew that the task of providing additional arable land for an increasing population was so formidable that only the state was capable of it. This conflict between distrust of the state and dependence on it was reflected in a vacillation between blind submission to the few relatively stable governments and apathy and despair under the irresponsible and inefficient governments.

Foreign rule had a direct responsibility for Egypt's failure to develop an indigenous middle class, a lack that continued after independence. The system of capitulations had led to an almost complete foreign monopoly over Egyptian commerce and to a similar, although lesser, foreign influence in industrial activity. Commerce and industry, the backbone of a politically active urban middle class, were in effect prohibited activities for Egyptians.

The absence of an Egyptian middle class had important political effects, perhaps the most important of which was Egypt's failure to develop genuine democratic institutions. Here, of course, we are subscribing to the belief that middle classes are essential to the development of democratic political systems. But even if this theory is exaggerated, one can easily see how the absence of a middle class could cause social and political unrest in any country. In Egypt, as perhaps elsewhere, social unrest due to the absence of a genuine middle class had been an aspect of city life, not of rural agricultural life. The Egyptian peasant was, and still is, politically less active than the city inhabitant. He was tied to the land, too poor, and very much under the control of the big landowner.

THE POLITICAL IMPACT OF FOREIGN RULE: NATIONALISM

In political terms, nationalism was Egypt's most significant reaction to foreign, particularly European, rule. It did not, however, become an influential political force until the beginning of the twentieth century. Prior to that, the intellectual class was the main, perhaps the only, politically active class supporting the forces of Egyptian nationalism. It was not until a few years before independence (1922) that nationalism received the support of the Egyptian masses.

The Intellectual Background. During the latter part of the nineteenth century, the nationalist movement was preoccupied primarily with the formulation of political ideas and with discussions of intellectual questions. In its intellectual or philosophical aspects, Egyptian nationalism emerged from a larger religious movement whose aim was the rejuvenation of Islam. In time, however, nationalism became independent of religion and took on a more secular form, although in Egypt politics remained one of the areas of activity of religion.

This larger religious movement was particularly concerned with how Islam could be modified and interpreted to make it suitable for modern life. At the heart of this question, however, was the political destiny of Egypt, for the revival of Islam was considered essential for the political awakening of Egypt, and the two objectives were intimately related in the minds of Egyptian intellectuals. This assumed relationship gave the Egyptian national movement its strong religious character.

The problem of Islamic revival gave rise to three schools of thought during the last quarter of the nineteenth century.[13] The first of these believed that Islam as a religious doctrine was unchangeable because it was God's revelation and should be the same regardless of the time element involved. This conservative-traditionalist approach held that there was nothing wrong with Islam itself and that it was the Muslim people who had gone astray and who needed to return to the commandments of their religion. The future of Egypt, therefore, required the Egyptian people to live up to the standards, moral and otherwise, of their religion; only in this way could Egypt hope to become a strong and progressive country.

The second school of thought espoused an essentially secularist position influenced by European example. It held that Islam had become obsolete and was not responsive to the needs of modern society. It was, therefore, an obstacle to progress, in Egypt and elsewhere, and should be confined to the regulation of personal relationships so that it would act only indirectly for the good of society; public and political matters should be outside the jurisdiction of religion.

The third school of thought was really a synthesis of the first two. It rejected both the theory that Islamic doctrine was unchangeable and the theory that Islam had become outmoded and was no longer suitable for modern society; it held that the religion could be reinterpreted to suit the needs of modern societies. What was needed was a reinterpretation that would make it a progressive, instead of a conservative and obstructive, philosophy. The appeal of the moderate approach was that it neither discarded the significance of religion as a sociopolitical force nor denied the possibility of progress under the Islamic banner.

It was this last school of thought which had the greatest impact upon later Egyptian nationalism. Owing to the efforts of its leader and champion, Mohammed Abdu, it became the intellectual-theoretical foundation of the nationalist movement of the nineteenth century. This foundation was to become the springboard of twentieth-century nationalism from which all efforts for the achievement of Egyptian independence were made.

Mohammed Abdu. Mohammed Abdu, of Egyptian peasant stock, was an articulate intellectual and a graduate of the famous Muslim university of al-Azhar. Early in his life he was influenced by the teaching of the revolutionary Persian scholar Afghani, who advocated the modernization of Islam and the unification of the Muslim countries. Abdu, however, formulated his own theories and pursued a more moderate political approach, especially with regard to the problems of Egypt. Thus, although intellectually he was a revolutionary, politically he was a gradualist who believed

13. See Jamal Mohammed Ahmed, *The Intellectual Origins of Egyptian Nationalism* (London: Oxford University Press, 1960), p. 41.

in the importance of social and economic reforms as necessary steps toward the achievement of political goals.

Many of the great political figures of Egypt had their first serious intellectual training under Abdu. Some of them were close associates; a few were his disciples. But the main contribution of Abdu was the creation of that intellectual environment which preceded the beginning of twentieth-century nationalism and which intensified the political curiosities of many Egyptian leaders.

Mustafa Kamil. Among those affected by this intellectual environment was Mustafa Kamil (1874–1908), whose political activity had a great impact upon Egyptian nationalism. Kamil received his education in France, where he acquired an enthusiasm for almost everything French and a dislike for almost anything British. Upon his return to Egypt, he became active in the national movement, contributing to it what he had learned in France about the art of propaganda.[14]

In 1907, Kamil gave Egypt its first political party with a serious national platform. Earlier political parties had not had genuine programs designed for nationwide consumption. Named the National party, after its predecessor of 1879, Kamil's party was organized nationally through a central committee and locally through branch offices. It was the first Egyptian party to attempt to reach the grassroots of Egyptian political life. Its program consisted of four elements: the establishment of parliamentary government; a declaration of independence for Egypt and the Sudan; the introduction of educational reforms; and the modification of the capitulations.

Kamil attempted to unite Egyptians of all classes and religious backgrounds in a strong national movement. Conscious of the major obstacles confronting Egyptian nationalism—mainly disunity among the educated and ignorance among the masses—he spent much of his time talking to students and making plans for the establishment of schools and universities. After his death in 1908 his party continued to play an important role in Egyptian policies, although it had to share the political arena with other parties and even accept an inferior position to some of them.

The Party Movements. In 1907, the year that the National party was organized, two other parties appeared on the political scene; all three were instruments in the nationalist movement during the period before the outbreak of World War I.[15]

The People's party (the Umma party) was composed of a group of prominent men who believed that the independence of Egypt could be achieved by a gradual process involving cooperation with the British and

14. Christina Phelps Harris, *Nationalism and Revolution in Egypt: The Role of the Muslim Brotherhood* (London: Mouton & Co., 1964), pp. 68–70.

15. Ahmed, *The Intellectual Origins*, pp. 76–82.

the introduction of social reform. Kamil disagreed with this gradualism and believed that Britain should evacuate Egypt immediately. Many anxious nationalists were suspicious of the Umma party's policy of cooperation with the British, for they had given up hope that Britain would ever honor its repeated promises to leave the country. Nevertheless, the People's party considered itself the best proof that Egyptians had become politically mature and pragmatic.

The third important party was the Constitutional Reform party organized by Aly Yusuf, a dynamic journalist. This group supported Kamil's demand for evacuation but favored persuasion over revolution to achieve that goal. The Constitutional Reform party was conservative in the sense that it support khedivial authority. Its program, however, envisaged a representative democracy for Egypt thereby giving rise to suspicions among other conservatives that the traditional authority of the khedive might be lessened in the process of installing democratic institutions. The resulting misunderstanding, coupled with doubt about the real aims of Yusuf with respect to power, contributed to the downfall of the party and its leader.

Because the other parties were moderate and gradualist, only Kamil's party seemed to embody the ideals of the more articulate nationalists. Kamil was the most popular national leader in Egypt, and when he died in 1908 he was mourned by the whole nation; even his political enemies recognized his immense popularity and stature.

Ahmad Lutfi. There was, however, one other Egyptian who deserves mention, for he had a unique outlook and a unique personality. Ahmad Lutfi al-Sayyid (henceforth Lutfi) differed from all other Egyptian leaders in that he made social reform the central theme of his efforts. He was interested in the reconstruction of the Egyptian personality which he believed lacked the essential elements of modernity. He understood the Egyptian national character in a very profound way, although his criticism of his people was sometimes harsh and bitter.[16]

Lutfi believed that the general level of Egyptian morality was low and that a kind of cowardice had crept into the Egyptian personality. He maintained that unless the standards of public morality and the intellectual level of Egyptians were raised Egypt could not hope to become strong and be able to solve its problems.

Foreign rule, he believed, had destroyed Egypt's chances of developing a democracy and had given the Egyptian a feeling of inferiority from which he could not be easily freed. Consequently, much of Egyptian life was characterized by a kind of hypocrisy which compelled people to submit to the rule of autocrat and foreigner alike.

Lutfi knew that it would take a long time before the Egyptian character

16. Ahmed, *The Intellectual Origins,* pp. 85–112.

and personality could be modified. This is why his intellectual activity and his interest in social reform overshadowed his interest in politics. Lutfi did not develop systematic theories about social reform or politics, but his contribution had profound impact upon Egyptian life and thinking. He was inspired and to a great degree guided by the theories of such thinkers as Aristotle, Locke, Rousseau, Voltaire, and John Stuart Mill. His study of these men's ideas convinced him that there was a strong need to develop an Egyptian philosophy based on the history and culture of Egypt. No nation, he insisted, could be strong without having a philosophy of its own, and this was exactly what Egypt lacked and what Europe had.

CHAPTER 6

EGYPT UNDER
THE MONARCHY

WORLD War I gave the Egyptian national movement additional impetus and a new orientation. For the first time the masses of the Egyptian people were willing to identify themselves with it. They had become aware of the real political status of Egypt as a British protectorate, a status they considered to be a mark of inferiority.

What caused this increased political awareness among the Egyptian masses? One cause, of course, was the common experience of the war, which brought home to all Egyptians that their domination by Britain meant that the British could use them to promote their own interests. Because of her dependent status, for instance, Egypt could not remain a neutral in the war and was compelled to fight the Turks with whom it shared the Islamic religion. In addition, the war brought martial law, which was difficult for most Egyptians, especially because the military administration was too rigid in handling civilian problems and too demanding for a people who had, in terms of material rewards, very little to spare.

In addition to increasing mass support for the nationalist movement, the war years also brought about a social revolution in Egypt.[1] An abrupt and unplanned redistribution of wealth had occurred as a result of industries that had been established to fill the need created by the disruption of trade during the war. A small class of newly rich industrialists emerged, and at the same time a growing class of industrial workers also appeared. These new social groups did not destroy the old social structure based on an agricultural economy, but they did increase the elements of tension in city life. This tension became an important aspect of political life in Egypt immediately after the war.

1. Jean and Simonne Lacouture, *Egypt in Transition* (New York: Criterion Books, 1958), p. 83.

124

THE REVOLUTION AGAINST BRITAIN

The restlessness caused by wartime changes was ultimately to provide the fuel for a revolt against Britain. The immediate causes, however, were two policy statements that seemed to promise much to Egypt. The first was a declaration by Britain and France issued on November 7, 1918, which promised that the peoples of the Ottoman provinces liberated by the war would have their choice of government.[2] The Egyptian nationalists thought that, since their country had until the outbreak of the war been technically part of the Ottoman Empire, the benefit from the joint declaration would accrue to Egypt in the same manner as it would to the other Ottoman provinces. The second statement was the enunciation of the principle of self-determination by President Wilson in his famous Fourteen Points declaration of January 1918. Although they were later ignored by Britain and France, these two declarations paved the way for nationalist demands for independence.

The Nationalist Leadership. Such demands were voiced by the various nationalist leaders of whom Saad Zaghlul became the most popular and the best known. Indeed, until the 1952 coup, Egyptians considered Zaghlul the savior of Egypt and believed him to be the one to win their country her independence. Zaghlul (1860–1927) was of peasant stock, like his great predecessors Arabi and Abdu. Early in his youth he fought with Arabi in the famous Battle of Tel-el-Kebir (September 13, 1882), in which the Egyptian army was defeated by the British. He was also a disciple of Abdu and an associate of this great Egyptian: from him he learned the art of writing and to him he owed his early political moderation. Zaghlul received his education at the Islamic University of al-Azhar and later studied law. His career in the courts was outstanding but was interrupted by his acceptance of several high-level positions in the government and also by his interest in the politics of his country. Lord Evelyn Cromer, the British agent and consul-general in Egypt from 1883 to 1907, thought highly of Zaghlul's qualifications and personal integrity. Consequently, he appointed him minister of education in 1906, at a time when students were becoming politically active and restless; and in 1910, after Cromer's departure from Egypt, the British continued to rely on him as minister of justice.

Zaghlul became disenchanted with the British when Egypt became a protectorate in 1914, but he did not become anti-British until he learned of Britain's intention to continue the protectorate status of Egypt after the

2. Text in George Antonius, *The Arab Awakening: The Story of the Arab National Movement* (New York: Lippincott, 1939), Appendix E, pp. 433–34.

war. Prior to that time, he cooperated with them and was able to serve in their administration with cautious loyalty.

When World War I was ended by the signing of the armistice in November 1918, Zaghlul, at the head of a nationalist delegation, requested the British high commissioner in Egypt, Sir Reginald Wingate, to be allowed to leave for London in order to present the Egyptian case concerning his country's future status. His request was turned down by the British government in London, and a crisis ensued. The incident provoked Egyptian nationalism into militancy, and the Egyptian delegation which was organized for the purpose of negotiating with Britain became the spokesmen of the national movement for independence. The delegation was known in Egypt by the Arabic word *al-Wafd* (the delegation), which became the name of the political party organized by Zaghlul in 1924. Between 1918 and 1924, however, the Wafd was something like a national committee whose purpose was to secure independence for Egypt.

THE LAUNCHING OF THE REVOLUTION

Zaghlul's agitation for independence caused his deportation to the Mediterranean island of Malta early in 1919, along with his close associates in the Wafd. This was the signal for the revolution. The nationalists turned to violence, and the whole Egyptian nation was ready to act against the British. For the first time in the history of the national movement, the Egyptian peasant was aroused sufficiently to participate in a national effort such as the revolution. Muslims as well as Copts (Christians), men as well as women, and Egyptians of all social classes were part of the revolution. Egypt seemed to be united and determined.

The British reacted by sending Field Marshal Lord Allenby to Egypt in 1919 to deal with the new situation. Allenby was able to pacify the nationalists temporarily by releasing Zaghlul and his colleagues so that they could present the Egyptian case at the peace conference. In Egypt and abroad, the nationalists organized an intensive propaganda campaign to support the efforts of Zaghlul. Meanwhile, however, there were signs that negotiations with the British might fail. For one thing, the delegation received the news that the United States had formally recognized the British protectorate over Egypt.

The Milner Report. Another strong indication that the British government was not yet willing to abandon its position in Egypt was that the Milner Mission, sent to Egypt under the leadership of Lord Milner to study the causes of unrest, was not empowered to propose a change in the protectorate status of Egypt as a possible solution. The mission was boycotted by the Egyptians upon its arrival in Egypt on December 7, 1919, and after it left Egypt for London in March 1920, the Egyptian delegation in Paris became convinced of the futility of its efforts to persuade the meeting of the big powers of the legitimacy of the Egyptian position. Consequently, the delegation left Paris for London with the intention of continuing the struggle there. It had agreed to confront the Milner Mission and to explore the possibilities of a solution to the Egyptian problem. Negotiations, however, produced nothing, and the crisis deepened.

Surprisingly, however, the "Milner Report," which was prepared by the mission under the most difficult circumstances, was favorable to Egypt. It pointed out that the Egyptian people had every reason to feel insecure about the future of their country in view of the fact that Britain had been uncertain about its Egyptian policy. It warned that unless Britain found a solution, Egypt would continue to be united in its opposition and resistance to British dominance. Finally, it exceeded the limits of its commission, recommending that the protectorate be ended, and proposing instead a bilateral treaty giving Britain safeguards against the disruption of imperial communication and the deterioration of the status of the foreign communities.

The Milner Report had important effects upon both the British policy-makers and the Egyptian nationalists. In Britain both public opinion and government began to move toward a new policy that would give Egypt its independence. Lord Allenby gave the principles contained in the Milner Report his wholehearted support. On the Egyptian side, however, the reaction to the report was negative. It was not easy to convince the leaders of the revolution of the immediate benefits which would result from a negotiated settlement. One difficulty arose from the fact that Zaghlul had become a national hero, very conscious of his responsibilities to the revolutionary movement and to Egyptian public opinion. Since both latter elements had moved to a radical political position, thanks to Britain's procrastination in declaring her better intentions, Zaghlul's own position had to be similarly adjusted; otherwise his leadership would have suffered a setback. There was also the development of rivalry to Zaghlul's leadership encouraged by the British themselves and supported by the nominal ruler of Egypt, Ahmed Fuad (1868–1936).[3] It is not clear, however, which came first, Zaghlul's radicalism or British opposition to his leadership.

The Granting of Independence. Zaghlul continued his agitation against the British, and violence was intensified during the last months of 1921. The extremists in the revolution were more willing than the moderate revolutionaries to indulge in excessive violence and unjust activity. Fortunately, these extremists were a small minority, and they were either denounced or

3. The British kept the khedives of Egypt in office after Egypt became a protectorate (1914). Fuad became the khedive in 1917 and acquired the title of king in 1922.

not recognized by Zaghlul and other moderates among the revolutionaries.

But Zaghlul was deported a second time in December 1921, leaving the revolution unrestrained and giving the terrorist wing of the revolutionary movement a freer hand. The high commissioner, Lord Allenby, threatened to resign unless the British government showed some appreciation of the realities of the Egyptian situation. On February 3, 1922, he left for England to explain these realities to the British cabinet and to attempt to find new solutions. When he returned to Egypt at the end of the month, he had with him just the solution he needed: the decision of the British government to give Egypt her independence.

After nearly two thousand years Egypt had become independent, and direct foreign control had come to an end. At long last, Britain had come around to a realistic position, and it did not need the Egyptian party to negotiate what it had already decided. The independence of Egypt was the outcome of a unilateral declaration made by Britain. The text of the declaration, made public on February 28, 1922, declared the end of the protectorate and the beginning of Egyptian independence.[4] However, the British government reserved full control over matters pertaining to the security of the communications of the British Empire in Egypt, the defense of Egypt against direct or indirect foreign aggression, foreign minorities, and the Sudan. Consequently, the independence of Egypt and her sovereignty were limited by these areas of British jurisdiction and control.

CONSTITUTIONAL GOVERNMENT

The declaration of independence temporarily disrupted the unity of the nationalist movement. Two men, Ismail Sudki and Mohammed Mahmoud, who with Zaghlul were prominent among the fifteen men who signed the original Wafd declaration, deserted Zaghlul and formed their own political parties. They were to play an important role in Egyptian politics before as well as after the death of Zaghlul.

The deportation of Zaghlul just two months before the declaration was issued seemed to have been part of a British strategy which aimed at the encouragement of opposition to the Wafd leadership so that it would be possible to negotiate a treaty with the government of Egypt and also to give the new constitution, which was to be drafted soon, a chance for approval and implementation. For the time being, this strategy was successful, and the moderate nationalists were able to give Egypt a constitutional document in April 1923. But the absence of Zaghlul permitted the Egyptian monarch to have a much stronger position in the new government than

4. J. C. Hurewitz, ed., *Diplomacy in the Near and Middle East, A Documentary Record: 1914–1956* (Princeton: Van Nostrand, 1956), vol. II, pp. 102–3.

would have been possible if Zaghlul had been present. The king was able to influence the drafting of the constitution in his own favor and consequently became the focal point in the new structure of power. Later on, his position became highly controversial, and the monarchy became a thorny problem for Egyptian democracy.

Under the 1923 Constitution, the king shared legislative power with a Senate and a Chamber of Deputies. He alone possessed the executive power. He could veto legislative acts, although the legislature had the power to override the royal veto by a two-thirds majority within one month following the veto decision or by an ordinary majority during the next session. Of greater significance to the king's power perhaps, was his right to dissolve the legislature, provided he did not exercise this right twice for the same reason. The king was also empowered to declare war and, with some limitations, to make peace.

In addition to all this, the Constitution authorized the monarch to appoint the ministers in his government, although these ministers are also made responsible to the legislature, thus making the cabinet's position extremely difficult in case of serious disagreements between king and Parliament. Finally, the Constitution permitted the king to appoint two-fifths of the Senate, the upper house of the legislature.

Thus, it was not a constitutional monarchy which Egypt acquired shortly after independence, but a government in which the monarch, not the prime minister, was the predominant figure. Between 1923 and 1952, Egypt was to experience the effects of a bitter struggle between autocratic monarchs and popular prime ministers. The alternative to popular governments was to be a coalition between cabinets and palace against the will of the people as expressed in the popularly elected Parliament.

The Wafd in Power. The adoption of the Constitution in 1923 did not end the nationalist struggle against the British and the palace. It was a weakness of British political strategy to assume that Egyptian affairs would improve with the creation of a constitutional instrument. The moderate nationalists were unable to rally the people behind them, and they themselves were far from united. As a result, the British had to allow Zaghlul to return to Egypt before the first national elections, which were to be held in 1924. They hoped that Zaghlul would accept the declaration and the constitution as a *fait accompli* and that he would be realistic enough to realize the necessity of negotiating a treaty with them. But the decision to release Zaghlul was not entirely an expedient one. The British sincerely wanted to negotiate with a government that represented the people, and they knew full well that without Zaghlul in the contest the elections would not be more than a farce.

When Zaghlul returned to Egypt in September 1923, he was determined to win the election if for no other reason than to prove that nothing could be done in Egypt that did not receive his approval, for he believed he was the undisputed leader of the people. The outcome of the election left no doubt that he was right. Out of 214 seats in the Chamber of Deputies, his party won 190. But the fact remained that Zaghlul did, at least indirectly, recognize the Constitution and the declaration, so that this part of British strategy was successful.

But British hopes for an immediate conclusion of a treaty proved too optimistic. Zaghlul, now the prime minister, was willing to negotiate but showed definite dislike and resentment to the four "reserved points" in the declaration of independence. He had no intention of accepting anything less than full sovereignty.

The British seemed willing enough to make further concessions. The Labour party was in power, and it was prepared to pursue a more liberal policy than previous governments so long as British interests were guaranteed. Although the British government made no formal commitments prior to negotiations, it was willing to consider the possibility of withdrawing British troops from Cairo and Alexandria and of abandoning its assumed responsibility for protecting foreign citizens in Egypt in return for a military alliance with that country.

But Britain would not yield as much as Zaghlul wished, and his demand for immediate and complete evacuation of British troops foredoomed his visit to London in September 1924.

The Assassination of Sir Lee Stack. Zaghlul had to return to Cairo with no negotiations undertaken at all. His return marked the beginning of new troubles: Egyptians began to demonstrate in protest against the British, and acts of violence were committed by mobs.

There were two issues that troubled the Egyptians and made difficult the possibility of an accord between them and the British. The first was the continued presence of British troops in the country, which was regarded by the Egyptians as a denial of the reality of independence. The second issue was the Sudan. Egyptians complained that Britain had ignored Egypt, her partner in the Sudan. More important, however, was the Egyptians' fear for their water supply, which could be threatened by the British control of the Sudan.

In the course of these developments, Sir Lee Stack, governor-general of the Sudan, was assassinated in Cairo on November 19, 1924. The assassin was not apprehended, and his identity remained unknown. However, the incident touched off a new chain of events. Lord Allenby presented Zaghlul, who was then prime minister, with a note [5] demanding the withdrawal of Egyptian troops from the Sudan. The note also warned the Egyptian

5. Hurewitz, vol. II, p. 130.

government that there would be no limitations on the quantities of water to be used for the irrigation of the Gezira in the Sudan. Previously, such limitations existed by the mutual agreement of the two governments, and they were necessary for the effective use of the Nile waters.

The regulation of the waters of the Nile was a matter of intense interest to Egypt. Control of the Sudan by another power could endanger Egypt's economic security, which relies very heavily upon the Nile, the lifeline of Egyptian agriculture.

Allenby's note to Zaghlul, which was in the form of an ultimatum, made it definite that decisions regarding the exploitation of the Nile waters would be made not by Egypt but by Britain by virtue of her presence in the Sudan; and this assertion of power served to prove the Egyptian argument regarding the dangers of non-Egyptian control of the Sudan. There was now a stronger desire in Egypt for insisting upon Egyptian rights with regard to her southern neighbor.

Lord Allenby overreacted to the assassination. The conditions he laid down in the ultimatum were not only unfair but also excessively punitive and politically unrealistic. Furthermore, the Egyptian government's responsibility for the incident was indirect and related only to its function as the agency of order and peace. Zaghlul was genuinely sorry for the turn of events after the assassination but believed the ultimatum was extremely unreasonable. He resigned as prime minister soon after the assassination.

Palace Governments. The resignation of Zaghlul's government was followed by the formation of a series of puppet governments subservient to the wishes of the king. Whenever such governments were formed, whether under King Fuad (1923–36) or under his son, Farouk (1936–52), they were the result either of the suspension of the Constitution or of manipulated elections.

The British were quite aware of this dilemma, and their position was very difficult, for they desired to deal with a government that represented the people. They did not want to identify themselves with palace government, lest they become associated with unconstitutionality and arbitrariness, but they could not deal with Zaghlul, and finding a third alternative was not easy as long as Zaghlul was the chief political power in Egypt and as long as he remained unwilling to cooperate.

When it became clear that the existing alternatives were Zaghlul or puppet governments, the British decided to encourage the development of a third force which would stand between the Wafd and the palace and be independent of both. This third force was also supposed to be independent of the British themselves. In the meantime, the palace under King Fuad was busy organizing its own "front" party, the Union party (the Ittihad), which it hoped would win elections and thereby give legitimacy to palace governments. In addition to the British "third force" and the Union party, another political group was of significance. This was a party of liberal constitutionalists, founded by Adli, a former prime minister. This group had a program of social reform, but it never had the popularity which the Wafd enjoyed over the years. It opposed the Wafd, and at the same time it was trying not to be closely identified with the palace. Although the British had nothing to do with the formation of this group, they considered the possibility of cooperating with it.

Thus, the division of power and influence was uncertain, and a deadlock was reached. At this point, Ismail Sidki, who became minister of interior in the government which took power after the resignation of Zaghlul's government, left Zaghlul to become part of the opposition to the Wafd. He was determined to rig the next elections in an effort to eliminate the Wafd party. He had appointed several of his supporters to the provincial administration of Egypt to ensure the manipulation of the electoral process. Parliament was dissolved on December 24, 1924, and the new elections were to take place in March 1925. In these elections, the Wafd obtained 102 seats while the parties opposed to Zaghlul's leadership obtained 108 seats. Thus, despite Sidki's efforts to rig the elections, the Zaghlulists were able to secure a few seats less than a majority. Moreover, it was revealed that a number of the non-Wafd legislators were actually Zaghlulists who somehow disguised their political identity during the elections. This was evident in the elections of the president of the Chamber of Deputies and the other officials of the house. The Wafdists filled all these positions, and Zaghlul himself became president.

As a result of these complications, and to prevent the formation of a Wafdist government, the king ordered the dissolution of the new Parliament on March 26, a few days after the election. But the next elections, held thirteen months later, in May 1926, returned the Wafd with a majority this time, having 144 seats out of 201. The threat of British intervention, however, forced the Wafdists to accept a coalition government, with Adli, the liberal constitutionalist leader, as prime minister. An uneasy truce between the Wafdists and the liberal constitutionalists lasted for almost a year, until April 1927.

In June 1925, Lord Allenby left his post as high commissioner and was succeeded by Lord Lloyd. Lloyd seemed to believe that cooperation with the Wafd was almost impossible and found himself, therefore, compelled to interfere in the formation of governments in Egypt. Zaghlul, on the other hand, was fully aware of the fact that an extreme form of British intervention could make the position of Egypt even worse. Therefore, he maintained his general policy regarding the negotiations of an Anglo-Egyptian treaty as well as his opposition to the palace with sufficient flexibility so that the political situation would not cause the British to resort to extreme measures. This was the general political situation when Zaghlul died in August 1927.

Mustafa Nahas. After Zaghlul's death, Mustafa Nahas became the leader of the Wafd, inheriting the political controversies between his party and the palace as well as those involving Egypt's relations with Britain. Like his predecessor, Nahas was of a peasant background, was an outstanding orator, and had a great appeal with the masses. He became prime minister in March 1928, but he proved to be as stubborn as his predecessor about the Wafd relation with the palace. Consequently, his government was short-lived.

The next government was formed by Mahmoud Pasha who, like Sidki, was among those original members of the Wafd who became disenchanted with Zaghlul's leadership and left him to join the anti-Wafd political groupings. He was a liberal constitutionalist until he began to dislike some of Adli's policies, when he became an independent. As prime minister, he earned the reputation of being an excellent administrator. His efficient administration succeeded in introducing a few reforms and in establishing the conditions for security and order. His government, however, like all governments which were not Wafdist, did not have the backing of the people. It was also difficult for him to rule because the legislature had been dissolved by royal decree one month after the resignation of the Nahas government.

By this time, it had become routine for the monarch to suppress the Constitution whenever the political situation was not to his liking or whenever he became exasperated with the democratic process. For a while Lord Lloyd shared the monarch's feelings about the Wafd, and he was willing to ignore constitutional provisions in return for anti-Wafd and pro-British governments. But during the summer of 1929 the new Labour government of Britain appointed, as Lord Lloyd's successor, Sir Percy Loraine, who was formerly British ambassador to Ankara. With this change in British personalities, the desire of the Labour government to negotiate a treaty with an Egyptian government that represented the people was once again a compelling reason for holding new elections, this time in December 1929.

But the new elections were no more than a repetition of previous ones, with the same results: a Wafdist majority followed by the formation of a Wafdist government. The electoral contest became somewhat ridiculous, not because of its authenticity, but because of the monarch's attitude toward it. Given this attitude, the elections brought nothing new, although they were slightly different in the sense that they were the first to endorse the new leadership of the Wafd. Nahas became prime minister, and a fresh attempt was made to negotiate an Anglo-Egyptian treaty.

The negotiations, too, seemed to be part of the monotony that charac-terized both Egypt's internal political developments and her relations with Britain since the adoption of the Constitution in 1923. The British offered Nahas the same concessions which had previously been made to two for-mer prime ministers. Perhaps Nahas saw no reason why he should accept the same deal from the British as the one offered to his predecessors who were not the representatives of the people. Furthermore, he had no other means of proving to his people that he was a better bargainer and that he was able to give Egypt a better choice. Nahas had hoped that Britain would accept his demand for the unlimited immigration of Egyptians into the Sudan. As this was not acceptable to the British, negotiations between the two parties broke down.

Suspension of the Constitution. Nor was the tension between the Wafd and the palace reduced after the election. As a matter of fact, the domestic situation became worse in June 1930, when Nahas decided to submit for the approval of King Fuad a legislative proposal which would penalize any minister who acted in violation of the Constitution. The proposal would enable him to pressure non-Wafdist ministers to submit to the will of the legislature (which they were constitutionally bound to obey and where the Wafd usually had a majority) rather than to the king. It was obvious that Nahas intended by this means to reduce the monarch's influence over the ministers by drawing him into another political battle, from which Nahas hoped the Wafd would emerge the victor.

There is no doubt that Nahas was justified in feeling that such measures were necessary. King Fuad's record showed that he had in the past acted arbitrarily and against the will of the majority. Nevertheless, he could only consider the legislative proposal an act of provocation, and as expected, he refused to approve the proposal. Nahas resigned, and a crisis ensued in which Nahas and the Wafd were defeated. The king asked Sidki to form a government, Parliament was dissolved, and the Constitution of 1923 was abrogated. There were riots in the streets, but the appearance of British warships in the port of Alexandria served as a warning that Britain meant business. It was then possible for the king and the new government to set the stage for a future in which the Wafd would not be able to participate. A new Constitution was promulgated by a royal decree and a new electoral law was similarly put forth. Naturally, the two instruments were designed to keep the Wafd away from the center of power and to allow the palace to enjoy virtual rule over the country.

From May 1930, when Nahas resigned, until 1936, the Wafd was out of power. Sidki was prime minister until January 1933, and his government enjoyed the longest tenure among all the governments that followed the adoption of the Constitution in 1923. To be sure, Sidki's government had a majority in Parliament but only after it had arranged to win the election, held in May 1931, under an unscrupulous 1930 electoral law.

Egypt under Sidki experienced "a period of convalescence." [6] The continuous struggle and the tiring rivalries between the Wafd, the palace, and the British meant that little attention had been given to domestic problems; and the country suffered from an economic depression during the early 1930's. It was, therefore, the task of Sidki's government, having succeeded in suppressing the Wafd, to concentrate upon the domestic conditions of the country.

Sidki was an able man who was determined to show political strength and independent judgment. He opposed the Wafd and ignored the palace. The result was a growth in his personal power, which, of course, irritated the king, who had no intention of replacing one strong man by another. Relations between Fuad and Sidki grew progressively worse until Sidki was finally obliged to resign in January 1933.

After a succession of palace governments, the Wafd began to show signs of making trouble again. Popular unrest in the form of street riots was instigated by the Wafd organization, and in 1935 the outcry was for the restoration of the 1923 Constitution. The new opposition to the palace included men who had formerly been enemies—Sidki, Mahmoud, and, of course, Nahas—but these prominent politicians were united only against palace despotism. They had little else in common. However, they succeeded in making Fuad restore the Constitution of 1923.

King Fuad died in April 1936. His only son, Farouk, was still a minor, and the situation created by Fuad's death required urgent decisions regarding the immediate future. This was accomplished by the call for new elections to be held under the original electoral law which was suspended in 1933. The elections, of course, enabled the Wafd to win, as usual, by a substantial majority. Subsequently, Nahas became prime minister, and the Wafd was back in power.

THE ANGLO-EGYPTIAN TREATY OF 1936

It was against this background of internal developments that the negotiation of an Anglo-Egyptian treaty finally was possible. Nahas and his party were in control of both the government and the palace. The Regency Council, which was to exercise the royal prerogatives on behalf of Farouk, was the creation of the Wafd government. Thus, one party in the old triangular struggle became temporarily inactive. It was now up to Nahas and the British government to resolve the problems between the two countries.

The possibility of reaching an agreement was reinforced by new interna-

6. Tom Little, *Egypt* (London: Ernest Benn Ltd., 1958), p. 148.

tional developments. Mussolini's attack on Ethiopia in East Africa, and the Italian presence in Libya, Egypt's western neighbor, changed the attitudes of Egypt and Britain toward each other. Britain was to realize more than ever before Egypt's importance to her military position in Africa and the Mediterranean. At the same time, Britain was to appreciate fully the inescapable need for maintaining friendship with the Egyptian people who, if they were belligerent toward Britain, could disrupt her security during an actual confrontation with Italy or any other power. Britain, therefore, was prepared to do everything possible to secure a mutually beneficial treaty agreement with the Egyptian government—one which would guarantee her security while giving Egypt full sovereignty.

Too, the Italian invasion of Ethiopia made Egypt realize that her own security was at stake: What would she do if Mussolini decided to invade her territory? Egypt knew well that she alone could not check the Italians; therefore, she had to decide whether she preferred the Italians or the British. The choice was obvious, since replacing the British by the Italians at a time when the former were willing to make important concessions that would limit their territory of occupation would be foolish if not ridiculous. Consequently, Egypt also was ready to negotiate and settle the outstanding issues between herself and Great Britain.

In August 1936, an agreement was reached, and the long struggle was finally ended. The treaty was confirmed by the parliaments of the two countries amidst jubilation. Suddenly "startled British troops in Egypt were greeted with cheers instead of brickbats." [7] It seemed, at the time, that a new era of peace and stability had begun.

Provisions of the Treaty. The 1936 Anglo-Egyptian Treaty [8] terminated the military occupation of Egypt. However, there were two important reservations to this provision: (1) British forces were permitted to be stationed in the "vicinity of the Canal"; and (2) "in the event of war, imminent menace of the war, or apprehended international emergency," Britain would be entitled to certain privileges pertaining to communication and military operations.

As to the Suez Canal, British troops could be maintained in its area only for the purpose of defending it. The treaty declared emphatically that such a privilege would not "constitute in any manner an occupation" nor would it "prejudice the sovereign rights of Egypt." Furthermore, the canal would remain an integral part of Egypt. The treaty also mentioned that whenever, in the opinion of both parties, the Egyptian army was deemed capable of insuring "the liberty and entire security of navigation of the Canal" and the presence of British forces was no longer necessary, such forces would

7. Little, *Egypt,* p. 150.
8. Text of treaty in Hurewitz, vol. II, Doc. 61, pp. 203–11.

leave. It is important to remember that the decision regarding the capabilities of the Egyptian army belonged to both. In case there were differences of opinion on this matter, the question would then be submitted to the Council of the League of Nations.

In the event of war, or threat of war, Egypt was obligated to provide Britain with needed facilities including such things as ports, airfields, and communications facilities. It would be "up to the Egyptian Government" to take other necessary measures to fulfill its obligations, such as a declaration of martial law and censorship.

On the question of the Sudan, the treaty re-established the provisions of the condominium created by the Anglo-Egyptian Convention of 1899. (These provisions had been largely ignored by Britain.) As we explained earlier, the term "condominium" was applied to the joint British-Egyptian rule over the Sudan. The boundary lines between Egypt and the Sudan, which were not known previously, were drawn by the terms of the 1899 convention, and the 1936 treaty recognized such boundaries as well as all other aspects of the condominium. And the problem of the free immigration of Egyptians to the Sudan was solved. This problem, we should recall, was the reason for the discontinuation of negotiations between the British and the previous government of Nahas. The treaty recognized only one limitation upon the free immigration of Egyptians to the Sudan and that was "for reasons of public order and health."

The 1936 treaty also dealt with the capitulation system. Britain agreed to use its influence to persuade the capitulatory powers to abolish their privileges. This was accomplished by the Montreux Convention [9] of January 1937. The agreement, however, stipulated two important limits on Egypt's relations to foreign nationals. The first recognized a transitional period of twelve years, during which the Mixed Courts would continue to exist and would have jurisdiction in criminal cases affecting foreigners. (The Consular Courts would be limited to cases dealing with the personal status of foreigners.) The second limit required Egypt not to discriminate, in terms of legislation, against foreigners.

The treaty established an alliance between the two countries to consolidate their friendship as well as "their cordial understanding and their good relations." Both countries pledged not to conclude political treaties with other countries that were not consistent with their treaty; and in case of war each party would come to the aid of the other. On this last point, however, prior consultations between the two countries were required and so also there were reservations with respect to attempts to settle disputes in accordance with the Covenant of the League of Nations. It seemed that Britain considered the alliance to be the most important aspect of the

9. Text of Montreux Convention in *U.S. Treaty Series*, No. 939.

treaty, for it was the only part that was not permitted to be affected by treaty revision. Perhaps as a measure of good will, Britain promised to support Egypt's request for admission to the League of Nations, and this was accomplished in 1937.

The treaty was intended to last for twenty years, until 1956, at the end of which period the two parties were to negotiate a new agreement. In case this was not possible and there were problems regarding revision, the two countries would then submit their differences to the League of Nations. Revision was also possible after ten years, provided both countries agreed to its necessity.

Implications of the Treaty. Did Egypt gain in 1936 something she could not have gained in an earlier year? What concessions did Britain make in 1936 which she would have refused to make earlier? What were the gains for Britain? Finally, was the 1936 treaty worth the long and bitter struggle between the two countries since 1922?

There is no doubt that both Egypt and Britain gained substantially from the 1936 treaty. In the case of Britain, her interests in the Suez Canal and the Sudan were recognized and were well protected under the treaty arrangements. She also received additional guarantees and privileges to further protect these interests during an international crisis or war. And, of course, the treaty guaranteed the security of her imperial communications systems, which were so vital to her Far Eastern trade and her strategic interests in the Middle East.

On the other hand, Egyptian gains could not be measured except on the basis of her position after 1882, when Britain first occupied her territory. Otherwise, anything short of full independence and full sovereignty could hardly be considered a gain. Furthermore, the 1936 treaty reflected the power position of the two countries, in which Egypt was the inferior and, therefore, the one with the lesser bargaining power. If the agreement is viewed from this angle, Egypt could not have gotten more than she did. She had only one other alternative in the situation: to accept the continuation of the *status quo*. But the *status quo* was worse than the treaty. Under it Egypt suffered British intervention in her domestic politics, British troops were not limited to the canal area, and Egyptian troops in the Sudan were withdrawn after the assassination of Sir Lee Stack.

Under the treaty, Egypt could hope to be in charge of her domestic if not her international situation. The only thing she had to fear was an international crisis or a war in which Britain would be involved, for such an event could bring Britain back into the domestic situation, and this is what actually happened toward the end of World War II.

THE EFFECTS OF THE TREATY: 1936–1939

The abolition of the capitulations brought about a significant change in government finance, by making it possible for the first time for the government to levy direct taxes on personal incomes and commercial profits and thereby increase its revenues.[10] Prior to the end of capitulations, Egyptian governments derived revenues from indirect taxes such as customs duties. The capitulation system had virtually exempted foreigners from the payment of taxes and at the same time had made it impossible for the government to levy direct tax on Egyptians, who understandably would have resented paying taxes foreigners did not have to pay. However, the impact of the abolition of the capitulations should not be exaggerated. Although there were improvements in government finance, these improvements were limited by government inexperience in assessing and collecting taxes and also by the negative attitudes of the people, especially the powerful landlords.

With the disappearance of foreign privilege, the prestige of Egyptian citizenship increased. It became a matter of expedience for foreigners to seek Egyptian citizenship, although a large number of them still preferred their existing national identities. The shift of power from the British to the Egyptians restored Egyptian self-confidence and contributed to the development of a high morale and a sense of integrity among the people.

There were also important developments in the internal political situation between 1936 and 1939. The old rivalries between Wafd and palace reappeared. King Farouk had come of age in 1937, and he was to fall under the influence of a "palace clique," [11] causing Nahas, the prime minister, great discomfort. This time, however, the palace had greater advantages over the Wafd. The youthfulness of the monarch was most appealing to the Egyptian masses and was somehow considered to be a sign of political innocence. Consequently, the young king had a strong chance of creating a good image, one that would have been very different from his father's.

Nahas, of course, showed poor judgment and poor timing in deciding to oppose the new king as he had his father, Faud, assuming that his popularity would carry him through.

The 1936 treaty had rendered pointless the Wafd's most potent political weapons: agitation and effective opposition. Now that the party was in power and the British were no longer a factor in domestic politics, there was no political capital to be gained from agitation or opposition. Moreover, the Wafd itself no longer enjoyed the kind of internal unity it had

10. John Marlowe, *Anglo-Egyptian Relations 1800–1953* (London: The Cresset Press, 1954), pp. 310–11.
11. Little, *Egypt,* p. 156.

before the treaty, when the British presence enforced such unity. The rivalry between Nahas and the king angered some of his important lieutenants, especially Ahmed Maher and Mahmoud Nokrashi who later were to become prime ministers. These men believed that it was high time for the Wafd to make a real effort to develop a constitutional monarchy in Egypt. They believed that the youthfulness of the king and his inexperience in politics created a good chance of success. Nevertheless, Nahas was determined to limit the power of the monarch, and both Maher and Nokrashi were expelled from the party. Consequently, the two men formed a new party, the Saad Wafd (after Saad Zaghlul), and proclaimed themselves the true successors of Zaghlul. Nahas, they claimed, had betrayed the old leader.

Nahas was dismissed by the king in December 1937. His successor was an old veteran politician, Mahmoud, a liberal Constitutionalist. The new government was really a coalition composed of Saadists, the newly formed party, constitutionalists, and independents. Since Mahmoud could not govern without a majority in the Parliament, an election was held in April 1938. In this election the Wafd won 12 seats, the Constitutionalists 99, and the Saadists 84. The elections were rigged [12] by the government, but it was the first time the Wafd lost an election held under the 1923 Constitution.

WORLD WAR II: THE RETURN OF THE BRITISH

The outbreak of World War II in September 1939 brought Britain back into Egyptian internal politics, and gradually the old hostilities between Egypt and Great Britain were revived and Egyptian nationalism was reawakened.

When the war began, British troops, which under the 1936 treaty were supposed to withdraw to the Canal Zone, were still in occupation of strategic points in and around the cities of Cairo and Alexandria. Their departure from these areas was delayed by the inability of the Egyptian government to construct, as was required by the treaty, the physical facilities needed for the stationing of the troops. Of course, the war made such arrangements unnecessary and, instead, required the Egyptian government, again under the terms of the 1936 treaty, to provide additional assistance to Britain in dealing with the problems of the war.

The Egyptian government, then under the leadership of Ali Maher, brother of Ahmed Maher, founder of the Saadist party, cooperated with the British to the extent required by the treaty. Thus, throughout most of the war Egypt remained neutral.

12. Little, *Egypt*, p. 157.

There were, however, certain internal pressures which threatened to make the position of Britain extremely complicated and caused Britain to intervene in Egyptian internal policies. The Egyptian people were concerned about the economic situation of their country during the war, and, understandably, there were those who doubted there would be any benefits for Egypt from the war. The shortage of food was an important factor in this Egyptian dilemma. Although many Egyptians became wealthy as a result of the war, most Egyptians were hard hit by the rise of prices of basic commodities.

The British also feared King Farouk, whose sentiments were on the side of Germany and Italy. Farouk knew, however, that he had no choice but to adhere to the 1936 Treaty provisions, and so he decided to do so, but without becoming deeply committed to the British, so that Egypt would not be harmed in case of a German victory. Ali Maher was for this cautious policy too.

There were also groups who actively oppposed cooperation with the British. Among them were the Muslim Brothers, a fanatic religious movement of whom we shall have more to say later. This group advocated the establishment of an Islamic state for all Muslims and accepted violence as a method for achieving its goals. By 1939 it had become a strong and important political force in the country, and its influence was being felt in the universities as well as in the armed forces.

Lord Killearn, the British ambassador to Egypt, was overly sensitive to the anti-British aspects of Egyptian public opinion. His fears led him to pursue highhanded policies with regard to Egyptian internal affairs. In June 1940, for instance, he forced the resignation of Ali Maher, the prime minister, because of his extremely cautious war policy. And when Axis forces were advancing in North Africa toward Egypt in February 1942, he demanded that the king appoint Nahas as prime minister. Lord Killearn felt that since the danger was imminent, Nahas would be in better command of his people than any one else and that his cooperation with the British under these circumstances would be more fruitful. King Farouk procrastinated, and Killearn issued an ultimatum. The situation reached a high point of tension when Farouk rejected the ultimatum and the ambassador threatened to force his abdication unless he retracted by appointing Nahas. On February 4, 1942 Killearn surrounded the royal palace with British troops and entered the palace to inform the king that he had only two choices: he could either abdicate or immediately appoint Nahas. The king chose the lesser of the two evils and appointed Nahas.

This episode in Egyptian history has been commemorated as a day of humiliation for all Egyptians. Killearn's action lowered the prestige of Nahas, although the latter was able to secure a large majority of seats in the Chamber of Deputies in the elections held in March 1942. Nationalists became disenchanted with the Wafd leadership; some of them turned to radical groups for leadership, groups like the Muslim Brotherhood, the Communist party, and other Socialist parties. Conspiratorial organizations were also formed in the armed forces.

In addition to its impact upon public opinion, Killearn's intervention policy made the 1936 treaty extremely unpopular. Whereas the people had once thought of it as marking the beginning of a new era in Egyptian history, they now became aware of the immense power it conferred upon Britain during times of war or international crisis. They began to understand that their country was not fully sovereign and in reality was not even independent. The treaty, therefore, became a source of hate for the large majority of Egyptian nationalists.

THE WARTIME FORTUNES OF THE WAFD

Of course, the return of Nahas to power under these circumstances revived Farouk's dislike for him and his party. Farouk was determined to get rid of Nahas at the first opportunity, and on October 8, 1944, while the British ambassador was out of the country, Nahas was dismissed, after he had been in office for more than two and a half years.

By the end of 1944, the Wafd had lost much of its popularity. It had become the party of the wealthy landlords and the party of the privileged. Paradoxically, its popularity usually increased while it was out of power and in opposition mainly because it knew how to manipulate issues and appeal to the masses. Of course, its powerful local organizations in the provinces were important sources of strength for the national leadership and succeeded over the years in establishing roots in the local communities. They became important in the sociopolitical structures of these communities. Political patronage and the ability to bestow favors upon friends and political allies had assisted them in attaining power.

But when the party was in power, the governments it controlled were characterized by inefficiency and corruption.[13] Governmental authority was used to promote the private interests of some of the leaders of the party. Most people considered Nahas to be honest and straightforward but deplored the fact that he was unable to limit the power of his lieutenants, some of whom became wealthier at the expense of the poor and the powerless. The wife of Nahas had the reputation of being a dominating woman, and many people believed she used her husband to promote the selfish interests of her relatives.

Ironically, Nahas usually left office, whether by resignation or removal,

13. Little, *Egypt*, p. 165.

before the situation got bad enough to seriously hurt his personal reputation and prestige. The impact of corruption and inefficiency was felt after the Wafd government had left, and succeeding governments were blamed for bad governments and bad politics. Even when the Wafd was blamed for some of these things, it somehow managed to recuperate and regain popularity.

When Farouk dismissed Nahas in 1944, the Wafd had already been further weakened by the loss of several outstanding leaders, who had been expelled by Nahas in an effort to eliminate dissension within his party. Among these leaders was Makram Obeid, the secretary-general of the party and often minister of finance in Wafd governments. Soon after his dismissal he formed a party of his own, the Ketla party; and when Nahas was forced to step down, Obeid's party joined the Saadist party in a coalition government under Ahmed Maher, the Saadist leader.

Unlike his brother Ali, Ahmed Maher favored declaration of war on Germany. He wanted his country to be able to participate in the peace conferences after the war to protect her interests effectively. He did not want a repetition of Egypt's dilemma after World War I, when she was not included in the Versailles Conference. Thus in February 1945, the Maher government declared war against Germany. Unfortunately, however, Maher was cut down by the bullets of an assassin as he was leaving the Chamber of Deputies after he had secured that chamber's confirmation of the declaration of war. His successor, Nokrashi, also a Saadist leader, firmly believed that Maher was killed by the Muslim Brotherhood. The postwar period revealed the immense hatred and fierce struggle between this radical group and the government.

THE MUSLIM BROTHERHOOD

Ideology. The Muslim Brotherhood was founded by Hasan al-Banna in 1928 at Ismailia, a town located in the Suez Canal area. Originally a religious movement with very little interest in politics, its main object was the revival of Islam as the guiding principle of life for all Muslim societies and the reconstruction of these societies in accordance with the commandments of the Koran and the teachings of the Prophet, Mohammed.

As such, the basic ideology of the Brotherhood was simple, and it was this simplicity which made it attractive to a great number of adherents. The ordinary Muslim had no difficulty understanding the need for establishing a way of life whose legal, social, and political structure conformed to his religious principles and requirements.

However, when it came to the specific application of Muslim principles, a complicated problem developed. The Muslim Brotherhood tried to avoid this kind of problem by insisting upon a literal interpretation of the religious doctrine. It maintained that Koranic principles were easy to understand and that their meaning could not be confused. Of course, this fallacy was, ultimately, the cause of the intellectual stagnation and rigidity which characterized the Brotherhood. It was also the seed of authoritarianism within the organization itself and in its relations with the outside.

The Brotherhood believed that progress and modernization could be achieved under the Islamic doctrine, and al-Banna repeatedly emphasized the need to raise the standard of living in Muslim societies and the necessity of eliminating poverty. He also encouraged the development of science, which he argued would not and could not pose any serious challenge to religious truths. The establishment of schools was an important priority in the Brotherhood's plan of action. As a matter of fact, several schools were actually established by the Brotherhood itself, and al-Banna taught at these schools occasionally.

The Brotherhood's progressive outlook was accentuated by its interest in physical fitness programs for its members, insisting that a great nation was a healthy nation. But the idea of physical fitness was expanded to include military training. This latter type of training was necessary to support the Brotherhood's concept of *jihad* (a holy war in defense of Islam). Al-Banna saw a need for military readiness in order to be able to defend the religion against external as well as internal threat.

While al-Banna and his Brotherhood did not fear modernism, they declared secularism and Western influence to be the enemies of Islam. Al-Banna believed that secularization and Westernization were not necessary to achieve modernization, and that modernization must be an integral part of Islamic reform. It should not be achieved in contradiction to the Islamic doctrine.

Economically, al-Banna maintained, the Islamic system was unique: it was neither capitalistic nor communistic and avoided the evils of both systems.[14] It was based on the idea of cooperation, and justice was its guiding principle. Moreover, it was democratic. From a Western point of view, this last assertion seems strange when coupled with al-Banna's demand that political parties should be abolished. According to al-Banna, political parties were based upon dissension, whereas democracy was essentially a system based upon cooperation.

Strict adherence to the Muslim moral code was considered by the Brotherhood to be of utmost importance. To compel such adherence, al-Banna demanded the enforcement of the Shariah (religious law), especially with regard to penalties for crimes. Thus, illicit sex should be punished by stoning the offender; thieves should be punished by the amputa-

14. *Middle East Affairs*, December, 1954, p. 379.

tion of their hands; and so on, in accordance with the Islamic penal laws. In addition, the Brotherhood prohibited such activities as dancing, gambling, drinking alcoholic beverages, and going to movie houses and theaters.

It is obvious from all this that the Brotherhood, in spite of its claim to being modern and progressive, was a conservative social movement. It could not be anything but a conservative force, for it proposed a return to a religious order which had long been obsolete. The societies it was attempting to reconstruct along religious lines had gone too far in the direction of secular socioeconomic development; it would be an impossible task to bring them back to the extreme religious position.

The political program of the Brotherhood was vague and even more unrealistic than its social and economic outlook. Al-Banna frequently referred to the re-establishment of the caliphate, but he never made clear whether the caliph would be the religious head or the political head of Muslim society. We do know, however, that the Brotherhood advocated the establishment of a single Muslim nation, to be governed by the same law and the same system of mores. This was a logical ideological position in view of Islam's universal character. The Muslim Brotherhood made it clear that under Muslim law there was no difference between an Arab and a non-Arab as long as they were both Muslim. Non-Muslims would have the usual guarantees of Islamic law, such as the freedom to worship; such guarantees, of course, were not sufficient, by modern standards, to constitute full citizenship rights for religious minorities.

The Brotherhood maintained that Muslim internationalism was not at odds with Arab nationalism, or even Egyptian nationalism, since the interests of the Egyptians were the same as those of the other Muslims. Consequently, Muslim Brothers were called upon to fight for the causes of Egypt, the Arabs, and other Muslim countries with the same vehemence and the same loyalty.

Political Activities of the Brotherhood. Evidence that the movement was beginning to appeal to a large number of Egyptians [15] and al-Banna's growing interest in politics forced the Brotherhood to enter Egyptian politics in the early 1930's. By 1936, the Brotherhood was no longer just a religious movement dedicated to the revival of Islamic principles but an important political movement with all the characteristics of a political party. The first opportunity to bring the Brotherhood into the limelight of politics was in 1936, at the beginning of the Palestine Arab rebellion. Al-Banna became active in raising funds and recruiting volunteers to aid his Muslim brethren in Palestine. Suddenly, Egyptian politicians began to real-

15. Christina Phelps Harris, *Nationalism and Revolution in Egypt: The Role of the Muslim Brotherhood* (London: Oxford University Press, 1960), p. 161.

ize the power potential of the Brotherhood, and they sought the support of al-Banna and his organization. Among these politicians was Ali Maher, who was the prime minister of Egypt in 1940, when the idea of cooperation among Arab countries was gaining support in Egyptian official circles. Maher saw the possibility of support from the Brotherhood in his efforts to make Egypt the leader of the Arab world. After 1940, al-Banna became more involved in the politics of his country and he had the prestige of commanding a number of followers in Syria, Lebanon, Jordan, Iraq, and even Pakistan and Persia. In 1942, when Nahas came to power, al-Banna reluctantly supported the new prime minister in return for a promise to introduce legislation to deal with vice. The promise was kept, and al-Banna made political capital out of it by claiming that he had sacrificed a share in power for this legislation which was an important item in the Brotherhood's reform plan.

After the dismissal of Nahas in 1944, the Brotherhood declared itself to be the enemy of all Egyptian parties, including the Wafd. By now, al-Banna had gained stature and his organization had real power in Egypt. At this point, the Brotherhood turned to the use of force and gradually gained the reputation of being a subversive organization. It was suspected of assassinating Ahmed Maher who, it will be recalled, was shot in February 1945. Assassination plots continued to characterize the postwar period, and the Brotherhood was a primary suspect in these plots. The climax came in December 1948, when Nokrashi was assassinated in the Ministry of the Interior. Ibrahim Abdel Hadi, who succeeded to the leadership of the Saadist party and to the office of prime minister, took severe measures against the Brotherhood, culminating in the assassination of al-Banna himself in February 1949. There was no doubt that the assassination of al-Banna was instigated by Abdel Hadi, as the trials, which took place in 1953 under the government of the 1952 revolution, revealed. Thus, the Muslim Brotherhood represented, in the postwar period, the greatest threat to political stability and to Egyptian governments. Indeed, it was a threat to the monarchy and the entire governmental system. If it had not been for the military coup of 1952, the Brotherhood might have succeeded in capturing political power in Egypt.

POSTWAR AND PREREVOLUTIONARY POLITICS

The postwar period marked the beginning of the end for the monarchical regime in Egypt and was characterized by violence, assassination, and radical politics. It seemed as if the Egyptian people had become tired of such old but persistent problems as their relations with Britain, the struggle between king and Wafd, and the influence of the wealthy classes in the government. They wanted something new—a new order perhaps, or, at any rate, a new kind of men to run their government and solve their problems.

King Farouk. The deterioration of the political situation during the postwar period was caused in part by the decline of King Farouk's personal reputation, which in turn was caused by the weakness of his character, by his immorality, and by his disregard of the public interest.

King Farouk had a chance to become a popular figure in Egypt during the first few years after his ascendance to the throne in 1937, but he never availed himself of the opportunity. His strong interest in pleasure overshadowed his interest in his country. Gradually, he fell under the influence of a group of palace advisers whose members were mostly foreign and who had been appointed by the king himself. Farouk's reliance on them might have been motivated partly by his fear of the Wafd and partly by his peculiar tendencies. There were a few Egyptians among Farouk's advisers who, while serving him loyally, tried to limit his extravagance and correct his mistakes, but they were unable to overcome his reckless attitude.

Of course, Farouk alone could not have been the sole reason for the fall of the monarchy in Egypt. Certain crucial problems, some of them new and some of them old, were also responsible. We could perhaps say that the way Farouk handled these problems was a more important contribution to the downfall of the monarchy than the issue of his personal fitness to rule.

The Palestine Problem. There was, first and foremost, the problem of Palestine and the role of Egypt in the development of the Palestinian crisis. Egypt's concern for the Arabs of Palestine, or for that matter for the Arabs as a whole, had not been strong in the past. Egyptian nationalism, rather than Arab nationalism, was the motivating force behind the political events in the country's modern history. But during World War II, Egyptian governments became interested in the idea of establishing a regional organization to promote cooperation among the Arab countries. The prime movers behind this idea were the British, who were concerned about their postwar position in the Middle East and believed that the formation of an Arab League would be in their interest as well as in the interest of the Arabs themselves. In any case, the Arab League was established in March 1945, and Egypt immediately assumed the role of leader in the new organization.

When on May 15, 1948, British troops withdrew from Palestine and the Palestinian Jews declared the establishment of the State of Israel, the Arab League became involved in the war now known as the Arab-Israeli war. Nokrashi, who was the Saadist prime minister of Egypt at the time, doubted the readiness of his country for such an adventure; but King Farouk saw an opportunity to enhance his position as leader of the Arab world. He, therefore, favored the idea of military intervention in Palestine, for which he had the support of Egyptian radical groups, especially the Muslim Brotherhood, who were pressing for an all-out war with the newly created Jewish state. These radical groups were able to rouse Egyptian public opinion in favor of war, and Nokrashi could not, under these circumstances, but follow suit.

And so Egypt became involved in a war with Israel, that failed. The events themselves do not concern us here, but the implications of the failure for Egypt do. To Arabs who had considered Egypt the strongest Arab country, the failure of Egypt to defeat Israel was viewed as a failure of all Arabs. Within Egypt, the defeat lowered the prestige of the men in power while giving the radical groups an effective political weapon to be used against the king and the government. More important was the feeling of shame which the Egyptian army acquired as a result of its defeat; and when rumors spread that the Egyptian army was fighting the war with defective weapons, this feeling of shame turned into anger and frustration. Conspiratorial groups within the armed forces became determined to avenge the honor of Egypt by doing something drastic about the power structure in the country.

Postwar Relations with Britain. A second major problem contributing to political instability during the postwar period, and to the failure of the monarchy as well, was the deterioration of Egypt's relations with Great Britain. We discussed earlier how World War II made the 1936 Anglo-Egyptian Treaty unpopular in Egypt. After the war, Egypt made an effort to have the treaty revised in line with nationalist aspirations and demands. Sidki, who became the Saadist prime minister in February 1946, upon the resignation of Nokrashi, appointed a negotiating team representing the major political groups. The Wafd, however, was left out because it had insisted on leading the Egyptian party in any negotiations with Britain.

The Sidki government was able to secure a draft treaty from Britain, known as the Sidki-Bevan agreement. Britain agreed to withdraw its troops from all areas outside the canal zone by March 31, 1947 and from the zone itself by September 1949. The Anglo-Egyptian alliance, it was further agreed, would continue. This meant that both countries would cooperate through a Joint Board of Defense in case Egypt was attacked by a third party or in case Britain was involved in a war as a result of attack on the neighboring countries of the Middle East.

On the question of the Sudan, the draft treaty was vague. It referred to a common policy which would operate "within the framework of the unity between the Sudan and Egypt under the common crown of Egypt," and which would also recognize the right of the Sudanese eventually to decide the future status of their country. Until this last objective was achieved, the agreement of 1899 would continue in force. The vagueness of these provisions almost immediately caused serious misunderstandings. The Egyptians thought that the unity between the Sudan and Egypt was permanent, whereas Britain believed that the right of the Sudanese to determine the future status of their country had a priority over the "framework of unity" of the two countries. Which interpretation was the correct one was, admittedly, a complicated question. On the one hand, the draft treaty did not expressly make self-determination by the Sudanese a condition for the continuation of unity between the Sudan and Egypt. On the other hand, self-determination would be meaningless if it were restricted, as the Egyptian party seemed to infer, by a permanent unity between the two countries. Unity with Egypt would be impossible if the Sudanese were to decide in favor of independence and full sovereignty for their country.

The Sudanese issue and the activity of antigovernment groups, mainly the Wafd and the Brotherhood, insured the death of the draft treaty as well as the resignation of the Sidki government in December 1946.

Nokrashi, who returned to office with Sidki's resignation, realized the futility of negotiation, in view of the determination of the Wafd to wreck all possibilities of reaching an agreement with Britain. Consequently, he decided to submit the Egyptian case to the United Nations Security Council. This was done in July 1947. The Security Council was unable to do anything beyond calling upon Egypt and Britain to resume negotiations. The Council's indecision was perhaps caused by the fact that many of its members had treaty obligations in various parts of the world and were afraid that a decision on the Anglo-Egyptian dispute might through setting a precedent create serious problems for them. The Soviet Union's reluctance to support the Egyptian side stemmed from its opposition to Egypt's attempt to control the Sudan.

Internal Affairs: 1947–50. The years that followed the collapse of negotiations between Britain and Egypt were a time of internal political turmoil mostly created by the radical groups. By the beginning of 1950, Egypt was in serious difficulty: she had been defeated in the Arab-Israeli war (1948–49); Nokrashi had been assassinated (December 28, 1948); al-Banna had also been assassinated (February 13, 1949); and Prime Minister Abdel Hadi, who came to power after the assassination of Nokrashi (and devised the assassination of al-Banna), had been forced to resign in July 1949. The popularity of Farouk was at its lowest. In 1948, he had divorced his popular Queen Farida, and rumors about his mistreatment of her were widely circulated. The following passage aptly summarizes the political situation at the beginning of 1950: "Egypt consisted of a hated King, a hated Government, and a sullen, docile people permeated by groups plotting rebellion in secret. The end was near. It only required the folly of the King and a new period of Wafd misrule to bring it about." [16]

The Abrogation of the 1936 Treaty. This "period of Wafd misrule" began in January 1950. At this time, the Wafd, tired of opposition, was willing to make peace with the palace; and the king, who sensed danger in the prevailing political situation, was equally willing to come to terms with the Wafd rather than risk his life or position at the hands of the radical groups. Behind the scenes and in an unofficial way the British embassy encouraged both parties to declare friendship. Thus when the Saadist Abdel Hadi resigned as prime minister, King Farouk asked Hussein Sirry, an independent, to form an interim government for the purpose of holding general elections. These elections were held in January 1950, and the Wafd was able to secure 228 seats out of 319 in the Chamber of Deputies.

Although the new Wafd government began its term of office by announcing a number of social reforms, it nevertheless soon became known for its corruption and mismanagement of public affairs. As if to add fuel to the fire, Nahas declared in November 1950 his determination to wrestle with the British until he secured complete evacuation of their troops as well as complete unity with the Sudan. From a nationalist point of view, it was an extremely difficult task.

When the Nahas government decided (October 8, 1951) to abrogate the 1936 treaty unilaterally, it became obvious that the Wafd government would be involved in a life-and-death struggle with the British. If it succeeded in driving the British out, something which would have required either military action or a boycott over a long period of time, nationalist support would prolong its life and raise its stature. On the other hand, if it failed, Egyptians would most certainly look elsewhere for leadership.

Gradually, after the abrogation of the 1936 treaty, the Wafd government began to lose control of the political situation. Nationalist feelings and strong determination on the part of the Egyptian people to settle once and for all Egypt's problems with Britain took matters out of the leaders' hands. Violence erupted in the Suez Canal area, and civilian volunteers were engaged in actual warfare with the British troops. There were casualties on both sides, and many university students were killed in the fighting.

Finally, on Friday, January 25, 1952, the situation reached its climax. British troops surrounded the police headquarters in Ismailia and demanded the surrender of its occupants. The Egyptian police force refused the British ultimatum, and a fierce battle ensued. The Egyptians were defeated after they had fought with great courage, and the Egyptian casualties were very high—because the Ismailia police force was short of the ammunition needed for its survival. In any case, the mob which took control of the streets of Cairo the following day, "Black Saturday," believed that the

16. Little, *Egypt*, p. 179.

Ismailia police force had been short of ammunition and that the Wafd government had betrayed the revolution. Turning its anger against buildings that housed foreign companies, movie houses, restaurants, night clubs, and hotels, the mob set them afire, and by noon Cairo was ablaze.

There were no policemen on hand to stop the mob from burning the city, and the army was not available until late in the day. The circumstances which accompanied these events remain ambiguous even today. A whole city was on fire, and no one knew how it started or who was responsible for it. There were rumors that King Farouk instigated the event as an excuse for dismissing the Wafd government. While the rumors had no basis in trustworthy sources, they were strengthened by the fact that the king did order the dismissal of the government on Sunday, January 27.

The failure of the Wafd government in its struggle against the British was a great disappointment to the masses of Egyptian people, who began to feel the need for stronger and more dynamic leadership. Before the end of the year (1952) such a leadership was in control of the country.

CHAPTER 7

EGYPT UNDER NASSER

T H E coup d'état which took place on July 23, 1952, marked the beginning of a significant period in Egyptian history. The leaders of the new regime and contemporary scholars refer to this event as "the Egyptian Revolution." A military coup may or may not be revolutionary, depending on whether it is successful in introducing important changes in the institutional life of society. The Egyptian military takeover was a revolutionary event, for the new regime did attempt, in some instances sucessfully, to reconstruct society and to give it a new outlook and new goals. It remains for future historians to judge the implications and the scope of these changes.

THE PREREVOLUTIONARY ERA

What prompted the 1952 revolution? The preceding two chapters were intended to provide, among other things, background for the answer to this important question. Foreign rule, no doubt, was a factor. In addition to intensifying Egyptian nationalism, it was indirectly responsible for frustrating the indigenous forces of constructive reform to the extent that they became preoccupied with protest rather than with the development of positive attitudes toward government.

Foreign rule, however, cannot be blamed for all the ills of Egypt. Strictly internal problems, as well, contributed to the deterioration of political conditions prior to the 1952 revolution. Egypt's experiment in parliamentary democracy had not been successful. Neither the political parties nor the monarchy had any understanding of public responsibility; both were more interested in obtaining and monopolizing political power than in using it for the benefit of the people. Thus no reform of major consequence was introduced between independence (1922) and the coup of 1952. The peasants, who constituted the majority of Egyptian society and who were for centuries in desperate need, received very little attention from political parties or governments. There was also the problem of corruption, a social disease that inflicted governments, political parties, and the monarch. Even the Wafd, the most popular party in the country, was not untouched by corruption and political irresponsibility. And the reform groups were uncompromising and unrealistic. By their radicalism and extremism, they destroyed their chances of participating in the political process. In short, there was no political group capable of giving Egypt a responsible government.

The monarch, who could have eased the effects of this crucial problem by providing wise leadership, was himself deeply involved in the feuds of the political parties. Consequently, a political vacuum was in existence long before 1952. This vacuum was made more dangerous by a widening gap between the fabulously rich upper class and the extremely poor lower class. The middle class was too small and insignificant to bridge the gap and eliminate the dangerous social tension. Thus, Egypt was ready for revolution.

THE MILITARY COUP

In 1952, the army was the only public agency politically able to save the country from further decline and national deterioration. The Muslim Brothers, for instance, could not have done it without the assistance of the armed forces, and they were temporarily incapacitated since the death of their leader, Hasan al-Banna, in 1949.

Secret conspiratorial organizations within the armed forces, formed in protest against political and social conditions in the country, had existed for many years before the revolution. One of these, a group of eleven young officers (average age thirty-three) called the Free Officers, seized power on July 23, 1952—almost inadvertently, it would seem.

The Free Officers, like many Egyptian nationalists, were dissatisfied with the social and political conditions of their country. They were extremely sensitive to British dominance, especially since this dominance had diminished the responsibilities of the Egyptian army and lowered its prestige. But more than this, their military pride had been insulted by the government's mishandling of the Palestinian war of 1948. Most of them, like Nasser, had been involved in the war, and they did not forget the lessons they learned from their participation. Their desire to act against the government was intensified after the burning of Cairo and the chaos which followed.

The Free Officers were fearful, however, that their youthfulness might be a serious obstacle to the success of the revolution. Therefore they chose General Mohammed Naguib, who was known to have sympathized with their cause and who was also disliked by the government and the monarch, to be the titular head of the movement.

Taking advantage of the absence of the cabinet and the king, who were spending the summer in Alexandria, Egypt's second capital, the Free Officers moved to take over the strategic places in Cairo. They occupied army headquarters (while the General Staff was meeting to discuss ways to eliminate conspiracy in the armed forces) and captured several high-ranking officers, thus eliminating the risks of a complicated search. Capturing the headquarters also gave them control of the army's system of communication, from which the group could transmit their orders to all military units outside the capital.

These young revolutionary officers, however, had not anticipated the events that confronted them after the day the coup took place. Their hope had been that by a show of force they would compel the government to accept demands for reform. No one was more surprised than they, perhaps, to discover that the vast majority of the armed forces were willing to follow them, and that in a matter of hours they were in effective command of Egypt's entire military. They received another jolt the next day, when they discovered that the Egyptian people were more than pleased with the coup, news of which had been broadcast over the captured radio by a member of the group.

They were not only surprised; they were unprepared. The Free Officers had little or no experience in civilian government; moreover, they shared no common ideology or political philosophy. No program of action existed beyond a vague and general idea that reforms were needed. Consequently, the group had to cope with problems of governing on an *ad hoc* basis and learn the art of government through their own experience.

CONSOLIDATION OF POWER

The success of the coup raised the question of the future of the monarch. One group in the Free Officers wanted to try Farouk for his crimes against the Constitution and the people. Nasser, however, was able to convince his colleagues that a better alternative would be to force his abdication and require him to leave the country. This was done on July 26, 1952, only three days after the coup. Theoretically, therefore, Egypt continued to have a monarchical system, but with Fuad II, Farouk's six-month-old son, as the new king. Since Fuad II was a minor, a Regency Council consisting of three men was appointed, supposedly to exercise the constitutional powers of the king. Of course, this Regency Council became no more than the nominal head of state.

Before the abdicaton of Farouk, the Free Officers had insisted upon the appointment of Ali Maher to the office of prime minister. This veteran politician, we should recall, had held the same office before. His brother, Ahmed Maher, had also been prime minister but was assassinated in 1945, allegedly because of his sympathies with the Allies during World War II.

Ali, unlike his brother Ahmed, belonged to no political party and had established a national reputation of being honest and competent.

However, the Free Officers soon became disappointed with the new prime minister, who was essentially conservative and, although honest, a product of the old regime. He could not appreciate the need, as felt by the military, for radical reform and revolutionary action. Nevertheless, since the officers were not yet sure about the future of their revolution and since they were still toying with the idea of returning to constitutional government, Maher was allowed to continue in office until September 7, 1952, when the Free Officers replaced him with Naguib.

In the meantime, the Free Officers were able to begin a few reforms. During the first week of the revolution, they ordered the political parties to purge themselves of corrupt elements as a condition for the continuation of their legal existence. They also promised, and actually began, a war against favoritism and corruption in government, and titles of nobility were abolished. Measures were taken to investigate and prosecute those responsible for the assassination of Hasan al-Banna, the former leader of the Muslim Brotherhood, and such steps were also taken against those responsible for the mishandling of the Palestinian war.

During the first six months, other reforms, largely economic, were introduced. Rent and the prices of food were lowered, and a progressive tax was established. New labor laws and a law fixing minimum wages in agriculture were introduced, and an agrarian reform law (which we will discuss later) was put into effect.

With the exception of the Agrarian Reform Law, the initial policies of the new regime were not radical. However, they gave the impression that the new military leadership was serious and well intentioned, that it would end irresponsible behavior in government, and that honesty and purposefulness would characterize the future government of Egypt.

But the reforming spirit of the new leaders also revealed their inclination to transform the coup into a dictatorship. They repeatedly declared their intention of holding elections and of returning to constitutional government; but they found it expedient, if not necessary, to tighten control and gradually assume total power. They claimed that they had initially desired to cooperate with politicians and political parties but had found these elements too corrupt to be dealt with. They claimed that the country was in desperate need of a forceful government with concrete programs and that no politician or group of politicians of the old regime saw this need.

Although not devoid of truth, these arguments cannot obscure the fact that the Free Officers had gotten a taste of political power, liked it, and wanted more of it. Nevertheless, their reasons were not entirely selfish, for they were serious about their aims. They wanted to transform Egypt's political and social institutions, and although they were uncertain about how to attain this objective, they believed they would succeed if they were given the opportunity.

The assumption of total power by the military took place gradually, beginning late in 1952, when power was transferred to a newly created body known as the Revolutionary Command Council (R.C.C.). This body consisted of the Free Officers themselves, under the chairmanship of General Naguib. Decisions were made by a majority vote; each member, including the chairman, had only one vote. The civilian cabinet, the official executive of the government, continued to exist (also under the chairmanship of Naguib), but the R.C.C. was the more important body. The establishment of the R.C.C. was followed (February 10, 1953) by a declaration of the beginning of a transitional period of three years, during which time the government was to rule by decree, and after which constitutional government was to be resumed. An interim constitution was promulgated with the declaration, presumably to give legal sanctions to existing institutions. The final step in the process of assuming power took place on June 18, 1953, when Egypt became a republic and the monarchy came to an end. Naguib became the first president and retained his position as prime minister.

RESTRICTION OF CIVIL LIBERTIES

The political transformation of Egypt from a monarchy to a republic was accompanied by severe limitations upon civil liberties. Opposition to the new regime was not allowed; political parties were declared illegal. The Constitution of 1923 was abrogated, and martial law remained in force until 1956. The press was controlled, and the whole nation was mobilized to support and uphold the revolution. Political prisoners of the old regime were freed, but new prisoners replaced them, and show trials—mockeries of justice—were held to deal with opponents of the new regime and supporters of the old regime. Perhaps the only redeeming element in Egypt's loss of freedom was that the new regime was a benevolent dictatorship and that the status of freedom had not been much better under the old regime.

THE NASSER-NAGUIB CONTROVERSY

By the summer of 1953 the R.C.C. was well entrenched, but within the ranks of the council a serious rift was developing between the inexperienced, youthful Nasser and the older, more moderate Naguib, who had become the symbol of the revolution. Nasser commanded the army and also had the backing of the majority in the R.C.C.; the young officers who engineered the 1952 coup believed that Nasser and not Naguib was their real leader.[1]

The roles the two men played in the stages before the 1952 coup are not clear. In his book *Egypt's Destiny* [2] Naguib claims that he was part of the Free Officers' group before the coup and that he participated in planning the revolution. On the other hand, Anwar Sadat, a member of the R.C.C., reports in his book *Revolt on the Nile* [3] that Naguib did not know about the coup until it had been executed. Most scholars either accept Sadat's statement or generally agree that Nasser was the "original mastermind behind the coup." [4]

Nevertheless, Naguib had become popular among the people, and this popularity was the main obstacle confronting Nasser in his quest for power. Thus, when Naguib submitted his resignation in February 1954, protesting the R.C.C.'s refusal to grant him sufficient powers to govern Egypt during the transitional period, the people of Egypt expressed their confidence in him by demonstrating against the R.C.C. After three days, the R.C.C. had to ask Naguib to return to the position of president, although the office of prime minister was left for Nasser. This experience showed that Nasser could not command the people without Naguib, but it was also true that Naguib could not control the army without Nasser.

But whereas Nasser and the army had the military power to silence all opposition and to compel, if necessary, the people's obedience, Naguib's popularity could not alone sustain him in power for a long time, especially in a country with a strong authoritarian tradition. Thus, Naguib was naïve to overestimate the value of his popularity.[5] Nasser knew all this, and he also knew that it was but a matter of time before Naguib's popularity would decline, becoming an unimportant factor. He realized that his control of the army would ultimately make him the undisputed leader of the revolution, at which time he could shore up his popular image. The efficacy of his reforms, his honesty, and his determination were assets. Moreover, he had great plans for his country, and he believed this alone should bring him the gratitude of millions of Egyptians.

Nasser began to seek popular support almost immediately after Naguib's return to the presidency. First he arranged pro-Nasser demonstrations in

1. About the details of the conflict between Nasser and Naguib see Keith Wheelock, *Nasser's New Egypt* (New York: Frederick A. Praeger, 1960), pp. 28–36.
2. Mohammed Naguib, *Egypt's Destiny* (New York: Doubleday & Co., 1955), p. 30.
3. Anwar El Sadat, *Revolt on the Nile* (London: Alan Wingate, 1957), pp. 109–19.
4. Malcolm H. Kerr, *Egypt Under Nasser* (New York: Foreign Policy Association, 1963), p. 10.
5. "Change of Leadership," *The World Today*, February, 1955, vol. XI, 52.

the hope that they would mislead opposition groups into believing that the people were deserting Naguib for him and the R.C.C. When this strategy failed, he made (March 5, and also March 25, 1954) several promises regarding an early return to constitutional government. He promised to call for an elected constitutional assembly, the lifting of censorship, and the end of martial law. However, Nasser soon realized that the fulfillment of these promises might endanger his position. Therefore, he was quick to declare that the transitional period would continue until January 1956, as had been planned.

Nasser then turned to the consolidation of his power within the government. In April 1954, Major Khalid Mohieddine, who had supported Naguib during the February crisis—and who was suspected of being a Communist—was sent to Europe at the expense of the government. Two other members of the R.C.C. were dropped from the leadership group. On April 18, Nasser reorganized his cabinet to include all the members of the R.C.C. with the exception of two, who were given important responsibilities outside the cabinet.

The final step in Nasser's acquisition of total power began on October 26, 1954, when an attempt was made on his life while he was addressing a mass rally in Alexandria. The would-be assassin was a member of the Muslim Brotherhood, and the Nasser government brought the leaders of the Muslim Brotherhood and all collaborators in the assassination plot to trial. Strangely enough, the trials revealed information connecting Naguib with the leaders of the plot. Whether Naguib was involved no one knows. Nevertheless, it justified removing Naguib from office and putting him under house arrest (November 14, 1954).

CONSTITUTIONALISM

In Egypt, as in all the Arab countries, constitutions are little more than signs of Western influence. They have no place in the traditions of Arab societies: neither the people nor the politicians appreciate their value or understand their purpose. They exist mainly because they give the appearance of orderliness, modernity, and perhaps progressiveness. Furthermore, and most importantly, they are intended to give the impression that the dominant regime is democratic. Few authoritarian regimes are willing to admit the authoritarian character of their institutions, and even totalitarian Communist systems deny their authoritarianism; rather, they profess a democratic philosophy that is superior in its basic elements and goals to the democracies of the Western world. Arab constitutions are similarly important insofar as they constitute the moral justification of the political regimes.

The Egyptian Constitution is remembered whenever the man or men in power are being discredited: opposition groups turn to the constitutional limitations upon the powers of government only in this negative, critical sense. However, when governments are popular, or when opposition is nonexistent, constitutions do not guide the government's actions. Thus, King Farouk was rightly criticized for abuse of the Constitution, but popular Wafdist governments were not required to respect the Constitution, especially with regard to the rights of individuals and political minorities. Similarly, after the Nasser regime had established itself in power, there was little talk about the illegality of governmental policies. To those who liked Nasser, the Constitution was no longer important, and Nasser could do what he liked. To those who did not like Nasser, the Constitution would be important, at least until Nasser was out and they were in.

THE PRESENT CONSTITUTION

The present Egyptian Constitution was created in 1964. It is substantially the same as the document proclaimed in 1956,[6] with a few added features that are interesting.

The 1964 Constitution [7] establishes a Socialist economy for Egypt—something the 1956 document did not do. The Egyptian state is proclaimed to be a Socialist state based upon an alliance of the "working powers of the people." The alliance consists of "farmers, workers, soldiers, intellectuals, and national capital." Furthermore, the law recognizes three forms of ownership: state, cooperative, and private. Article 13 guarantees the people's control over, and supervision of, the three types of ownership. It requires the private sector of the economy to operate within the limits of the national economic plan and without exploitation. Also, the use of capital is always conditioned by the demands of the public interest. Although private ownership is protected by the Constitution, its social functions may be determined by statute. The expropriation of property is possible but requires adequate compensation. The 1964 Constitution retains the provision of the 1956 law which allowed the state to fix the maximum limits of private ownership.

From the above one can conclude that the extent and capacity of private ownership depends on the will of the political agencies of the state rather than on the Constitution itself. Socialism, we should add, has become an

6. Text in *Middle East Affairs,* VII (February, 1956), 68–81.
7. Amos J. Peaslee, *Constitutions of Nations* (The Hague, Netherlands: Martinus Nijhoff, 1965), vol. I, pp. 988–1008.

important aspect of Egyptian constitutional theory; it is considered an essential element of Egyptian life. Thus, Article 23 makes it the responsibility of the armed forces of Egypt to protect "the socialist gains" of the people.

The 1964 Constitution introduces new changes in the executive and legislative branches of the government but does not change the all-powerful position of the president as established in the 1956 Constitution. The position of prime minister, which did not exist under the 1956 law, is added by the 1964 law. However, although the prime minister shares responsibility with the president, he may not challenge his authority. He is appointed and may be dismissed by the president, and although he usually presides over the meetings of the Council of Ministers, the president can take charge of these meetings if he wants to. The president has the power to introduce legislation in the National Assembly, to veto legislative proposals passed by that body, and to order its dissolution, provided new elections are held within sixty days and he does not dissolve the new Assembly for the same reason. In addition, he can declare a state of emergency and rule by decree. And there are other cases in which he can rule by decree, although sometimes the approval of the Assembly is required, at least ultimately.

The 1956 Constitution permitted the National Assembly to force the resignation of individual ministers but not the entire ministry. (There was no prime minister under the 1956 law.) However, the prime minister and the ministers are now both collectively and individually responsible to the Assembly, which by a vote of no confidence can compel their resignation. It is important to note that when the legislature compels the resignation of the prime minister and the ministers collectively or individually, the president's tenure is not affected in any way. The only way to get rid of the president is by impeachment—a process limited to charges of high treason or disloyalty to the Republic.

THE UNITED ARAB REPUBLIC: 1958–1961

In 1958 a new Arab state was established out of two formerly independent countries, Syria and Egypt. The unification of the two countries was prompted primarily by Syria's fear of the Communist party, which had gained sufficient influence in the Syrian army to enable it to challenge the country's legitimate and nationalist government. Although Nasser did not initially favor unity with Syria, he was persuaded to change his mind. Consequently, plans for the merger were announced on February 1, 1958, and on March 5 a provisional constitution for the new state, the United Arab Republic, was declared.

The governmental structure of the newly created state was similar to that of Egypt prior to the union. At the national level, there was a National Assembly and an Executive Council headed by the president of the republic. Similar bodies were established at the regional level for each country. (Egypt became known as the Southern region and Syria as the Northern region.) The union was not based upon a federal principle; rather, it was a unitary state with power concentrated at the national level and with the president the dominant political figure. The National Assembly had six hundred seats, four hundred for Egypt and two hundred for Syria. The system of elections was overcomplicated, but the National Union, the only licensed party in the two regions, controlled the electoral process. Of course, this party was organized and controlled by Nasser, who was elected president of the new republic on February 21, 1958. For most of its existence (1958–61), the United Arab Republic was actually governed by executive decree, and the legislative bodies created by the provisional constitution were nothing more than rubber stamps.

Syrian officers in September 1961 disrupted the union in a successful coup. Thus, the hopes of the Arab nationalists to develop the republic into a larger Arab union were destroyed, perhaps permanently. Why did the experiment in Arab unity fail? The most significant causes, perhaps, were the institutional and cultural differences between the countries—of which neither country was sufficiently aware. For example, French rule in Syria (1920–43) had left its mark upon the political and legal institutions of that country; British rule in Egypt (1882–1922) had had a different set of influences upon Egypt. There were also temperamental political differences between the Syrian and the Egyptian people. The Syrians had difficulties submitting to political authority; the Egyptians were more submissive. Perhaps this is why Syria was politically less stable than Egypt.

During the period of unity, the Syrians became resentful of Nasser's authoritarian, highly centralized system of control. Through his Syrian protégé, Abdul Hamid al-Sarraj, his political opponents were severely dealt with. Syrians had to accept an inferior position to Egyptians in the conduct of their own affairs, and many of them began to think that the union was not a partnership but an Egyptian experiment in colonial rule.

Geography also contributed to the failure of the union. The two countries were separated by a common enemy, Israel, and by the Mediterranean Sea. From a purely administrative point of view, it was difficult, if not impossible, to rule Syria from Cairo. Of course, the union being one of a unitary state made the administrative task even more complicated.

The economic policies of Nasser were the last straw in the series of events which culminated in Syria's defection from the United Arab Republic. In 1961 Syria's banks and a number of her private enterprises were nationalized, alienating the already irritated business and conservative elements of Syrian society. These elements found an important ally in the high command of the Syrian army, which by this time (September 1961) resented Egyptian overlordship in the military establishment. It is important to remember that before the union the Syrian army had assumed a major political role in Syrian affairs; its inferior role under the union was difficult to accept. The political alliance between conservative businessmen and the army brought about the military coup of 1961 which ended the republic.

THE PROBLEM OF DEMOCRACY

Western observers often raise important questions about democracy in underdeveloped countries and criticize the authoritarian character of political life in these countries. In doing so, they tend to judge foreign systems by their own cultural and political standards, not realizing that in many parts of the world established traditions and unique historical forces make it difficult for democracies of the Western type to develop. They also fail to realize that what may not be suitable and desirable for their own countries is very often the best alternative—or the only alternative—available to other people and other countries. This is not to argue that authoritarian regimes are better than democratic regimes but rather to point out that, when authoritarianism exists, there are powerful causes for its existence.

No student of history would have expected the Egyptian revolution to be the beginning of democracy in Egypt. On the contrary, most historians were not surprised to see the authoritarian tradition continue to characterize the political system after 1952. They knew that the parliamentary system which existed in Egypt between 1923 and 1952 was a complete failure. Political parties, which Westerners think are important elements in their democracies, did not, in Egypt, fulfill their responsibilities as pillars of democracy or as guardians of the public interest. Nor was constitutionalism, another element of Western democracy, a vital element in the tradition of the country. Consequently, political democracy in Egypt was doomed long before the coming of the revolution in 1952.

NASSER'S POLITICAL PHILOSOPHY

Nasser strengthened traditional authoritarianism by tightening the political system and by centralizing the administrative bureaucracy. He believed he was giving Egypt something she needed for a long time: an honest government with a serious purpose. If he were not to consolidate his position and centralize the political system, the old, corrupt regime would have returned to power and commenced another period of misrule. He therefore believed it was his responsibility to protect the people by preventing this from happening.

Furthermore, Nasser believed his country was not ready for democracy, an argument often advanced by many Arab intellectuals with regard to the future of democracy in their countries. It raises perplexing questions: When will they be ready, or will they ever be ready? Sometimes one wonders whether the argument reflects genuine concern about democracy or whether it is made only to isolate Western opposition to and suspicion of such regimes. It may also be that the argument is intended to provide a moral justification for authoritarianism by arguing that it is neccessary as well as temporary.

But whatever the merits and faults of these arguments, we are well advised to consider them irrelevant. The fact is that authoritarianism, like democracy, is the product of a complex situation and that it exists in the same way as democracy, that is, as part of the intricate workings of a society's life.

In any case, Nasser thought a transitional period was essential (1) to prevent a return to old methods and the old regime; (2) to launch revolutionary reforms which would put the country in the right direction; and (3) to prepare the people for responsible democracy while giving them the needed opportunity to reconstruct their social and political institutions.

Nasser makes a distinction between social and political democracy, the latter being impossible without first establishing the former. For him, social democracy implies a fluid social structure, without which political democracy cannot exist. Nasser maintains that the class structure that existed under the old regime was too rigid and that this rigidity was in fact responsible for the failure of that regime. This is why his government accepted the important responsibility of eradicating social distinctions and great economic inequalities. While arguing along these lines, Nasser discovers a common dimension among democracy, nationalism, and socialism: each is based on a concept of public interest. Of course, the relationship between them remains theoretical so long as democracy is not a reality in Egypt.

Nasser, it should be emphasized, formulates a concept of democracy to defend his regime against attack from foreign critics, who frequently criticize him for being a dictator. Ironically, he need not be apologetic when it comes to the domestic, political implications of democracy, because the Egyptian people rarely make democracy an important issue. For them, democracy exists whenever the government pursues and fulfills national aspirations and national goals. It does not matter to them whether such a government is elected or not. They believe that since their aspirations are known it is unnecessary to have political institutions such as a parliament or a political party to discover them. Consequently, any regime that pursues these aspirations acts in accordance with the will of the people.

Why are these aspirations and goals so clearly visible? The answer, the argument continues, lies in the fact that the Egyptian people have fought for their attainment so hard and so long that they have become known to every Egyptian, generation after generation. Egyptian aspirations include such things as independence through expulsion of imperial interests, elimination of corruption in government, and a fair share for all citizens of the country's wealth and benefits.

This argument assumes that representative government and democratic procedures are necessary only in the countries where the national will is not always known; thus, some kind of a procedure is needed to discover it. Of course, this argument implies and assumes that public policy, aspirations, and goals are different names for the same thing and that they are static and absolute. Because of this, there is no disagreement as to what they are.

We know, however, that democracy involves much more than the achievement of a few goals such as independence, social justice, and honest government. Public policy is not a simple matter, and there is always disagreement over what constitutes the public interest. Furthermore, aspirations, goals, and policy, although interrelated, are not always identical. Consequently, Egyptian attitudes toward democracy oversimplify a highly complex process and give priority to a few national goals while ignoring almost everything else. In reality, these attitudes are not related to democracy but mostly to national aspirations. Egyptians argue that a leader who pursues national goals expresses the will of the people regardless of whether he allows political parties to operate or whether he is elected by the people. Therefore, a benevolent dictatorship is itself democratic. Although this statement is self-contradictory, it is nevertheless representative of Egyptian attitudes toward democracy. It also reflects similar attitudes in many other underdeveloped countries which have similar problems and aspirations.

While analyzing the contradictions in the Egyptian argument about democracy is helpful, we should be careful not to allow the discrepancies over the meaning of democracy to determine our attitudes toward the Egyptian regime. It should not be too difficult for us to understand how a country can, under certain circumstances, be so preoccupied with a few highly important goals that its comprehension of the whole concept of democratic government is confused. Democracy, after all, is the most difficult form of government, and countries that are mainly concerned with the attainment of certain goals usually find a democratic system of government too difficult to practice, even if it is possible to assume that these societies understand democracy and that there are no other obstacles to the application of democratic principles.

THE ECONOMY

Egypt's economic problems are even more serious than her political difficulties. Most Egyptians live in extreme poverty and ignorance. Per capita income in 1965 was less than $132 (as compared, for instance, with Britain's $1,439 and France's $1,379).[8] Economic improvements, especially with regard to the food supply, are usually offset by the growth of population of 2 per cent per year. (In 1897 Egypt had approximately nine million people; in 1965 it had over twenty-nine million.) In addition, Egypt's arable land amounts to less than 4 per cent of the country's total land area of 386,000 square miles, and about 60 per cent of the population lives and farms on this 4 per cent. Furthermore, in spite of recent emphasis on industrialization, cash crops still account for approximately 90 per cent of Egypt's exports. Thus, "Too many people on too little watered land is a fact of life in Egypt which presents any Egyptian government with desperate economic problems." [9] And improvements in the agricultural output, although possible, are limited because "yields per acre in Egypt are already among the highest in the world." [10]

Nasser's government thus has concluded that the creation of sources of wealth other than agricultural is the only way out of the economic dilemma. However, the recent emphasis on industrialization has not overlooked the possibility of increasing agricultural production by making more land cultivable. To do this, the Nasser government had to give a high priority to land-reclamation projects and spend a large proportion of Egypt's capital on such projects.

LAND-RECLAMATION PROJECTS

The highly publicized and internationally controversial Aswan Dam is the most important reclamation project and is essentially a multipurpose project. Designed to increase Egypt's cultivable land by two million acres by creating a reservoir of water covering an area of 739 square miles—the dam's primary purpose—it will also establish the largest power station in the world. This power station will increase Egypt's electric power tenfold, making it possible for Nasser's government to enlarge the country's industrial base.

The financing of the project involved many political complications of international significance, which we will discuss elsewhere. However, it can

8. *The New York Times,* April 16, 1967, p. 17.
9. Georgiana G. Stevens, *Egypt: Yesterday and Today* (New York: Holt, Rinehart & Winston, 1963), p. 135.
10. Kerr, *Egypt Under Nasser,* p. 18.

be said here that in addition to its economic significance, this extremely ambitious project is an important national goal and has great symbolic and psychological importance to the Egyptian people.

Other projects of lesser importance were initiated by the Nasser regime during the 1950's. Among these is the Liberation Province, which was to be composed of model agricultural settlements on reclaimed desert land.[11] In 1954, approximately 54,000 acres were allocated for this experiment. Reclamation was made possible by construction of a canal to carry water from the Nile. However, it is believed that this canal will not be able to provide Liberation Province with sufficient quantities of water over a long period of time, and the completion of the Aswan Dam is necessary for its success.

Much publicity was given to the Liberation Province. The Egyptian government invited many people, especially newsmen, from neighboring Arab countries to visit the province. Some were impressed and returned to their countries attesting to the great accomplishment of the Nasser regime. Obviously, the experiment is a major program when judged by Middle Eastern standards. But final judgment must be postponed, because—based upon Egypt's economic ability and the project's economic rewards—Liberation Province is too costly. Also, its future is in doubt because the settlers' enthusiasm for it has declined.

A third reclamation project is the New Valley. Drilling by army engineers in the Western Desert had revealed underground water in this area. However, whether there is a sufficient quantity of water for land-reclamation purposes is still unknown.[12]

The Soviet Union and the United States had contributed to similar reclamation projects. In 1965, the Soviet Union undertook to grant a loan for a reclamation project which would convert 200,000 acres of desert land into cultivable land.[13] Since 1953, the United States has assisted Egypt in reclamation projects in the Faiyum Province, southwest of Cairo, and in the Abis area, southeast of Alexandria. Under a program of cooperation between the Egyptian government and the American Point Four Program, the United States contributed $11.5 million toward the development of Faiyum and Abis projects. Egypt's contribution was $21 million.[14]

LAND REFORM

About the only program the revolutionary officers of 1952 were sure was necessary was a land-reform measure which would protect the Egyptian

11. For more details see Stevens, *Egypt: Yesterday and Today*, p. 145.

12. Stevens, *Egypt: Yesterday and Today*, p. 146.

13. *The New International Year Book: 1965* (New York: Funk & Wagnalls, 1966), p. 492.

14. Stevens, *Egypt: Yesterday and Today*, p. 147.

peasant and establish a maximum for land ownership. The problem can best be explained by a careful look at the following 1952 figures. The total number of landowners then was 2,800,000, and the total area of cultivable land was less than 6,000,000 feddans (1 feddan = 1.038 acres). However, 2,000,000 of these owners had less than one feddan each, and half a million had less than five feddans (5.2 acres) each. Only 11,000 people owned one-third of all the cultivable land of Egypt.[15]

Since the small farmer could not make a decent living from his plot, he had no alternative but to rent additional land from the big farmer. But because land yields were high, land rent was also extremely high. Furthermore, the price of cotton—Egypt's major crop in the world market—was often extremely high by Egyptian standards, and the big landowner acquired a large income from the sale of cotton. Consequently, his desire to rent out land was limited, and the small farmer continued to suffer from exploitation by the big landlords.

To remedy this situation, the revolutionary government issued, in September 1952, the Agrarian Reform Law. This law limited individual holdings to 207 acres; it allowed families up to 104 additional acres, which could be retained by the owner's children provided no child received more than 52 acres. Anything in excess was either to be sold by the original owner directly to other individuals or be given to the state in return for a thirty-year government bond. Direct sale had to be made before October 31, 1953; government bonds were to yield the owner 3 per cent interest. The land was assessed at a value equal to its tax value, which had been assessed by the former regime at an extremely low rate; thus, the big landowner who had been able to influence the tax assessor of the old regime received a low price for his property under the new agrarian law.

The government planned to resell the land it acquired to peasants, in parcels of three to five acres. The buyer was to pay for his new property in easy installments, and he received government assistance in the way of credit, marketing facilities, and technical knowhow. In other words, the government intended to provide the new owner with some guidance as to how he could increase the productivity of his land.

However, so few landowners held more than the total allowable 207 acres that only 7 per cent of the arable land (and approximately two thousand landowners) were affected by the law. By the summer of 1961, 446,340 acres had been redistributed by the government, but this arrangement had no effect on agricultural production. Consequently, a governmental decree of July 1961 reduced the limit of individual holdings to 104 acres.

The 1952 Agrarian Reform Law also tackled the problem of high rent

15. *The Middle East and North Africa 1964–65*, p. 646.

and low wages. A ceiling was imposed on land rent, and a minimum wage for hired farm labor was fixed at 18 piasters (about 50 cents) per day for men and 10 piasters for women. Although this wage minimum is very small by American standards, it was adequate by Egyptian standards.

When evaluating the impact of the Agrarian Reform Law upon Egypt's economy, we should not forget the magnitude of the problems which this law was trying to deal with. Thus, the reform's benefits to the whole economy could not be expected to be substantial. A fundamental problem, of course, is that Egypt's population has been increasing at the rate of 600,000 a year, thereby minimizing some of the positive effects of the reform law upon Egypt's economy. Also, since the yield of land was already among the highest in the world, the land-redistribution program did not increase agricultural production; instead, it resulted in the redistribution of income. Nevertheless, the recipients of the new land benefited from the reform measures. And, of course, the destruction of the old aristocracy of Egypt was among the goals of the new middle-class-oriented regime; the Agrarian Reform Law crushed Egypt's traditional social stratification.

NASSER'S ARAB SOCIALISM

Nasser's socialism is not an elaborate economic theory: rather, it has been a pragmatic program designed to do four important things: (1) implement the protest against concentration of economic power in the hands of a small group that wielded too much power under the monarchy; (2) realize the desire of the revolutionary regime to establish social justice and improve the social and economic conditions of the lower classes; (3) realize, also, the regime's desire to modernize and industrialize the country and to bring her up to the level of the advanced countries; and (4) make effective the regime's protest against Western capitalism, which Nasser considered to be imperialistic and exploitative.[16]

Nasser's socialism differs from Marxist socialism in several significant ways: it rejects the theory of economic determinism and the theory of the class struggle; it establishes a nonproletarian dictatorship as the political system of Egypt; and it leaves the ownership of land in private hands while exerting substantial government control over the agricultural sector of the economy.

Nasser's socialism also differs from Soviet socialism. In economic development, for example, Nasser seems unwilling to concentrate on heavy industry, fearing that such a policy would require too much sacrifice on the part of the people, as it required of the Soviet people in the 1930's. An

16. For more details on the subject of Arab socialism see G. H. Torrey and J. F. Devlin, "Arab Socialism," *Modernization of the Arab World,* ed. Jack H. Thompson and Robert D. Reischaur (Princeton: Van Nostrand, 1966), pp. 178–96.

emphasis on heavy industry would require the postponement of satisfying immediate and temporary demands, including that for consumer goods. Nasser is very conscious of the fact that his people suffered for too long under the old regimes and that they deserve relief from their burdens.

Public ownership of the means of production and the enlargement of government's role in the economy did not take place in Egypt until 1960, when the National Bank of Egypt, a commercial bank founded in 1898, was fully nationalized. Prior to this time, the government was content to leave domestic industry and finance in private hands; nationalization was limited to foreign-owned firms and the Suez Canal. However, once begun, the nationalization program proceeded rapidly. In June 1960, the press was nationalized, and the Cairo bus services were placed under municipal control. A year later, cotton exporting firms were nationalized. In July 1961, the state acquired varying degrees of control over 275 industries and trading agencies; all banks and insurance companies were nationalized; and a steeply progressive tax system was adopted. Industrial companies were required to distribute 25 per cent of their profits to their workers and to assign workers' representatives two seats on their boards of directors.

By the end of 1961, the means of finance, production, and exchange were controlled by the government, which also owned one-third of the distributive trades. By the end of 1963, very little was left to private enterprise: only agriculture and the wholesale and retail trades were not government owned. Socialism had become a reality.

INDUSTRIALIZATION AND TRADE

Since 1957, industrialization in Egypt has proceeded in accordance with a series of five-year plans. The first plan, coming into effect in July 1957, invested £E 230 million (U.S. dollars = £E 0.348 official rate) in industry, mainly in textiles, motor vehicles, cement, and phosphates. This plan was absorbed by another, still more ambitious, five-year plan launched in 1960, which provided for an investment of £E 459 million. The second plan emphasized small-scale industry, whereas the first had stressed consumer goods. According to government sources, the 1960–65 plan had an average growth rate in the industrial sector of 815 per cent.[17]

Egyptian sources rely on national-income and value-of-production figures for economic data. This is a crude basis of evaluation because it could very easily conceal inefficiency and bad planning.[18] However, there is no doubt that the revolutionary leaders of Egypt are determined to industrialize the country and to improve its economic conditions. Thus the seven-year plan which began in 1965 emphasized capital goods.

17. *The Egyptian Gazette,* August 4, 1966, p. 5.
18. Peter Mansfield, *Nasser's Egypt* (Baltimore: Penguin Books, 1965), p. 145.

The Egyptian leaders are also aware of the importance of foreign trade and of the promotion of exports to the success of industrial development. The General Trade Organization, established in 1962 to regulate both imports and exports,[19] is invested with the responsibility of providing capital as well as consumer goods, raw materials, and auxiliary products. Perhaps its most crucial task is to increase exports for the purpose of acquiring as much foreign exchange as possible. This task has been complicated by the impact of the Arab-Israeli war.

Since 1966 there has been a tendency toward centralizing trade controls. Commodity boards were established for every group of industrial products, and they were given the responsibility of investigating trade offers and selecting the most suitable of such offers. The work of government departments concerned with foreign trade is integrated by a council at the ministerial level.

In spite of improvements in the trade organization, Egypt has been running a trade deficit. In 1957 this deficit was reduced by import restrictions, but in 1958 it resumed its upward movement. One problem is that Egypt must buy more things than she can sell: she imports wheat, fertilizers, and also a large variety of equipment and machinery needed for development projects. On the other hand, Egypt's exports are not as diversified as her imports, partly because she must rely on cotton, her major crop. When this fails, as in 1966, when bad weather reduced the yield of cotton, so do exports; but exports rose in 1967, when new aerial spraying techniques and better weather improved the yields.

Egypt's balance-of-payments situation is not good. There have been instances when the lack of foreign exchange hindered production; but the situation from 1957 to 1967 would have been worse if it were not for the steady increase in the Suez Canal revenues. However, the 1967 war with Israel resulted in the closing of the canal for shipping. This in turn resulted in the loss of nearly $300 million in annual Suez Canal revenues. Had it not been for the subsidy of about $280 million from Saudi Arabia, Kuwait, and Libya, which offset the loss, Egypt's economic problems would have been enormous. The 1967 war also affected the tourist industry, which had been an important potential for increasing foreign-currency income. It forced the government to reconsider its plans to spend $80 million for tourism and new hotel construction by 1972.

EGYPTIAN FOREIGN POLICY

In his book, *The Philosophy of the Revolution,* Nasser refers to a "group of circles" in which, so to speak, Egyptian foreign policy oper-

19. *The Egyptian Gazette,* July 25, 1966, p. 5.

ates.[20] The first circle is the Arab world, which is "as much of us as we are a part of it." The African continent is the second circle, "in which fate has placed us." And finally the Muslim world, "with which we are tied by bonds which are not only forged by religious faith but also tightened by history." According to Nasser, these circles are Egypt's "theater of activity."

ARAB POLICY

Geographically, the "Arab world" comprises a large portion of the Muslim world. The Muslim peoples outside the Arab world, especially the Turkish people, have not been significantly susceptible to Nasser's influence. Pakistan's friendly attitude toward the Arabs has not been motivated by Egypt's revolutionary regime. Thus, of the three circles the Arab world is the most important. It is also the area in which Egyptian influence has been the greatest, for the Arab countries share a common language, a common religion (with the possible exception of Lebanon), and a common history.

Nasser's Concept of the Arab Alliance. History provides ample evidence that the leaders of Egypt were normally *Egyptian* nationalists, not Arab nationalists. Arabi, Zaghlul, Kamil, and Lutfi, all mentioned earlier, are examples. Mohammed Ali, however, who ruled Egypt during the first half of the nineteenth century and who was neither Egyptian nor Arab, espoused a Pan-Arab policy whose object was to build an Arab empire. But his policy had nothing to do with Arab nationalism, which did not develop until the end of the nineteenth century. It was motivated by his personal ambition to become a world leader and by his desire to use the Arabic-speaking peoples against the Turks in an effort to destroy Ottoman supremacy in the Middle East. Although it failed, Mohammed Ali's policy was a rational one for an Egyptian leader who aspired to world prominence. The assistance of her Arab neighbors would make Egypt appear much stronger on the world political scene than she could hope to be without them.

Nasser, who was anxious to become a great hero, discovered that a modified version of Ali's policy could make him a leader of world stature. Initially, however, he conceived of the establishment of a strong Arab alliance (rather than an Arab empire) under Egypt's leadership and guidance. Such an alliance, he believed, would enhance Egypt's international position and would also enable her to counteract British influence more effectively than if she remained alone. Nasser did not introduce this policy immediately after the 1952 revolution, however. At that time, the leaders of the revolu-

20. Gamal Abdel Nasser, *The Philosophy of the Revolution* (Buffalo: Smith, Keynes & Marshal, 1959), p. 59.

tion were nationalists whose main concern was Egypt. They did not formulate an Arab policy of significance until eighteen months later.

Nasser pursued his Arab policies for approximately three years, from 1955 to 1958. The more he became involved in Arab affairs, the more he ran into serious difficulties with his alliance policy. He was challenged mainly by Nuri Said, the pro-Western prime minister of Iraq, who, in January 1955, committed his country to an agreement, also signed by Turkey, which became the basis for the Baghdad Pact, a Middle Eastern defense organization supported by Great Britain and, indirectly, by the United States.[21]

Nasser opposed the pact on the grounds that it was a form of Western interference in Arab affairs as well as an attempt on the part of Western imperialism to divide the Arab world. He preferred the establishment of an Arab defense organization under the Arab League.

Nasser denounced the Iraqi leader as a reactionary stooge of Western imperialism. All of Egypt's propaganda machinery—the best in the Arab world—was put behind Nasser's opposition to the Baghdad Pact. The immediate impact of this was to make Nasser the great hero of the Arab nationalists throughout the Arab world, including Iraq itself. These nationalists, eager to free their countries from Western influence and desiring the unification of the Arab states in a single national state, saw in Nasser a potential leader. However, Nasser at this point neither advocated nor desired more than an Arab alliance; the idea of Arab unity under a single state was not part of his thinking or planning.

Several other important incidents contributed to Nasser's hero image, providing evidence to Arab nationalists that he was not only an independent and brave leader but a shrewd statesman who could successfully challenge the Western powers. His independence was demonstrated by his decision in September 1955 to purchase large quantities of arms from Czechoslovakia and by his recognition of Communist China in May 1956. His reputation as a statesman was established in the nationalists' minds when he nationalized the Suez Canal on July 26, 1956. The Suez crisis increased his popularity immensely in Egypt and throughout the Arab world.

But the policy of alliance, although beneficial to Egypt, split the Arab world into two camps—liberal nationalist and conservative monarchist. The liberals' strength came from the support of the Arab masses. In the Fertile Crescent area, only Syria belonged to this camp, although a substantial conservative element, opposed to Nasser, also existed there. The conservative group included Saudi Arabia, Jordan, and Iraq, although Nasser had much support from the people of these countries. The governments

21. For more details on Nasser's Arab policy see Chapter 3 in Mansfield, *Nasser's Egypt*, pp. 53–76.

of the conservative countries were basically opposed to Nasser, especially during 1957, because they feared that the success of the Arab nationalists would result in the abolition of their monarchical regimes. Their fear was justified in view of the fact that the Arab nationalists were republican.

Lebanon, a republican state, constituted a special category. It was pro-Western and desired to preserve its independence against the trend toward unification. Consequently, Lebanon leaned toward conservatism, although it really had no genuine sympathies with the conservative monarchies.

Nasser's Concept of Arab Unity. We mentioned earlier that Nasser, though the hero of the Arab nationalists, did not believe in a single Arab national state; this was the main difference between him and his followers and admirers in the neighboring Arab countries. But the growth of his reputation and popularity after the Suez crisis was a major factor in his conversion to Arab nationalism. By the end of 1957, it was clear that Nasser had become the most powerful figure in the Middle East: nothing could happen without taking into account his views and his desires. However, the alliance policy was incapable of properly exploiting this new political stature. Any alliance is essentially a relationship between governments, not peoples, and in the Arab Middle East there were more governments opposed to Nasser than aligned with him. His personal power and his popularity was with the people, but this popularity could not be used for political gain through the policy of alliance. Something new was needed.

This something new was a call for the unification of the Arab states. The groundwork for the change in Nasser's views on unification was laid by his popularity and by his appeal to the Arab masses. But it took some effort on the part of others to make this change possible for Nasser, who still doubted the workability of the new policy. The effort was made by the Baath party of Syria, which was a major force in the 1957 coalition government of Syria; their motivation was, primarily, fear of a possible Communist takeover in Syria.

The establishment of the United Arab Republic, discussed earlier, marked the end of Nasser's alliance policy and the beginning of his new policy of Arab unity. The new policy insisted on the dissolution of the existing Arab states in favor of a political merger with the United Arab Republic under the presidency of Nasser. This, of course, meant that the Arab monarchical regimes could not exist as they did under the alliance system. Also, Lebanon could not preserve her independence or sovereignty. Consequently, it was to be expected that the attack on the leaders of the conservative Arab camp would be intensified after 1958.

Problems of the Arab Unity Policy. The struggle was in fact intensified, and for at least a short time in 1958 there was a possibility that Nasser might succeed in annexing Lebanon and Iraq. A civil war in Lebanon in

May 1958 involved pro-Nasser elements. Although these elements failed to destroy Lebanon's independence, Nasser's influence in Lebanon remained strong even after the settlement of the civil war.

In Iraq, a military coup by Brigadier General Abdul Karim Kassem on July 14, 1958, lent hope that Iraq would seek closer ties with Egypt, especially since Kassem's deputy, Colonel Arif, announced shortly after the coup that he would favor an immediate Iraqi-Egyptian merger. Unfortunately for both Nasser and the Arab nationalists, Kassem had no intention of jeopardizing his leadership in Iraq by such a merger. Consequently, Arif was jailed, and any hope for a union with Nasser's United Arab Republic disappeared.

Nasser's ambitions in Lebanon and Iraq collapsed, but his failure in Syria was even worse. The Syrian military coup of September 1961 ended the union between the two countries and proved that Nasser's more ambitious policy of Arab unity would be far more difficult to implement than his earlier policy of Arab alliance. Obviously, a revision of the policy of Arab unity was necessary after 1961. Nasser's experience in the U.A.R. taught him an important lesson: Arab unity was impossible as long as the Arab states continued to have serious differences in their social systems. The failure of the republic, Nasser believed, was due to Syrian opposition to his 1961 socialistic reforms. Consequently, the merger of Arab states should be preceded by a transitional period during which the social systems of the merging states would have to be modified until they became similar. Only then could Arab unity survive and endure.

This new approach to Arab unity was used on April 17, 1963, when Egypt, Syria, and Iraq agreed to join in a federal union. The decision was made possible by an anti-Kassem coup in Iraq (February 9, 1963) and another coup in Syria (March 1963), which brought the Arab nationalists to power in the two countries. The three countries agreed to establish a federal state after a transitional period of twenty months, the purpose of which was to bring their social systems closer together.

Nasser's idea of a transitional period proved to be sound. One month after the three countries agreed to federate, Egypt felt obliged to revoke her decision regarding the new federal union because, Nasser declared, Egypt could no longer cooperate with the Baath party, which dominated the governments of Syria and Iraq. The reason was obvious: the Baath party, although it also advocated Arab unity, did not want Nasser to dominate the union. Plans for the federal state were therefore suspended, and the Arab world was now more divided than ever before: in addition to the Nasserite and conservative groups, there was a third, an anti-Nasser Pan-Arab element, which included the Baathists and others.

The Yemeni War. Nasser's failure to unite the Arabs was not his only problem with the Arab countries; more pressing was his involvement in the Yemeni war which broke out in September 1962. The war followed a military coup, led by Yemeni General Abdullah Sallal, that succeeded in overthrowing the monarchy. However, the ousted monarch, Imam Badr, escaped from the capital and, gathering around him tribes loyal to him, regained control of much of the country. Egypt aided Sallal's republican regime, while Saudi Arabia, herself a monarchy, helped Imam Badr in his quest to regain his throne as well as the capital. Neither the Sallal forces nor the Badr forces were able to achieve a final military victory, and Yemeni territory was divided without the conclusion of a peace treaty.

Nasser's difficulty in the Yemeni war consisted of the fact that he committed one-third of his army to support the Yemeni republican regime. This was an expensive operation, especially since the war continued much longer than was anticipated. Efforts during 1966 and early 1967 to settle it were unsuccessful. However, after Egypt's defeat by Israel in June 1967, it became necessary for Egypt to concentrate on defending her own territory against Israeli military threat and Egyptian troops were withdrawn from Yemen. An agreement to end the five-year civil war in Yemen was reached on August 31, 1967, between President Nasser and King Faisal of Saudi Arabia. A committee consisting of three Arab states—Iraq, Morocco, and the Sudan—was formed to supervise the withdrawal of Egyptian troops from Yemen and the end of Saudi Arabia's assistance to royalist Yemenis. By January 1968, Egypt was no longer militarily involved in Yemen.

EGYPT AND GREAT BRITAIN

In 1952, when the military coup took place in Egypt, Anglo-Egyptian relations were at their worst, and the new Egyptian regime inherited many unsettled problems, including the crucial question of the Suez Canal. However, during the first two years of its existence, the military junta was preoccupied with establishing control over the country; it did not involve itself in such highly controversial foreign-policy issues as Egypt's relations with Britain for fear of endangering its domestic power position.

Later, however, it became possible for Egypt to enter into negotiations with Britain, and in July 1954 the countries signed a treaty in which Britain agreed to withdraw her troops from the Suez Canal within twenty months.[22] Egypt agreed to allow British troops to return to the Suez in case of an attack on any member of the Arab League or on Turkey. She also agreed to honor the provisions in the Constantinople Convention of 1888 guaranteeing freedom of navigation.

Although the 1954 treaty was a reasonable settlement of a complicated

22. Text of the treaty in J. C. Hurewitz, ed., *Diplomacy in the Near and Middle East* (Princeton: Van Nostrand, 1956), vol. II, pp. 383–84.

and serious situation, in terms of domestic implication it did very little for Nasser. The Muslim Brotherhood argued that if the 1936 Anglo-Egyptian Treaty was allowed to run its course (it was abrogated in 1951 by the Wafd government), it would have expired in 1956; this meant that the 1954 treaty did not acquire any additional benefits for Egypt. While this argument wrongly assumed the automatic withdrawal of British troops upon the expiration of the 1936 treaty, it had some appeal in certain segments of Egyptian society. Nevertheless, the 1954 agreement created optimism about the future of Anglo-Egyptian relations. British troops were withdrawn from the canal zone by the beginning of 1956. Furthermore, Britain, along with the United States and the World Bank, promised to help finance the enormous Aswan Dam project.

The Suez Crisis. The optimism for the future of Anglo-Egyptian relations vanished with British sponsorship of the Baghdad Pact early in 1955, and a major crisis developed when Nasser decided, on July 26, 1956, to nationalize the Suez Canal Company. This decision was prompted by American Secretary of State John Foster Dulles' announcement of the withdrawal of the United States offer to assist in financing the Aswan Dam. Secretary Dulles believed that Egypt's economy could not sustain such a costly project and that the economic benefits to be derived from the project were doubtful. Nasser claimed that nationalization of the company was necessary to enable Egypt to obtain the revenues needed for financing the dam project since the United States was no longer willing to help. However, there is evidence that Nasser was considering nationalization before the Aswan Dam controversy began.[23]

Britain's reaction to the nationalization of the company was violent. The conservative government of Anthony Eden considered the canal to be of vital importance to Great Britain, and no doubt the canal also had symbolic meaning to the British insofar as it reminded them of their great imperial past. Nasser promised to compensate the owners of the company (Britain controlled 44 per cent of the company's stocks); but Eden was worried about the possible effect on British shipping, which in 1955 had accounted for 28.3 per cent of the total canal tonnage. Also, the Eden government held the view that Nasser had no legal right to nationalize the company, claiming that the canal had a special status under the 1888 Constantinople Convention.[24] Eden, therefore, was determined to prevent Egypt's unilateral control of the Suez even if he had to use force.

23. Wheelock, *Nasser's New Egypt,* p. 238.
24. For details regarding the British argument as well as the implication of the Suez crisis upon British domestic politics see James B. Christoph, "The Suez Crisis," *Cases in Comparative Politics* (Boston: Little, Brown and Company, 1965), pp. 90–124.

The Egyptian argument [25] was that the Suez Canal was an Egyptian company subject to Egyptian laws; that compensation was offered to the company shareholders; that the nationalization decision would not interfere with freedom of navigation; and that the 1888 Constantinople Convention did not explicitly require the company to maintain freedom of passage through the canal.

However, Britain, France, and the United States refused to accept the Egyptian argument. They insisted that the canal remain under international control, and at their request, an international conference of twenty-two nations met in London in August 1956. The convention proposed the establishment of an international board to consist of Egypt and eighteen other users of the canal, to take charge of its management and development. A committee of five, under the chairmanship of Prime Minister Menzies of Australia, was sent to persuade Nasser to accept the decisions of the conference. Nasser refused on the grounds that they compromised Egyptian sovereignty.

When the first attempt failed, Secretary of State Dulles proposed a new plan, which would establish a Suez Canal Users Association consisting of maritime nations using the canal. The association would hire its own canal pilots and charge fees for its services. The expenses of its operations would come out of revenue from its fees and the remaining portion of such revenue would be paid to Egypt. This second plan was only slightly different from the first, and it was approved by another London conference on September 21, 1956.

Before Nasser could consider the second plan, however, Dulles made known the fact that the United States would not be prepared to back the plan by force. This, of course, frustrated the British hope that Nasser might yield to American pressure in the form of possible joint military intervention. A last attempt for a peaceful solution failed in October when the Soviet Union vetoed a United Nations Security Council resolution calling for negotiations on the basis of the principle of international control of the canal.

With the failure of these efforts, military intervention by at least Britain became a serious possibility. France was willing to participate because she was irritated by Nasser's financial and military aid to the Algerian rebels. Israel, claiming Nasser was menacing her security by attacks on her borders, was also anxious "to teach Nasser a lesson." Consequently, the three countries became involved in the events of October 1956 which culminated in a serious international crisis. Whether all three were in "collusion" prior to the events of October remains questionable for lack of conclusive evidence, although the uncertainty applies only to Israel's role. There is ample

25. Wheelock, *op. cit.*, p. 239.

evidence that at least France and Britain had a prior agreement regarding the invasion of Egypt; and in the case of Israel there is "a great deal of circumstantial evidence" pointing in the same direction.[26]

The events leading up to the invasion are easily recounted. On October 29, Israeli forces crossed the Egyptian borders and moved swiftly in the direction of the canal; the next day, Britain and France gave both Egypt and Israel an ultimatum demanding that their forces remain at a ten-mile distance from either side of the canal. On October 31, the Anglo-French invasion began.

The impact of these events upon the international situation was enormous: there was an uproar of resentment and emotion in every Arab city and town, including those in the anti-Nasser states; the Soviet Union threatened to bomb London and Paris with rocket missiles and send "volunteers" to help Egypt; and the Afro-Asian states denounced the invading countries as imperialists. In Great Britain domestic opposition was serious enough to endanger the political future of the Eden government. Most important, however, was the opposition of the United States, a position which was extremely difficult for her. On the one hand, the United States resented the fact that Britain and France did not consult her prior to their decision to invade Egypt. On the other, she disliked being forced to be on the same side of the controversy as her adversary, the Soviet Union.

The almost unanimous opposition of the world community was too great for the invaders to ignore. The Anglo-French effort collapsed, and Israel was forced, owing to American pressure, to withdraw behind the original boundary line. Perhaps the most important factor in the collapse was the United States threat to impose economic sanctions against the invading countries. Soviet threats also contributed to the Anglo-French setback, reminding the world of the dangers of a general war in the Middle East. Furthermore, the General Assembly of the United Nations, with unprecedented speed, ordered the invading countries to withdraw their forces from Egypt immediately. On November 6, one week after the invasion was started, Britain complied with these orders, and the other invading countries followed suit. The Suez war was over. Although Nasser lost the battle against the invaders because of his poor military showing, he won the war and proved that he was either a brilliant statesman or a lucky gambler.

EGYPT AND THE UNITED STATES

John S. Badeau, United States ambassador to Egypt from 1961 to 1964, once pointed out that American relations with Egypt had been beset by a

---

26. John G. Stoessinger, *The Might of Nations* (New York: Random House, 1965), p. 122.

"crisis of confidence" [27]—the product of misconceptions and suspicions between two countries regarding each other's policies. Both countries were responsible for the development of the crisis, and both needed to make a strenuous effort to improve relations and promote friendship. However, they must first understand the difficulties which created the "crisis of confidence" before they could hope for improvement.

American Contribution to the Crisis of Confidence. One of these difficulties has been the unpredictability of United States policy toward Egypt, which had been characterized by sudden and frequent shifts in position. From 1952, when the Egyptian revolution took place, until 1955, when Egypt began to purchase arms from Czechoslovakia, the United States attempted to pursue and promote friendly relations with Egypt. But thereafter and until shortly before the end of the Eisenhower administration, the United States attempted to isolate Egypt from her Arab neighbors and reduce her influence in the Middle East and Africa.

Then when, according to Badeau, this policy failed (since Nasser's influence during much of this period increased), the United States began, gradually and cautiously, to make friendly overtures to Egypt. But this new policy was not pursued vigorously until the coming of the Kennedy administration in January 1961.

United States support to the anti-Nasser Arab states was one source of trouble, but Egypt's lack of confidence in the United States was caused primarily by the latter's policy and attitude toward Israel. Egypt, as well as the other Arab countries, believes that the creation of the State of Israel would have been virtually impossible had it not been for the support which Palestinian Jews received from American Jews and from the United States government. Furthermore, most Egyptians believe that the United States would not pursue an independent Middle East policy—based on her own national interest—because of pressure from American Jews, who, according to these Egyptians, wield too much influence and power in American politics. As long as the Arab-Israeli dispute continued to have an important place in American electoral campaigns, they believed the United States would not understand the Arab point of view. The possibility of clarifying the other issues between the two countries exists, but to lessen the impact of the Israeli issue is most difficult.

Egyptian Contribution to the Crisis of Confidence. Egypt too shares responsibility for the mutual suspicion which has characterized Egyptian-American relations. The United States has been irritated by Egyptian med-

27. John S. Badeau, "U.S.A. and U.A.R.: A Crisis in Confidence," *Foreign Affairs*, January, 1965, pp. 281–96. I am indebted to Professor Badeau's excellent study for many of the observations that follow in this section.

dling in the affairs of other countries. Some of this meddling is unjustified, although the Nasser regime feels that it is its duty to export Egypt's revolution to countries which still suffer from colonial rule. However, Egyptian interference in the affairs of other countries does not always serve the interests of Egypt, and the United States cannot understand this aspect of Nasser's foreign policy. At any rate, Nasser's activities in the Arab world and Africa very often conflict with United States policies there, creating friction, annoyance, and frustration between the two countries.

Furthermore, the United States cannot understand why Egypt, with her need for economic assistance, spends so much of her revenue on propaganda at home and abroad and in attempts to help other revolutionary regimes in pursuing anti-Western policies. Also, the United States considers Nasser's acceptance of Soviet economic assistance as a dangerous policy that could result in the total dependence of Egypt upon the Soviet Union. Of course, the Egyptian army is armed by the Soviet Union; that in itself is a dangerous situation, since the Egyptian army is in control of political power.

The "crisis of confidence" is a stumbling block in the improvement of American-Egyptian relations. Badeau believes the two countries can eliminate some of the conflicts in their relations since many of their interests are reconcilable as well as compatible. He also believes the task of improving these relations is not easy but that the policy-makers in the two countries must try.

The Eisenhower Doctrine. Immediately after the Suez crisis, there was hope that the United States image in Egypt might change. However, it soon became clear that United States opposition to the Anglo-French invasion had not been intended to introduce a friendly policy toward Egypt but was a reluctant course of action necessitated by the exigencies of international relations and by America's own sense of security and morality. As soon as the crisis was over, the United States reverted to the policy of isolation and opposition to the Nasser regime. The United States refused to assist Egypt in providing medicine for her injured during the ill-fated invasion and declined her request for 435,000 tons of American wheat and flour. Egyptian assets in the United States were frozen, making it impossible for Egypt to purchase the medicine and the wheat she urgently needed; and $55 million worth of food authorized under the 1956–57 CARE program was not delivered, food which had been destined to provide free lunches for three million Egyptian schoolchildren.

The withdrawal of American food assistance to Egypt created an excellent opportunity for the Soviet Union to extend its influence in the Middle East. Thus by the end of 1958, the Soviet state had given the United Arab Republic (Syria and Egypt) more than $600 million in long-term, low-interest credits.[28] Clearly, the Soviet Union was replacing the West as the major source of economic aid for Egypt; Soviet aid exceeded American Point Four aid to all the Arab countries combined.

Early in 1957, the United States, which had become concerned with the seriousness of the Middle Eastern situation, decided to contain Soviet influence in the area by winning the support of those Arab states whose leaders were opposed to communism and its chief ally, Nasser's nationalism. This strategy and policy, proclaimed in March 1957, was known as the Eisenhower Doctrine.

The doctrine declared that the United States would render economic and military assistance to any Middle Eastern country that desired protection against "overt armed aggression from any nation controlled by International Communism." In reality, the doctrine added very little that was new except perhaps to emphasize United States determination to limit Communist influence in the area. It also served to remind the countries of the Middle East that such was the policy of the United States and that no country should underestimate its implications.

Immediately after the formulation of the Eisenhower Doctrine, the United States government sent a "mission" to the Middle East to explain the doctrine to government leaders and to solicit their support. King Saud of Saudi Arabia was the first Arab ruler to endorse the Eisenhower Doctrine openly—ironically, after he had signed with Egypt, Jordan, and Syria an Arab Solidarity Agreement designed to limit British influence in Jordan. The Arab nations of the Middle East became divided over the Eisenhower Doctrine, and this was perhaps the doctrine's major accomplishment.

But Nasser's popularity in the Arab world after his Suez political victory was too strong to be challenged. He was supported by public opinion in most Arab countries; and this, of course, prevented the Iraqi and Saudi Arabian leadership from lining up support for the Eisenhower Doctrine. In fact, King Saud had to relinquish much of his power to his brother Prince Faisal who at the time was friendly with Nasser. Also, Nuri Said of Iraq, who perhaps would have otherwise endorsed the doctrine, was unable to do so because of domestic opposition.

In Jordan the situation was more serious. Unrest among the people, going so far as an attempt to overthrow King Husain, forced upon the United States her first need to put the Eisenhower Doctrine into operation. When King Husain announced the existence in Jordan of a Communist plot backed by Egypt, the United States rushed the Sixth Fleet to the eastern Mediterranean and announced her readiness to save, by force if necessary,

28. Richard H. Nolte, "United States Policy and the Middle East," *The United States and the Middle East,* ed. Georgiana G. Stevens (Englewood Cliffs: Prentice-Hall, 1964), p. 164.

Jordan's integrity and independence. Husain was saved, but even so he was unable to officially endorse the Eisenhower Doctrine, which by now had become a highly controversial issue in Arab politics.

Arab nationalists, as well as the Communists, intensified their anti-American activities in the spring and summer of 1957, thereby bringing about the second round in the implementation of the Eisenhower Doctrine. This time the United States became concerned about Communist influence in Syria, which had grown as a result of Syria's acceptance of large quantities of arms from the Soviet Union and as a consequence of apparent Communist infiltration of the military and political agencies. An American task force appeared off the Syrian coast, and Turkey mobilized her forces along the Syrian border with United States consent. Of course, that Syria did not become Communist was not a result of the United States threat of intervention; rather, it was because of Nasser's acceptance of union with Syria and his subsequent suppression of the Syrian Communist party.[29]

The third round in the controversy over the Eisenhower Doctrine began in Lebanon in the spring of 1958. Although the causes of the civil war which broke out in Lebanon at that time were complex, President Camille Chamoun's endorsement of the doctrine in 1957 was certainly an important factor in the political events immediately preceding the war. Upon Chamoun's request, the United States had no choice but to honor her commitments under the doctrine and land troops in Lebanon. The pro-Nasser groups in the civil war were defeated, but a neutral government led by one of the Nasserite leaders of the revolution was formed and repudiated the Eisenhower Doctrine.

By the end of 1958, it became obvious to the United States that the Eisenhower Doctrine was not successful. Thereafter, the United States began to cultivate, as cautiously as possible, better relations with Nasser. President Kennedy desired to improve American relations with Egypt, but he also expected Nasser to reciprocate. In 1962 the political environment was suitable for such improvements. Nasser, for instance, showed a less belligerent attitude toward the United States, and furthermore, he became less sympathetic to African extremists, who were a source of trouble to United States African policy. More important perhaps was Nasser's attitude toward the United States during the Cuban missile crisis; his controlled press showed some sympathy for the American position. As a result of these new Egyptian attempts to show moderation in international relations, the United States was able to increase the amounts of economic aid to Egypt and to show a similar desire to improve her relations with that country.

For a while, it appeared that Kennedy's popularity in Egypt would bal-

29. Nolte, *The United States*, p. 168.

ance the negative impact of the "crisis of confidence" which previously characterized American-Egyptian relations. However, in 1967 the Johnson administration, which initially tried to continue the Kennedy policy in the Middle East, was faced with the dilemma of a new war between Israel and the Arab countries. It took a pro-Israel position; consequently, Egypt severed diplomatic relations with the United States. As 1969 began, the relations of the two countries were at their worst, Soviet influence in Egypt had increased, and the danger of a Communist takeover in Egypt, Syria, Algeria, and Iraq also increased. The Arab Middle East was becoming less susceptible to American influence than it was at any time since World War II.

POSITIVE NEUTRALITY

The official foreign policy of Egypt is based upon Nasser's concept of "positive neutrality." In its simplest form, this concept means nonalignment in the struggle for power among nations. As such, it is a "response to bipolarity," which is considered by Nasser to be a dangerous power relationship if left unchecked by neutral and small nations. However, some Arab political theorists distinguish between positive and legal neutrality.[30] They maintain that positive neutrality allows Egypt to take a stand on international issues, whereas legal neutrality—the Swiss type of neutrality—is in fact negative, since it usually results in the isolation of the legally neutral state. According to these arguments, legal neutrality, which is quite capable of assisting in reducing international tension, nevertheless curtails the ability of the neutral state to pursue a flexible foreign policy. Positive neutrality, on the other hand, results in no such restrictions. The only condition it requires for its own validity is that the adherent state should not commit itself permanently to either side in the international power struggle.

The first time positive neutrality became the announced official policy of Egypt was in 1956, during the Suez crisis.[31] In 1957, it became associated with Nasser's Arab policy in the sense that it was considered to be in the best interest of not only Egypt but all the Arab states as well. Gradually, Arab nationalists began to see this policy as an instrument of attaining Arab unity. They believed that neither the Soviet Union nor the United States wished to see the Arab states unified. Soviet assistance to the Arab nationalists was viewed to emanate from Soviet interest in driving the Western powers out of the Middle East; such interest, however, was not based upon that country's desire to see the Arabs united.

30. Leonard Binder, *The Ideological Revolution in the Middle East* (New York: John Wiley & Sons, 1964), p. 242.
31. *Ibid.*, p. 243.

In applying his concept of positive neutrality, Nasser insistently and consistently opposed joining military pacts and alliances which were in any way identified with the international power struggle. Military pacts which bind member states to one bloc against another were considered by the Egyptian leader to be not only dangerous but also contrary to the principle of nonalignment. This is the reason for Nasser's opposition to the Baghdad Pact. More interesting, however, is his opposition to any kind of "international economic grouping," which he considered as "the means used by the strong to destroy all attempts or endeavor for progress by others." [32] Economic imperialism, for Nasser, is just as detrimental to the interests of the neutral and small nations as is military imperialism.

Nonalignment also meant joining hands with the other nations who believed in neutrality.[33] Even before positive neutrality became Nasser's official foreign policy, Egypt was one of the most conspicuous and effective participants in the first Afro-Asian Conference which met in Bandung, Indonesia, in April 1955. Thereafter, Nasser was able to share the limelight of world leadership with old neutralists like Tito of Yugoslavia and Nehru of India.

There is no doubt that Nasser's activities in the conferences of the nonaligned nations won him many friends and admirers. He also profited from his activities in the various African conferences of the late 1950's and early 1960's. Thus, after Egypt was defeated by Israel in June 1967, many of his neutral friends in Asia and Africa came to his aid in the political battles which were fought in the Security Council and the General Assembly of the United Nations. Their voices carried a great deal of moral weight although less political influence and power.

CONCLUSION

To understand the Nasser regime we should understand Egyptian history. Foreign domination and a corrupt monarchical regime in Egypt were the main reasons for the Egyptian revolution of 1952. And they were also the two situations against which the Nasser regime reacted with forcefulness and bitterness. It was therefore natural for Nasser to emphasize honesty in government and anti-imperialism in foreign policy. The former policy was difficult to implement, and its success was limited: governmental bureaucracy had a long history of corruption. His anti-imperialism

32. The United Arab Republic, Information Department, *The Year Book: 1965,* p. 19.
33. For details regarding the various international conferences in which Egypt participated see *ibid.,* pp. 50–60.

was reflected in the regime's foreign policy and in the anti-Western attitudes of the Egyptian leaders.

Nasser's foreign policy, with its emphasis on Arab independence and Arab unity, made him popular in many Arab countries, especially among the masses. At the same time, it made him many enemies, mainly among the conservative Arab leaders and those Egyptians who were reared in the tradition of Egyptian rather than Arab nationalism.

Perhaps the most difficult domestic problem for the Nasser regime was the application of "Arab socialism." In theory, socialism is very appealing to a revolutionary regime in a country previously dominated by a small class of aristocrats. But in application, socialism might not be so appealing, at least as far as some people are concerned. In Egypt, the old business community, the old landlord class, and some intellectuals were hurt by Nasser's socialism. Certain ethnic minorities, such as the Greeks, Armenians, and Jews were also hurt because they had business interests in Egypt. Nevertheless, some people benefited from the introduction of a socialistic program. Among them were the army officers, who acquired a privileged status. Many of these army officers used their influence to put their relatives in positions of power in the socialistic enterprise.

However, there is no doubt about Nasser's personal integrity and his personal honesty. In spite of his many mistakes, many Egyptians admire his personal qualities. Not even the defeat of the 1967 Arab-Israeli war could substantially diminish his popularity or destroy his power position in Egypt. Thus, when he offered to resign in June 1967, millions of people in Egypt and outside demanded his return. Nasser's popularity in Egypt and the Arab world has never been matched by another leader. And it is very unlikely that his popularity will disappear in the near future.

CHAPTER 8

IRAQ

THE ancient name of Iraq is Mesopotamia—the "land between the rivers"—where man established and developed several highly complex civilizations, some of the oldest in history. The peoples that lived in that region contributed to human civilization a great wealth of knowledge. The Sumerians, for instance, who once controlled the southern part of Mesopotamia, are credited with inventing the cuneiform system—one of the earliest forms of writing. The Babylonians under their great ruler Hammurabi gave man a highly sophisticated code of law, which later influenced his theories on jurisprudence. And the Assyrians, known for their military innovations, also contributed greatly to man's culture in architecture, sculpture, and administration. All of these peoples spread their rule over the large portions of the Near and Middle East and were among the founders of human civilization.

What made possible the development of a complex civilization in Mesopotamia was, of course, the existence of the great Tigris and Euphrates rivers, whose waters flow into the Persian Gulf. They were for Mesopotamia what the Nile was for Egypt—the lifeline of its agricultural economy. In the valleys of these rivers, irrigation schemes and water-control systems were developed; land was made fertile; and the area became suitable for the development of higher forms of civilization.

Many foreign conquerors became interested in Mesopotamia: Persians, Greeks, Romans, Arabs, Mongols, and Ottomans. The country lacked natural frontiers and was vulnerable to attack, especially in the western part. In modern times foreign interest in Iraq has been based upon the country's strategic position and economic resources—of which, of course, oil has been a primary ingredient.

ARAB RULE

The Arab conquest of Mesopotamia began in 634, and it was the Arabs who gave the land its present name. At that time, Mecca was the center of an Arab-Muslim empire, but following a civil war and the assassination in 661 of Ali, the fourth caliph of the Muslim state, Damascus (in Syria) became the new center of the empire. The civil war reflected the existence of a strong rivalry between Iraq and Syria, both of which wished to dominate the Arab empire.[1] The victory of Syria forced Iraq to oppose the established leadership in Damascus, and Iraq became a base of activity for the dissenters. For instance, the followers of the slain caliph, Ali, organized themselves in Iraq, where they became known as "the Party of Ali." When, in 680, Ali's son, Husain, was killed fighting against the Damascus leadership, the party of Ali received a religious status in addition to being a political movement. The Arabic name for the new religious sect was Shi'ite. It must be remembered that the Shi'ites were Muslims who differed from their Orthodox (Sunnite) coreligionists only in certain interpretations of the creed and in some rituals.

The Umayyad dynasty ruled the Arab empire from Damascus; it existed for less than a century, from 661 to 750. Many of its subject people converted to Islam, some out of religious conviction and some for the economic and social advantages which the new religion conferred upon its adherents.[2] However, the converts contributed to the decline of Umayyad rule, since they no longer had to pay the poll tax required of non-Muslims. The converts were also a source of strength for the Shi'ites who had to moderate their views to compete for new members. When Umayyad rule came to an end in 750, the political center of gravity shifted to Iraq, where a new Arab dynasty, the Abbassid, was established.

Under Abbassid rule, Iraq prospered. Commerce and industry flourished, and there was a lucrative trade between India and the Near East. Philosophy, science, and literature flourished. The Abbassid period marked the height of Arab glory.

The Abbassid caliphs were absolute autocrats. They relied upon armed forces and an elaborate bureaucracy to govern their vast empire. However, the empire was always threatened by ethnic and religious divisions, which were most pronounced and most dangerous at the political center, Baghdad. The Abbassid rulers believed Islam would unite the empire, but the religion was not a sufficient force for unity. Thus, after the death of the legendary Caliph Harun al-Rashid in 809, a conflict for leadership developed between Persia and Iraq that marked the beginning of the end of the Abbassid empire. A civil war broke out between Persia and Iraq, with Rashid's two sons each receiving the support of one country. Persia was defeated and gradually withdrew from the empire. In addition, many prin-

1. *The Middle East and North Africa, 1966–67* (London: Europa Publications, 1966), p. 263.
2. *The Middle East and North Africa,* 1966–67, p. 263.

cipalities were established in the eastern part of the empire that were virtually independent of the authority in Baghdad. And in the west other provinces began to break away: Spain in 756, Morocco in 788, Tunisia in 800,
and Egypt in 868.

The fall of Abbassid rule was gradual. It began when the military commanders and the imperial guard gained influence over the caliph until they
were able to control him. These commanders were mostly Turkish Mamelukes whose ancestors had been slaves in the caliph's guard. Finally, the
Mongols, under Hulagu, grandson of Genghis Khan, captured Baghdad in
1258. This was a devastating event for Iraq: "The material and artistic
production of centuries was swept away. The commercial life of the city
[Baghdad], so long a center of trade with the East, was crippled. Iraq
itself was laid waste and—a tragedy from which the country has not yet
recovered—the canal system, upon which the prosperity of the land depended, fell into ruin." [3]

The Abbassid ruler fled to Cairo, where he was recognized as the spiritual leader but not as the political head of the state. Iraq entered a period
of political chaos and social disintegration, and nearly two centuries passed
before a new power—the Ottoman Turks—was established in the area
between Persia and Asia Minor. The Turks captured Cairo in 1517 and
forced the last Abbassid caliph to give up his spiritual position. Thereafter,
the Turkish ruler was both caliph and sultan—both the spiritual and political head of the Islamic state. In 1534, Baghdad was captured by the Ottomans, and, with the exception of a brief period of Persian control in the
seventeenth century, Iraq remained under the Ottomans until World
War I.

OTTOMAN RULE

Under the Ottoman Turks, Iraq was in constant turmoil. The sultan at
Istanbul had great difficulty governing the country. There were religious
divisions and rivalries: northern Iraq was predominantly Sunnite Muslim,
the south was largely Shi'ite, and Baghdad was under the influence of both
sects. Second, nomad tribes were a constant threat to settled communities
in Iraq. The nomads of the delta region and the Persian frontiers revolted
several times. Finally, Persia continued to be interested in Iraq. The Persian attempt to penetrate Iraq reached its height between 1578 and 1590,
although it was not until 1623 that Persian capture of Baghdad was
achieved under Shah Abbas (1587–1629). Ottoman control, however,
was re-established in 1638.

Iraq never regained the glory of her Abbassid past. The Ottomans were

3. George L. Harris, *Iraq* (New York: Frederick A. Praeger, 1958), p. 19.

not anxious to revive this illustrious period of Iraqi history, and during Ottoman rule the country stagnated politically and culturally, in spite of the fact that in the 1870's an attempt was made by Midhat Pasha, a Turkish viceroy in Baghdad, to reform the administration and recognize the potential wealth of Iraq.

The Turkish system of government was extremely inefficient. It paid little attention to the masses of impoverished people. High governmental positions were in the hands of Turkish officials and an elite of local dignitaries, both of whom mercilessly exploited the people. The central government in Istanbul was satisfied so long as it obtained the required taxes and was able to maintain political control. However, their control was often nominal, and real power was exercised mostly by the local officials. No consideration was given to the economic unity of the Tigris-Euphrates Valley. Economic integration was completely lacking, and the country was divided administratively as well. It was split into three major districts known as vilayets: Mosul, Baghdad, and Basra. Each district was governed independently, and this political fragmentation accentuated the problem of economic disintegration. Although Iraq had never existed as one political entity, she had been many times the center of great empires. Under the Turks, however, she was neither a political entity nor an important political center.

BRITISH RULE

Western influence had been present in Iraq long before the disintegration of the Ottoman Empire. Britain and France had commercial interests in the Persian Gulf early in the nineteenth century, and both countries had diplomatic representatives in a few Iraqi cities. In addition, both France and Italy maintained religious ties with the area. Mainly, however, early Western influence was felt in Iraq in the reforming spirit of a few Turkish officials who were able to introduce some programs of social and administrative reform. In addition to Midhat Pasha, other Turks attempted to introduce Western programs to modernize the Ottoman Empire. However, more direct and more meaningful contact between Iraq and the West was not possible until World War I.

The Occupation. Britain's interest in Iraq up to and during World War I was complex. Turkey's alliance with Germany posed strategic questions throughout the Middle East. During the war it became necessary for Britain to invade Iraq in an attempt to bring about the ultimate defeat of Turkey. Second, Britain needed Iraq to protect her oil interests in southern Persia. And lastly, Iraq, like Iran, was important for the security of India. British troops invaded Iraq in November 1914 and succeeded in capturing the important southern city of Basra. In March 1917 they occupied Baghdad. The northern part of Iraq, which included the city and province of Mosul, was not occupied until a few days after the Armistice of Mudros, which was signed on October 30, 1918. The Turks had to withdraw from the area, although they protested the British violation of the armistice, and they continued to claim territorial rights in northern Iraq for the next eight years.

The Establishment of the Mandate. The occupation confronted Britain with two difficult problems: first, to establish boundary lines for an Iraqi state; second, to determine its political status.

The problem of boundaries arose because Iraq had never been a separate political entity, and her frontiers were artificial. There were no natural boundaries between Iraq and her western neighbors. In addition, it was necessary to clarify the legal status of the province of Mosul, which was contested by Turkey. These problems were solved, however, through the negotiation of a number of treaties with Iraq's neighbors. The May 1922 Treaty of Mohammara and subsequent agreements settled Iraq's boundaries with Saudi Arabia. A large neutral zone was created on the western frontier of Kuwait. In 1925 the League of Nations recommended the inclusion of Mosul in the territory of Iraq, and the following year a treaty was concluded between Britain, Turkey, and Iraq in which the League's recommendation was accepted.

The second problem, the determination of the political status of Iraq, was dealt with gradually. In a conference held at San Remo in April 1920, the Allied powers agreed to place Iraq under a British mandate, which continued in effect until Iraq gained her independence in 1932. In October 1920, the British terminated their military rule in Iraq and allowed the formation of an Iraqi Council of State. The council was to govern with the advice of a group of British officials under the leadership of a high commissioner.

On August 23, 1921, Iraq became a Kingdom without affecting her status as a British mandate territory. The decision to establish a monarchical regime in Iraq was taken in the Cairo Conference of March 1921. Winston Churchill, then Britain's colonial secretary, was instrumental in the decision. The candidate selected for the throne was Faisal Ibn Husain, the former king of Syria who had been dethroned by the French. Faisal's appointment was later confirmed by "a hastily improvised nation-wide referendum." [4] His coronation took place on August 23, 1921.

Finally, Iraq received her first electoral law in May 1922, and in March 1924 a Constituent Assembly was held to approve an organic law which

4. Stephen Longrigg and Frank Steakes, *Iraq* (New York: Frederick A. Praeger, 1958), p. 84.

became the Constitution of the Kingdom of Iraq. The Constitution was officially promulgated on March 21, 1925. Although the new law was often ignored and violated, it was officially in effect until the fall of the monarchy in 1958. We will therefore discuss it briefly with the hope that some understanding of the legal framework of the state may be gained.

THE MONARCHICAL CONSTITUTION

The 1925 constitutional document consisted of ten parts and 125 articles.[5] It contained what might be called a bill of rights, which included many guarantees of freedoms and rights similar to those in Western constitutions. The rights of minorities were protected, and all citizens were equal before the law. The document also established the organization of the state and defined the powers of governmental agencies.

Under the Constitution, the king was the chief of state. Although sovereignty belonged to the people, it was intrusted by them to the king and his heirs. In addition, the king possessed important powers. He could dissolve Parliament and veto its acts. When Parliament was not in session, the king issued decrees which had the force of law, but such decrees would have to be ultimately approved by the legislature if they were to continue in effect. The prime minister was appointed by the king, who also had the constitutional power to remove him. Furthermore, the Constitution empowered the monarch to declare war without the consent of Parliament, although he could not conclude treaties without ratification by the legislature. Thus, the Iraqi monarch had legal powers to govern the country without too much interference from governmental agencies. This, however, should not be construed to mean that he was an absolute monarch, since the Constitution created a legislative body with important if limited responsibilities.

The Constitution intended the prime minister and a Council of Ministers (similar to the British cabinet) to be the working executive in the government. In theory, these two agencies were responsible to the king as well as to Parliament, which consisted of a Senate and a Chamber of Deputies. The Chamber of Deputies, the lower house, could under the Constitution compel the resignation of the Council by a vote of nonconfidence. In practice, however, the Council dominated the legislature. Between 1925 and 1958, not a single Council was overthrown by the legislature.[6]

Between 1921 and 1956, Iraq had more than fifty governments, that is,

5. See text in Amos J. Peaslee, *Constitutions of Nations* (The Hague, Netherlands: Martinus Nijhoff, 1956), pp. 412–32.
6. H. B. Sharabi, *Government and Politics of the Middle East in the Twentieth Century* (Princeton: Van Nostrand, 1962), p. 151.

Councils of Ministers. The average life span of the Council was seven and a half months. During this period, Iraq was governed by a small political elite: the total number of persons who occupied positions in the first fifty Councils has been estimated at only 150.[7] The oligarchic character of Iraqi politics before the military coup of 1958 was, therefore, very strong. This phenomenon can also be substantiated by the fact that between 1925 and 1958 only one parliament was allowed to complete its four-year term. Iraq had fifteen elected Chambers of Deputies during that period.[8]

Of the two parliamentary chambers, the Senate was appointed by the monarch. The Constitution limited its membership to a maximum of one-fourth the size of the Chamber of Deputies. Senators served for a period of eight years, and they were eligible for reappointment. Of course, the Senate could not legislate alone while the Chamber was dissolved. Furthermore, it did not have the power to vote nonconfidence in the government and thereby force it to resign; this power belonged to the lower house only. Nevertheless, the Senate was ordinarily more critical of the government than the Chamber of Deputies which, as mentioned earlier, never used its power to force the resignation of governments.[9] Perhaps the reason for the difference was in the composition of the Senate, which included former ministers and prime ministers, who usually looked with envy upon the government of the day.

Members of the Chamber of Deputies were elected by the people according to the ratio of one deputy for every twenty thousand citizens. The Constitution insisted upon the representation of Christian and Jewish minorities. The duration of a legislative session was only six months in each calendar year; consequently, for six months of each year the country was governed by royal decrees.

Only deputies could introduce nonfinancial laws. Senators could not. Financial bills could be introduced only by the government. However, no legislative proposal could become law unless the two houses of Parliament approved it. If one house twice rejected a proposal which the other house approved, a joint session of the two chambers decided the issue by a two-thirds majority. In this case, it is obvious that the lower house had the advantage.

INDEPENDENCE

The British mandate in Iraq lasted for twelve years, from 1920 to 1932. From the beginning, the British had faced opposition and resistance from

7. Harris, *Iraq*, p. 118.
8. Sharabi, *Government and Politics*, p. 151.
9. Harris, *Iraq*, p. 121.

many elements of Iraqi society. A national war of liberation, which took place in July 1920, was caused by many factors. The politically conscious Iraqis resented the fact that their country was occupied by a foreign power. Arab nationalist sentiment had begun to assert itself, and in the last few years in the life of the Ottoman Empire, contact between Arab nationalist groups was established and many secret organizations were formed.

In spite of the fact that Iraq benefited more under the British than under the Turks, improvements after the establishment of the mandate were very limited. Of course, the British task of building Iraq's economy after centuries of stagnation was not an easy one. In addition, Britain was not sure about continuing the mandate in Iraq; she suspected that a different arrangement might be better for both countries. Whatever arrangement was to be adopted, however, Britain wanted to preserve her economic and strategic interests in Iraq. Thus in the 1930 Anglo-Iraqi Treaty of Alliance, Britain agreed to grant Iraq her independence as soon as it became possible for Iraq to become a member of the League of Nations. League membership was achieved in 1932, and with that Iraq became independent.

But Iraq's independence was not really total, as it was limited by her obligations to Great Britain under the 1930 Treaty of Alliance, which went into effect on October 3, 1932. These obligations included mutual aid and free passage for British troops during war, full consultation in foreign affairs, and the maintenance of two British air bases in Iraq.

Internal Politics 1932–40. Until 1933 the predominant figure in Iraqi politics was King Faisal Ibn Husain. Although he was not an Iraqi by birth, Faisal was able to moderate the conflicting interests of Iraqi groups, and this was perhaps his strongest political virtue. The conflicts between Shi'ite and Sunnite, between tribal and rural elements on the one hand and the urban elements on the other, between conservatives and liberals, and finally between the Arab nationalists and the British, were all explosive situations which he restrained very admirably.

The British liked Faisal and considered him to be a great asset. While sympathizing with the cause of the Arab nationalists, he was cautious lest a major crisis would develop between them and the British. He had learned a good lesson from his experience in Syria, where he had been king before being dethroned by the French. He knew that small countries could not win against major powers, so that in Iraq he adopted the policy of attaining national goals gradually. While this policy did not make him popular in Iraq, it did establish him as a respected monarch. Only after his sudden death in September 1933 did the Iraqis begin to remember him as their beloved monarch. And thus, ironically, Faisal gained popularity after his death.

Faisal's death created a political vacuum which his son and heir to the throne, Ghazi, could not fill. The new king was more popular than his father, but he lacked his wisdom and political foresight. Furthermore, the role of moderator of conflicts which his father played so well was not Ghazi's forte. Consequently, the Iraqi politicians competed to fill the vacuum left by the death of Faisal. The competition was rough and involved the use of the army to gain control of the government.

In 1936, Iraq had her first military coup d'état. The conflict which precipitated the coup was between personalities in the government as well as between the conservative-traditionalists and the liberal-reformists. The issue of reform, however, was lost in the squabble for power which followed the coup. Personal feuds caused political instability, and in the short span of five years (1936–41), a total of seven coups and countercoups took place.

In 1936, King Ghazi died in an automobile accident. He had espoused many national causes, and his death gave rise to rumors that he had been killed by the British. Violence broke out, especially in the city of Mosul, where the mob murdered the British consul. The government declared martial law in the city, and disturbances were quelled by force.

In accordance with the Constitution, Ghazi's son, Faisal II, was declared king, but because he was still a minor, Parliament appointed his uncle Abdul Ilah as regent. The prince was pro-Western and, of course, a believer in gradualism in economic and social change. He lacked, however, the wisdom of Faisal I and the popular appeal of Ghazi. Soon he would align himself with Iraq's small political elite, thereby committing the mistake of tying the future of the monarchy to the future of this elite. In the experience of other countries—Egypt, for instance—this rigidity was detrimental to the monarchy. The monarchs of Iran and Jordan were more flexible and were able to survive by shifting their alignments and changing their policies.

POLITICS DURING WORLD WAR II

The outbreak of World War II raised two important questions in Iraq: (1) Would the interests of Iraq be served better by neutrality or by taking sides? (2) What was the extent of Iraq's commitment to Great Britain? These questions became serious after the fall of France in June 1940.

Divisions over the Question of Neutrality. Some Iraqi leaders believed that Germany would win the war and that, consequently, Iraq should remain neutral so that a German victory would not deprive her of her sovereignty. The leader of this group was Rashid Ali al-Gailani, a former prime minister who had never been enchanted with Iraq's friendship with

Britain. The weakness of this position, of course, was that Great Britain might not accept Iraq's neutrality.

However, the majority of the Iraqi politicians were pro-British and believed that it was in the best interest of Iraq to side with the Allies. The spokesman of this majority was Nuri Said, a shrewd statesman who would later become Iraq's best known politician until the 1958 coup ended his career as well as his life.

While the neutrality debate was going on, a group of Arab nationalists from Syria and Palestine were actively lobbying for an Iraqi policy sympathetic to the Axis powers. These nationalists were exiles from their own countries, where they had led unsuccessful revolutions against the occupation powers, Britain in Palestine and France in Syria. Their leader was Amin al-Husaini, the mufti (a high religious official) of Jerusalem, who in the 1930's instigated an abortive revolt against the British. He was a hero among Arab nationalists. He believed that the British had betrayed his people by breaking promises they made to the Arabs during World War I. Furthermore, Amin was understandably concerned about the British policy that had enabled a large number of Jews to immigrate to Palestine.

The Regime of Rashid Ali al-Gailani. The struggle for power between the neutralists and the pro-British factions (complicated by the effectiveness of German and Italian propaganda in Iraq) became serious.[10] The British were naturally alarmed, and the urgency of the situation prompted the regent to call for unity in a special meeting of Iraq's prominent leaders. The result was the formation of a national government under Rashid Ali al-Gailani, with Nuri Said as foreign minister. Unfortunately, the feud continued within the national government, which became ineffective and disunited.

In June 1940, Britain invoked the Treaty of Alliance of 1930 and requested Iraq to permit the landing of troops in Basra. These troops were destined to go to Haifa in Palestine. Rashid's government approved the British request on condition that the troops would not be stationed in Iraq or stay there for any length of time. Rashid was trying to limit Iraq's obligations under the Treaty of Alliance so he could maintain a neutral policy.

However, as this policy became difficult because of the continuing struggle within the government, Rashid began to move toward the position of the mufti's nationalists. Although most Iraqi politicians were still against a pro-Axis war policy, the army was behind the Rashid-Amin group and the German and Italian governments. An effort was made to secure from

10. For more details on al-Gailani's regime see the excellent study of Majid Khadduri, *Independent Iraq 1932–1958: A Study in Iraqi Politics* (2nd ed.; London: Oxford University Press, 1960), pp. 159–258.

the two Axis powers written guarantees for safeguarding Arab right to independence and sovereignty.

For the British, things had gone too far in Iraq; they pressured the regent into requesting Prime Minister Rashid's resignation. Knowing that the army was behind him, Rashid refused, and the regent left the capital. He went to another part of Iraq where he hoped to use troops loyal to him to force Rashid to give up the government. Nuri Said, who had resigned as foreign minister in protest against the government's neutral policy, was now in open opposition to the Rashid government.

With the prospect of imminent civil war, Rashid finally resigned on January 31, 1941. The regent returned to Baghdad, and a new government was formed under the leadership of General Taha al-Hashimi, the minister of defense in the previous government. However, another crisis developed when the regent insisted upon the retirement of the army officers who supported Rashid. These officers expressed their determination to remain in their posts, and when Taha failed to induce the regent to change his mind, they ordered their troops to surround the royal palace. The regent managed to escape; he appeared later in Transjordan, where a relative of his was the ruling prince. There he was joined by Nuri Said and other loyal Iraqi politicians.

At this point, a constitutional crisis developed. The formation of a new government required a royal decree, and the regent was not in the country. Rashid and his military supporters had no alternative but to call the Iraqi Parliament, have that body depose the regent, appoint a new one, and thereby pave the way for a new government to be formed through the initiative of the new regent. This procedure was specious, but it gave Rashid's acts a façade of constitutionality. In any case, on April 10, 1941, a new regent, Sharif Sharaf, a distant relative of the deposed regent, was appointed. Of course, Rashid became the head of the new government.

The Downfall of Rashid. The British became exceedingly alarmed at Rashid's return to power, for their military purposes required an Iraqi government that was pro-British. Germany would be more than glad to have control over Iraq and Iran, both for their territory and for their oil. Britain was determined not to let this happen.

The Rashid government announced its intention to honor Iraq's international commitments, including its obligation to Britain, but it was clear to the British that, under Rashid, Iraq would ultimately side with Germany and Italy. Knowing that the Iraqi government was already in communication with the German and Italian governments, they decided that the situation was serious enough to warrant military intervention.

On April 29, 1941, British troops landed in Basra, and a thirty-day war followed. The Iraqi army was no match for the invading forces, who were assisted by the Arab Legion of Transjordan. It lacked equipment, training, and good strategists. The Iraqi air force was destroyed in the first few days of fighting, and the Iraqi government never received the expected assistance of Germany, partly because the Germans were unable to provide it and partly because the Germans believed that the Iraqi "revolution" had come prematurely. Having failed to make good his pro-Axis policy, Rashid fled to Iran to save his life and went from there to Germany. Some of his lieutenants were captured and later tried for their crimes against the constitutional order; others were able to join their leader in exile. The mufti of Jerusalem and many of his lieutenants also went to Germany.

Thus Iraq, like Iran and Egypt, failed to assert its independence from the British. The governments of these countries learned the hard way the same lesson that Faisal I had learned before them: a small power was no match for a big power.

THE POSTWAR PERIOD

The downfall of Rashid's regime returned the country to civilian rule. Immediately after the war, there was popular demand for democratic government. In 1945, the regent had promised that political parties would soon be permitted to exist, and the promise was fulfilled in April 1946, when five parties were allowed to operate. Other parties were established later, but in 1954 political parties were legally prohibited.

Political Parties. The five parties licensed in 1946 were the Independence party, the Liberal party, the National Democratic party, the National Union party, and the People's party.[11] In 1947, the government suppressed the People's party and the National Union party because of their strong socialism and, in the case of the Union, also because of its anti-British and pro-Soviet policies. A year later, in 1948, the Liberal and the National Democratic parties, frustrated with the authoritarian character of the government, voluntarily stopped their political activity. Only the Independence party continued to exist.

The five parties represented the younger generation,[12] not the ruling elite of Iraq, which consisted of elder statesmen who were conservative, pro-Western, and firm believers in the monarchy. Naturally, this elite was suspicious of the newly established parties which were more liberal, and sometimes more nationalistic. The elder statesmen did not genuinely desire democratic government; they were used to an oligarchic government, which was authoritarian although not totalitarian. There were no doctrinal differences or even fundamental policy disagreements among the members of the

11. Khadduri, *Independent Iraq*, pp. 299–300.
12. Khadduri, *Independent Iraq*, p. 300.

elite. If there were any differences among them, they were personal and lasted only until each was satisfied with his share of power.

Consequently, the young political parties were ignored and occasionally suppressed. Soon, the elder statesmen saw the necessity of establishing their own parties so as to compete with the liberal parties and to give their regime a democratic façade. Nuri Said, for instance, founded the Constitutional Union party in 1949. Salih Jabr, the first Shi'ite member to become prime minister (in 1949), formed the Socialist Nation party in 1951. Salih's party had essentially the same political outlook as Nuri's, and in reality was not Socialist at all. Salih established it because of personal differences between himself and Nuri; both men were members of the same political elite.

In 1954, Nuri as prime minister outlawed all political parties including his own, a measure that proved disastrous since it contributed to the downfall of the monarchy in 1958. In 1956, opposition leaders requested from the government permission to establish the Congress party, which was in reality an alignment of the old Independence and National Democratic parties. When Nuri refused, the opposition leaders formed a secret organization, the National Union Front, which was a coalition of opposition groups and included the Communist party. The National Union Front agitated for greater freedom and for the legalization of political parties. Its failure to achieve these goals contributed to the frustration and disappointment that preceded the 1958 military coup. Political freedom was not achieved even after the coup, however. Clearly, Iraq's experiment in democracy was a failure, for the revolutionary regime which was established in 1958 was more oppressive than its predecessor. It was, however, a very different kind of regime, as we shall see later.

Internal Conflicts. The postwar period was no less turbulent than the prewar period. However, the causes of unrest in the postwar period were slightly different. First, the formation of political parties enabled opposition groups to influence public opinion and expose some of the weaknesses of Nuri Said's regime. The popularity of the ruling oligarchy was seriously diminished when it decided in 1954 to halt Iraq's limited experiment in democratic government. The intelligentsia no longer supported the authoritarian regime, and the alienation of this class by denying it participation in the political process was a mistake that contributed to the downfall of the regime.

The role of Nuri Said as the strong man of the regime during the 1950's was also an important source of discontent and conflict: he was criticized by all segments of Iraqi society except the political elite, whose leader he was. Nuri was in many respects an able statesman. Whether he was in office or working behind the scenes, he was able to influence Iraqi policies more than any other politician. He believed that the economic future of Iraq was great provided economic developments did not suffer from abrupt political change. In this belief, he was correct: Iraq was an underpopulated country with important natural resources. However, Nuri underestimated the significance of the noneconomic desires of his people. He had very little respect for public opinion, which he ignored and very often suppressed. He also underestimated the importance of Arab nationalism by charting a political course for his country which emphasized its relation with the "northern tier" states and Great Britain at the expense of Arab solidarity. His narrow outlook permitted events in the Arab world to disrupt Iraqi politics.

The Palestinian problem was a third frustrating issue in postwar Iraqi politics. This problem had contributed to political instability both before and during World War II, but in the postwar period it assumed new and greater dimensions. Iraq sent troops to Palestine to prevent the establishment of the State of Israel, and consequently the Iraqi government had to share responsibility for failure in Palestine. The people of Iraq never forgot the experience or forgave the ruling oligarchy for the defeat. Furthermore, many army officers believed that they had been betrayed by their government when they were fighting in Palestine, and the Palestine war was a significant factor in the coming of the military coup in 1958.

Finally, Iraq's foreign policy was a source of frustration for the nationalists, who could not understand why the ruling oligarchy was more interested in strengthening the country's ties with the West than with the Arab countries. Nuri received most of the blame for this foreign-policy orientation, but the whole regime was also held responsible.

The many facets of political instability were intermingled with the violent expressions of public sentiment. When the contents of a new treaty of alliance with Great Britain were made public on January 16, 1948, riots and demonstrations broke out in which college students participated. The government was forced to repudiate the treaty.

There was also an uprising in November 1952, caused mainly by public concern over elections. Iraq, it must be mentioned, had never had honest and free elections because the ruling oligarchy had always manipulated them. It was, therefore, natural for opposition groups to demand electoral reforms which would guarantee honest and free elections. Once the rioting had begun, it became impossible for the government to control the situation. The regent had to call upon the army chief of staff to form a government and to deal with the rioting. No reforms came out of the incident, of course, and the government was returned to the politicians.

Union with Jordan. When Nasser became the undisputed champion of Arab nationalism, hope for the unification of the Arab states also became strong. The political merger of Syria and Egypt on February 1, 1958, in what became the United Arab Republic, was the first step toward the realization of this hope. Although the merger was later disrupted, it had a strong impact upon the internal political situation in Iraq. There, the Arab nationalists acquired a new weapon with which to discredit the Iraqi regime. They accused it of obstructing Arab aspirations for unity.

The union between Iraq and Jordan, therefore, which was proclaimed only thirteen days after the proclamation of the United Arab Republic, should be viewed as a reaction to the success of the Nasserite Arab nationalists in Syria and Egypt. It was also a desperate move by the Hashimite family to save its thrones in Iraq and Jordan. Of course, it must be remembered that the conservative elements in the two countries supported the Hashimite family and were ready to defend it.

According to the constitutional arrangements worked out for the union of Iraq and Jordan in what was called the Arab Federation, each country was to retain its political institutions: king, parliament, and cabinet.[13] However, common federal institutions were added to both countries. Faisal II, the king of Iraq, became the head of the Federation, which also had a government headed by a prime minister. Nuri Said became the first federal prime minister. The Federation's legislative body consisted of an equal number of deputies from each country, to be chosen by their own parliaments.

Although each government was left a large degree of sovereignty over its own territory, many important functions were entrusted to the federal government, including foreign policy, diplomatic representation, defense, education, customs, and currency. The union agreement was designed to enable the two merging countries to cooperate in the economic sphere and to have one currency. It also stipulated that international agreements concluded prior to the establishment of the Federation would continue to be valid, but they would bind only the state which concluded them and not its partner. Thus, only Iraq was bound by the Baghdad Pact, and only Jordan was bound by its Armistice Agreement with Israel. However, international agreements concluded after the establishment of the union would become the responsibility of the federal government.

Jordan was expected to benefit most from the merger, since her economy would be strengthened by Iraq's substantial oil income. Also, although it contributed only 23 per cent of the population of the new state and 18 per cent of its territory, Jordan obtained equal representation in the Parliament of the Federation. In addition, Iraq was to assume 80 per cent of the expenses of the new state. Finally, Amman and Baghdad were to alternate

13. See the text of the Iraq-Jordan Federation Agreement in *Middle East Affairs,* IX (1958), 111–13.

as capitals of the Federation, each being the capital for six months each year.

The Arab Federation was formed to compete with the United Arab Republic for political power in the Arab world. Its proclamation agreement stipulated that other states could join the union and that the question concerning the headship of the federal state was subject to reconsideration. Although both Arab unions were later dissolved, the Arab Federation seemed to be the more natural of the two, and the one with the better chance of succeeding. Unlike Syria and Egypt, which were separated geographically by Israel and Jordan, the Arab Federation united two countries which had similar political institutions, and which were ruled by the Hashimite family. Both had experienced British rule before they became sovereign and independent.

Unfortunately, the Federation was not popular with Arab nationalists, especially in Jordan, where a large percentage of the population was of Palestinian origin.[14] The nationalists were more interested in the question of leadership and personalities than in the question of unity, and this was one of the main reasons for the failure of both unions. They distrusted monarchical regimes in general and the Hashimite royal family in particular. They criticized the foreign policies of Iraq and Jordan prior to unification and believed similar policies would continue under the Federation. Finally, they wanted revolutionary leaders to transform Arab society, continue the unification process, and regain Arab rights in Palestine. In 1958, only Nasser seemed to fit their description of a revolutionary leader; he was the idol of Arab nationalists.

The Downfall of the Monarchy. In spite of the fact that the economic conditions in Iraq improved between 1952 and 1958, owing mainly to the increase in the oil revenues, public tension still existed. And this tension was aggravated by the United Arab Republic's anti-Hashimite propaganda. Also, the 1958 disturbances in Lebanon were followed by rumors in Iraq and Jordan that the federation countries might invade Syria, which was considered to be responsible for the Lebanese crisis. This and other factors contributed to dissatisfaction and resentment in the armed forces of Iraq.

On July 14, 1958, a military coup took place in Iraq, headed by Brigadier General Abdul Karim Kassem and Colonel Abdul Salam Arif. The military units of these two officers had been ordered into Jordan, presumably on a special assignment. Instead of passing through Baghdad, however, they executed the conspiratorial plans of Kassem and Arif, capturing the city and bringing down the government.

14. M. Perlmann, "Fusion and Confusion, Arab Mergers and Realignments," *Middle East Affairs,* IX (1958), 128.

Kassem, according to his own admission, became antimonarchist in 1934, when he joined the army, but he did not think of overthrowing the government until the Suez crisis.[15] The idea of the coup entered his mind after meetings with some Syrian officers in Jordan. His collaborator, Arif, had his own separate conspiratorial organization, but he cooperated with Kassem. Later, Arif's membership in the Baath party was revealed.

The coup was violent. Almost all members of the Iraqi royal family were killed, including the young king, his mother, and the crown prince. Nuri Said escaped temporarily but was tracked down by a mob and brutally murdered. Many of the civilian and military leaders of the old regime were arrested and tried.

Of course, the coup brought an end to the Arab Federation. The Hashimite family continued to rule Jordan through King Husain, who initially entertained the idea of intervening in the Iraqi situation but dropped it under the pressure of public opinion from both Iraq and Jordan. Consequently, the fall of the monarchy ushered in a new era in Iraqi history, but one which would become as turbulent and unstable as its predecessor.

THE KASSEM REGIME

Iraq became a republic as a result of the coup. A Council of Sovereignty, consisting of three members, a Sunnite, a Shi'ite, and a Kurd (belonging to a non-Arab minority), was established to exercise presidential authority, and a Cabinet was formed to exercise both executive and legislative powers. Kassem became the prime minister and held the posts of minister of defense and commander-in-chief of the armed forces. His collaborator, Arif, was minister of interior and deputy commander-in-chief. Among the members of the Cabinet, there were two Baathists, one Marxist, and one Kurd.

Martial law was declared by the new regime; the leaders of the old regime were jailed; and its opponents freed. Leaders of Communist front organizations were allowed to return from exile; and Rashid Ali al-Gailani, who had lived until then in Saudi Arabia, and Mustafa Barzani, the leader of the Kurdish rebellion (1943–45), were also given permission to return.

Internal Struggles for Power. Shortly after the new rulers took power, a struggle developed which seriously threatened their regime. Although Kassem was not deposed until 1963, the experience made clear the fact that Iraq was a difficult country to rule.

The struggle for power took place among the four political parties repre-

15. F. R. C. Bagley, "Iraq's Revolution," *International Journal*, XIV (1958–59), 288.

sented in the Kassem government: the Communists, the Baathists, the National Democrats, and the Istiqlalists (followers of the Independence party).[16] The Communist party had always been prohibited, and Nuri Said considered it a dangerous movement. The Baathist party believed in the political unity for all the Arab countries and in the nationhood of Arabic-speaking peoples. Its central authority was in Damascus, the capital of Syria. The National Democratic party and the Independence party were among the five parties which were organized in 1946. Although they were banned in 1954, they continued their activity in secret. The National Democratic party advocated mild social reform. The Independence party had its origin among the followers of Rashid Ali al-Gailani. What these parties had in common was their hatred of the old regime, but very little else. Under such circumstances, there would obviously be difficulty for Kassem to maintain unity in his government.

The question of Arab unification was the major point over which the various groups were to quarrel. Should Iraq remain independent, at least for the time being, or immediately merge with Syria and Egypt in the United Arab Republic? The issue involved political parties as well as personalities. Arif, Kassem's junior partner in the coup, wanted immediate union with the other two Arab countries. As mentioned earlier, he was a Baathist and an admirer of Nasser. He was supported by the Istiqlalists but opposed by the Communists and the Social Democrats. The Communists hoped that in time they might be able to subvert the Kassem regime. The Social Democrats believed that Iraq would lose more than she would gain if she were to join in the Arab union; they were afraid that under the union Iraq would have to share her oil wealth with the other two countries. Kassem himself was in no mood to give up his leadership to play second fiddle to Nasser, who would naturally remain the president of the U.A.R.

The showdown came during September 1958. On September 12, Arif was removed as deputy commander-in-chief, and on September 30 he was relieved of all other official duties. He was, however, appointed as Iraq's ambassador to West Germany, a move obviously designed to keep him away from the seat of government. Arif spent some time traveling in Europe, but he never visited Bonn, the place of his new assignment. Instead, he returned to Baghdad on November 24, where he was immediately put under arrest and later tried for conspiring against the regime. A kangaroo court sentenced him to death, but Kassem commuted the sentence.

The internment of Arif and his collaborators did not put an end to Arab

16. Don Peretz, *The Middle East Today* (New York: Holt, Rinehart & Winston, 1965), pp. 391–92. For further study of the struggle for power in Iraq see Benjamin Shwadran, *The Power Struggle in Iraq* (New York: Council for Middle Eastern Affairs Press, 1960).

nationalist activity in Iraq. Nasser's propaganda continued to denounce Kassem as the betrayer of the Arab cause, urging the Iraqis to revolt. Furthermore, elements in the Iraqi army began to resent Kassem's stress on Iraqi nationalism, believing that he was using it to stay in power. These elements also feared Kassem's drift toward the left and the possibility of a Communist takeover.

On March 9, 1959, there was a rebellion in Mosul under the leadership of Colonel Shawwaf, who declared that the purpose of his "revolution" was the achievement of the real goals of the July 14 coup, which, he said, had been ignored by the Kassem regime. He called upon all Arab nationalists to support him and promised to march on Baghdad. However, the Iraqi air force bombed Mosul, bringing an end to the rebellion, and Shawwaf was killed by officers loyal to the regime.

The Mosul rebellion caused the Kassem regime to move further to the left, for Kassem believed that Nasser and the Western powers were behind it. Severe measures were taken against pro-Nasser elements in Iraq, and anti-Western policies began to characterize Iraq's foreign relations. It was clear, however, that the regime was in serious trouble, for its popular support had already been challenged by the nationalists.

The Kurdish Rebellion. Another major event that undermined the Kassem regime was the Kurdish rebellion which began in 1961 and continued sporadically until 1966. The Kurds are a nomadic people engaged mainly in agriculture, although they are also famous for carpet making, their main industry. The majority of them are fanatic Sunnite Muslims, and they are a warlike people who have always resisted foreign domination. They inhabit the northeastern part of Iraq but also live in parts of east Turkey, Soviet Armenia, and in northwestern Iran. In all, they number somewhere between 1,500,000 and 2,000,000; the Iraqi city of Sulaimania, in the northeast, is entirely populated by Kurds.

For centuries, the Kurds fought for their independence and sought autonomy from the Ottoman state. At the Paris Peace Conference of 1919 they demanded independent political status; and although they failed to secure it, they were able to get recognition in the 1921 Treaty of Sèvres for an autonomous Kurdish state. However, the Treaty of Lausanne (1923), which superseded the Sèvres treaty, said nothing about Kurdistan, their cherished state. Consequently, the Kurds were to revolt not only in Iraq, but also in other regions, especially Iran. They rose up in 1925, in 1930, and again in 1946. The last revolt was led by Mustafa Barzani, who, after its failure, lived in exile until 1958, when the new regime allowed him to return. The old regime had distributed Barzani's properties to other Kurds who favored cooperation with the Baghdad government. As a result, there were rivalries between the Barzani tribe and the pro-government elements.

This rivalry might have been one of the reasons for Barzani's decision to proclaim an independent Kurdish state in March 1961, and thereby unite the Kurds behind him.

But this was not his main reason. The Kurds had always insisted upon an independent or autonomous political status, and the government of Iraq had failed to honor its promises to grant them a measure of autonomy. Furthermore, since World War II the Soviet Union had encouraged the Kurds to demand their freedom. In 1961, many Kurdish politicians were in sympathy with communism.

The Kurdish rebellion of 1961 succeeded temporarily in disrupting the territorial unity of Iraq; by September 24, 1961, the rebellion had spread over one-third of the country. However, on October 10 the Government of Iraq declared that the Iraqi army was in control, and subsequently the government outlawed the democratic party of Kurdistan, which was founded by Barzani in 1958, and imposed many other restrictions.

There was much destruction of property in the towns and villages, and the rebellion was obviously very costly to the Kurds. However, they were able to show their solidarity and determination, for they had thrown more than twenty thousand men into the fighting and could claim that their rebellion was in reality a national uprising. Although their revolt was put down in the same year it began, the Kurds continued to press their demands for autonomy, and their demands were often accompanied with force even after the overthrow of Kassem's regime.

The Downfall of Kassem. Iraq under Kassem was very different from Iraq under the monarchy. Some of the policies of the Kassem regime and the changes it sought will be discussed later in this chapter. However, the nature of the challenges to the regime and its lack of popular support were the important factors in its political failure.

Although the Kassem government spent much energy in whipping up support for its policies, it failed to gain the support of the nationalists, who still desired unification with the other Arab states. The irony of a military coup is that it is likely to produce national heroes who are unwilling to give up their leadership. Unification processes, on the other hand, often require that the leaders sacrifice their power positions. Kassem, like Nasser and all the leaders of the Arab revolutionary regimes, did not desire to give up power after he had gotten a taste of it. Consequently, when it came to the question of Arab unity, Kassem was no improvement over the monarchical regime he had helped to destroy in 1958. The tension and anxieties of the Arab nationalists were intensified by Kassem's attitude toward Arab unity, and they were one reason for his downfall.

The Baathists, who were with Kassem in the 1958 revolution, were the engineers of the 1963 coup which resulted in his death. But though they were united first against the monarchical regime and then Kassem, they became divided after they took control of the government. The future of Arab unity remained uncertain.

The 1963 coup returned Arif, Kassem's erstwhile partner, to power. Arif became the president of the republic, and a Cabinet under Brigadier General Ahmed al-Bakr, also a Baathist, was created. The Baathist regime proceeded to purge the army and the country of pro-Kassem elements and took severe measures against Communists and their sympathizers. As usual, the coup was followed by further restrictions on freedom. Iraqi prisons, which under Nuri Said were filled by the opponents of the regime (especially the Communists), and under Kassem by his opponents (especially the Baathists), were now filled by the pro-Kassem elements, and once again by the Communists. It seemed as if the political men in Iraq had no choice except to be in power or prison. Whatever the choice, it was clear that the limitation of freedom was at its worst during Baathist rule.

THE ARIF REGIME

The military coup which took place on February 8, 1963 made no fundamental changes in the political and governmental structure of Iraq. The new regime declared its determination to achieve the basic objectives of the 1958 revolution, which it too said had been ignored by the Kassem regime. It announced its intention to pursue more vigorously an Arab policy designed to liberate the Arab countries and bring these countries closer together. In addition, it expressed a desire and determination to bring the Iraqi government closer to the people by seeking their support and fulfilling their ideals.

The Question of Arab Unity. Of course, everyone expected Arif to work to bring about an Iraqi union with Egypt and Syria. Immediately after the coup, negotiations with the Syrian and Egyptian governments were begun, and on April 17 an agreement for the federation of the three countries was signed. A transitional period of twenty months was to precede the actual establishment of the federation. During this period, however, relations between these countries changed, and the agreement was not enforced. A struggle for power within the Baathist party of Iraq was one of the reasons for the failure of realizing the federation agreement.

Two factions were involved in the struggle for power. The extremists believed that radical social reform in Iraq should precede plans for Arab unity. The moderates, who had the greater support in the armed forces, wanted closer ties with Egypt and were apprehensive about their relations with Syria. The dispute between the factions became critical when the extremists attempted a coup, late in 1963, in which the presidential palace was attacked by elements in their air force.

Consequently, President Arif assumed full powers on November 18, 1963, and a new Revolutionary Command Council was established. The extremists, who were in control of the National Guard, a paramilitary organization, attempted to stir up more trouble, but they were unsuccessful. Arif purged the Baathist party's extremists who had been encouraged by the Baathist party of Syria. As a result, the Syrian Revolutionary Council denounced Arif's policies as well as his regime.

In 1964, Arif took steps toward the establishment of union with Egypt. However, a constitutional document announced on May 4, 1964, established a period of three years during which time the status of the government would be provisional. Presumably, therefore, the regime desired gradual unification between the two countries rather than immediate and complete political integration. Thus, on May 26, the two countries agreed to establish a Joint Presidency Council to integrate their economic and military policies. On July 4, 1964, President Arif issued instructions to integrate all political parties in one organization to be called the Iraqi Arab Socialist Union. The new political organization was comparable to its Egyptian counterpart of the same name. Furthermore, the Iraqi government began to introduce socialistic programs, and many private establishments, banks, insurance companies, and industrial enterprises were nationalized. All of these measures were designed to make the institutions of Egypt and Iraq similar, so that the final step toward political integration could be taken. However, a second conflict over the speed of unification developed within the Arif government. Arif wanted to move slowly and to attain some sense of the people's reaction to the socialization program. Six Cabinet members were opposed to this policy and resigned in July 1965. Nevertheless, Arif designated Brigadier General Abdul Razzaq, a pro-Nasser officer, as the new prime minister. This proved to be a mistake, for Razzaq attempted a coup while Arif was attending an Arab conference in Casablanca. Had it not been for the president's brother, who was chief of staff of the Iraqi army, the coup might have succeeded.

Razzaq's abortive coup was a setback for plans to unify Egypt and Iraq. Although Arif did not discard altogether the possibility of union with Egypt sometime in the future, the question of unity was postponed indefinitely. The death of Arif in a helicopter crash on April 13, 1966 brought no drastic changes in policy. His brother, Abdul Rahman Arif, became the new president. Nor was there a drastic or fundamental change in Iraqi policies after the coup of July 1968, which was led by General Ahmad al-Bakr.

Although many contacts were made with various Arab countries to discuss Arab cooperation and unity, nothing came of them. However, in the few months following the defeat of the Arab armies by Israel in June 1967, Iraq showed more serious concern about the future of Arab unity. The humiliation which was borne by the Arab leaders as a result of their defeat in the war with Israel might become a new factor in Arab relations. Although the future was still uncertain toward the end of 1968, there were signs that Syria, Iraq, and Egypt were moving toward the left. Their policies became more anti-Western and more authoritarian.

The Settlement of the Kurdish Problem. As mentioned earlier, the Kurdish rebellion was quelled but did not end. Sporadic fighting occurred throughout the next four years, 1962–66. The Arif coup of 1963 was well received by Kurdish leaders, but these leaders made known their intention to continue the struggle until an agreeable settlement was possible.

An effort to settle the dispute was made in August 1963, when the Iraqi government offered the Kurds limited autonomy, a share of Iraq's oil revenue amounting to $56 million a year, and indemnities in the amount of $14 million for war losses. The Kurdish leaders rejected that offer, but in February 1964 agreed to a cease-fire with the stipulation that Kurdish rights and claims would be recognized in a new constitutional document. The Iraqi government also agreed to grant a general amnesty for the Kurds. This truce did not require the Kurdish tribesmen to lay down their arms. It was assumed that such a requirement would depend on a final solution to the Kurdish problem. In fact, sporadic fighting occurred during part of 1966, and the truce agreement proved to be of limited success only.

Nevertheless, the final solution was announced in June 1966, and Barzani, the leader of the rebellion, announced his consent to it. According to the terms of the settlement, the Iraqi government would recognize Kurdish nationalism as legitimate. The governmental process was to be decentralized so as to allow Kurdish control of their educational and municipal affairs. The Kurds were to be represented in Parliament and in the Cabinet in proportion to their numbers. In addition, more Kurds were to be recruited in the governmental services. Finally, the Kurds would in return lay down their arms and dissolve their rebel army.

THE ECONOMY

Economists consider Iraq to be one of the less developed countries of the Middle East, but they also consider it to be ideally suited for economic development. It has extensive resources, low population density in proportion to its resources, and capital.[17] The obstacles to economic progress include mainly the lack of knowhow and the persistence of archaic social attitudes. Since 1950, both of these problems have been attacked, but it

17. Fahim I. Qubain, *The Reconstruction of Iraq: 1950–57* (New York: Frederick A. Praeger, 1958), p. 254.

will take a long time before they are eliminated. It remains true, however, that the economic future of Iraq looks better than those of other countries of the Middle East.

Agriculture. Iraq is an agricultural country. It has land and water. The latter element comes from her two great rivers, the Tigris and the Euphrates, but their efficient use requires construction of massive projects for flood control, water storage, and irrigation. Of course, such projects need large amounts of capital. The great irrigation systems which were built thousands of years ago and were responsible for the prosperity of Mesopotamia, were destroyed by the Mongols, and ever since that time, the land of Iraq and its agriculture have been neglected. Only recently have there been serious efforts to revive agriculture by building adequate irrigation systems. Four dams were constructed between 1956 and 1961 alone, and they have been successful in providing protection against floods. Other irrigation schemes were initiated between 1961 and 1967; among them was the Eski-Mosul project introduced in 1963. It is estimated that by the time these projects are completed, the area of cultivated land in Iraq will have doubled.

The government has already shown interest in agricultural production and the distribution of land. So far, its policy has aimed at the creation of communities of small landholders. Land was given to the landless on condition that they would live on their new holdings. The government also encouraged the formation of cooperative societies and provided the new farmer with technical assistance and loans. These measures were part of the 1958 land-reform plan which was realized in a period of five years. Another feature of this plan was to set limits on landholdings. The maximum holding was six hundred acres for land watered by irrigation and twelve hundred acres for land watered by rain.

Industry. Until 1958, Iraqi governments had generally shown wisdom in their industrialization policies. Realizing that Iraq is not an overpopulated country, and that her agriculture is potentially sufficient to support her, they aimed at industrialization on a limited scale. In pursuing this policy, they were conscious of the severe handicap created by the lack of know-how.

Consequently, outside Baghdad, Iraq had few industries of significance in 1958. Among these were cement, date packing, cigarette manufacturing, spinning and weaving, shoe making, and chemicals. With the exception of the cement industry, most of these were small enterprises. In 1962, there were 1,162 enterprises employing ten or more persons. The greater number of industrial enterprises are found in Baghdad, the capital. A textile factory was built in 1958 at Mosul and employs twelve hundred workers, and a large sugar factory was also constructed. In 1961, a cigarette factory was opened in the Kurdish city of Sulaimania and the next year a shoe factory was opened at Kufa.

The revolutionary regimes of 1958 and 1963 put new emphasis on industrialization. The new leaders seemed to believe that past emphasis on agriculture was an imperialist policy designed to keep Iraq in backwardness. To them, power and industry were the same, and no country could hope to attain respectability in the international community without industrialization.[18] It was therefore to be expected that these regimes would invest more heavily in industry. Accordingly, the Development Plan for 1966–70 allocated 28 per cent of its budget to industrial development in comparison with 26 per cent for agriculture, which had been given priority by the old regime.

Industrialization has been encouraged by the recent discovery of deposits of iron ore, chromite, copper, lead, and zinc in the north. Iraq also has significant deposits of limestone, gypsum, salt, dolomite, phosphates, and sulphur. Nor should we forget Iraq's most precious natural resource— oil. Before the Arab-Israeli war of June 1967, oil accounted for about 94 per cent of the country's exports.

In recent years, emphasis has been placed on diversification of industry. The Development Plan of 1966–70 envisaged the establishment of a chemical-petrochemical complex and also a steel mill. Plans were made for the development of a metal industry, plastics, pharmaceuticals, and electrical appliances.[19]

Of course, the success of these plans is by no means assured. Industry is still in its infancy, accounting for only 10 per cent of the national income and engaging about the same proportion of the labor force. Secondly, its future is dependent upon the future of Iraqi socialism, which was introduced in the summer of 1964. At that time, all the big firms were put under state control, making the development of heavy industry a governmental responsibility. The future of industrialization also depends on the military commitments of the state. After the Arab defeat in the 1967 war with Israel, such commitments were expected to be heavy. The government of Iraq is now giving priority to the building of its military power, and this, of course, is expected to have a negative impact upon other investment. Lastly, industrialization—indeed the whole area of economic planning—is dependent upon the political stability of the country, and this stability is by no means certain.

Finally, Iraq's principal source of capital is oil, and oil is the country's

18. Kathleen M. Langley, *The Industrialization of Iraq* (Cambridge: Harvard University Press, 1961), p. 267.

19. E. Kanovsky, "Arab Economic Unity," *The Middle East Journal* (Spring, 1967), p. 228.

main hope for a successful economic development. Without it, Iraq's economic future would not be very different from that of other Middle Eastern countries which do not have oil.

Iraq is the eighth largest oil producer in the world and the fourth largest in the Middle East. Total production rose from 22 million tons in 1957 to 63.2 million tons in 1965. The Iraq Petroleum Company and its associates operate the oil industry. Under the 1952 oil agreement with the company, the government of Iraq received half of the oil company's profit. In 1965, this amounted to 131 million Iraqi dinars (I.D. 1 = £ sterling = $2.80). Until 1959, 70 per cent of the oil revenues went to the Development Board established in 1950 to take charge of economic development. However, the Kassem regime reduced this share to 50 per cent.

Immediately after the Arab-Israeli war of June 1967, Iraq cut oil shipments to the West. In an Arab oil conference meeting in Baghdad in August 1967, Iraq proposed a two-year ban on all oil exports to the Western countries that continued to support Israel after the June war. However, the Khartoum Arab Summit Conference of October 1967 rejected the proposal in favor of resumption of oil shipments to the West. Another outcome of the war was the development of closer ties between Iraq and France, which took a pro-Arab position in the aftermath of the Arab-Israeli war. France is providing military equipment to Iraq and receiving economic advantages in return. One of these advantages is oil. And as the year 1969 began, France was the only Western country with significant economic advantages in Iraq.

CHAPTER 9

ISRAEL: THE MAKING
OF A NATION

J E W I S H national independence in what was known as the "Land of Israel" ended in 63 B.C. From that time on Jews dreamed of returning to what they believed was their "Promised Land." But their dream did not come true until 1948, when the State of Israel was established.

The dispersion of the Jews and their persecution were dramatic events in the political movements that brought about the modern State of Israel. Just as dramatic, however, is the story of the land they left after the Romans destroyed their political identity; for while the Jews were cherishing the hope of returning to Palestine, the political identity of the land itself changed several times.

After the Romans conquered Jerusalem, many Jews were sold into slavery. Those who remained free stayed on with the hope of regaining political independence. They made several attempts but failed, and after revolts in two different periods, A.D. 66–73 and A.D. 132–135, the Roman rulers renewed their persecution and no longer permitted Jews to reside in the city of Jerusalem. Moreover, the Romans changed both the name of the city and the country. Jerusalem became Aeolia Capitalina and Judea was called "Palestine." After each revolt, many Jews emigrated to the various Mediterranean countries, but some chose to settle in Galilee, the northern part of Palestine, where they were allowed a measure of political autonomy.

Flanked by the fertile valleys of the Nile to the west and the Euphrates to the east, "Palestine was tossed like a ball from Empire to Empire." Palestine was controlled by the Romans and their successors, the Byzantine Christians (320–614), and the Persians then controlled Palestine for a brief period. The Byzantines were able to return in 628, when they massacred a large number of Jews. Ten years later, the Arabs conquered Palestine and ruled it until 1071, when the Seljuks were able to wrest power from them.

212

In 1099, the Holy Land was occupied by the Crusaders, but the Latin kingdom they established was destroyed by the Muslims in 1187. Following the Muslim conquest, the area fell under the control of the Tartars in 1244 and then of the Mongols in 1259. A year later the Mameluke sultans of Egypt defeated the Mongols. In 1517, the Ottoman Turks conquered the area, and maintained their rule for over four hundred years. Finally, the defeat of Turkey by the Allied nations in World War I brought the whole area known as the Levant under British military occupation. In 1920, the League of Nations assigned Palestine to Great Britain as a mandate territory, which it remained until the establishment of the State of Israel in 1948.

JEWISH IMMIGRATION TO PALESTINE

It is estimated that 50,000 Jews resided in Palestine in 1900 and that the Jewish population of the entire world was 11,000,000.[1] Thus, less than one-one hundredth of the Jewish population of the world lived in Palestine. The percentage, of course, indicates that outside Jewish interest in Palestine was extremely limited. Most Jews knew that the Muslim Turks, who were in control of Palestine, usually resisted the admission into Palestine of a religiously and culturally alien people like the Jews. However, Jewish demands upon the sultan of Turkey were partially met by the admission of 25,000 Jews between 1882 and 1903. The greater number of these immigrants came from eastern Europe. A second reason was that Palestine was not considered by the Jews of other countries to be a land of opportunity. It was a primitive agricultural country, and European Jews had little interest in farming, perhaps because for centuries they had been prohibited from engaging in this pursuit. Mainly for these reasons, Jews preferred to immigrate to more prosperous countries—the United States, England, Argentina, and countries of western Europe.

The Zionist movement, which attempted to create a political consciousness among the Jews of Europe, was eventually able to stir Jewish interest in the Holy Land. However, there were formidable political obstacles confronting the movement's efforts to bring about mass immigration of Jews to Palestine. For instance, the Arab people of Palestine were becoming politically conscious, and it was feared that they might resist such mass immigration. Zionist pressure upon the British government succeeded in persuading the British to issue the famous Balfour Declaration of 1917 prom-

1. *Statistical Abstract of Israel, 1963* (Jerusalem: Central Bureau of Statistics, 1963), p. 18.

ising "a national home" for the Jews in Palestine.[2] Although the exact interpretation of the term "a national home" later became a highly controversial matter, the document was a major victory for the Zionist movement, for it meant that the British government would thereafter facilitate the mass immigration of Jews to Palestine.

In 1918, only one-tenth of the total population of Palestine of nearly 700,000 was Jewish; the rest was Arab, both Christian and Muslim. However, by 1926 the Jewish population had grown by about 250 per cent compared to what it was in 1918. The increase in the Jewish population alarmed the Palestinian Arabs, but the Zionist leaders, who desired to hasten the establishment of a Jewish state, were not satisfied. Nevertheless, by 1932 there were 200,000 Jews living in Palestine, about 17 per cent of the country's population.[3]

The Zionist movement wanted to create a Jewish majority in Palestine, or at least to establish a large enough proportion of the population on which to argue the necessity of establishing a Jewish state. This goal was gradually being attained. Between 1932 and 1939, 225,000 Jews were admitted into the country, bringing the Jewish population up to nearly half a million and about 30 per cent of the total population. This sudden Jewish interest in Palestine was caused mainly by the depression of the 1930's in Europe and the United States, which made it difficult, if not impossible, for Jews to immigrate to these areas.

In the mid-1930's, Arab opposition to Jewish immigration became violent, causing the British government to issue in 1939 a White Paper restricting Jewish immigration to Palestine to a maximum of 75,000 in the next five years.[4] The White Paper also stipulated that immigration after the five-year period would be based upon the consent of the Palestinian Arabs. More disturbing to Zionist leaders was the paper's promise to establish in the next decade an independent Palestinian—not Jewish—state, in which, of course, the Arabs would have a majority. This meant that the Zionist hope for establishing their own state in Palestine would not be realized. The White Paper policy was strictly adhered to during World War II. However, large-scale Jewish immigration was carried out by illegal means, and this was stimulated by Hitler's policy of persecution.

After the war, the political situation in Palestine was extremely dangerous. Jewish terrorists attacked the British, and a period of violence ensued. Consequently, in 1947 the British turned the problem of Palestine over to

2. Text in J. C. Hurewitz, ed., *Diplomacy in the Near and Middle East; A Documentary Record: 1914–1956* (Princeton: Van Nostrand, 1956), vol. II, p. 25.

3. For figures on Jewish immigration and a brief but useful analysis of the subject, see the first two chapters in Leonard J. Fein, *Politics in Israel* (Boston: Little, Brown and Company, 1967), pp. 9–66.

4. Text in Hurewitz, vol. II, p. 218.

the United Nations. On November 29, 1947 the General Assembly v
to partition Palestine into two states, one Jewish and one Arab. The S
of Israel came into being on May 14, 1948. At the time it was proclaime
30 per cent of the population of Palestine was Jewish; the rest was Arab
The success of Zionism, therefore, can be measured by the fact that it was
able to organize the mass immigration of Jews and manipulate all the relevant political forces on behalf of a Jewish minority that wanted a Jewish
state.

POLITICAL ZIONISM

Zionism is a movement whose object is the reconstruction of the Jewish
nation. As mentioned earlier, some Jews had always yearned to return to
Palestine. This "Messianic vision" of returning to the Promised Land was
essentially based upon religious beliefs, yet its implications were largely
political, since Palestine was Arab and the return of the Jews required the
overcoming of a natural and understandable Arab opposition. In a sense,
therefore, the Zionist movement provided the political means by which its
religious goal could be achieved.

The difficulty facing the Zionist movement at the turn of this century was
that most Jews did not want to re-enter Palestine. Some Jews believed that
their return to Palestine depended on an act of God, and they thought that
such efforts of man were virtually sacrilegious. Others believed that the
solution of their dilemma depended on their own willingness to assimilate
with different national cultures. The liberal attitudes toward Jews in the
eighteenth and nineteenth centuries made this theory very appealing to
Jews, especially to those from western Europe. Finally, there were those
who were concerned that Zionism might cause the non-Jew to doubt the
Jew's loyalty to his country of birth or citizenship. This, they believed, was
the most significant and most dangerous implication of Zionism.

In the past, certain Jewish leaders expressed alarm at Jewish apathy
about their religious and cultural identity. Moses Mendelssohn (1729–
86), for instance, saw a threat to Jewish religious culture and advocated
the strengthening of the religious values. This kind of concern produced
Zionist political ideas. One of these was the belief that if the Jewish reli-
gious-cultural identity were to be preserved, a territorial base was a necessity. Palestine was not necessarily the only territory which could fulfill the
goal of Jewish survival. Sociologically speaking, any territory could accomplish this objective. However, from a religious point of view, Palestine was
the ideal place since she answered the religious as well as the cultural needs
of the Jews. Furthermore, eastern European Jews favored Palestine
because many of them had already gone there.

The Zionist movement remained largely theoretical until the 1890's when Theodor Herzl (1860–1904) became its leader. Herzl, who was born in Budapest but lived later in Vienna and then in Paris, was a journalist. He became famous as a result of a pamphlet, "The Jewish State," which he wrote in 1896.[5] In his early years an advocate of Jewish assimilation, he, like many of his Jewish contemporaries, became converted to Zionism as a result of the Dreyfus Affair,[6] when he came to believe that "Jews could overcome anti-Semitism only by becoming sovereign over a given territory."[7] Herzl was uncommitted about the location of a Jewish state, although he thought Argentina and Palestine were possible sites.

The First Zionist Congress met in 1897 in Basel under Herzl's leadership and resolved on the creation of a Jewish home in Palestine. Subsequently Herzl, as the first president of the organization, set out to secure a charter from the Turkish sultan which would permit the Zionists to organize Jewish colonization in Palestine. But the sultan rejected his request, an event which in essence warned the Zionists that the road to Palestine would be long and arduous.

But the Zionist movement was by no means united in its goal to create an independent Jewish state in Palestine. Early in 1901, Ahad Ha'am (Asher Ginsberg), a Jewish social philosopher, argued a theory of "cultural Zionism" which emphasized Jewish culture over political involvement. Ginsberg believed that the settlement of Jews was a more urgent matter than the question of "political self-government in Palestine" and that the former should not depend on the latter.[8]

A more serious issue divided the Zionists in 1905. The British offered the Jews the possibility of making Uganda, East Africa, their national home; and the question was to be decided in the 1905 meeting of the Zionist Congress. Although the majority favored rejecting the British offer, a minority known as the "Territorialists," led by Israel Zangwill (1864–1926),[9] withdrew from the conference on the grounds that the urgency of the Jewish problem required immediate refuge for the Jews.

Zionist leaders fought over many other issues, but none of the disputes

5. See T. Herzl, *The Jewish State* (New York: American Zionist Emergency Council, 1946).

6. This involved the false arrest and the imprisonment of Captain Alfred Dreyfus (1859–1935) by French authorities in 1894. Dreyfus, a French Jew, was exonerated in 1906. The incident caused many Jews to believe that anti-Semitism was for them a fact of life even in the liberal and democratic countries of the West.

7. Marver H. Bernstein, *The Politics of Israel: The First Decade of Statehood* (Princeton: Princeton University Press, 1957), p. 7.

8. Bernstein, *The Politics of Israel*, p. 8.

9. Zangwill was an English author of the Jewish faith. He wrote several books: *Children of the Ghetto* (1892), *Dreamers of the Ghetto* (1898), *Merely Mary Ann* (1893), *The Melting Pot* (1914), *The Principle of Nationalities* (1917), and finally *Chosen Peoples* (1918).

prevented the movement from being effective and dynamic. Zionism achieved an extremely impressive record of accomplishment in a very difficult task—one that some people thought impossible—under Chaim Weizmann, who assumed leadership in the World Zionist Movement after 1920. Weizmann believed in "synthetic Zionism," the theory that colonization was attainable by diplomatic action. His approach was responsible for the increase in Jewish immigration to Palestine in the early years of the British mandate.

But whatever the successes of the Zionist movement, it is also true that without the cooperation of the British before 1939, Zionism would have had greater difficulties in furthering its aims. We will, therefore, consider the mandate system as it existed between 1920 and 1948.

THE BRITISH MANDATE

Palestine was governed by Turkey as a province of Syria. The population had been preponderantly Arab since shortly after the conquest by the Arabs in the seventh century; the Palestine Jewish community numbered no more than twenty-five thousand in 1880.

Under the Turks, Palestine enjoyed a large degree of political autonomy. Economically, however, she was a neglected territory. Her agriculture was primitive and so was her transportation system. Thus, when the British were preparing to establish their mandate system in 1920, they found the country on the verge of political and economic bankruptcy. The three years of British occupation, from 1917 to 1920, had been a period of transition, but the military administration had been unable to cope with the many problems besetting Palestinian life.

It was the crucial task of the British mandate to reconstruct the economy and to provide the country with an efficient and responsible governmental system. But the British were handicapped by the promises and counterpromises they had made to the Palestinian Jews and Arabs. As a reward for the valuable assistance the Arabs rendered to the Allied forces during World War I, the British made them a number of promises. In 1917, they made promises to the Jews which seemed to conflict with their previous commitments to the Arabs, and the provisions of the mandate [10] embodied the Balfour commitments to the Jews. This situation, of course, caused bitter controversy among the British, Arabs, and Jews, and eliminated all hope of establishing stability in Palestine during the mandate period. Moreover, the energies of Palestinians were dissipated by their quarrels, so that it was impossible for them to create political institutions and guide them to maturity.

The three parties involved inevitably disagreed on the future of Pales-

10. Hurewitz, vol. II, p. 106.

tine. The Zionists believed that the establishment of a Jewish national home should be the principal object of British rule. Accordingly, the Jews demanded that the British government do all it could to honor its commitments under the Balfour Declaration and the mandate agreement. As time went on, the Zionists began to insist that the term "national home," which was used repeatedly in these documents, meant the establishment of a state for the Jews. The Arabs, on the other hand, believed that the country belonged to them, since they were in the majority, and that the British and the Zionists were determining the future of their country without their approval or participation.[11]

The British were caught in the middle, and their policy fluctuated between pro-Zionist and pro-Arab positions. However, before World War II, the British decided that their true interest was with the Arabs; and as we have already seen they issued the White Paper in 1939. After the war, American pressure forced them to take a neutral position.

In the period of hesitation and procrastination, Palestine was ruled according to the familiar British colonial pattern. At the apex of the governmental pyramid was a high commissioner who possessed extensive executive and legislative powers. He was assisted by an all-British Executive Council composed of senior civil servants. The court system enjoyed some degree of independence: it was headed by a British chief justice, but Arab, Jewish, and British judges and magistrates were part of the judicial branch. However, few Arabs and Jews were able to reach high positions in the administration, and they were always under a British senior official.

In terms of their ratio to the whole population of Palestine, the Muslim Arabs were underrepresented in the government service, and the Jews and Christian Arabs were overrepresented. This disparity was due in part to the fact that the Muslims were behind the other two groups in social development and education. Possibly, too, the British were applying the old principle of "divide and rule" in order to maintain political control over the three groups.

The British failure to establish institutions of self-government in Palestine was partly due to their indecision and lack of consistency. Had they not, for instance, commenced their rule by confusing the Arabs and Jews about their intentions, they might have succeeded in inducing these two parties to cooperate for their common interests, although such cooperation would have been very difficult to achieve. The Arabs were uncompromising, underappreciative of potential British contribution, and doubtful of

11. The Arabs proposed, on several occasions, the establishment in Palestine of an Arab state with adequate safeguards for Jewish citizens. Within this Arab state, the Jews would be able to enjoy the fulfillment of their cultural and religious aspirations. See George Antonius, *The Arab Awakening* (London: Hamish Hamilton, 1938), p. 410.

British sincerity. The Jews wanted a separate social and political existence and showed little interest in any joint endeavor with the Arabs. They were preoccupied with their plans to establish their home in Palestine.

Nevertheless, the British twice attempted to develop self-government in Palestine. In 1922, the high commissioner revealed plans for the establishment of an elected advisory body with quasi-legislative functions representing the three major Palestinian groups, Muslim, Christian, and Jewish. The Arabs boycotted the elections, and the plan was dropped. In 1932, a similar plan was announced, and this time both Arabs and Jews rejected it. The Arabs wanted to give the proposed body real legislative powers and objected to the high commissioner's right of an absolute veto of the acts of the advisory council. The Jews rejected the plan because they did not want "to enter a council dominated by an Arab majority." [12]

THE EMERGENCE OF ISRAEL

Under the mandate, the Jewish community in Palestine was a state within a state. Jewish quasi-governmental institutions existed alongside the mandatory regime for more than a quarter of a century. Jews received training in self-government under these institutions, and this training and background was of immense value to them when they were able to establish their sovereignty over the greatest part of Palestine. Unlike the Palestinian Arabs, who lacked adequate experience in self-government, partly because the British would not allow a community government for the Arabs,[13] the Jews had no difficulty ruling themselves in 1948.

Jewish Political Institutions. Under the mandate, there were two Jewish political institutions: the Community Government and the Jewish Agency. The first took charge of the internal affairs of the Jewish community. It consisted of an elected Assembly as the equivalent of a national legislature in sovereign states, a National Council which exercised the power of the Assembly between sessions, and an Executive Council which was the administration of the Community Government.

The Assembly was elected by all Jews over twenty years of age having at least three months' residence in Palestine. (Women had acquired the right to vote in Assembly elections in spite of bitter opposition from the ultra-orthodox Jews.) Between 1920 and 1947 four elections took place, in 1920, 1925, 1931, and 1944. The size of the Assembly fluctuated from a high of 314 deputies in 1920 to a low of 71 in 1931. Elections were based

12. Bernstein, *The Politics of Israel,* p. 19.
13. The British allowed the Arabs to elect local municipal councils, but these councils had very little power. Matters pertaining to education and police were under central British control.

on proportional representation, and twenty political parties contested the elections of 1920. Twenty-eight parties contested the elections in 1925, sixteen those in 1931, and twenty-four those in 1944. By 1948, the system of proportional representation and multiparty politics had become part of the tradition of the Palestinian Jews. The National Council was appointed by the Assembly from among its members, and the Executive Council was chosen by the National Council from among its members.

Because the Community Government did not have the power to tax the Jews of Palestine and because it was not officially recognized by the British, its effectiveness and involvement were limited. However, this situation began to change after 1927, when the mandate government recognized it and conferred upon it the power to tax. Gradually the Community Government initiated various public services and programs, such as administering social welfare, settling labor-management disputes, and dealing with employment and unemployment.

The second major political institution, the Jewish Agency, had no problem being recognized by the mandate government, since Article 4 of the mandate agreement called for its establishment. According to this agreement, the Agency's responsibility was "to take part in the development of the country" as well as to assist the mandate government "in such economic, social, and other matters as may affect the establishment of the Jewish national home." [14] Between 1922 and 1929, the Agency's authority was exercised by the Zionist Organization. However, this arrangement was not satisfactory to the non-Zionists who, although they had accepted the idea of a Jewish home in Palestine, did not believe in the establishment of a Jewish state. In 1929, the Jewish Agency included non-Zionists for the first time since its establishment; this was due to the efforts of Chaim Weizmann, who had sought their cooperation mainly because of their potential financial support. The Jewish Agency became the official spokesman for the Palestinian Jews.

The structure of the Jewish Agency was similar to that of the Community Government. It had a council of 224 members who met once every two years to formulate the broad lines of policy and to elect an administrative commitee. The Agency was headed by the president of the Zionist Organization and was organized into departments which took charge of its political and administrative activities. In time, the Agency became more significant than the Community Government. Its international political activity, its responsibility for Jewish immigration, and the fact that the mandate government considered it the spokesman for the Jews were factors in this development. In fact, the executive department of the Agency became comparable to the organization of sovereign states and performed similar functions. Thus, when the State of Israel was established in 1948, the

14. Text in Hurewitz, vol. II, p. 106.

Agency's executive department was easily transformed into governmental units.

Very important is the fact that the Agency was one of the sponsors of the Haganah, a "defense force" organized to defend the Jewish community against Arab attacks. In reality, the Haganah was much more than a small defensive militia, as was demonstrated by its later successful defense of the territory of Israel against attack by Arab regular armies.

The Partition of Palestine. Immediately after the end of World War II, violence broke out between the Jews and the British. The situation became so serious that the Labour government of Great Britain referred the Palestinian problem to the United Nations. On April 28, 1947, the General Assembly met in a special session to explore possible solutions to that problem. On May 15, a special committee on Palestine was established. UNSCOP, as the committee became known, held hearings in Palestine and some Arab countries to gather information and to listen to views regarding the Palestinian situation. The committee also visited displaced-persons camps in Europe. It concluded that Palestine should be partitioned into two states, one Arab and the other Jewish. This conclusion was reported to the General Assembly in September 1947.

The General Assembly discussed the commitee's majority and minority reports for a period of two months. The majority report embodied the partition plan, the minority report proposed the establishment in Palestine of one federal state which would unite an "Arab province" and a "Jewish province." It was supported by three members of UNSCOP: Yugoslavia, India, and Iran. In these debates, Great Britain strongly opposed partition, and so did all the Arab states, who favored a unitary Arab state in Palestine. The Soviet Union and the United States favored partition.

The adoption of a plan required a two-thirds majority in the Assembly. As it turned out, the influence which the United States exerted over the Latin American countries was decisive, and the partition plan was chosen on November 29, 1948. The famous Resolution 181 (11) [15] passed by a vote of 33 to 13, with the Arab and Muslim states, Cuba, Greece, and India opposed. Great Britain abstained.

According to the resolution, the mandate for Palestine was to be terminated, and the British armed forces were to be withdrawn no later than August 1, 1948. Separate Arab and Jewish states were to be established; the Jewish state was to receive 55 per cent of the total area of Palestine. Jerusalem was given an international status under the United Nations Trusteeship Council. In addition, the resolution provided for the establishment of an economic and social union between the two states. This union would promote joint economic programs such as irrigation projects, soil

15. United Nations, Official Records of the Second Session of the General Assembly, *Resolutions* (A/519, Jan. 8, 1948 [Lake Success, 1950]), pp. 131–50.

conservation, interstate communication, currency regulations, and a customs union.

Statehood. Shortly after the partition decision, the British government announced that it would terminate the mandate on May 15, 1948, but that it would not participate in the execution of the United Nations decision. The Jewish Agency informed the United Nations that it planned to proclaim the Jewish state as soon as the mandate ended. This proclamation was made on May 14, 1948, which became the official date for the establishment of the new State of Israel. The National Council of the Jewish Community Government elected David Ben-Gurion as prime minister of Israel's provisional government. Ben-Gurion, who was born in Russian-occupied Poland in 1886, had emigrated to Palestine in 1906, when he became active in the Zionist movement. Prior to the Proclamation of Independence he was the chairman of the Jewish Agency and head of its security department. A cabinet was also nominated by the council, representing the political parties of the Jewish community. Weizmann, head of the Zionist Organization, became the first president of Israel.

Since the State of Israel was born in a belligerent environment and was threatened by the Arab states which opposed the partition of Palestine, it became necessary for the new state to seek recognition of its sovereignty by members of the world community. The first nation to recognize Israel was the United States, which did so on May 14, the day Israel was established. Four days later the Soviet Union followed suit, and by February 1, 1949, thirty-three countries had recognized Israel, including Britain.

The next step in Israel's efforts to gain acceptance as a sovereign state was to seek admission to the United Nations. An application for admission was filed on November 29, 1948, but it failed to receive sufficient votes in the Security Council. The Arab-Israeli war which was going on at that time was the primary reason for the rejection of the application. However, when the armistice agreement between Egypt and Israel was signed on February 24, 1949, Israel renewed its application for admission, and on March 4 the Security Council voted 9 to 1 for admission; Egypt opposed admission and Britain abstained. The formal procedure for admission was concluded on May 11, when the General Assembly accepted the Security Council's recommendation for the admission of Israel, and Israel became the fifty-ninth member of the United Nations.

THE ARAB-ISRAELI WAR OF 1948–1949

In the years before the establishment of the State of Israel, the Arabs of Palestine saw the large-scale immigration of Jews as a threat to their majority status and as an intrusion upon their national rights and security.

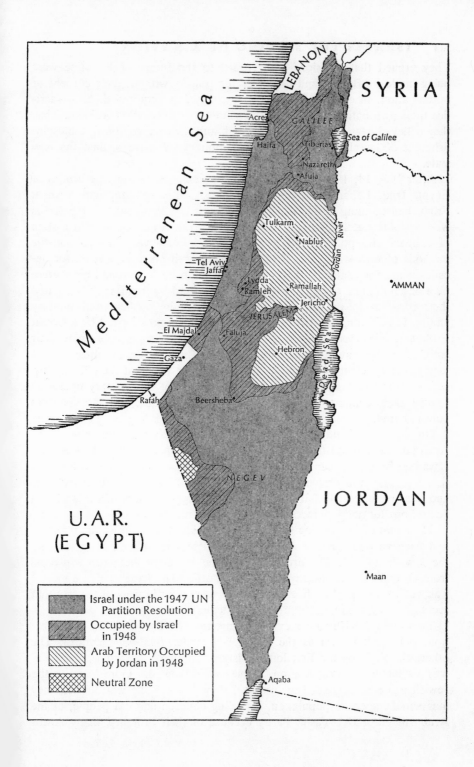

Mediterranean Sea

SYRIA

LEBANON

Acre
GALILEE
Haifa
Tiberias
Sea of Galilee
Nazareth
Afula

Tulkarm
Nablus

Tel Aviv
Jaffa
Lydda
Ramleh
Ramallah
Jericho
JERUSALEM
AMMAN
El Majdal
Faluja
Hebron
Gaza
Dead Sea
Rafah
Beersheba

NEGEV

JORDAN

U.A.R.
(EGYPT)

Maan

Jordan River

Israel under the 1947 UN
Partition Resolution

Occupied by Israel
in 1948

Arab Territory Occupied
by Jordan in 1948

Neutral Zone

Aqaba

They argued that decisions with regard to the future of Palestine were being made by Britain and the other big powers without their consent or participation. In essence, such decisions, they felt, required them to sacrifice their own national rights for the solution of the Jewish problem. This, they believed, was unfair as well as cruel, and their opposition to the establishment of Israel took the form of a military offensive against the new state.

After May 14, 1948, the Arab offensive included the regular armies of Egypt, Iraq, Lebanon, Saudi Arabia, Syria, Transjordan, and Yemen. From the beginning of this attack, however, it was apparent that the Arabs were not adequately prepared. Most of the Arab countries were in a state of cultural and political transformation and knew very little about the methods of war, which they had not experienced on a large scale for decades if not for centuries. They lacked common leadership and a coherent plan of action, and some of them were still bound by treaties which limited their freedom to pursue independent policies in political and military affairs. In addition, the Arab armies were trained and supplied by different European countries, and it was very difficult for them to coordinate their activities or to draw up a common strategy. But perhaps the most serious factor in the defeat of the Arab armies was the fact that their leadership seriously underestimated Israel. They thought that the military operation against their common enemy would be brief, because the Israelis were outnumbered.

On the other hand, the Israelis were well organized and united. The Arab attack involved their very survival as a people and as a new nation. Jews had waited for centuries to fulfill their religious dream, and now that they had made this dream a reality they must defend it with all their power and their resources: to fail would be a catastrophe from which there could be no hope for national recovery and religious revival.

The brunt of the fighting fell on the Haganah, which during the mandate had been an underground militia organized by the Labor Federation and the Jewish Agency. The arms used by the Haganah had been smuggled from abroad or made locally in secret factories. The Israeli defense system was well developed, but the mobile forces were poor in view of the fact that secrecy during the mandate prevented adequate training.

Two other Jewish forces existed. One, the National Military Organization, popularly known as the *Irgun,* was under right-wing control. The other, the Fighters for Freedom of Israel, popularly known as the *Lehi,* was a chauvinistic organization. These two militias did more harm to the Jewish cause than good. For instance, they shocked the world when they massacred the entire population, including children and old people, of the Arab village of Der Yasin. Partly because of their brutality, many Arabs fled their villages and towns, hoping to return after the Arab armies had driven the Israelis out.

The war lasted nearly eight months and ended with Arab defeat. During these months, the United Nations tried but failed to secure a cease-fire. The U.N. representative, Swedish Count Folke Bernadotte, lost his life at the hands of an Israeli assassin while attempting to bring peace to the warring parties. Armistice agreements between Israel and the Arab states were finally concluded during 1949, beginning with the Egyptian-Israeli Armistice Agreement of February 24, but no peace treaty was signed.

The outcome of the war was beneficial for Israel. She was able to add 2,500 square miles to the territory assigned to her under the United Nations partition resolution. The remaining portion of Palestine went to Jordan and Egypt. Jordan gained control of 2,200 square miles along the western bank of the Jordan, and Egypt acquired the Gaza strip, a twenty-eight-mile stretch of land in southern Palestine along the Mediterranean coast. These territories would have been part of the Arab state had the partition resolution been enforced.

The Arab defeat resulted in the displacement of nearly one million Arabs who fled Israel during the war. The reasons these refugees left their homes are still not certain. The Israeli government claimed that the Arab states had urged the refugees to leave both for tactical reasons and to discredit Israel in the eyes of other nations. But the Arab states argued that the Arab Palestinians were driven out of their villages to make room for Jews coming to Israel from other parts of the world.

In spite of the fact that the refugee problem remains unsolved and a peace treaty with the Arabs has never been signed, Israeli statehood is now a reality which the Arabs cannot ignore, although they can refuse to recognize Israel's existence as they have done since 1948.

ISRAEL'S POLITICAL INSTITUTIONS

The United Nations resolution of November 29, 1947, required each of the two new states to hold elections for a constituent assembly within two months following the withdrawal of British forces. The resolution also required the two states to establish a legislature to be elected on the basis of proportional representation and an executive to be responsible to the legislature.

The Declaration of the Establishment of the State of Israel, proclaimed on May 14, 1948, stated that an elected constituent assembly would adopt a constitution before October 1, 1948, thereby reaffirming the intent of the resolution. However, owing to Arab-Israeli hostilities, the deadline prescribed by the declaration was not met, and permanent governmental institutions were not officially instituted until March 8, 1949, when the first Knesset (Parliament) came into being. In the meantime, political life in Israel was directed by a provisional government. Authority was vested in a Provisional State Council of thirty-eight members, representing the various political parties of Israel, and an executive which was referred to as the Government. These two agencies were in existence prior to statehood, but on May 14, 1948, they received the new status of Provisional Government. On May 19 the Provisional State Council enacted the Law and Administration Ordinance which transformed the Provisional Council into a national legislature and the Government into a Cabinet similar to executive bodies in countries having parliamentary systems. In the Cabinet seven political parties were represented by thirteen ministers holding twenty portfolios. The Cabinet was authorized to develop its own procedures and methods for carrying out the acts of the legislature.

The government was given special powers to be able to cope with the unusual circumstances of the war. The State Council could declare a state of emergency, in which case the Cabinet would authorize one of its members, presumably the prime minister, to issue decrees that had the force of law. However, these decrees were valid only for three months unless extended by the State Council, which had the power to end the state of emergency.

A state of emergency was declared on May 19, 1948, and it continued even after the establishment of the permanent government in March 1949. This did not mean that the legislature abandoned its law-making functions. Since the duration of a state of emergency was controlled by the legislature, the Cabinet received authority only in those areas which were related to national security.

The Constitution. Elections for a constituent assembly were held on January 25, 1949. Two weeks earlier, the State Council had enacted the Constituent Assembly (Transition) Ordinance which provided for the transfer of the Council's power to the elected Constituent Assembly. Matters dealing with the electoral process were also prescribed by this ordinance. Furthermore, the Constituent Assembly's membership was fixed at 120. Election results showed that the Constituent Assembly would represent twelve political parties and would include twelve women and three Israeli Arabs. There were in the Assembly thirty-five farmers, nineteen union officials, eighteen writers, and twelve lawyers. More than a hundred members were emigrants to Palestine.[16]

The major responsibility of the Constituent Assembly was to enact a

16. See the outstanding work of Oscar Kraines, *Government and Politics in Israel* (Boston: Houghton Mifflin, 1961), p. 25. I am indebted to Mr. Kraines for much of the factual material in this chapter.

fundamental law for Israel, which it did on February 16, 1949, when it enacted the "Transition Law." Known as the "small Constitution," the law consists of fifteen brief sections organizing the basic institutions of the state. The Transition Law was not considered to be a true constitution, for arguments about the adoption of a constitution continued after its enactment. Ben-Gurion and his Mapai party opposed the adoption of a written constitution, favoring an evolutionary constitutional process similar to that of Britain. The Mapai maintained that in Britain this evolutionary process was compatible with the development of democracy and that such could also be the case in Israel. Furthermore, if Israel were to have a written constitution anyway, the Mapai argued, then it would be better to wait until Arab hostilities had ceased and the people had become more stable and settled. Ben-Gurion also believed that a written constitution at this early stage in Israel's development would seriously jeopardize Israeli unity because religious conflicts with regard to legal principles could produce political tension at a time when the very existence of the Israeli state was being threatened by the Arabs.

Those who wanted a written constitution believed in its necessity as a guarantee of personal freedoms and rights. Constitutionalism in the twentieth century, they argued, had developed effective means for flexibility and adaptability.

The supporters of evolutionary constitutionalism won the battle, and on June 13, 1950, the Knesset resolved to allow a constitution to develop gradually. However, specific enactment of "fundamental laws" by the legislature was required for this process. Ultimately, therefore, Israel would have a complete constitutional document embodying the separate enactment of "fundamental laws."

Although the Knesset never distinguished between fundamental and ordinary laws, the Constitution of Israel is based upon a number of laws similar to the Transition Law of 1949. As in the British constitutional system, Israel's Knesset can enact a constitutional law by the same simple majority required to enact an ordinary law. Consequently, the distinction between the two must depend upon their subject matter. If an act deals with aspects of the political system which elsewhere are considered to be part of the Constitution, they will be so regarded by the Israelis. But though Israel has no formal constitution like most other modern states, it does not lack the inclinations toward order and system.

THE LEGISLATURE

The Constituent Assembly, which as we said was elected on January 25, 1949, primarily to adopt a constitution, decided on March 8 to transform itself into a Knesset. This body is patterned after the British Parliament, and the similarities between them are numerous. For instance, Parliament is supreme in both governmental systems: legally and technically, the British and Israeli legislatures have unlimited powers. Politically, however, public opinion and the people's sense of democracy serve as restrictions upon their powers. Another similarity is that in neither country can a court of law declare parliamentary acts unconstitutional. Moreover, both legislative bodies have the power to enact constitutional laws.

These similarities are not accidental, for from the turn of this century, the Zionist movement had preferred the British parliamentary system to those of other European countries. The British mandate also influenced Jewish institutions and concepts of government. Furthermore, when the Israeli state was proclaimed in May 1948, its leaders decided—or perhaps found it more convenient and more natural—to retain, as much as was feasible, the laws which already existed. These laws would be modified, of course, in response to conditions and needs.

One main difference between the two parliaments is that, whereas the British institution is bicameral, Israel's is unicameral. Also, while British politics is characterized by a two-party system, Israeli is a multiparty country. Finally, British elections are based on single-member districts, whereas Israeli legislators are elected on the principle of proportional representation. Under the latter system, each political party places before the voters a list of candidates—usually for all the seats in the Knesset—and obtains a percentage of seats equal to the percentage of votes cast for it in the election.

Parliamentary Membership. To be a member of the Knesset a person must be a citizen, be at least twenty-one years of age, and be able to secure a place on a party list. Once elected, a member is entitled to certain material benefits such as a base salary (considered substantial by Israeli standards), travel allowances, and free mailing privileges. He may not accept a salary in addition to this. A member is also entitled to a "subsistence allowance," which depends on his place of residence and, since 1956, on the number of meetings he attends each month.

Members of the Cabinet may hold seats in the Knesset or may be chosen by the prime minister from outside the legislature. People in certain offices and occupations are prohibited from becoming members of the Knesset. Among these are the president of the republic, judges, clergymen, senior civil servants, and army officers.

Knesset members are entitled to certain immunities. They are not liable to prosecution for any action emanating from their official duties as members of the Knesset. The Immunity Law of 1951 stipulates that the withdrawal of immunity from a member is possible only by Knesset decision, and not by the decision of the member himself or any other person or authority. When a request for the withdrawal of a member's immunity is submitted to the speaker, the member is given an opportunity to state his case before the "House Committee," which has jurisdiction over these matters. If immunity is withdrawn, the member is then treated as any other citizen. If a member is involved in a criminal act, only the attorney-general may apply for withdrawal of immunity. On other grounds, the Government or any member of the Knesset may request withdrawal of immunity. Of course, if the member is caught in the act of committing a crime he can be arrested, but the arresting officer must notify the speaker of the Knesset, and he cannot detain him for more than ten days without the Knesset's approval.

The Organization of the Knesset. The speaker is the presiding officer of the Knesset. Like his British counterpart, he enjoys immense prestige among his colleagues and in the country. He is elected by a majority of Knesset members. He is expected to chair the meetings and be an impartial arbitrator of disputes regarding order and procedure. He cannot, therefore, participate in debate and discussion, although he has the important power of ruling on points of order. If there is an objection to his ruling, an appeal is usually made to an Interpretation Committee which consists of himself, the deputy speaker, and five members of the Knesset selected by the House Committee. The Interpretation Committee cannot overrule the speaker, but it can establish a precedent binding on subsequent (similar) situations.[17] To overrule the speaker, a majority vote in the Knesset is required.

The speaker is not required to belong to the government's political party, since Israeli governments are always coalition governments and no party has ever had a majority in the Knesset. The speaker, however, is usually a man known for his fairness, integrity, and knowledge of the legislative process. In the Knesset, he is assisted by a number of deputies, and one of them usually acts for him during his absence. In addition, there is also the clerk, who is sometimes referred to as the secretary-general of the Knesset, and he is assisted by a number of deputy clerks and a technical staff.

In addition to these officials, the Knesset has a committee system. There are usually nine specialized standing committees. The House Committee, sometimes known as the Knesset Committee, formulates the standing orders and rules of procedure of the Knesset and the other standing committees. It is also responsible for matters pertaining to the conduct of members, such as requests for withdrawal of immunity. Moreover, any subject which is not under the jurisdiction of the other committees usually falls to the House Committee.

The Finance Committee is in charge of fiscal policy and state property.

17. Kraines, *Government and Politics,* p. 38.

The Constitution, Law and Justice Committee is in charge of constitutional and legal matters as well as the administration of justice. The Economic Committee is in charge of agriculture, industry, trade, transportation, and all other aspects of the economic system as they relate to governmental responsibility. The Labor Committee has jurisdiction over housing, public works, and, of course, labor. Police, local government, citizenship, and immigration are areas which fall under the jurisdiction of the Home Affairs Committee. The Foreign Affairs and Security Committee is responsible for defense and foreign relations. There is a committee in charge of education and cultural affairs; finally, the Public Service Committee handles social services, health, and war victims.

Representation on these committees of political parties in the Knesset is guaranteed and is determined by the party's relative strength in the Knesset. In the cases of the Finance Committee and the Foreign Affairs and Security Committee, a party has to have at least eight seats in the Knesset to be entitled to membership. This requirement was designed to keep Communists out of these two important committees. Committee assignments are made by the Organization Committee, which is an *ad hoc* committee of twenty-eight members elected by the Knesset. The Organization Committee also nominates the chairmen of the standing committees, the Knesset giving the final approval.

There are about fifteen members on each committee, except that the House Committee and the Constitution, Law and Justice Committee have twenty-three members each. Committees recommend measures to the entire membership of the Knesset by majority vote. Chairmen do not have to belong to the government party, and a member of the Cabinet may also be a member of a committee provided he is a member of the Knesset. As mentioned before, the Israeli system allows ministers to run for election for seats in the Knesset.

THE LEGISLATIVE PROCESS

As a matter of practice, the initiation of legislation is part of the government's responsibilities, although there is no rule that prohibits members of the Knesset from introducing laws. Private-member bills may be introduced once every two weeks, but the vast majority of enacted laws have been introduced by the government.

Drafting government bills involves three steps. A bill is first worded by the ministry that has jurisdiction over its content. Second, the Ministry of Justice reviews it for legality and form. Third, the Cabinet votes on it before it is presented to the speaker of the Knesset. Sometimes a Cabinet committee looks into the bill before the whole Cabinet votes on it.

On the floor of the Knesset, the proposal is given three "readings." The first usually opens with a speech by the minister or ministers who support the bill. Open debate follows the government's presentation, and debate time is divided among the political parties on the basis of their relative strength in the Knesset. The total allotted time for debate varies, but is always determined by the House Committee. The speaker enforces adherence to the time schedule. After debate is concluded, the Knesset decides that the bill be rejected, that it be sent back to the government for further consideration, or that it be referred to a standing committee. The last alternative is the most common practice.

At the Standing Committee stage after the first reading, government ministers are questioned about the bill. Sometimes they are requested to furnish the committee with documents and other information. After the committee has voted on the bill, it reports its conclusions to the Knesset. Usually, the committee submits to the Knesset a majority and a minority report. On the floor of the Knesset, the bill receives a second reading, at which time it is debated and voted upon clause by clause. Amendments are discussed and voted upon at this stage. Finally, a third reading takes place and the bill is voted on as a whole, usually without amendment. If a majority of the members who are present votes for it, the bill becomes law. Of course, the prime minister, the minister in charge of the bill, and the president of the republic must sign the bill. As mentioned earlier, none of these officials can veto a law passed by the Knesset.

Legislative Supervision of the Government. The Cabinet is held accountable to the Knesset. No Cabinet may be formed that does not receive the Knesset's vote of confidence, nor can it continue in office if the Knesset votes to withdraw confidence. But although the Knesset can get rid of the government, the government cannot get rid of the Knesset, and this fact—that Parliament may not be dissolved by the Cabinet—is another important difference between the British and Israeli parliamentary systems. Although this adds to the prestige and power of the Knesset, it has obvious disadvantages. No political party, so far at least, has been able to acquire a majority of seats in the Knesset, and political parties may, after all, not agree on the formation of a government. In Britain the way out of such a dilemma is through new elections, but this is possible in Israel only if the Knesset decides to dissolve itself.

The danger, however, has been only a theoretical one in Israel up to now. So far the Israelis have managed to form governments, and the Knesset has shown some willingness to dissolve itself when confronted with an unusual situation, such as on March 8, 1961, during the incident known as the "Lavon Affair." [18]

18. The incident goes back to 1954 and involved the then minister of defense, Pinhas Lavon. When in October 1954 the Egyptian government announced the uncovering of an Israeli spy ring in Cairo, Lavon resigned his post. Rumors had it that

The Knesset also exercises a degree of control over the government by means of interrogations conducted during the "Question Time," which is the first half-hour of Knesset meetings. In this connection, a member has the right to submit written questions to ministers in the government concerning any aspect of policy. The speaker transmits the question to the appropriate minister, who is then required to answer during the Question Time and within two weeks. The Question Time gives members and political parties an opportunity to censure the government on issues that have important implications for the country. Censure does not require the government to resign, but it is an important method by which the Knesset attracts people's attention to governmental policies. It also serves a democratic purpose by allowing criticism of governmental policy, and sometimes it forces the government to reveal information which members of the Knesset think should be brought to the people's attention.

Finally, supervision of the administration is accomplished through Knesset control over the government's fiscal policy. The government must submit budget proposals before the beginning of the fiscal year on April 1. In practice, the Knesset tentatively approves the income provisions of proposals before the beginning of the fiscal year and deals with the expenditures in a more leisurely fashion. In the meantime, the government can spend up to one-fourth of the amount it proposed to the Knesset. The Knesset usually approves expenditures during the first three months of the fiscal year. The state comptroller, who is an arm of the Knesset, audits government accounts and insures fiscal responsibility.

THE EXECUTIVE

The organization of the executive branch of the government is based on that in European parliamentary systems. Executive powers are exercised by a Cabinet officially referred to as the Government. The prime minister, although technically a peer among peers, is in fact the most important man in the Cabinet. He is the head of the government and the man responsible for the execution of the laws. The head of state is the president of the republic, but his responsibilities are mainly ceremonial.

The Transition Law of 1949—the "small Constitution"—failed to detail the organization and responsibilities of the executive branch. We are therefore compelled to analyze these matters on the bases of both law and prac-

---

he was responsible for the security operation in Egypt and that he failed to consult his subordinates in the Defense Ministry regarding its activity. In 1960, a Cabinet committee investigated the whole affair and found Lavon innocent of the charges. The affair drove a wedge in Mapai's ranks mainly because of Ben-Gurion's insistence that the case be reopened, this time before a court of law. See Eliahu Salpeter, "Israel Knesset Elections," *Middle East Affairs*, XII (November, 1961), 263–66.

tice, relying more upon the latter, which seems to provide a realistic picture of the working of the Israeli executive.

The President. Israeli law makes no specific reference to the qualifications of the president. Presumably, therefore, the president can be a man or a woman of any age, and he or she does not even have to be a citizen. Furthermore, there is no requirement that the president be a member of the Knesset.

According to the Presidential Tenure Law of 1951, the president's term of office is five years. In 1964 the Knesset enacted a "basic law" which limited the president's tenure to two terms. The president is elected by the Knesset by an absolute majority on the first two ballots or by a simple majority if there are more than two ballots. However, endorsement by at least ten members of the Knesset is required for the nomination of a president, and the nomination should be accompanied by the nominee's written consent. Also, no Knesset member may consent to the nomination of more than one candidate.

The first president, Chaim Weizmann, was elected on February 16, 1949, after he had served as provisional president of the state. Weizmann died in office on November 9, 1952. The second, Izhak Ben-Zvi, was elected in December 1952; he died in April 1963 while serving his third term as president. The incumbent president, Shneur Zalman Shazar, was elected on May 21, 1963. These three men, especially Weizmann, transformed the presidency into a position of prestige and dignity even though the office carries with it no significant political or executive powers.

The duties of the president include the appointment of Israel's diplomatic and consular representatives, the state comptroller, and certain judges such as justices of the Supreme Court and the religious courts. However, these officials are appointed upon the recommendation of the appropriate ministers in the government, and in the case of the comptroller the House Committee of the Knesset. In addition, the president receives the credentials of the diplomatic representatives of foreign countries and ratifies treaties after they have been confirmed by the Knesset. He also may pardon convicted persons.

All of these powers are obviously limited by the required participation of other officials and agencies in the government. Perhaps a potentially more important presidential power is the power to appoint the prime minister. When the position of prime minister becomes for any reason vacant, the president consults with the leaders of the political parties in order to select someone who can secure a majority in the Knesset. Since no political party has so far been able to control a majority of seats in the Knesset, the president's task in choosing a candidate is not an easy one. However, this responsibility has been made less difficult by the fact that the Mapai party has been able to form coalition governments and therefore secure for itself the position of prime minister. When this situation changes, the president's role in designating a candidate for the office will become more important.

The Government. In theory, the prime minister selects members of his Cabinet and distributes government portfolios. There is no legal requirement that members of the Cabinet hold seats in the Knesset, although they usually do. In practice, the power of the prime minister to choose members of the Cabinet is limited because he has to negotiate with the other parties to secure majority support in the Knesset. Since no party has ever had a majority, coalition governments have become the established pattern of Israeli life. Consequently, the prime minister is often compelled to compromise his party's policies and even his party's principles in order to form a government.

Such compromising is not altogether bad, and in Israel it has become a force for moderation. However, the Israeli Cabinet system is based on a principle of collective responsibility, for the Cabinet as a whole is responsible to the Knesset. This principle is very often abused or ignored because of the difficulty of getting the coalition parties to agree on all aspects of governmental policy.

Violation of the principle of collective responsibility has been a frequent problem, and as a result many governments have been compelled to resign. In 1951, Ben-Gurion resigned because of the refusal of the United Religious Front, a partner in the coalition, to support him over the issue of religious education for the immigrants. In 1952, the government resigned over the question of women's conscription into the armed forces. And in 1959, Ben-Gurion's government resigned because the parties in the coalition refused to support Ben-Gurion and the Mapai party over the issue of selling arms to West Germany. Thus, the fact that certain minor parties have been willing to join coalition governments with Mapai does not mean that governments are guaranteed the stability and unity that are vital in a parliamentary system.

The effectiveness of Israeli governments depends very much on the person who occupies the position of prime minister. Under Ben-Gurion, who was the predominant figure in the government during the first decade of Israeli existence, Israeli governments exhibited a degree of strength and effectiveness, although not much in the way of stability and continuity. Ben-Gurion belonged to the older generation of Zionists, was one of the initiators of Israeli statehood, and, owing to his dynamic personality, was also the man who led the Israelis through the most difficult time of their political life. No doubt, historians will consider him the architect of the Israeli state in spite of the fact that his political star began to decline early in the 1960's.

Basically, the prime minister has two difficulties: one is to keep his Cabinet together; the other is to keep the Knesset in line, or at least to prevent that body from voting his government out of office. Ben-Gurion was more successful in dealing with the Knesset than with his Cabinets. He impressed upon Knesset members the need for government support during national crisis. Such a crisis, of course, was continuous because of Arab hostility. The fact that opposition groups in the Knesset are themselves rarely united was another asset to Ben-Gurion and other prime ministers. Discipline within the party groups, combined with ideological differences between them, has resulted in the disunity of the opposition in the Knesset. Thus the danger of government instability comes not from the Knesset but from within the Cabinet itself. As long as the prime minister is able to manage his Cabinet, he is assured of a reasonable degree of continuity.

Nevertheless, danger does exist, and if there is anything that characterizes Israeli political life today, it is Cabinet crisis.[19] Fortunately for Israel, the crisis has not become chaos. And the main reason has been the awareness of the Israelis themselves of the danger that comes from the neighboring Arab countries. If they were to quarrel among themselves, their very existence would be jeopardized. Only the future can tell whether the Israelis will be able to solve the problem of Cabinet crisis after external danger has disappeared.

THE LAW AND THE COURTS

Because Israel is a young state, its legal system is derived from many sources. Foreign influence is apparent in its law, court structure, and judicial precepts. In the area of personal relations, for instance, Ottoman influence exists. The religious courts which functioned under the mandate system, and which were originally established by the Ottoman Empire, were continued in the Israeli legal system. These courts decide cases involving such matters as marriage and divorce. Israeli statute law is also influenced by the regulation and ordinances enacted by the mandate authorities. In addition, the Israeli legal system accepts British principles of common law and equity as well as the doctrine of *stare decisis,* that is, the doctrine of judicial precedent.

However, although these elements still constitute a major part of the Israeli legal system, they have been continually modified since the establishment of the state. Israeli practice, for example, insists that British common law must suit the Israeli circumstances; if it does not, the necessary adjustments are made. The same rule applies to British legislation, which is being replaced by Israeli legislation and will ultimately disappear.

19. Kraines, *Government and Politics,* p. 117.

Since the Knesset is supreme, there are no legal limitations upon its powers; its enactments supersede all others, regardless of their source or authority. Thus the religious courts, which enjoy autonomous existence, do not violate this principle of Knesset supremacy because their authority derives from the Knesset.

Court Structure. The structure of Israeli courts is simple. The lower courts have been borrowed from the mandate system. They consist of four District Courts, which exist in the principal cities of Israel, and of twenty-four Magistrate's Courts. The Magistrate's Courts have jurisdiction over minor crimes and cases involving small monetary claims. The District Courts have both original and appellate jurisdictions. The first type of jurisdiction is unlimited with the exception, of course, of cases which fall within the jurisdiction of the lower courts and such specialized courts as the military courts. The second type of jurisdiction involves the reviewing of cases decided in the Magistrate's Courts.

The Supreme Court is Israel's highest court. It is composed of a president, who is the chief justice; a deputy president; and eight other judges. The court has two divisions; a Court of Appeal, which receives cases from the District Courts; and the High Court of Justice, which deals with petitions for writs, such as habeas corpus, and with matters pertaining to governmental jurisdiction.

These three types of court, the Magistrate, the District, and the two divisions of the Supreme Court, constitute the structure of Israel's regular and secular court system. In addition, there are religious courts of the recognized communities of Israel. Many bitter conflicts have developed over the role of the Jewish religious courts, known as the Rabbinical Courts. Basically, the controversy stems from situations where religious law and interpretations are in direct opposition to secular attitudes and trends in Israeli life. Often, the difficulty arises from confusion regarding the limits of religious and secular jurisdictions. For instance, when the Rabbinical Council insisted that it had the authority to determine whether children of mixed marriages were of the Jewish nationality or not, the Ministry of Interior refused to acknowledge the validity of the argument and insisted upon its right to decide such matters. After a long and bitter conflict, this question was settled in favor of the religious courts.

Organizationally, the Israeli courts are part of the Ministry of Justice, but they do enjoy independence within the department. The minister of justice performs certain administrative responsibilities in connection with the courts; for example, he determines regulations governing judicial procedures and practices. He does not appoint the judges of the secular courts, although he participates in these appointments as chairman of the Appointment Committee. In addition to the minister of justice, the Appointment

Committee consists of the president of the Supreme Court, one other member of the Cabinet, two members of the Knesset, and two members of the Bar Association. Appointments of judges are made by the president of the republic upon the recommendation of the Appointment Committee.

The appointment procedure for judges of the religious courts is similar to that for the appointment of secular judges, except that the Appointment Committee has a different membership and of course the qualifications for prospective appointees are different. The religious courts are under the jurisdiction of the minister of religious affairs, whose responsibilities are similar to those of the minister of justice with regard to the secular courts.

POLITICAL PARTIES

The majority of Israel's political parties originated in Europe long before the establishment of Israel. This fact explains some of the peculiarities of Israel's political parties today. Unlike political parties elsewhere, Israeli parties in other countries did not aspire to political power: this would have been an impossible goal. The parties were organized for a more fundamental purpose—the establishment of a national home for the Jews. Furthermore, since these political parties had given their loyalties to no state and had functioned outside a governmental frame of reference, they found themselves assuming, in relation to their Jewish communities, responsibilities normally performed by governments. They thus became quasi-governmental institutions that symbolized Jewish authority and embodied community ideals. The Jews considered their parties either as quasi-governments or as social movements.

Thus, when the Jewish state was finally established in 1948, Jews found it difficult to view their parties the way parties are viewed in most Western countries, mainly as instruments for the attainment of common political goals. Instead, they overemphasized their role as instruments for the attainment of material benefits, such as jobs and economic security. "The parties of Israel were therefore transformed from political movements into what may be called economic trusts." [20]

Under the mandate, Jewish political parties continued to function as quasi-governmental institutions. They intensified their economic and social activities, establishing agricultural settlements, cooperatives, banks, insurance agencies, youth organizations, and recreational facilities. Some of them even had a militia.

Multiplicity of Political Parties. There are several reasons why Israel has a multiparty system. Most of them have to do with their European and

20. Joseph Badi, *The Government of the State of Israel* (New York: Twayne Publishers, 1963), p. 42.

Palestinian social and political environments of their origin. Of great significance is the fact that the Jews were—and still are—a heterogeneous group; parties, therefore, are an aspect of Jewish cultural and social diversity. They were also the Zionist movement's mainspring and mainstay, for they made it possible for Jews of different backgrounds to affiliate with, and give their loyalties to, Zionism. Had it not been for them, this movement would have failed. In time, however, the Zionist movement itself perpetuated the Jewish multiparty system, since its survival depended upon its grasp of the fact that the Jews were not a homogeneous group.

Jews were also divided between secularism and orthodoxy. The secularists were modernists who believed in the separation of church and state; the orthodox Jews believed that the future Jewish society—and later, the Israeli society—should be governed by the tenets of the religion and must conform to religious law. This division continued to characterize the Jewish view of society even after the establishment of the Israeli state.

A second source of conflict and division was Jewish differences about what was the best economic system for Israel. Some Jews, mostly from Russian and east European backgrounds, were Socialists, but they did not agree on which type of socialism would best suit Jewish life and society. Consequently, the Socialists were of many varieties: Marxists, Syndicalists, and Social Revolutionaries, to mention only a few. Others believed the capitalist system to be the ideal. Still others believed in a mixed economy, that is, in a welfare state.

Jews were also divided ideologically between nationalists and internationalists. The nationalists were preoccupied with the question of Jewish destiny as a people and as a state. This group contained both moderate nationalists and extremist and narrow-minded chauvinists. The internationalists, on the other hand, believed in some kind of an international order, of which the Jews must become a part and for which they should make sacrifices. As with the nationalists, the internationalists included a variety of ideological differences, the most significant group being the Communist Jews, who believed neither in Zionism nor in the State of Israel.

The cultural and ideological differences among Jews are not the only reasons for the multiparty system of Israel. Proportional representation, which has characterized Jewish elections since the beginning of the Zionist movement, is another important one. This system was required by the United Nations resolution which partitioned Palestine and was adopted by Israel for all of its Knesset elections.

The multiparty system has many implications for Israel; it necessitates the establishment of coalition governments which have become a basic feature of Israel's political system. Also, partisan politics in the Knesset and in the Cabinet often results in the development of national crisis, and this is also characteristic of the Israeli system.

Since candidates for the Knesset are nominated by the political parties, the party machine acquires much power over its members in the Knesset. The same condition helps intensify rivalries among the parties themselves, and the rivalries are further aggravated by the fact that the parties have had to compete for the immigrant vote, which in 1955 was three-fourths of the eligible votes.

Israeli voters do not vote directly for the Knesset candidates; they vote for party lists. Consequently, members of the Knesset owe allegiance not to the voters but to their political parties. They have no direct contact with their constituencies. "To many of them, party activity seems to be more important than legislation." [21] Parties not only control their members in the Knesset but they emphasize the importance of party membership. In Israel, the ratio of party members to voters is usually high, sometimes amounting to one member for each three voters. [22] One reason for this is the reliance of citizens upon political parties for their economic security. Parties are influential in securing employment, housing, and other social benefits for citizens, and in this respect they resemble the American city bosses of the 1920's and 1930's. [23] One evil of this situation has been the deterioration of the quality of government and civil service employees.

The Major Parties. Israeli parties can be classified into four main categories: (1) the labor parties, which include Mapai (the Labor party of Israel), Achdut Ha'avodah (Labor Unity party), and Mapam (United Workers' party); (2) the conservative parties, which consist of the Liberal party and the Herut (Freedom) Movement; (3) the religious parties, which consist of the National Religious party, Agudat Israel (Association of Israel), and Poalei Agudat Israel (Workers of the Association of Israel); and (4) other parties, which include the Communist party and the Arab parties.

Achdut Ha'avodah was originally a faction within Mapai, but separated from it in 1944. In 1948 it joined Mapam, only to separate from it in 1954 to become independent again. Achdut Ha'avodah has trouble pursuing realistic policies, and this seems to threaten its political future. Generally, it advocates a Socialist program, and its main influence is in the trade unions.

Mapam, established in 1948, is antireligious and Socialist. Although it is

21. Bernstein, *The Politics of Israel,* p. 55.
22. Benjamin Akzin, "The Role of Parties in Israeli Democracy," *Journal of Politics,* XVII (November, 1955), 515.
23. However, Israeli parties are oligarchic, although a degree of internal democracy does exist.

influenced by Marxism, it advocates a neutral foreign policy. It also advocates large-scale immigration, equal rights for Israel's Arab minority, freeing the labor movement from government control, and guaranteed higher wages for labor. It appeals to urban workers as well as professional people, but in the main it is a kibbutz (agricultural settlement) party.

The Liberal party before 1961 consisted of the General Zionists and the Progressive party. The General Zionists believed in private enterprise and were strongly opposed to the Histadrut, Israel's Federation of Labor, which they claimed had become a state within a state. The Progressive party, primarily a nonideological, middle-class party, believed that a mixed economy was the best economic system for Israel. Its position, therefore, is in the middle, somewhere between socialism and capitalism. The two groups were united in the election of 1961, but their union was not successful partly because it failed to employ a sound campaign strategy. Another factor in their failure was their campaign for Nahum Goldman, an American Jew and head of the World Zionist Organization, as an alternative to Ben-Gurion. Goldman, who was expected to head the party ticket and settle in Israel, showed little inclination to do so, and the party, therefore, had no leadership.[24] In 1965, the Liberal party formed a bloc with the Herut (Freedom) Movement, but seven Knesset members split the bloc by forming a new group, called the Independent Liberal party.

The National Religious party was founded in 1956 to unite a number of religious groups. Although the party usually has bargaining power in the Knesset and the government, its mass appeal is limited. Factionalism, personal feuds, and rivalries characterize its internal organization. Some of these factions, which originated in Europe, are anti-Zionist; others are Zionists. However, they all believe in the strict adherence to Jewish religion and tradition and that the Constitution of Israel should be based on Jewish religious law. These religious groups have been a source of governmental instability because of their opposition to secularism.

The Communist party of Israel is heir to the Palestine Communist party, which was established in 1919. The party is dominated by the Soviet Union and adheres to Soviet policies. Basically, therefore, it is anti-Zionist and anti-Israeli. However, in recent years it has advocated a policy of neutralism and peace with the Arab countries. Of course, the party follows Marxist doctrine; however, the party's success with the Israeli laborer is limited. It has some appeal among the Arabs of Israel, especially those situated in the Galilee area, where severe restrictions are placed upon their freedom by the Israeli government, which claims that such restrictions are necessitated by security considerations.

Mapai. Mapai is Israel's largest party. In the six elections between 1949

24. Salpeter, *Middle East Affairs,* XII, 268.

and 1968, Mapai's strength in the Knesset was as follows: 46 seats in 1949, 45 in 1951, 40 in 1955, 47 in 1959, 42 in 1961, and 43 in 1965. Mapai has never had a clear majority in the Knesset, but it has always maintained more seats than any other party. In 1965, Mapai received 37 per cent of the vote, and this percentage is about average for all previous elections.

Mapai's control of Israel's political life is not limited to its control of the government. It has influence in the Jewish Agency, which solicits financial aid for Israel from foreign sources. The Agency's budget in 1958–59 was about one-eighth of the government's budget in the previous year.[25] Foreign aid is vital to Israel, and the significance of the Agency's contribution makes it politically influential. Furthermore, since under Israeli law new immigrants acquire citizenship and the right to vote immediately after their arrival in Israel, the Agency's control over Jewish immigration assumes additional political significance to Mapai, even though the other political parties are represented in the Agency's political organs.

Mapai also possesses controlling influence over the Histadrut, Israel's Federation of Labor. This national union is important in the politics of Israel since it comprises about 75 per cent of the country's employed labor. Mapai party members usually receive over 50 per cent, an absolute majority, of votes in Histadrut elections.

This party is mildly socialistic and strongly Zionist. Many of its more dogmatic socialistic principles were tuned down after statehood, primarily a result of the practical experience Mapai gained from its dominant position in Israeli governments. Today, the party is pragmatic, and this perhaps is one reason why it has been more successful than the other parties. On the other hand, it has not been able to gain majority control in the Knesset. In this regard, the fact that the voters of Israel are basically ideological [26] and the lack of public consensus on domestic issues are important factors.

In international relations, Mapai desires not to be identified with either camp in the international struggle; but this has not been easy because of Israel's economic dependence on the United States. Consequently, Mapai, and therefore the government of Israel, has been compelled to pursue a pro-Western foreign policy. With regard to Israel's relations with the neighboring Arab countries, Mapai has advocated a strong defensive military policy but has refrained from accepting the idea of preventive war as advocated by the Herut party, Israel's second largest party. In 1956, however, Mapai did not hesitate to make the decision to invade the Sinai Penin-

25. Amitai Etzioni, "Alternative Ways to Democracy: The Example of Israel," *Political Science Quarterly*, LXXIV (June, 1959), 198.

26. Aaron Antonovsky, "Classification of Forms, Political Ideologies, and the Man in the Street," *Public Opinion Quarterly* (Spring, 1966), p. 114.

sula, although it had to withdraw from this Egyptian-controlled territory under pressure from the United States. And it did not hesitate to push its boundaries outward in June 1967.

Until 1955, the organization of Mapai was highly centralized. Led by Ben-Gurion, it was dominated by a group of veteran Zionists who had immigrated from Russia and eastern Europe. Levi Eshkol, who succeeded Ben-Gurion to the prime ministership in 1963, attempted to reconcile the position of the party's "old guard," the *vattikim,* with the position of the "young" in the party, the *tzerim.*[27] It would be a matter of time until the *tzerim,* led by men like Abba Eban, Moshe Dayan, and Simon Peres, would control the party organization and transform it into a more modernistic and future-looking structure.

The transformation of the party has been accompanied by unhappy and difficult experiences. In 1965, for instance, Ben-Gurion came out of his retirement to challenge Eshkol's leadership of Mapai. He insisted on certain demands which Eshkol and the party's central committee considered unacceptable. These demands included the reopening of the "Lavon Affair," the discontinuation of Mapai's alliance with Achdut Ha'avodah, the leftist Labor party, and the replacing of proportional representation with single-member districts. The rejection of these demands by the party's new leadership caused a split within the ranks. Ben-Gurion formed his own party, the Israel Party List, or Rafi for its Hebrew initials. In the November elections, Rafi obtained ten seats in the Knesset while Mapai won 43 seats, one seat more than it had held before the elections.

In 1967, after the war with the Arab countries, the four labor parties, including Rafi, felt obliged to support Prime Minister Eshkol and to close ranks behind him. The experience has been beneficial to most of them. In fact, Achdut Ha'avodah decided in November 1967 to merge with Mapai, and in December Rafi followed suit. Of course, Ben-Gurion did not approve Rafi's policy of merger with Mapai for there remained "personal and moral" reasons for his disagreements with Eshkol's leadership of the government. It is believed that Rafi was induced by Dayan, the defense minister, who hopes to succeed Eshkol to the prime ministership. And the same reason applies to Achdut Ha'avodah's decision to join Mapai. The party's leader and minister of labor, Yigal Allon, also aspired to Eshkol's job. Mapam, the fourth labor party, remained independent, but Eshkol seemed interested in uniting the party with his own.[28]

The sudden and somewhat mysterious death of Eshkol in the spring of 1969 intensified the rivalries among the contenders for the office of prime

27. See Jon Kimche, "Succession and the Legacy in Israel," *Journal of International Affairs,* XVII–XVIII (1964), 43–53.
28. *Time,* December 22, 1967, p. 28.

minister. However, these rivalries were less sharpened by the contenders' agreement to wait until after the election, to be held in the fall of 1969. In the meantime, Golda Meir, an "old guard" Zionist, was selected to serve as interim prime minister.

What happens to Mapai in the future will certainly affect the whole future of Israeli politics. Should the multiparty system continue, the *status quo* would also continue. If a two-party system develops (although there is no reason to believe at the present time that it will), it would be hard to predict the implications of the change upon the power position of Mapai. One thing remains certain: whatever is the future of Israel's party system, Mapai will continue in an important role, if not a dominant one.

CHAPTER 10

ISRAEL: ECONOMIC LIFE AND FOREIGN POLICY

ECONOMICS and foreign relations are Israel's most important areas of public policy. They are vital for the security of the state. Economic power is essential for the sustenance of military power capable of safeguarding the country's territorial integrity. It is also important for enabling Israel to absorb the large number of Jewish immigrants who come to the country every year.

Israel's regional position, being surrounded by enemy states, requires for security a friendly international environment. Although Israel has been so far able to protect itself against its Arab enemies, it needs the assistance of other countries for arms, money, and moral support. Furthermore, such assistance might become more urgent as the Arab countries increase their military strength. Thus the future of Israel demands an effective foreign policy as well as a strong economy.

THE ECONOMY

Israel is the most economically advanced country of the Middle East, and it has the highest per capita income in that area ($1,069 in 1965).[1] Furthermore, the Israeli government predicts that the country will achieve economic independence during the next few years. Whether this ambitious goal will be realized or not is an intricate question, but one thing is certain: the Israelis are determined to transform their economy into a highly efficient system, and their country into a showcase of the Middle Eastern world.

1. In 1965 the per capita income of Britain was $1,439; France, $1,379; Belgium, $1,368; and Italy, $885. *The New York Times,* April 16, 1967, p. 17. In 1961 Israel's per capita income was $602, in contrast with Egypt's $118; Syria, $152; Lebanon, $308; Jordan, $110; and Turkey, $192. Robert B. Pettengill, "Population Control to Accelerate Economic Progress in the Middle East," in *The Contemporary Middle East,* ed. Benjamin Riulin and Joseph S. Szyliowicz (New York: Random House, 1965), p. 385.

Reasons for Economic Success. Israel is already the most progressive Middle Eastern country, even though it has not yet accomplished its goal of self-sufficiency and is still economically less developed than the advanced countries of the West. Why is it ahead of the other Middle Eastern countries? The answer to this question can be easily provided.

First, their long history of persecution made the Jews depend on themselves for economic and social well-being; they had to work harder to accomplish the things which majority ethnic groups obtained with less effort. This is almost always the natural outcome where a self-conscious minority —and the Jews were such a minority—is discriminated against and excluded from the mainstream of a country's national life. Persecution increased the determination of the Jews to survive and excel.

Secondly, the Jews of Israel are mostly immigrants; in 1964, 63 per cent of the country's population had been born elsewhere. Immigrants usually have a strong incentive for material success, for without such promise it is not likely they would immigrate at all. It is true that the Jews who came to Palestine, and later to Israel, were motivated religiously, politically, and culturally; but once in Palestine their biggest challenge, in addition to the establishment of their state, was economic. And when the Jewish state was finally established, their challenge was to maintain it. To do so, economic survival was the overriding necessity.

Thirdly, the Jews who immigrated to Palestine had an almost fanatic psychological need to prove to the Gentile world that they were worthy of an advanced level of human existence. Israel to them was the great experiment; it was the place for the development of their national identity and for the establishment of their independent national existence. This psychological factor affected not only the Jews who made Palestine their home but also the Jews who remained in the Diaspora (areas outside Palestine). The latter made heavy financial contributions to Israel to help her build her economy. Without their generous contributions, Israeli economic progress would not have been possible.

Another reason for the quick advance of Israel is that the knowhow, which most other countries of the Middle East lack, is abundant in Israel. This knowhow was perhaps the key to Israel's economic transformation. The Jews who came to Palestine between 1919 and 1948 were primarily European and American. (At the time Israel became a state, the European and American elements of the population accounted for about 54.8 per cent in contrast with 9.8 per cent Afro-Asian. The remaining 35.4 per cent were born in Palestine.) [2] Thus in 1948 the culture of Israel was primarily

2. Between 1919 and 1948, 89.6 per cent of the total number of immigrants came from Europe and America, but between 1948 and 1962 the Afro-Asian element was greater than the Anglo-American, 54.6 per cent in contrast with 45.4 per cent. See

European. In spite of the fact that after 1948 the Afro-Asian element became the more predominant in the population, the European Jews still had the stronger cultural influence, and remained predominant in economic and political activities.

Lastly, Israel had made one of her major objectives the admission and absorption of more Jews, a factor that contributed to the development of Israeli awareness of the need for rapid economic progress. The Jewish state estimates that by 1970 it will have a population of 3,000,000. This means that the 650,000 who were already in the country in 1948 have had to bear the economic burden of a huge population increase. The first few years after statehood saw an increase of 140 per cent in the population. Obviously, the need to provide for the transportation and settlement of the newcomers has been the major preoccupation of the new state.

And so the will to work hard and the determination to succeed were the main factors in the story behind Israeli economic accomplishments. But while there were numerous positive forces assisting Israel in her economic endeavors, there were serious obstacles as well. Some of them were formidable, and some still imperil the future of Israel. Others should be considered as temporary, and solutions to them are either forthcoming or have already been introduced.

Obstacles to Progress. Among the most important obstacles is one we have already considered as an incentive: immigration. Although immigration had the effect of awakening the Israelis to the need for rapid economic progress, it also presented a host of economic problems. Enormous amounts of money were needed to bear the cost of transporting and settling the immigrants. Large amounts of capital were imported for this purpose, but the influx of people has been so great that the import of capital has generally lagged behind.[3] Consequently, Israel was compelled to economize whenever possible, and the early years of Israeli life were characterized by high taxation, strict rationing, and shortages of food and housing.[4] Furthermore, the local industries developed during the mandate period for local consumption were inadequate to meet demands resulting from the sudden increase in the immigration rate. The solution to this problem required a great increase in productivity and the import of essential items of consumption.

The necessary increase in productivity, however, was handicapped by the value systems of some Israelis, specifically the so-called Oriental Jew,

---

Leonard J. Fein, *Politics in Israel* (Boston: Little, Brown and Company, 1967), pp. 37–38.

3. S. N. Einsenstadt, "Israel: Traditional and Modern Social Values and Economic Development," in *The Contemporary Middle East, op. cit.,* p. 397.

4. L. F. Rushbrook Williams, *The State of Israel* (London: Faber and Faber Ltd., 1957), p. 106.

who came from the Afro-Asian countries. This problem did not affect only the newcomer but also some of the *Sabra,* or the Israel-born Jews. The new social setting required adjustment to mechanization in industry, but the Orientals were used to ancient methods of production. Also, they had negative attitudes toward work which made the task of adjustment even more difficult. However, these problems were sometimes temporary, and training programs and the pressures of the new environment combined to reduce their effect.

The Israeli social setting also demanded the development of new skills. The need for food required specialization in farming, but since the Jews in the Diaspora had usually been barred from farming, agricultural knowledge was lacking among immigrant groups. Very few wanted to be farmers, yet the country was in desperate need for farmers. Consequently, immigrants were settled on the land without ever having been involved in farming. Despite these difficulties, however, they did very well: the index of the value of agricultural production doubled between 1957 and 1962.

While the problem of skills was being solved, another problematic situation was developing. The present occupational structure shows a definite relationship between the origin of the Jewish immigrant and the type of job he is likely to have. Statistics show that 22 per cent of the Sephardic-Oriental immigrants are agricultural workers while only 11 per cent of the Ashkenazi (European) immigrants are engaged in this type of work. Also, the percentages of the Ashkenazi newcomers who are engaged in professional and managerial occupations is much higher than the percentages of the Sephardis in these same occupations.[5]

The Problem of Trade Deficit. In addition to immigration problems, Israel has a serious trade deficit. In 1949, this deficit was valued at $224.5 million; by 1951 it had reached $335 million. Subsequently and until 1956, the deficit declined, but in the aftermath of the Suez crisis it began to rise again. In 1965, it was $405 million.

Israel attempted to remedy this situation by increasing her exports, which actually began to grow in 1956, and in 1965 they reached a value of $429 million. The value of exports in 1949 had been only $28.5 million. The Israelis might be able to increase their exports by stimulating the citrus industry, which was seriously damaged during the War of Independence. In 1965, citrus fruit was the second largest export item, valued at about $154 million. However, while the value of exports was going up, so was the value of imports, from about $253 million in 1949 to about $835 million in 1965. Thus, the trade deficit was still critical.

5. Aryeh Rubenstein, "Israel's Integration Problem," *The Contemporary Middle East, op. cit.,* p. 389. The Sephardi is a Jew who descends from the Spanish Jews who were driven out of Spain in A.D. 1492 by the famous Inquisition.

What makes the Israeli deficit so serious is the part that consumer-goods imports play in it. Israeli consumer industry has not been able to reduce this much in spite of the increase in its output. Israel's comsumption rate continues to climb at a pace that offsets much of the positive effects of its high investment rate.[6] Here again, the continuous flow of immigration is a major factor in the continually rising consumption.

The trade deficit would have had very serious consequences on Israel's economy had it not been for the inflow of foreign capital, which in 1965 amounted to $565 million.[7] By the end of the first decade after statehood, American grants-in-aid alone amounted to more than $500 million. Israel also receives generous contributions from the Jewish communities in other countries, and revenues from the sale of Israeli bonds. Furthermore, between 1952 and 1964, West Germany made annual payments totaling $715 million toward the cost of resettling in Israel 300,000 refugees from Nazi persecution. The German indemnities were paid to Israel in the form of goods and services, and they were an important element in the foreign-exchange budget of Israel. In addition to the reparation deliveries, West Germany, under her laws of restitution and indemnification, still pays, in Germany currency, Israeli citizens who had been affected by the Nazi regime.

But the German reparations ceased in 1964, and contributions from the Jewish community outside Israel cannot last indefinitely. Indeed, there is concern that contributions might seriously decline, and this concern was the subject of Ben-Gurion's visit to the United States in March 1967. All this seems to indicate that unless Israel solves its trade deficit in the near future it might become a critical problem. The negotiation of agreements for tariff concessions will be helpful. An agreement with the European Economic Community was concluded recently, but it should not be expected to have a spectacular impact on the deficit. Tariff agreements alone will not balance Israel's external trade, although they might help expand the foreign market for her products.

AGRICULTURE

For a people who lack specialization in agriculture, the progress has been outstanding. Israel has already become self-sufficient in products such as vegetables, potatoes, fruit, eggs, poultry, milk, and other dairy products. In fact, many of these products are now exported in large quantities. Other

6. L. Berger, "An Industrial Program—And an Absorption Program," *The Israel Yearbook, 1960,* p. 41.

7. Oded Remba, "The Middle East in 1962—An Economic Survey: II," *Middle Eastern Affairs,* XIV (May, 1963), 142.

crops, introduced to achieve greater self-sufficiency and to expand export trade, have also been successful. In 1953, for example, Israel discovered that it could grow good quality cotton, and today this cotton supplies a substantial portion of Israel's needs. Sugar beets were introduced in 1951 and are now processed in newly constructed factories. However, Israel still needs to increase her meat output and also her output of grain, sugar, wood, and timber.

The Farm Surplus Problem. Israel's success in increasing its agricultural output has resulted in a problem of surplus similar to that of the United States. The general price level went up, while in many instances high production levels resulted in slight price rises or a drop in prices of agricultural products. Thus, there was disparity between the farmers' incomes and industrial workers' incomes. To relieve the farmers, the Israeli government has extended to agriculture substantial direct and indirect subsidies. As the American experience has shown, this cannot be considered a sound long-term solution to the problem of low parity.

The Problem of Water Scarcity. Recently the Israeli government has realized that the natural resources of the country are more limited than had been thought. Although over 60 per cent of the land of Israel is desert, many people had believed that new colonization could continue indefinitely, but this belief has been totally discarded. Governmental research has shown that the Negev, the vast desert expanse in the south, is mostly uncultivable, and "unless some revolutionary new discoveries are made in social science," the Negev would remain a desert.[8] Too, such extensive land reclamation would require enormous capital expenditure.[9]

Israel's critical problem is not the scarcity of land; the main obstacle to further development is the lack of enough water to irrigate the cultivable land. A Water Administration has been created to control the supply and consumption of water. It has also been exploring means by which the water supply can be increased and conserved. One of the most controversial projects dealing with the problem of water supply is the one known as the Johnston Plan which was proposed in 1953 by the United States. Although the project never became a reality, it is an important study in Arab-Israeli relations.

The Johnston Plan: 1953–56. Zionist leaders have always been aware of the problem of water shortage in Palestine. At the beginning of this century they showed interest in the Litani River, a river entirely within the boundaries of Lebanon, and attempted to have the boundaries of Palestine adjusted so that the water of this river could be used in Palestine. In the

8. *The Israel Yearbook,* 1960, p. 189.
9. *The Israel Yearbook,* 1960, p. 189.

1920's they pressed the British and the French to incorporate into Palestine the southern part of Lebanon up to Sidon. This would have given Palestine control over the reservoir of the Jordan River.

Zionist efforts in this regard have not been successful; the Litani River was not included nor was the drainage area of the Jordan River. But this experience was to become a factor in Arab suspicion of Israeli intentions with regard to the Jordan Valley Authority, which was proposed by the American Johnston Plan. The Arabs claimed that Zionist plans always lacked respect for other people's rights and interests. As to the Johnston Plan itself, the Arabs felt that it was more of a political project than it was economic. Its purpose, they believed, was to establish a degree of economic cooperation between Israel and the Arabs that might eventually lead to political cooperation.

The economic purpose of the plan, however, was to exploit the water of the Jordan River for the benefit of Syria, Jordan, and Israel. The project also envisaged the possibility of settling 200,000 refugees on the irrigated land. Of course, the idea of inducing cooperation between Israel and the Arabs was implicit in the Johnston Plan.[10]

According to the project, Lake Tiberias would be maintained as the reservoir for the river's water, and electric power generators would be located in a number of places in the area. The water was to be used within the area of the project itself and not in any other place. This area would include both sides of the Jordan River, and the Huleh and Yarmuk regions. Israel would obtain 35 per cent of the water, Syria and Jordan the rest.

Eric Johnston, the United States diplomat, was an extremely able and artful negotiator. It is to his credit that the Arabs were induced to consider the plan at all, since their attitude toward cooperation with Israel was usually negative. Negotiations, however, went on for three years, and during this time the Arabs and the Israelis prepared their own proposals for the exploitation of the Jordan River's water. These two proposals disagreed in many respects, but it should not be forgotten that both parties were at least willing to explore the possibilities of cooperating in a joint project.

The Israeli proposal, known as the Cotton Plan, provided for the diversion of the Litani River into the Jordan River so as to increase the latter's water supply. Second, it proposed the transfer of Jordan River water to the Negev area through pipelines. Half the total amount of water would be allocated to Israel; the other half would go to Jordan and Syria. Finally, the hydroelectric generator would be located in Israel.

The Arab plan proposed giving Israel only 20 per cent of the water and insisted that the water would be used only in the reservoir area and not sent

10. Earl Berger, *The Covenant and the Sword, Arab-Israeli Relations, 1948–56* (London: Routledge and Kegan Paul Ltd., 1965), p. 136.

to the Negev. Third, a high dam to be used for storage would be constructed in Arab territory instead of at Lake Tiberias, which is in Israel.

The two plans also differed markedly on the subject of supervision and management of the Authority. The Arabs would not accept any direct contact with the Israelis. Consequently, they preferred United Nations supervision of the project. But Israel would not agree to such supervision "on the ground that it was an unsatisfactory organization to work with." [11]

In spite of the differences in their proposals, the two parties were able to reach a compromise according to which the United Nations would supervise the construction of the project only; the United States would pay two-thirds of the total cost, which was estimated at $200 million; the storage site could be located in the Yarmuk area; Israel would be given 40 per cent of the water; and she would be allowed to use the water in the Negev area. But the supervision question remained unsettled.

The project was killed by the political situation which developed in the Middle East during 1955 and 1956. The Baghdad Pact and the conflicts which resulted from it contributed to its demise, as did Egypt's secret arms negotiations with the Soviet Union and, in 1956, the development of the Suez crisis. Nevertheless, the death of the Johnston Plan provided us with the important lessons that in the Middle East political conflict is detrimental to economic plans and that the political has precedence over the economic.

THE COLLECTIVE SETTLEMENTS

The significance of collective farming in Israel can be seen in the fact that, in 1961, about 59 per cent of the total farm population lived in collective settlements. The remainder lived in villages and owned private farms.

Israeli cooperative agriculture is of three types: (1) the settlement of smallholders known as mashav oudim; (2) the cooperative settlement known as mashav shitufi; and (3) the kibbutz (group) settlement. Of the three types, the kibbutz is the best known and the one that has received the most publicity.

These three collective settlements are usually affiliated with Israel's Federation of Labor (the Histadrut). Originally, they were "utopian" movements designed to express the Jewish pioneering spirit which existed in the days when Palestine was under British mandate.

Physical factors contributed to their development. As mentioned earlier, many Jews were not trained in agriculture and preferred to live in cities. When they had to take up farming as an occupation, they chose places where land was fertile and the environment was not excessively harsh. But

11. Earl Berger, *The Covenant*, p. 141.

this left unexploited the usually less fertile land found inland from the coastal areas of Palestine. Life in these places was very lonely; the Israelis' solution to this problem was the collective idea of social and economic existence. This idea created a pioneering spirit among some immigrants and lessened their fear of the harsh environment of the less fertile and more isolated areas of Palestine.

The Socialist ideas of immigrants coming to Palestine from eastern and central Europe played a significant part in changing the self-interested and materialistic outlook on life, which they feared would not be suitable in the Palestinian environment, where sacrifice and selflessness were the requisite qualities.[12] The immigrant from these areas also spread Socialist ideas of egalitarianism. The collective settlement was the ideal method for the fusion of Zionism and socialism. "The double-pronged objective of the Kibbutz movement was to build a Jewish homeland and a Jewish socialist state in Palestine." [13]

Finally, there was a military purpose in establishing the collective settlements. Originally, these settlements were located in areas near Arab towns and villages, where there was danger of Arab hostility. The collective settlements were viewed as outposts for defense of the centers of Jewish population in Palestine. In the Arab-Israeli war of 1948, many collective settlements were useful not only as defensive posts but as offensive military units.

The three types of collective differ mostly in the relationship of the individual to the group. In the mashav oudim, the family remains an economic unit, and production and consumption are determined by individual families. The cooperative authority controls the marketing of products and is in charge of machinery and supplies. It is the most conservative form of collective settlement in that it retains some aspects of private farming and its traditional social institutions.

The mashav shitufi, the most recent type to develop, stands between the two other types of collective settlement. Economically, it resembles the kibbutz, in which production, marketing, and management are communal. Socially, it resembles the mashav oudim in which the family structure is traditional and collective life is less apparent than in the kibbutz.

The Kibbutz. In the kibbutz, there is the greatest control of the economic and social activities of members. Production, consumption, and marketing are all communal. The rule (Marxist) is "from each according to his ability and to each according to his needs." Members of the kibbutz

12. Alan D. Crown, "The Changing World of the Kibbutz," *Middle East Journal,* XIX (Autumn, 1965), 424.
13. Boris Stern, *The Kibbutz That Was* (Washington, D.C.: Public Affairs Press, 1965), p. 2.

receive no wages, and the kibbutz' economy is moneyless. Kibbutzim are supposed to utilize only the labor of their members, and in the early stages of their development they adhered to this rule. However, they have now developed economically to the point where hired labor has become a necessity, and these workers receive money for their services. This conflict with the principle of "self-labor" upon which the kibbutz system is based is justified on the grounds that hired workers are employed only in nonprofit types of production such as building and construction. (Buildings are nonprofit because they are public property and have no rent value.) The production of consumer goods, where hired workers are not employed, yields profit, not for the members themselves but for the kibbutz' economy.[14]

In the kibbutz, the economic security of the members is guaranteed. The family as a unit has no economic functions. Children belong to the kibbutz, and their education is the responsibility of the kibbutz. Members eat together in communal dining halls. Children have quarters and other facilities separate from their families.

The kibbutz lacks some aspects of politically organized communities. There are, for instance, no policemen and no judges. Criminals in the kibbutz are rare, and the only punishment is expulsion from the kibbutz. Minor offenses are dealt with by conveying to the offender the membership's disapproval of him, which is usually expressed by a refusal to communicate with him socially. It should be remembered that the members are conditioned to accept a system of mores conducive to cooperation and discipline.

In the past, the kibbutz' culture emphasized the sovereignty of the group, modesty, and austerity. Recently, however, individualistic tendencies and a desire for material things have become apparent. Signs of gradual change in many aspects of the traditional kibbutz system are becoming more and more visible.

Manufacturing has become part of the economic activity of the kibbutz. By 1951 the plywood plant at Afikim was already the largest and most modern in the Middle East. And since 1958, manufacturing in the kibbutzim has grown so rapidly that it has created a labor shortage in agriculture. In the older kibbutzim, the share of manufacturing in the kibbutz income is greater than that of agriculture. The change reflects trends in the national economy.

In recent years, the kibbutz has declined, and it is no longer a leading institution. There are two main reasons for this. First, the establishment of the Jewish state in 1948 made many of the aims of the kibbutz movement unnecessary. The state has an army to protect its frontiers, and Israeli agriculture is yielding a surplus, at least as far as some commodities are con-

14. Crown, *Middle East Journal*, XIX, 429.

cerned. Furthermore, the state now relies less on voluntary organizations, such as the kibbutz, as a result of growth in its own capabilities. In addition, the new Jewish immigrant is less interested in the idealism of the kibbutz than he is in his own material well-being. He now looks to the state for his economic security instead of to the kibbutz.

The kibbutz should be considered as a unique social experiment. Economically, the kibbutzim still offer certain definite advantages to their members. For instance, they have "flexibility in man power and resources," and this makes their economies adaptable to market conditions.[15] Consequently, many of them have been able to provide a fairly good standard of living for their members. Also, since members of the kibbutz receive no wages, there are no income taxes. True, the kibbutz itself pays an income tax, being a producer, but the tax applies only to its net profit. Hence the kibbutz can deduct the cost of supporting its members, who are without income and therefore are dependent upon the kibbutz.

ISRAEL'S GENERAL FEDERATION OF LABOR

The Histadrut (General Federation of Labor) is Israel's largest labor organization. Many of its critics, mainly Israel's right-wing parties, believe that it is a "state within a state." [16] The Histadrut is a powerful union, and it plays a significant role in Israel's social, economic, and political life. With the government and the Jewish Agency, it controls two-thirds of all economic activity in Israel. These three constitute the public sector of the Israeli economy, which is predominant since only one-third of the country's economic activity is controlled by private enterprise. Furthermore, Mapai, the dominant political party, also controls the Histadrut. In fact, Mapai exercises greater control over the Histadrut than it does over the government. Consequently, many of the activities which in other countries are controlled either by the government or by private enterprise are in Israel controlled by the Histadrut. For instance, health insurance is provided mainly by the Histadrut; the worker's sick fund of the Histadrut, Kupat Holim, is Israel's largest medical organization. It covers more than three-fourths of the country's population and is available to anyone, not only to members of the Histadrut for whom the insurance is mandatory. Although the government and employers contribute to it, this insurance is very much like programs in Socialist countries, except that it is controlled by the union rather than by the government.

Some people believe that the Histadrut's medical insurance should be nationalized or turned over to an agency independent of the union. But

---

15. Crown, *Middle East Journal*, XIX, 433.
16. Edwin Samuel, "The Histadrut," *Political Quarterly*, XXXI (April–June, 1960), 175.

Histadrut involvement in such activities as the insurance antedate the establishment of the State of Israel. In fact, it is because there was no Jewish state to deal with such matters before 1948 that the Histadrut, which was established in 1920, was able to get involved in them.

Organizing Workers. The Histadrut is primarily a trade union, and as such it is open to "all workers who live by their own labor without exploiting the labor of others." Throughout almost all of its history, about 75 per cent of Jewish workers have been members. The percentage has been maintained in spite of the increase in the Jewish population of the country.[17]

In 1964, the Histadrut had 872,000 members, including 250,000 members in Israel's agricultural settlement (affiliated through the Agricultural Workers' Union), 261,000 wives who had membership by virtue of their husband's eligibility, and 35,000 Arab workers. There were, in addition, 100,000 members under eighteen years of age who were affiliated through the Organization of Working and Student Youth. By special agreements two separate religious unions are also affiliated. In all, the Histadrut speaks for nearly 90 per cent of all wage earners in Israel.

Every four years, the members participate in the election of the Histadrut Convention, which is the union's highest authority. Since the convention is large and meets infrequently, the General Council elected by it acts as the authority between conventions. The Council itself, however, meets only twice a year to decide serious disputes between union authorities. It elects an Executive Committee which meets at least once a month to deal with major policy issues. The day-to-day aspects of administration are the responsibility of an Executive Bureau, appointed by the Executive Committee from among its own members. The Executive Committee also appoints the secretary-general of the Histadrut, who becomes the Committee's chairman as well as the chairman of the Bureau.

Locally, the Federation is represented by numerous workers' committees elected by the workers in industrial plants and offices. Between the highest and lowest levels of organization there is an intermediary level of labor councils that represent members in a specific area regardless of the type of work they do. Generally, these councils approve or disapprove decisions to strike made by local unions.

About forty national unions are affiliated with the Histadrut, operating as departmental units within the Federation. Their members are also members of the Histadrut, and the affiliation of individual members with the Histadrut is direct, not indirect as in the case of Britain's Trade Union Congress. The Histadrut organizes a variety of professions, including doc-

17. Margaret L. Plunkett, "The Histadrut: The General Federation of Jewish Labor in Israel," *Industrial and Labor Relations Review*, XI (Oct.–July, 1957–58), 166.

tors, lawyers, nurses, teachers, civil servants, actors, musicians, social scientists, and psychologists. The vast majority of its members, however, are manual workers.[18]

Other Responsibilities. In addition to being a worker's union, the Histadrut is an entrepreneur. When it functions as an entrepreneur, the Histadrut becomes the General Cooperative Association of Jewish Workers. However, membership in the Histadrut and the Association is identical. The Executive Committee of the Histadrut appoints some of the members of the Association's governing board; the other members are elected by the various economic enterprises constituting the Association. In turn, the Association appoints a number of members, varying with the enterprise, who serve on the boards of the enterprises. In theory, the Association has a veto power with regard to the policies of the economic enterprises. In reality, however, they enjoy a large degree of autonomy.

Originally, the Histadrut's enterprising activity was based upon the cooperative principle, but today it is both capitalistic and cooperative.[19] The direct economic activity of the Histadrut covers almost every aspect of the economy, but traditionally the emphasis had been on building and construction. However, in the mid 1950's, the Histadrut began to show an interest in heavy industry. By 1960, the Association was responsible for more than half of the basic heavy industry in the country. In addition to the direct economic activity of the Association, there are numerous other activities in which the Association is in partnership with private capital. In many of these instances, foreign capital is involved, for the Association has always encouraged cooperation with foreign investors.

Approximately 60 per cent of the Histadrut's revenues from membership dues go to maintain a network of social-welfare institutions. We have already mentioned its medical insurance and medical organization. In addition, the union maintains a widow's fund, a pension fund, and a fund for invalids. Also, it provides its members with social security benefits through the collective agreements it negotiates with employers.

Furthermore, (the Histadrut maintains a number of institutions to train new immigrants) The union considers such training to be essential for the integration of the immigrants as well as a benefit for the economy. It is also interested in raising the cultural standards of the working class. The youth organization mentioned earlier was designed to provide the young people, both students and workers, with social and cultural necessities. The Education and Culture Center of the Histadrut attempts to raise the cultural standards of the members by conducting seminars and offering special courses. Finally, the Histadrut owns and operates a publishing house. Most impor-

18. Samuel, *Political Quarterly,* p. 175.
19. Plunkett, *op. cit.,* pp. 161–62.

tant, the Histadrut publishes Israel's largest morning newspaper, *Davar*.

Thus the Histadrut is a special kind of union, and it is a vital Israeli institution. Only the state ranks higher in importance. But if it is an exaggeration to say that the Histadrut is "a state within a state," it is close to the truth to say that the Histadrut is a government unto itself or that it has many of the attributes of governmental institutions.

FOREIGN-POLICY GOALS

Israel's foreign policy has had three main objectives which are essential for her survival as a nation and as a state.[20] Without their attainment Israel almost certainly cannot maintain her sovereign existence.

Arab Recognition. The first goal of Israel's foreign policy is to secure Arab recognition. Without such recognition her borders will remain unsettled, and her territory will always be under attack from her Arab neighbors who believe that the establishment of the Israeli state in 1948 violated the rights of the Arab majority in Palestine.

If peaceful relations could be established between her and the Arab countries, Israel would be able to acquire immediate and significant benefits. First, she would be able to pursue a more independent policy in the East-West struggle. At the present time, this independence is impossible, because Israel relies heavily on the United States both economically and for security. If she did not need this aid she would undoubtedly pursue a neutral policy in world affairs.

Secondly, peaceful relations with the Arab countries might result in the establishment of economic cooperation among Middle Eastern countries. This would give Israel an important market for her products, one closer to her industrial plants than the European and African markets. Possibly she would be able to exploit some of the natural resources of the Arab world.

Thus, there can be no doubt that Arab recognition of Israel would result in great benefits for Israel. Without such recognition, Israeli institutions cannot be normalized and will always reflect the uncertainties of the future. And the psychological makeup of her citizens will also be influenced by a constant sense of crisis. Without Arab recognition of her sovereign status Israel will become a nation of worriers as it has already become a nation of warriors. Although this might not be altogether bad, no nation wants to exist for a long time under the constant threat of war.

Although Israel is aware of the significance of Arab recognition to her security and to her political and economic future, she often pursues policies toward the Arab countries that are inconsistent with this objective.

20. See the excellent work of Nadav Safran, *The United States and Israel* (Cambridge: Harvard University Press, 1963), pp. 212–13.

For instance, Israel's anti-Arab propaganda has gone far beyond what is necessary for her to obtain economic and military assistance from the Western countries. Especially in the United States, such propaganda has almost succeeded in creating the image of an Arab monster with whom no nation can hope to have peace. The success of Israeli propaganda has reduced the chances of peace in the Middle East. While it is understandable that Israel should take all precautions against the Arab threat, including the use of propaganda and military preparedness, it is the extent of that propaganda which raises the issue of how much of it is really necessary. Ironically, the intensity and effectiveness of Israel's anti-Arab propaganda have made it difficult for that state to pursue more rationally her own goal of securing Arab recognition of her sovereignty. She has been influenced by her own propaganda. Consequently, peace, which should be the real object of her policy, has become for her a necessary evil only.

Both Israel and the Arabs contributed to the condition of belligerency in the area. Of course, Arab determination to destroy Israel is an important factor in this situation. Equally important is Israeli excessiveness and over-reaction. There is also Israel's refusal to allow the Palestinian Arab refugees back to their homes in Israel. Thus, if the Arabs are guilty of being troublesome on the question of peace in the Middle East, Israel is equally guilty of pursuing policies inconsistent with her alleged desire for peace.

The Goal of Promoting Jewish Immigration. The second goal of Israel's foreign policy is the promotion of mass Jewish immigration; the ultimate aim is to bring all the world's Jews to Israel. In 1965, only 15 per cent of the world's Jews lived in Israel. From this fact, it is clear that the achievement of this objective will require great effort. Even if all Jews could be persuaded to move to Israel, the transportation and settlement of immigrants would continue to be very costly operations. Another implication of Jewish immigration is cultural. Although Zionist leaders were aware of cultural differences among Jews, they underestimated the impact of these differences upon Israel's social existence. Israel in fact does not have an integrated culture. In spite of the existence of certain unifying forces, which are basically political and religious, Israel does not yet constitute a nation. The cultural differences, for instance, between the so-called Oriental Jews (the Afro-Asian) and the European Jews are so great that some scholars wonder if in fact there is not more than one Israeli nation.[21]

These two categories of Jews are further divided into subgroups, mostly in accordance with their country of origin. In addition, another division separates those who were born in Israel—the *Sabra* Jews—and those who were not. The former category is dominated by Jews of Oriental descent;

21. Safran, *The United States,* pp. 72–78.

those born in Israel of European descent are in the minority. This group (the *Sabra* Jews) is highly publicized as the model of the "new Jew" who is supposed to possess admirable qualities and who is different from his ancestors. Although such publicity exaggerates the differences between the *Sabra* Jew and his ancestors, the "new Jew" is considered to be the hope of Israel and the one to lead her in the future.

The cultural differences among the Israeli Jews are alarming because they are accentuated by economic and political differences. For instance, the average income of the Israeli "European" family is much higher than the average income of the "Oriental" family. The last group also rates lower in matters pertaining to educational levels, housing facilities, the civil service, the officers' corps, and the professions. Moreover, the gap between the two groups "is consciously felt and expressed" by their members.[22]

In addition to its domestic implications, Israel's immigration policy has equally important external implications—particularly with respect to Jews who do not want to immigrate. United States Jews, especially, differentiate between their status as citizens of the United States and their obligations toward the State of Israel. They wish to help Israel in any way possible, but they have no intention of renouncing their American citizenship. Their position is in conflict with Israel's policy of ultimately making the country the home of all Jews. Early in 1967, the resulting problem was the subject of a bitter controversy between Ben-Gurion, who was on a visit to the United States, and American Jews. Ben-Gurion maintained that a Jew was not really a Jew unless he was willing to make Israel his permanent home.

Israel's immigration policy raises the question of whether she can absorb a large number of Jews without expanding her territory. This question frightens the neighboring Arab countries, who maintain that Israel's immigration policy must ultimately force her to enlarge her territory at the expense of the Arabs. This, of course, has been another important element in the Arab argument that Israel's stated goal of peace is not sincere. The Arabs claim that it is designed to pacify the Arabs until it becomes possible for Israel to force the enlargement of her territory. The Israelis argue that Israel's capacity to absorb a large number of newcomers is much greater than the Arabs realize and that their country's technology is capable of accommodating the newcomers.

Israel also wants immigration because she considers the growth of her population to be an asset rather than a liability. She maintains that the new immigrants will enhance her economic development and will strengthen her military power. Of course, this assumes that the country's future economic performance will be similar to that in the past. Such an argument may or

22. Safran, *The United States*, p. 77.

may not be valid. Thus, a decline in the rate of immigration, during the early months of 1967, was caused by unemployment, which was estimated at 100,000.[23]

The Goal of Rapid Economic Development. Israel's goal of rapid economic development is the most important of the three goals of her foreign policy. Economic development is a goal of all countries of the modern world, but in Israel, it is a prerequisite to the success of her immigration policy as well as to the fulfillment of her desire to pursue a neutral foreign policy. In other words, Israel's future—indeed, her survival—depends on her economic achievements. Very few states are as conscious of the interdependence of economics and national security as the State of Israel.

One aspect of the Israeli economy which necessarily relates to her foreign policy is foreign capital. Total foreign capital averaged between 15 and 20 per cent of the gross national product in the years 1950 to 1960, and during that period the rate of net investment in Israel was about the same as capital inflow. However, the investment rate was only a very small portion of the annual increase in the gross national product. Economic assistance to Israel, although great, does not account for the entire growth in the economy, which has been also influenced by the utilization of manpower and increased productivity.[24]

As mentioned earlier, Israel cannot rely on foreign capital indefinitely, and there are signs that the inflow of capital is declining. German reparations have already been halted and the American grants-in-aid have declined considerably. Sooner or later, therefore, Israeli consumption will have to be curtailed if Israel is to continue her present immigration and defense policies without affecting the rate of investment. To lower the rate of growth of personal income, which must be done to curtail consumption, will not be an easy task, for the Israelis have become accustomed to a high level of consumption.

Although Israel has large capital reserves, the decline in her capital inflow will make it exceedingly difficult for her to eliminate or appreciably reduce her trade deficit. This means that Israel must either reduce her imports, which might be politically undesirable if not impossible, or increase her exports. As mentioned earlier, Israel has tried to increase her exports, but the increase of imports has made the deficit problem almost a fact of economic life in Israel.

Thus, the most important goal of foreign policy, on which everything else seems to depend, is difficult to attain. So far Israel has a remarkable record of economic achievements considering the unfavorable conditions of progress. Nevertheless, its economic future seems to be uncertain and, con-

23. *The New York Times,* April 1, 1967, p. 4.
24. Fein, *Politics in Israel,* p. 213.

sequently, its political future also. One might say that Israel is a state that was born in crisis and one that will live in crisis, at least for some time.

THE UNITED STATES AND ISRAEL

The United States is in an awkward position in the Middle East; it is difficult for the United States to reconcile her economic and strategic interests in the area with her desire to help Israel. Economic and strategic considerations would seem to argue a United States policy favorable to the Arabs. On the other hand, United States commitments to Israel which were mostly the product of the political pressure of American Jews seem to compel her to pursue a friendly policy toward Israel. So long as the Arabs and the Israelis are in conflict with each other, the position of the United States in the Middle East will remain difficult.

Early Developments. Politically, the United States is a newcomer in the power struggle in the Middle East. Until World War I, American involvement in the Middle East was limited primarily to missionary and educational activities of citizens and private organizations. During Ottoman rule in the Middle East, American consular representatives tried to secure the benefits of the capitulation system for the Jews of Jerusalem. There was in Palestine a small number of American Jews, and American representatives to the Ottoman state tried, whenever possible, to save them from the effects of discriminatory Ottoman law. During World War I, when the Turkish government expelled many Palestinian Jews, the American navy provided their transportation.

The United States began to show some interest in the political future of the Middle East for a brief period during and after World War I, but this interest was limited. In October 1917, President Wilson declared his support of the Balfour Declaration when this document was at the drafting stage. This marked the beginning of pressure-group involvement in the Palestinian question. Zionist pressure was brought to bear upon the Wilson administration by Louis D. Brandeis, who was a personal friend of President Wilson. Counterpressure came from oil companies in the United States and also from anti-Zionist Jews. As to the oil companies, the object of their political pressure was clearly economic. They feared that American oil interests in the Middle East would be hurt by a pro-Zionist American policy. The anti-Zionist Jewish group was fearful that such a policy might expose the Jews of America to the charge of dual allegiance. The counterpressure was successful, and the Wilson administration, in discussing the future of Palestine with the other powers, ignored the Balfour Declaration.

After World War I, the United States returned to a policy of isolation, and American political interest in the Middle East was no longer apparent.

This was the beginning of a period in which the relationship of the United States to the Middle East was characterized by the economic interests of American citizens. During this period the United States government assisted private citizens and corporations in securing for themselves a share in the Middle East oil. In 1920, for instance, the American government was able to obtain for certain American companies more than a one-fourth share in the Iraq Petroleum Company.

Between the two world wars, an interesting political phenomenon developed: while the executive branch of the United States government showed very little interest in becoming politically involved in the Middle East, the legislative branch showed the opposite inclination. In 1922, for example, Congress passed a resolution in support of the Balfour Declaration; and in 1939 a group of congressmen protested the British White Paper which restricted Jewish immigration to Palestine.

In the meantime, the United States government was becoming concerned about American oil interest in the Middle East. In 1933, extensive oil concessions were obtained by American companies from the government of Saudi Arabia. During World War II, the great demand for American oil created fears that native oil reserves might be drained, and this fear increased the interest of the government in Middle East oil. The war period, however, brought about a new relationship between the United States and the Middle East. This relationship added to the economic interests of the United States the dilemma which resulted from Hitler's brutal policy toward the Jews. The American Jews, who until this time were divided between Zionist and anti-Zionist positions, were now mostly sympathetic toward Zionism. Of course, the persecution and extermination of their coreligionists under the Nazis was the reason for the turnabout in their position. Consequently, the Palestine question gradually assumed importance in the domestic politics of the United States. In the last two years of the war, Congress passed a number of resolutions urging the unrestricted immigration of Jews to Palestine and the establishment of a Jewish state in the mandate territory. In addition, President Roosevelt made similar assertions in the form of promises during the presidential campaign of 1944. However, he also promised Ibn Saud, the Saudi Arabian monarch, that the United States would take no action with regard to the Palestine question without full consultation with the Arabs. Thus the difficulty of reconciling Jewish interest in Palestine and American interest in Arab oil assumed new significance. During the war, the United States became aware of the immense strategic importance of the Middle East. Since the Arabs occupied much of this area, the strategic factor seemed to weigh heavily in favor of a favorable policy toward the Arab countries.

After the war, however, President Truman pursued an American policy favorable to the Jews. He was motivated by humanitarian reasons but mostly by political pressure which, he states in his memoirs, was put on him by Zionist friends. Both the State Department and the joint chiefs of staff were opposed to the Truman policy because of the economic and strategic interests in the Middle East, which could be endangered by a policy antagonistic to the Arabs.

When the partition plan was being discussed in the United Nations, it had the full backing of the United States, which, as mentioned earlier, used her influence to adopt the partition resolution. It is doubtful that this resolution could have become a reality had it not been for American pressure to secure the needed "votes" for its adoption. When the Arabs declared that they would use force to prevent the execution of the partition resolution, the position of the United States became exceedingly complicated. The civil war in Palestine finally convinced President Truman that the situation in the Middle East was becoming dangerous, and he instructed the American delegation to the United Nations to propose an alternative solution to the partition plan, one that would have involved the setting up of a United Nations trusteeship in Palestine. Thus, the United States had reversed its position.

But this reversal was only temporary. Military developments in the Palestinian war were the reason. The Jews of Palestine received arms from the Soviet Union, and they were able to reverse the tide of war in their favor. The United States, under these circumstances, decided to ignore the trusteeship proposal and, instead, recognize the State of Israel. One might say, therefore, that if it were not for the Arabs' poor showing in the civil war, the United States would have no choice but to abandon her pro-Jewish policy in Palestine.

After the establishment of the State of Israel, the American position in the Middle East did not become less complicated or less awkward. The Arab nationalists were later to become distrustful of American intentions. They argued that the American government tried to solve the Jewish problem at the expense of the Arabs, who had had nothing to do with the Jewish persecution during the war. While the argument that American help made the Jewish state possible was not devoid of truth, it ignores the Arab weaknesses and the Jewish solidarity, which were also factors in the establishment of the State of Israel.

More Recent Developments. After the establishment of the State of Israel, the first object of American foreign policy was to prevent the Arab-Israeli conflict from developing into a general war. The preservation of Israeli statehood was considered as important as the task of establishing peace in the area.

During the Truman administration, the United States was clearly partial to Israel. The State of Israel was a new state and therefore needed all the help she could get to survive, and inasmuch as she had already contributed to the creation of Israel, the United States felt obligated to help her through the most dangerous period of her life.

After the end of the Arab-Israeli war in 1949, the United States attempted to establish a more permanent policy in the Middle East. In 1950, she joined Britain and France in issuing a Tripartite Declaration for the purpose of maintaining peace and stability in the area through a kind of Middle Eastern balance of power. The three countries were determined to prevent an arms race which might result in the renewal of war between Israel and the Arab countries. They proposed, therefore, to control the supply of arms to the feuding countries and thus maintain a balance of arms.

In addition to its promise to prevent an arms imbalance, the declaration guaranteed the armistice boundaries of Israel. In reality, this meant that the United States would preserve the *status quo* on the Arab-Israeli issue. Furthermore, as long as the Arabs remained opposed to Israel, the American policy of preserving the *status quo* would run into great difficulties. The alternatives to this policy, however, would have been equally problematic, if not impossible. They would have involved an American policy unfavorable to the State of Israel.

In the 1950's the Eisenhower administration became concerned about the growing influence of the Soviet Union in the Middle East. Accordingly, the question of Communist infiltration of the Arab world became a prominent factor in the formulation of United States policy. The Baghdad Pact was intended to provide a solution to this problem; and later the Eisenhower Doctrine was formulated with the same purpose in mind. In spite of these measures, Soviet influence in the Middle East continued to grow. Part of this dilemma is that most Arabs consider Israel to be a more dangerous enemy than communism. Consequently, the Arab-Israeli issue is a formidable obstacle to United States efforts to combat Soviet influence in the Middle East. This influence increased substantially after June 1967 and has become a source of frustration to Arab nationalists. There is fear that this frustration might contribute to a failure of the Arab nationalists to establish political unity and thereby contribute to the success of a Communist takeover in either Syria or Iraq. This possibility seems to argue for an American policy of alliance with Arab nationalism, since the failure of Arab nationalism would enhance the political fortunes of the Communists. Such an alliance, however, would require the United States to abandon her support for the State of Israel, and since this is difficult, the danger of communism in the Middle East will continue to exist.

Until the Arab-Israeli war of 1967 the United States attempted to maintain friendly relations with both the Arabs and the Israelis. This was part of her policy of preserving the *status quo*. On occasions, however, the United States has checked the power of Israel when that state showed signs of going beyond the reasonable limits of her national security or when her policy seemed to threaten the balance of power. Thus, the United States protested strongly when Israel initially refused to obey the orders of the United Nations Truce Supervision Organization to halt work on a hydro-electric project in the demilitarized zone between Israel and Syria. The United States went as far as withholding aid to Israel, but the aid was resumed in October 1953 after Israel agreed to suspend work on the project. And in the United Nations, there have been instances when the United States joined other nations in censoring Israel for use of excessive force against some of her Arab neighbors. In the case of the Qibya incident of October 1953, in which many Arabs died at the hands of Israeli troops, the matter was brought to the Security Council at the initiative and demand of the United States. In an incident involving an Israeli attack upon Jordan (December 1966), the United States voted for a United Nations resolution condemning Israel for use of excessive force against Jordan.

The United States also attempted to check the use of power by the Arab countries. More than that, the United States has attemped to contain Nasser's influence in the Arab world, and we have seen in an earlier chapter on Egypt how by the end of 1958, the United States policy of containment was in trouble. But between 1958 and 1967, the United States made every effort, within the limits of her policy of preserving the *status quo,* to appease the Arab countries.

Until 1959, Israel received more aid from the United States than the Arab countries as a whole. Thereafter, however, the United States intensified her aid program to the Arab countries. In 1963, the United Arab Republic received approximately $220 million in aid from the United States.[25] It seemed as if the United States was willing to do her utmost to gain the friendship of the Arabs provided they did not jeopardize the security of Israel.

But the 1967 Arab-Israeli war made the position of the United States still more difficult. In that war the United States was pro-Israel, although there is no evidence to support the Arab charge that the United States aided Israel militarily. Politically, the United States supported most of the elements in the Israeli argument justifying that country's involvement in the war. Thus, she sided with Israel on the question of Egyptian blockade of the Gulf of Aqaba (May 1967) and maintained that the blockade was illegal. After the war, the United States agreed with Israel that territorial

25. Georgiana G. Stevens, ed., *The United States and the Middle East* (Englewood Cliffs: Prentice-Hall, 1964), p. 118.

gains as a result of the war should not be given up except as a part of general settlement of all outstanding issues of Arab-Israeli relations.

What will be the future of Arab-American relations is uncertain, although we can predict that they will not be better than they were before June 1967. Of course, the increase of Soviet influence in the area should continue to be the concern of the United States. As to Israeli-American relations, there will be no dramatic change in the future. The United States will continue to support Israel and guarantee her political existence, although she might later return to the pre-1967 policy of maintaining the *status quo* in the Middle East, however the *status quo* is defined.

CHAPTER 11

THE HASHIMITE
KINGDOM OF JORDAN

A S a political entity, Jordan did not exist before 1923. Carved out of the Syrian districts of the Ottoman Empire at that time, it was previously part of kingdoms and empires whose power extended beyond its boundaries. The country was nothing more than a rugged and backward area with no industry and little agriculture.

The establishment of the Jordanian state was not the outcome of nationalistic demands for an independent political identity. The people of Jordan were not conscious of any Jordanian identity, but rather considered themselves simply as Arabs. Their state was the product of a bargain between the British and Amir (Prince) Abdullah, the second son of King Husain of the Hejaz (later Saudi Arabia). And this bargain, as we shall see, was almost accidental.

The circumstances surrounding the establishment of the Jordanian state explain why the future of the country is uncertain today. Created by accident and lacking the economic and political conditions required for statehood, the state of Jordan could disappear as suddenly as it appeared.

STATEHOOD

During World War I, the Arabs of the Hejaz and Syria agreed to assist the Allied powers in destroying the Ottoman Empire, and the British made several ambiguous promises to their leader, Sharif Husain of Mecca (later king of the Hejaz). These promises, the Arabs believed, insured them independence and freedom. However, in spite of the promises, at the end of the war Britain and France divided the Fertile Crescent into spheres of influence. Jordan was included in the British zone.

In April 1920, the San Remo Conference gave Britain the Palestine mandate, while Syria was allotted to France. In December, France and Britain agreed to include Transjordan (the east of Jordan) in the Palestine mandate; the Zionists were happy about this decision since the Balfour Declaration of 1917 promised them a national home in Palestine.

In Syria, the French decided to force Faisal, the third son of Husain, out of Damascus and did not recognize him as king of Syria. In response to the French, Husain's second son, Abdullah, was in Amman (later the capital of Transjordan) preparing a campaign against the French to restore his family's rule in Syria. But before he set out, he met with Winston Churchill, then Britain's secretary of state for the colonies, who persuaded him to abandon the plans for his campaign against the French by offering him rule over the British mandated territory which later became Transjordan. This was the beginning of statehood for that territory. The new state was officially declared on May 26, 1923.

About the time of its establishment as a state, Transjordan had only 200,000 inhabitants, about 90 per cent of whom were Muslim Arabs living in nomadic or seminomadic conditions. It covered an area of 34,550 square miles of which only 3 per cent was fertile. It is, therefore, reasonable to assume that the Jordanian state was created without any justification except to balance regional and international interests in the Fertile Crescent.

The Amirate of Transjordan, as the new state was called, became autonomous under British mandate. However, its territory was excluded from the provisions of the mandate relating to the establishment of the Jewish national home. Although its frontiers were artificial, they were clearly defined except for the southern boundary which was contested by Saudi Arabia. But in 1927, the Treaty of Jidda settled this issue, and Saudi Arabia allowed Transjordan to retain the southern cities of Aqaba, Maan, and Tabuk.

In April 1923, the British government announced its willingness to recognize Transjordan as an independent state on condition that the latter would establish a constitutional system and recognize, in a formal agreement, Britain's interests in the area. The two countries signed a treaty in February 1928, and Transjordan became "independent." [1] However, this new status was merely formal. In reality, Transjordan continued to rely on Britain financially, politically, and militarily.

The treaty provided for the adoption of an organic law for Transjordan, and the law was promulgated in April 1928.[2] Under it, the head of state,

1. Text in Jacob C. Hurewitz, ed., *Diplomacy of the Near and Middle East, A Documentary Record: 1914-1956* (Princeton: Van Nostrand, 1956), vol. II, Doc. 52, p. 156.
2. Text in Helen Davis, ed., *Constitutions, Electoral Laws, Treaties of States in the Near and Middle East* (1st ed.; Durham, N.C.: Duke University Press, 1947), pp. 302-14.

called amir (prince), had greater powers than the legislative council; and the Executive Council, which was in charge of the administration, was responsible to the amir. Transjordan's obligations to Great Britain were reaffirmed in the constitutional document, including the acceptance of Britain's control over the country's international relations.

THE QUEST FOR INDEPENDENCE

Transjordan was a British creation. She was bound to Great Britain by the mandate system as well as by the terms of the 1928 treaty. The treaty gave Britain a great degree of control over Transjordan's foreign relations, her military affairs, and, more important, her finances. From the time of her establishment as a state, until, perhaps, the dismissal of the British commander of the Arab Legion in 1956, Jordanian politics was greatly influenced by the country's relations with Great Britain. This influence was a bone of contention between the Arab nationalists and the Hashimite family and was a significant factor in the uncertainty of political life in Jordan. Abdullah accepted British supremacy, believing that it was in his interest and in the interests of the other Arab countries to pursue a pro-British policy. He continued to hold this belief until he died in 1951 at the hands of an assassin.

Abdullah's pro-British policy earned him the respect of the Western world, which considered him a realist and a "reasonable" monarch. However, the same policy made him unpopular in the Arab world, which, after World War II, underwent intense nationalistic revival. The more extreme nationalists believed Abdullah had betrayed the Arab cause, and they hoped to eliminate him from Arab politics. They did not forget the role he played during World War II, when his Arab Legion helped the British against the nationalist government of Rashid Ali al-Gailani in Iraq. The Legion also participated in the British campaign against the Vichy regime in Syria. The Arab nationalists disliked Abdullah's war policies not because they were sympathetic with either Rashid or the Vichy French, but because they believed he let his alliance with Great Britain take priority over Arab affairs and interests. And the Arab nationalists abhorred Abdullah's acceptance of a position of subservience.

Nevertheless, Britain did attempt to show her appreciation of the assistance given by Abdullah during the war, and she did this without abandoning her predominant position in Transjordan. Thus, in 1946, she consented to a Treaty of Alliance with Transjordan in which the latter country was declared a fully independent state.[3] Subsequently, Abdullah was pro-

3. Davis, *Constitutions,* pp. 333–38.

claimed king, thereby abandoning his previous title of amir. The official name of Transjordan was changed to the Hashimite Kingdom of Transjordan.

Under the 1946 treaty, Britain retained the right to keep troops in Transjordan and continued to control the Arab Legion. It could be assumed, therefore, that the new treaty was only a slight improvement over the old one. The changes involved formalities which enhanced the position and prestige of King Abdullah, but the provisions concerning Transjordan's independence were largely theoretical.

A short time before Britain terminated the mandate over Palestine, she concluded, in March 1948, a new treaty with Transjordan.[4] The treaty allowed Britain to station troops at bases in Amman and Mafrak and stipulated that if Transjordan were attacked Great Britain would come to her assistance. In addition, Britain was to continue payment of annual subsidies to Transjordan.

Continuation of the British subsidies was an economic necessity since Transjordan was not economically self-sufficient, but this economic dependence was also the main obstacle to achievement of real independence. Had she not needed British money, Transjordan would have had little difficulty gaining control of her army.

However, finding another source of subsidies was not much of a solution either; for whoever subsidized her budget would also expect something in return. Clearly, the independence of the country is conditioned by her economic future, which is severely handicapped by limited resources. Until this problem is solved, the future of Transjordan will continue to be uncertain.

CONSTITUTIONAL DEVELOPMENTS

The 1928 organic law, which was amended in 1939, was replaced in 1946 by still another constitutional document.[5] Aside from the change in the title of the ruler and other minor changes, the 1946 Constitution was very similar to that of 1928. Very little change was introduced in the formal relationships of the governmental agencies, and the monarch remained powerful while the legislature continued to have only limited authority.

The annexation on April 24, 1950, of the Palestinian region known as the west bank and the death of Abdullah on July 20, 1951, necessitated a revision of the constitution. This revision was also desired by King Talal, who succeeded his father to the throne. Consequently, a new Constitution

4. Hurewitz, *Diplomacy*, vol. II, Doc. 89, pp. 296–99.
5. Davis, *Constitutions* (1953 edition), pp. 235–52.

was promulgated in January 1952.[6] The system which emerged was, at least in theory, based upon the principle of executive responsibility. The Cabinet became responsible to the legislature instead of to the monarch as in the previous constitutions.

Thus the patriarchal rule of Abdullah disappeared after his death. The new king, Talal, was mentally ill and could not exercise the royal prerogatives. On occasions, however, he attempted to introduce changes into the internal and foreign policies of his kingdom that were in contradiction to Abdullah's general political philosophy and strategy. Talal was known for his dislike of his father's policies, which he opposed while still a prince, and this opposition earned him popularity among the Arab nationalists. However, Talal's mental condition created a vacuum in the power structure, which was filled by conservative elder statesmen who were loyal to the Hashimite family. These statesmen controlled the Cabinet, which under Talal became a powerful governmental institution.

Although the conservative politicians were able to pull the country through the major crisis, created by Talal's illness, they could not hope to monopolize power for long. The Palestinian elements of the population constituted a large majority, and they were constantly pushing for reform and democracy. Their efforts were partially recognized in the 1952 Constitution.

Under the new Constitution the official name of the country was changed from the Hashimite Kingdom of Transjordan to the Hashimite Kingdom of Jordan. The new name recognized the territorial changes which resulted in the incorporation of the west bank after the Arab-Israeli war of 1948.

The 1952 Constitution gave additional powers to Parliament. Although in Jordan, as in the other Arab countries, constitutions have little meaning beyond establishing the formal structure of government, the new Constitution accepted the principle of executive responsibility, thereby making possible future developments in the informal structure of power. One should not conclude from this that the 1952 Constitution was designed to reduce the powers of the monarch. On the contrary, these powers remained substantially strong. The king, for instance, appoints and dismisses the prime minister, and he also appoints members of the upper house of the legislature (the Council of Notables). He can dissolve the Council of Representatives, the lower house, provided a new council is elected within four months. Finally, he can veto legislation, although his veto can be overridden by a two-thirds majority of both houses.

However, Parliament was given control of the Cabinet. If it votes non-

6. Amos J. Peaslee, ed., *Constitutions of Nations* (The Hague, Netherlands: Martinus Nijhof, 1956), vol. II, pp. 524–44.

confidence in the government, the latter agency must resign. In addition, laws vetoed by the king could, as mentioned, be overridden by Parliament. These two powers, if exercised, could become the basis of a genuine parliamentary system. But the relationships of monarch and Parliament are more complicated than they appear on the surface. They depend on the political circumstances and the personalities involved in the system. For instance, King Husain II, who was still a minor when his father abdicated, tended to rely on the elder statesmen in the early period of his reign. He found, however, that unless he learned the political game and exercised his authority as a monarch, his own life would be in danger. He ruled a country riddled with crises, and conspiracies were constantly being woven around him. Consequently, Husain assumed the full powers of his office, and until the Arab-Israeli war of 1967 he was considered the strong ruler of his country. Parliament was subservient to him.

THE POWER STRUCTURE: THE SOCIAL DIVISION

Prior to June 1967, two groups influenced affairs of state in Jordan and were involved in a power struggle: the Palestinians, a source of political instability; and the Transjordanians, a force for stability. A coalition between the Transjordanians and the army was not only the monarchy's main support but was the force which made possible the preservation of Jordan as a state.

The Palestinians. After the Arab-Israeli war of 1948, the portions of Palestine which did not go to Israel or Egypt went to Transjordan, which became known as Jordan. The term "west bank" was used to refer to this Palestinian area because it lies west of the Jordan River. Its inhabitants, including the Palestinian refugees who came to live in it, became citizens of Jordan. Before the Arab-Israeli war of 1967, which resulted in the occupation of the west bank by Israel, the new citizens of the west bank constituted a two-thirds of Jordan's population. They demanded more democracy in government and desired to dominate the country's politics. But the Palestinians's desire for democracy was not genuine. To them, democracy was a means to the establishment of their "rights in Palestine," and they needed to control the Jordanian government to help accomplish this objective.

The Palestinians were not loyal to the Hashimite monarchy and had no confidence in the statehood of Jordan. They considered the monarchical system to be too conservative, and selfish, and, moreover, they saw it as an obstacle to Arab unity. Thus, they believed, Jordan should not exist as a political entity. It had to rely on foreign aid for its survival, yet it was foreign influence, they argued, that was responsible for the establishment of the Israeli state and, therefore, for the creation of the Arab refugee problem.

King Husain maintained himself in power by limiting the influence of the Palestinians in the powerful organs of the state. Only when political circumstances made him feel secure did he rely on the liberal Palestinian elements, and when these circumstances changed he returned to his reliance on the conservative Transjordanians. This strategy was a very delicate one, and his reliance on the liberals in 1957 almost cost him his throne. But Husain always managed to survive. His courage and youthful appearance were undeniable assets, but it was his sense of timing that usually carried him through crises. This was his greatest political talent.

The Transjordanians. The Transjordanians inhabit the east bank. Unlike the Palestinians, who became Jordanians only after 1948, the Transjordanians had lived under Hashimite rule since its establishment in 1921. They had developed a loyalty to the Hashimite monarchs and acquired pride in their state.

Some Palestinians looked down on the Transjordanians, but the latter group believed that it was the one which embodied the true virtues of Arab life. Some Transjordanians felt that the Palestinians were ungrateful intruders. Moreover, the Palestinians, being better educated and possessing more skills than the Transjordanians, engendered in the Transjordanians an understandable insecurity and fear of competition. Husain's policy of not allowing the full participation of the Palestinians in the governmental process reduced this fear, but at the same time it created resentment among the Palestinians, whose numerical majority should have entitled them to far more power and participation.

For instance, with a two-thirds majority in the country, the Palestinians had only half the seats in Parliament. Nearly all the prime ministers of Jordan were either Transjordanians or Palestinians who had lived in Transjordan long before 1948 and had served Abdullah when he was still amir. Without any exception, all the chiefs of staff of the Jordan Arab army were Transjordanians. Finally, many governmental and commercial activities were carried on in Amman, which is on the east bank, by virtue of its being the capital; in this sense, the cities of the west bank, which were more suitable for those activities, were deprived of these benefits.

THE POWER STRUCTURE: THE ARMY

The Jordan Arab army, known as the Arab Legion before July 1956, was organized in 1923 mainly for the purpose of quieting the rebellious Bedouins. It was first commanded by F. G. Peake, a British officer, but John Bagot Glubb succeeded to the Legion's command in 1939. After the pacification of the Bedouins in 1933, the Legion was developed as a small force to support the British army and it participated in the Iraqi and Syrian campaigns during World War II in that capacity.

The Arab Legion was not intended to fight foreign wars without the British. Consequently, it was unable to achieve the objective of its 1948 military campaign against Israel. It was too small to be an effective offensive force. Furthermore, without its British officers, it was weak in military strategy and the use of modern military technology. Worst of all, the government of Jordan could not maintain it without British financial support. During the 1948 war with Israel, the British, not wishing to antagonize the United States whose sympathy was with Israel, pursued a policy of neutrality; and lack of British assistance, in terms of weapons, officers, and technical assistance proved to be crucial.[7]

In the 1967 war, the Jordan Arab army was much larger than it had been in 1948, but it was still much smaller than the Israeli army. The Arab officers who replaced the British in 1956 knew little about military strategy, and there was inadequate ammunition to fight a long war. Consequently, the Jordan army was defeated by the Israeli army for the second time.

In the domestic power struggle, the army traditionally played a conservative role; it was the backbone of the monarchy. However, when Husain dismissed Glubb, the British commander, in March 1956, and replaced him by an Arab, the Legion gradually became embroiled in politics. Abu Nuwar, whom Husain made the new chief of staff in May 1956, later conspired to overthrow the monarchy. The military coup which he engineered in April 1957, with the prime minister's support, failed. Apparently, King Husain had not considered his credentials, for Abu Nuwar was an Arab nationalist who believed neither in the monarchy nor in the state of Jordan.

After the attempted coup, the army returned to its traditionally nonpolitical role. It was to continue as the major force behind the monarchy and its loyalty to the Hashimites was assured by its Bedouin units, which had kept their tribal allegiance to the king. Like most Bedouins, these units believed that since Husain was a direct descendant of the prophet Mohammed disloyalty to him was a sinful act. In time of trouble, therefore, the king had always relied on his Bedouin regiments, who remain the greatest assurance against a military coup.

7. Upon the instructions of the British government, British officers serving in the Arab Legion were withdrawn on May 30, 1948. Henceforth, the effectiveness of the Arab Legion in the war was greatly diminished. See John Bagot Glubb, *A Soldier with the Arabs* (London: Hodder and Stoughton, 1957), pp. 135–36.

THE POWER STRUCTURE: POLITICAL PARTIES

In 1953, a law was enacted setting down the rules governing the establishment of political parties. It required political groups to secure a license from the Ministry of Interior.[8] In theory, a party could be licensed if its principles did not oppose Arab unity or if it did not encourage internal dissension. In practice, however, only conservative and moderate parties were licensed; extremist groups were not. In 1954, regulations were issued which authorized the Cabinet to disband existing parties and refuse to license new ones.

Thus in the elections of 1956—the only free elections held in Jordan [9]—only three of the seven parties were licensed. The others participated in the elections under new names or by the unofficial acceptance of the government. The three licensed parties were the National Socialist party, the Arab Baath party, and the Arab Constitutional party.[10]

The National Socialists believed in cooperation with Syria and Egypt, the end of Jordan's treaty with Great Britain, and a neutral foreign policy. Their leader was Sulaiman Nabulsi, who became prime minister after his party had secured a plurality in Parliament. Before Nabulsi was dismissed in April 1957, as a result of the abortive Nuwar coup which he supported, he was able to abrogate the 1948 treaty between Jordan and Great Britain. He also concluded an agreement with Egypt, Syria, and Saudi Arabia in which these three countries promised to pay Jordan $36 million annually as a replacement for the British subsidies, which were discontinued as a result of the abrogation of the treaty. Unfortunately, the agreement was ignored soon after its announcement, when relations among these countries became strained.

The Baath party, mentioned several times earlier, was a branch of the Syrian party known by the same name. It believed in Arab unity and socialism. Soon after the 1956 elections, the party drifted toward extremism and became involved in conspiracies against Husain. As a result the party was outlawed in 1957.

The Arab Constitutional party was the most conservative of the three licensed parties. Its influence depended on the personal political appeal of its leaders rather than on its mass following, which was very limited. The leaders of the party were mostly feudal landlords who were inclined to ac-

8. George L. Harris, *Jordan* (New Haven: HRAF Press, 1958), pp. 76–77.
9. H. B. Sharabi, *Government and Politics of the Middle East in the Twentieth Century* (Princeton: Van Nostrand, 1962), p. 186.
10. For more information on political parties, see Harris, *op. cit.,* pp. 76–84.

cept Egypt's leadership in Arab affairs. They also desired the fulfillment of Arab unity, but through an evolutionary process rather than through a revolution.

Nabulsi's National Socialist party disintegrated soon after the fall of his government. The Baath party continued to exist illegally, but suffered from internal dissension. Only the doctrinal parties were unaffected by the crisis of April 1957. This is perhaps because they had ideologies which carried them through difficult times and which inspired their work. Their followings were extremely limited, but they were well organized and their influence was disproportionate to their size.

Among the doctrinal parties, the Syrian Social Nationalist party and the Communist party were most significant. The SSNP was a branch of the Lebanese party known by the same name. It believed in a Fertile Crescent unity which would include Syria, Lebanon, Iraq, Jordan, and Palestine (now Israel). The party had difficulty finding mass support because of the upsurge of Arab nationalism in the 1950's and 1960's, and because of its belief in Syrian instead of Arab nationalism. However, the SSNP was highly organized, well disciplined, and had a small militia. The high ethical standards established and developed by its doctrine might play a role in its revival in the future. For the time being, however, the party must wait until its parent organization in Lebanon acquires the freedom to operate which it lost in 1961 after an abortive coup.

The Communist party of Jordan was a subversive organization dedicated to Marxist principles. Prior to June 5, 1967, the party's main support came from the west bank. It was active among the refugees, who were highly susceptible to subversive influence. The party followed Soviet leadership, and consequently it had a difficult time when the Soviet Union pursued a policy friendly to Israel. Most of the time, however—especially after the Suez crisis of 1956—it was able to identify its aspirations with those of the Arab nationalists; and the Soviet Union's policy was also in line with this strategy. From that time, the party's popularity and appeal increased. It was aligned with Arab nationalist forces before the Arab-Israel war of June 1967. It is difficult, however, to assess the impact of Arab defeat upon the future of the Communist movement in Jordan.

ECONOMIC DEVELOPMENTS

Two political events have had profound effects upon economic developments in Jordan: the 1948 annexation of the west bank and its loss to Israel in 1967. The effects of the annexation were positive in that Jordanian technology was advanced by the addition of the Palestinians to the population of Transjordan. On the negative side, the traditional economic system of

Transjordan was shaken to its roots and had to be transformed in a very short time, causing much economic dislocation. In 1948, Transjordan's population was not quite 400,000. In 1965, seventeen years after the merger, it was about 1,850,000, of which over 800,000 lived on the west bank, with 500,000 classified as refugees.[11] Consequently, the population of the Jordanian state increased almost five times in less than two decades. The capital city of Amman grew to almost ten times its pre-1948 size, from 30,000 to 300,000. Thus, it was many years before the two economies of the east and west banks were reasonably integrated, and even then many problems continued to pressure Jordan.

The west bank became the most productive region in Jordan, and its people were the most advanced. Consequently, its loss in 1967 was tantamount to an economic disaster. Reliable sources estimate that 38 per cent of the gross national product was lost, and about $200 million in foreign exchange.[12]

After the war, Jordan's finances were in danger. However, Saudi Arabia, Libya, and Kuwait promised Jordan an annual payment of $112 million to keep her from total economic disaster. In addition, Jordan is seeking new sources of finance as well as military aid. But so far she has been unable to make up for the loss of the west bank.

Agriculture. The chief economic activity is agriculture. However, although Jordan's territory was before 1967 (that is, including the west bank) about the size of the state of Indiana, only 5 per cent of her land was cultivable, mainly because of a lack of rainfall. The Jordanian government has built irrigation systems and has been assisted by the United States and other countries. In March 1967 the Ford Foundation contributed the modest amount of $43,000 for the purpose of opening arid lands for settlement in the Jordan Valley; and in April 1967 the United States Agency for International Development (AID) contributed $260,650 to help develop water resources.

Many farmers, especially on the west bank, relied on artesian wells for irrigation; but this kind of operation required considerable capital. Consequently, most farmers fell into debt trying to provide their land with water. Interest on loans had traditionally been very high, and profiteers exploited the farmers until the government stepped in. It passed laws enabling farmers to borrow at reasonable rates and pay back over reasonable periods of time; and it established the Jordanian Bank of Reconstruction and Development in 1951 to provide agricultural and industrial loans for the development of the economy. In April 1967, this bank merged with the

11. *The Middle East and North Africa, 1965–66* (London: Europa Publications, 1965), p. 314.
12. *The Christian Science Monitor,* October 21, 1967, p. 2.

Agricultural Credit Organization, which became the main source of credit for farmers.

Jordan's main agricultural product is wheat, but she is not self-sufficient. Consequently, early in 1967, the government contracted with the United States for the purchase of 60,000 tons of wheat. In fact, Jordan has had to import most of her flour and grain. In 1961, these imports alone accounted for more than the value of the country's exports for that year. However, Jordan usually did better in the area of fruit and vegetables. The west bank specialized in raising these crops, perhaps because its people had earlier learned the required techniques from the British. Of course, this asset has been lost to Jordan since 1967.

Industry. At present only small industries exist in Jordan, including the manufacture of cigarettes, soap, matches, cement, and sugar. Growth of large-scale industrialization or even small-scale but diversified industrialization is blocked by insufficient mineral wealth, including fuel; poor communication; lack of knowhow; and lack of capital.

Unlike her neighbor, Iraq, Jordan had no oil of any commercial importance. The government has signed agreements with several foreign companies to prospect for oil, but these efforts have not been successful. As for Jordan's other mineral deposits, lack of capital has made their exploitation very difficult. The Dead Sea contains large quantities of potash and bromine, and before 1948 the Palestine Potash Company ran a large operation for extracting potash; but its factory was destroyed by the 1948 war. Before the 1967 Arab-Israeli war, the Dead Sea shores belonged to both Jordan and Israel, and Jordan controlled the larger part of the sea. Lack of cooperation between the two countries made effective exploitation of the sea's minerals impossible. However, the rich deposits of phosphates found in the early 1960's around Amman have been exploited and phosphate products have been exported; in 1967, Turkey and India were among the buyers of Jordanian phosphates. There are also deposits of gypsum and manganese ore, but at present the exploitation of these deposits is still at the planning stage.

The lack of good communication is a problem that requires large amounts of capital for its solution. Jordan has no railways of significance. The Hejaz line, which runs from Damascus to the south of Jordan, needs repair to put it in use, and the 1967 war has made continuation of government reconstruction efforts difficult. The government has also spent large amounts of money on expanding the road network. The opening in 1960 of the Amman-Aqaba road was of great economic significance because it connected the capital with the country's only port. Other roads were constructed in the 1960's, but Jordan still needs more new roads and improvements of old roads.

More important, however, is the problem of establishing facilities for international trade. The road network cannot carry this kind of trade. Furthermore, Jordan's only sea outlet is at the Gulf of Aqaba, and the facilities at the port of Aqaba need enlargement. In 1956, initial improvement projects were begun, and by 1964, the port was equipped to handle about 70,000 tons a month. However, since most of Jordan's imports are received at Aqaba, the need to further develop the port continues. In March 1967, Jordan borrowed $1,600,000 from West Germany for this purpose.

As mentioned earlier, industrialization is also handicapped by lack of technical knowhow. The people's interest is mainly in agriculture, and interest in industrialization is limited. True, many Jordanians have been going to European and American universities to study technical specialties, but many students have concentrated in areas which the present stage of economic development in Jordan does not require. As a result, most of these students have been forced to give their services to technically more advanced countries or accept employment which has little to do with their training. Obviously, there is a need to establish a direct relationship between the type of industry the country needs and the type of technical training such industry requires. In addition to the problem of technology, Jordanians do not have the necessary organizational training needed for industrialization. Although the Palestinians were educated and had many skills, they were so only in relation to other Arabs. They had adequate training in administrative careers and agricultural activities but very little in industrial management and activity.

Finally, lack of capital is the most serious obstacle to industrialization. The country is poor. Individual income is generally too low to permit substantial private saving or investment. A minor exception is the income which comes to Jordanian families from their relatives employed in other Arab countries, such as Kuwait and Saudi Arabia, and from relatives who have immigrated to the United States, Europe, and Latin America. But most of this income, which is small, is used to sustain a decent standard of living, and is not invested in industrial projects. Moreover, families which are able to save have usually preferred to invest their money in building homes. Consequently, only the building industry has been growing. Other types of industry are few, and the task of industrialization has been left to the government, which is dependent on foreign financial sources. So far, however, such assistance has not enabled the economy to develop self-sufficiency.

THE OCCUPIED TERRITORY

The west bank was occupied by Israel during the war of June 1967. Although it is not certain what juridical status the occupied territory will have in the future, Israel's control over the area will not be relinquished until Jordan recognizes the State of Israel. Consequently, the possibility of another war between Israel and the Arab countries still exists.

The War and Its Aftermath. The people of the occupied territory were stunned by Israel's quick victory over the Arab armies. Prior to the war, they were confident that the Arab armies would win, and afterward they became convinced that Husain's army withdrew from the west bank without a good fight. The truth of the matter, however, was different. Husain's army did withdraw from certain areas of the west bank so as to concentrate on the military operations in Jerusalem, which were thought to be the most important from a strategic point of view, and the key to a total victory over Israel. Of course, when the Jordan Arab army withdrew from cities like Jenin, Tulkarm, Nablus, and Hebron, these cities fell without any serious resistance. It is, therefore, understandable that the people of these cities believe that Husain's army did not fight the Israelis.

While the Jordan army was withdrawing from these cities, minor battles were fought on the main highways of the west bank, and Israeli airplanes were able to prevent the concentration of Jordanian troops in the Jerusalem area by destroying them before they got to Jerusalem.

But in Jerusalem, the Jordanian army fought bitterly, although its forces were too small to defend the city. Again, the Israeli air force was instrumental in achieving a quick victory as was Israel's strategy of knocking out the Egyptian air force. Jordan had counted on Egypt for air cover, but Egypt's air power was destroyed in the first few hours of the war. Nevertheless, the Jordan Arab army fought with discipline and great courage.

There was no treason, as some people in the west bank believed, but there was a lack of foresight on the part of Husain, who was not prepared for the battle and underestimated Israeli military power. The people of the west bank complain that Husain was so afraid of the Palestinians that he was unwilling to arm or train them. Thus, when the Jordanian army withdrew from certain areas of the west bank, their inhabitants did not have weapons to fight with. Although this complaint is valid, it is doubtful that an armed civilian force would have changed the outcome of the war.

Israel's Policies in the Occupied Territory. Immediately after the war the west bank was put under military rule. For the first time in almost twenty years, Arabs and Jews faced each other outside battle grounds. The experience for both sides was both positive and negative, and no definite conclu-

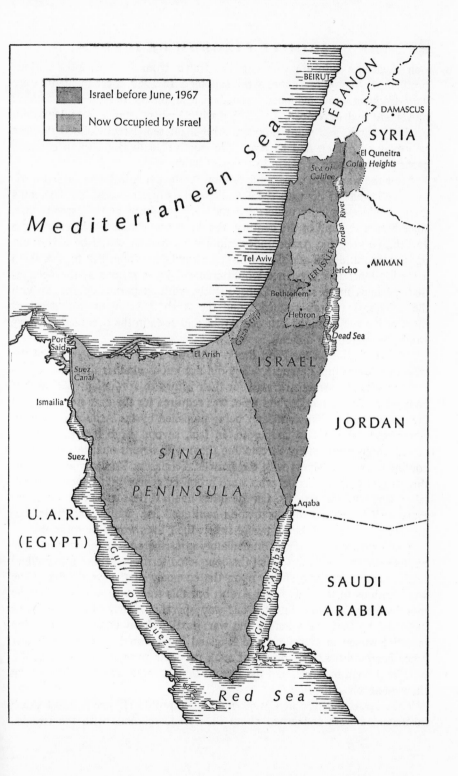

Israel before June, 1967

Now Occupied by Israel

BEIRUT

LEBANON

DAMASCUS

SYRIA

El Quneitra
Golan Heights

Sea of
Galilee

Jordan River

Mediterranean Sea

Tel Aviv

JERUSALEM

Jericho

AMMAN

Bethlehem

Hebron

Gaza Strip

Dead Sea

Port
Said

El Arish

ISRAEL

Suez
Canal

Ismailia

JORDAN

Suez

S I N A I

P E N I N S U L A

Aqaba

U. A. R.

(EGYPT)

Gulf of Suez

Gulf of Aqaba

SAUDI

ARABIA

Red   Sea

sion regarding future peace can be drawn from it. The most serious problem that Israel faced was Arab sabotage. In 1969, these incidents were very frequent, and evidence existed that a highly organized resistance movement had developed. In dealing with Arab resistance, Israel was excessively harsh, and many innocent Arabs suffered. Israel claimed that the only way to put an end to Arab "destructive" activities was to create a general atmosphere of alarm in the west bank.

After the war there were some million Arabs living in the occupied territory, and what to do with them was Israel's biggest headache. To annex them would eventually undermine the very existence of the Israeli state, since before the end of the century, the Arab population would exceed the Jewish. To keep the Arabs under military occupation would be a very expensive operation; in addition, resistance would continue. But to give them a semi-independent existence would create risks as serious as the occupation, perhaps more serious. Consequently, without permanent peace with the neighboring Arab countries and the Arab Palestinians, the development of normal relations between Arabs and Jews in the occupied territory would be extremely difficult.

Arab Attitudes on the West Bank. After the 1967 war, the Arabs of the west bank were in a dilemma. They did not know whether they should cooperate with the Israelis or wait for their return to Jordanian rule. If they cooperated with Israel beyond what was required for the bare necessities of life, they stood a chance of later being punished by the Arab commandos, who urged them not to cooperate. In fact, several Arab businessmen received anonymous letters threatening them with severe punishment if they continued to do business with the Israelis. Damascus Radio voiced similar threats and named persons who were promised severe punishment for collaborating with the Israelis. On the other hand, if the Arabs did not cooperate with Israel and the occupation continued for many years, their economic and social well-being would suffer; their lives would be miserable.

The Economic Situation. Immediately after the end of the war, a large number of Israelis came to visit the conquered territory. These tourists had temporary but positive effects upon the economy of the west bank. They were anxious to trade with the Arabs, but this trade was, for the first few months after the war, almost a one-way operation. They bought products imported by the Arabs before the war: textiles from Damascus, clothing material woven in Germany and England but tailored locally, and many other commodities. The prices of such products were much lower in the west bank than in Israel, and the Israelis bought more from the Arabs than they could sell to them.

Thus Arab businessmen were making a profit. However, most Arab businessmen were concerned about their trade relations with the Israelis.

Aside from the political situation, the economic outlook also favored the Israelis, for the west bank was cut off from Arab markets, and therefore its supplier had to be Israel. There were few factories in the west bank to supply the Arab shopkeeper, and when his stock of goods was sold, he had to buy from Israeli producers at high prices. Arab incomes did not rise with the prices of products, and the Arabs of the west bank suffered economically. Thus, unless Israel pursues a liberal policy in the occupied territory, Arab economic problems will have serious political implications.

Unlike the shopkeeper, who, at least temporarily, was making profit from trade, the farmer in the west bank suffered immediately. There was little demand for many of his products, and in the summer of 1967, he found himself with a surplus. The reason is obvious: the Israelis themselves had a surplus of farm products, and the Arab markets, where the farmers of the west bank sold their surplus, were not expected to remain open. True, there was illicit trade between the west and the east banks, but it was a risky and inadequate operation. Moreover, the Israelis, who ignored the illicit trade before December 1967, became more strict in preventing it. The only solution to the farm problem of the west bank was to find new outlets for agricultural products. But implementing such a solution will not be easy, since Israel herself has for some time had a surplus problem.

CONCLUSION

The future of Jordan remains uncertain. The main problem is economic: Jordan cannot sustain itself without outside financial assistance. But there are other factors relevant to the Jordanian dilemma. Jordan's independence is threatened by internal and external pressures of Arab nationalism. The desire of the Arab nationalists to unify the Arab states is in contradiction to the principle of Jordanian sovereignty. Furthermore, the Arab Commando groups, which became powerful after June 1967, are now an important political force. In 1969, they were Husain's main concern and worry.

Jordan's ties with the West have been criticized by those who desire to establish an Arab common front against the State of Israel. Their argument is that Israel is the enemy of the Arabs and that her friendship with the United States should preclude Arab cooperation with that country. To them, it does not make sense that one should be friendly with the friends of one's enemy.

Yet, it is possible that the independence of Jordan has survived because of Israel, which has often threatened to intervene in case of changes in the political identity of Jordan. Israel fears that the disappearance of Jordan's independence would increase the threat to Israel's own existence.

In her relations with the other Arab countries, Jordan is further handicapped by her monarchy. In the countries where Arab nationalists have been able to capture power—in Syria, Iraq, and Egypt—there is a strong dislike for monarchy. Arab nationalists believe that monarchical regimes in Jordan, Saudi Arabia, and elsewhere have cooperated with the imperialist powers that were responsible for dividing them and establishing the State of Israel. They also believe that economic and social progress is usually handicapped by the conservatism of the monarchy.

Yet Jordan continues to survive. The personality of Husain is an important factor in this survival. He is courageous, politically able, and determined. How long Husain will be able to hold on is a question that cannot be answered at this time. But one thing is definite: so long as the Arabs are divided among themselves and Israel continues to exist, Jordan's political status is not likely to change.

CHAPTER 12

THE STATE OF LEBANON

L E B A N O N is a small country, about half the size of the state of New Jersey. Yet it is the most advanced Arab country. Economically prosperous, Lebanon has been the commercial center of the eastern Mediterranean. It has the highest literacy rate in the region, and its universities and cultural institutions include the best in the Arab World.

Culturally and politically, the country is Western oriented. It has a relatively stable political system, and although its democracy leaves much to be desired, it is the most democratic country in the Middle East. Finally, its political democracy is associated with a dedication to the private enterprise system. Indeed, Lebanon is a unique country—at least by Middle Eastern standards.

THE HISTORICAL BACKGROUND

A small country on the eastern shores of the Mediterranean, Lebanon has had a rich history and an enduring civilization. Professor Philip K. Hitti, one of the foremost authorities on Lebanese history, once said about Lebanon that "its people can rightfully claim to be beneficiaries of all ages and benefactors of many." [1] Indeed, Lebanon's contributions to man's culture are far out of proportion to her population and territory.

Among Lebanon's early settlers were the Canaanites. The culture of these people "lay at the basis of the Aramean culture of Syria and of the Israelite of Palestine—all these being semitic." [2] Many aspects of Hebrew culture were influenced by the Canaanites.

The Phoenicians were the most outstanding Canaanites. Their name was given to them by the Greeks who knew them through their efficient trading. They invented the alphabet—perhaps the most outstanding invention of all times, for without writing the development of civilization would have been impossible. The Phoenicians were also known for their colonization and

1. Philip K. Hitti, *A History of Lebanon* (London: Macmillan, 1965), p. 2.
2. Hitti, *A History of Lebanon*, p. 2.

commercial activity. They had colonies on all sides of the Mediterranean, the best known of which was Carthage, the North African city that stood as a serious rival to Rome. Phoenician commercialism made possible cultural interaction between East and West and the spread of the Semitic culture in the Mediterranean basin.

Lebanon's history has always been closely associated with that of Syria. Before 331 B.C. Lebanon and Syria were subject to the military conquests of such great powers as the Egyptians, Babylons, Hittites, Assyrians, and Persians. But they retained degrees of cultural and political autonomy. Between 331 B.C. and A.D. 636, the two countries were part of the Greek, Roman, and Byzantine empires. It was during this period that Christianity appeared and became a mature religion. The most important contributions of Christianity to the way of life of the people in the area were its new values and its standards of ethics.

The Greeks attempted to Hellenize the regions they controlled; but their system of government in the eastern Mediterranean emphasized city autonomy, which contributed to political fragmentation and cultural diversity. The Romans brought with them their concept of law and their idea of empire. However, aside from these two elements, the same general conditions which existed under the Greeks were continued. Beirut became an important center for legal studies. The Byzantines adhered to the Greco-Roman tradition but emphasized the unity of state and church, persecuting Christians who were not Greek Orthodox.

In A.D. 636, the Arabs became the predominant power in Syria, but Lebanon, although "within the political orbit" of the Arabs, remained largely autonomous. While the neighboring countries became Muslim, the people of the mountainous region of Lebanon remained Christian. The cold climate there was an obstacle in the spreading of Islam.[3] Nevertheless, Arabic later became the predominant language of Lebanon and the means by which certain aspects of the local culture were changed.

During the century after 650, Damascus became the center of the Arab empire, and the eastern Mediterranean assumed political significance. Lebanon was not neglected by the Damascus leadership, as it was after 750 when the center of the Arab empire moved to Baghdad, but Lebanon enjoyed political autonomy under both Damascus and Baghdad. The coastal area in particular experienced cultural stagnation during Abbassid hegemony, but a limited revival took place in the tenth century. However, the rivalry between Cairo and Baghdad during the tenth century resulted in the political division of the region. The Shi'ite caliphate gained control of most of the coastal areas of the eastern Mediterranean.

During the tenth and eleventh centuries, Lebanon consisted of a number

3. Nicola A. Ziadeh, *Syria and Lebanon* (London: Ernest Benn Ltd., 1957), p. 30.

of local principalities. Consequently, it became vulnerable to conquest by the Crusaders, who remained in the eastern Mediterranean until the end of the thirteenth century, when the Mamelukes were able to drive them out. The Mamelukes controlled Egypt, Palestine, Lebanon, and Syria until the coming of Ottoman rule in the sixteenth century.

Between 1516 and 1864, the territory of what later became Lebanon was divided into two political divisions, both under Ottoman sovereignty. The northern area became part of the vilayet of Sidon. The eastern region of modern Lebanon formed part of the vilayet of Damascus. (In 1864, the vilayets of Tripoli and Sidon were merged into the newly created vilayet of Beirut.)

Four years before the merger of Tripoli and Sidon a new and separate political entity, commonly known as Mount Lebanon, was created. It included "that part of the present Lebanese territory which extends roughly from the watershed of the Lebanon to the sea, excluding the town of Beirut and the regions of Tripoli and Sidon." [4] From 1861 until 1915, Mount Lebanon was governed by a non-Lebanese Christian appointed by the Ottoman sultan. It was during this time that the term "Lebanon" was first used to refer to a specific political entity.

In the second half of the nineteenth century different forms of national consciousness developed in Lebanon. In the northern region, the Christian Maronites, a religious group affiliated with the Roman Catholic church, emphasized the Christian identity of Lebanon. Other Christians, such as the Greek Orthodox and the Greek Catholics, developed a concept of Syrian unity based upon the Arab heritage and culture. They advocated a secular nationalism and called for cooperation between Muslims and Christians. This nationalism was reinforced by an Arabic literary revival that took place in Lebanon in the second half of the nineteenth century.

Until the turn of this century the Muslims of Lebanon and Syria were very conscious of their Islamic identity and were loyal to the Turks, but their situation began to change after 1908 as a result of the centralist and racial policies of the Young Turks, who in that year won control of Ottoman power in Constantinople. The Muslims were rapidly developing a new kind of political consciousness—an Arab rather than Islamic nationalism. This nationalism, although new, was inspired by the earlier nationalism of the non-Maronite Christians of Lebanon.

Of course, Arab nationalist activity after 1908 culminated in the Arab revolt of 1916, which was supported by the Allied powers in World War I. It was successful in bringing about the disintegration of Ottoman power in the Arab Near East but failed, owing to the intervention of Britain and

4. Kamil S. Salibi, *The Modern History of Lebanon* (London: Weidenfeld and Nicolson, 1965), p. xii.

France, to assure the independence of the Fertile Crescent territory. After World War I, Syria and Lebanon became the responsibility of France.

LEBANON UNDER THE FRENCH MANDATE

During and shortly after World War I, the geographic area known as Syria—which includes present-day Syria, Lebanon, Palestine (now Israel), and Jordan—suffered most from European desire to establish control in the area. Most Syrians had hoped to become free of foreign control soon after their participation in the expulsion of the Turks. However, their hope was destroyed when it became clear that Britain and France had planned to establish their authority in the Near East.

On May 16, 1915, the two world powers concluded a secret agreement, commonly known as the Sykes-Picot Agreement,[5] in which they provided for the division of the Fertile Crescent into a number of zones. One of these zones was coastal Syria, which France was to control. Parts of present-day Lebanon were included in this zone.

This agreement was in conflict with the promises previously made by the representative of Britain, Sir Henry McMahon, to Sharif Husain, who later led the Arab revolt against the Turks. The conflict was caused mainly by Britain's desire to reconcile her interests and the interests of France in the Fertile Crescent. France's ambitions in Syria seemed irreconcilable with Arab national aspirations. Of course, the Christian Maronites were receptive to the idea of French control or a French mandate. Fearing they might become a minority in an Arab-Muslim unity, they naturally looked to Catholic France for protection and guidance.

The fate of the Ottoman Empire, of which Syria and Lebanon were parts, was discussed at the Paris Peace Conference in January 1919. Although early in its session the conference decided to separate the Arab territories from the Ottoman Empire and put them under the mandate system, it failed at the end to agree on the future of the Arab lands. However, in September 1919 Britain conceded to France the military occupation of coastal Syria, and she withdrew her troops for that purpose.

In 1920, at the San Remo Conference, Britain and France formally agreed to divide the Fertile Crescent. The southern half of geographical Syria was allotted to Great Britain; the northern half went to France. The two areas were to be governed as mandate territories. On July 25, French forces entered Damascus after defeating the Arabs at the famous Battle of Maisalun. Two years later the Council of the League of Nations approved

5. Text in Jacob C. Hurewitz, ed., *Diplomacy in the Near and Middle East, A Documentary Record: 1914–1956* (Princeton: Van Nostrand, 1956), vol. II, Doc. 10, pp. 18–22.

the text of the mandate for Syria and Lebanon, which went into effect in September 1923.[6]

According to the mandate, France was to govern Syria and Lebanon on behalf of the League of Nations, to which she was required to report annually. Controversies regarding the meaning of the mandate agreement were to be submitted to the Permanent Court of International Justice. Furthermore, France was required to establish an organic law for Syria and Lebanon after consultation with the local authorities; this law was to take into account the rights and interests of the people. Defense and foreign affairs were to become the responsibility of the mandatory power, which was obligated to develop self-government in Syria and Lebanon.

French authority in Syria and Lebanon was exercised by a high commissioner. Several indigenous governments were created to help him. French policy was opposed to the formation of a single government for all of Syria and Lebanon on the grounds of diversity of the population. As early as 1920 France had established the State of Greater Lebanon to include the cities and districts of Beirut, Tripoli, Sur, Saida, Baalbeck, Biqa, Rashaya, and Hasbaya. But the administrative arrangement was to be provisional. In 1922, Lebanon acquired a Representative Council, but the French high commissioner was the real power in the government. Furthermore, the formula for representation on the Council was constructed on religious lines, and the census which preceded the elections for the Council was not accurate.[7]

In fact, the weakest aspect of French rule was its failure to develop self-government in Syria and Lebanon. Critics of the French mandate charged that France failed her commitments under the mandate instrument by ruling Lebanon and Syria as if they were her colonies. In addition, these critics were at pains to point out that France had also failed to train the Lebanese and Syrians for public service.[8] There is a great deal of truth in these accusations, for France was generally inclined toward the centralization of the political system, not only in Lebanon and Syria, but in almost every place where French political authority existed. Moreover, one of the important characteristics of French rule and administration that it is too French, that it is too imbued with zeal for everything French and with contempt for indigenous cultures.

Yet France made certain contributions, mostly in the development of the communications system. In many areas of Lebanon and Syria, the French established civil government where there had been little or none under the

---

6. See Appendix D in Stephen Hemsley Longrigg, *Syria and Lebanon Under French Mandate* (London: Oxford University Press, 1958), pp. 376–80.
7. Longrigg, *Syria*, p. 127.
8. A. H. Hourani, *Syria and Lebanon: A Political Essay* (London: Oxford University Press, 1958), pp. 376–80.

Turks. Lebanon benefited from French road construction, which connected her towns and facilitated commercial activities. Schools were established, and she became the educational center of the Middle East. Unfortunately, the French neglected agricultural activities and education. Too, the semi-feudal structures of Syrian and Lebanese societies were left intact. In sum, we can say that while French culture appealed to many Lebanese, they were generally disappointed with French rule.

Technically speaking, the French mandate in Lebanon came to an end in June 1941, when the Free French proclaimed the independence of Syria and Lebanon. However, subsequent events showed France's reluctance to surrender control of these two countries. The people of Syria and Lebanon insisted on the complete and unqualified independence of their countries. Great Britain, the United States, and Russia were sympathetic as well as instrumental in bringing about the withdrawal of French troops from the two Levant states. The withdrawal was completed at the end of 1946, and Lebanon was left to administer her own affairs.

THE CONSTITUTION AND THE GOVERNMENTAL SYSTEM

In theory as well as in practice, the most powerful figure in the government of Lebanon is the president. He is elected by the Chamber of Deputies, Lebanon's unicameral legislature, by a two-thirds majority on the first ballot or an absolute majority on subsequent ballots. He serves for a term of six years, and the Constitution does not allow him to succeed himself in office.[9] In the past this prohibition has caused political crises. In 1952, President Bishara al-Khouri tried to have the Constitution amended so as to be able to succeed himself. He failed, but created a crisis which threatened the country's political stability. In 1958, President Camille Chamoun also attempted to have the Constitution amended, producing a civil war. Although Chamoun's attempt to succeed himself was not the only factor in the civil war, it was an important one. The next president, General Fuad Shihab, left office in 1964 without causing difficulties. The incumbent, President Charles Hilu, succeeded Shihab without incident, and his term of office will not expire until 1970.

The president is empowered to appoint and dismiss the prime minister and other ministers. He can call Parliament for a special session and adjourn it for a period not exceeding one month. With the Cabinet's consent, he can dissolve Parliament. In addition, he can veto legislation, although

9. For the text of the Constitution see Helen Miller Davis, ed., *Constitutions, Electoral Laws, Treaties of States in the Near and Middle East* (Durham, N.C.: Duke University Press, 1953), pp. 290–305.

Parliament can override his veto by an absolute majority of all members. The president also has an important decree power: he can declare in force a draft law deemed "urgent" by the Cabinet if Parliament does not act upon it within forty days of its introduction.

What makes the president so powerful is not only the scope of his constitutional powers but also the fact that he is not held accountable to the legislature for his acts, except for crimes and the violation of the Constitution. However, the prime minister and the other ministers are accountable to Parliament individually and collectively. But Cabinet changes are affected more often by the president than by Parliament. In fact, only once, in 1930, has a Cabinet ever been ousted by Parliament. Sometimes Cabinets fall because of the personal quarrels among their members.

There were forty-six Cabinets between 1926 (the year when Lebanon acquired its present Constitution) and 1964. The average life span of a Cabinet has been less than eight months. Nevertheless, Cabinet positions are limited to only a few men, many of whom continue from one cabinet to another. The 333 Cabinet positions that became vacant between 1926 and 1963 were filled from a "pool" of 134 individuals.[10]

The frequency of Lebanese Cabinets is reminiscent of French Cabinets during the third and fourth republics. However, while France had a strong and stable civil service to balance her political instability, Lebanon has no such advantage. This brings us to the important question regarding the role of government in the Lebanese society. According to Professor Malcolm Kerr, the Lebanese people subscribe to Lao-tze's saying that "the best government is the one whose existence is barely noted by the people." [11] This seems to explain why the ineffectiveness of Lebanese government does not have greater impact upon the life of the people. Furthermore, Lebanese Cabinets have as their main responsibility not "to create policy, nor to choose between clear-cut alternatives entailing the triumph of one set of demands over another, but to reflect faithfully and adjust the competing interests of various groups." [12] This too is a reason for the lack of responsiveness by the people to governmental instability.

The Lebanese political system has features of both presidential and parliamentary systems. In practice, the Lebanese president is even more powerful than he is in constitutional theory. Like the President of the United States, he is not politically accountable to the legislature. But unlike him he is almost always in control of the legislature, not through formal powers but through informal ones. According to Professor J. C. Hurewitz, the

10. Malcolm H. Kerr, "Political Decision Making in a Confessional Democracy," in *Politics in Lebanon,* ed. Leonard Binder (New York: John Wiley & Sons, 1966), p. 192.
11. Kerr, in *Politics in Lebanon,* p. 187.
12. Kerr, in *Politics in Lebanon,* p. 190.

Lebanese legislative body "has become the President's creature in a way that the Congress never has." [13] The parliamentary features of the Lebanese political system exist more in theory than in practice. For instance, the Chamber of Deputies elects the president. It also can compel the resignation of the Cabinet (but not the president), although it can be dissolved by the president and the Cabinet. These elements of the parliamentary system have not, as mentioned earlier, worked to the advantage of the legislature. In practice, therefore, the Lebanese political system remains essentially a presidential system.

THE POWER STRUCTURE: THE STATUS OF THE RELIGIOUS GROUPS

Lebanon is a country of religious minorities. Because of the lack of accurate census data, we cannot be sure how many people belong to any one group. The men in power since independence have a vested interest in retaining the power structure that developed during the nineteenth century; and this structure is based mainly on an equilibrium that grew out of the relationships among the religious groups of that time. The last official census was taken in 1932. Official estimates were taken in later years (the most comprehensive were those of 1943), but these were estimates only.

In spite of the lack of reliable information, we do know that none of the religious groups constitute a majority of the country's population. The largest groups are the Maronite Christians and the Sunnite Muslims. Officially, the Maronite is considered the larger of the two, but because of the higher Muslim birth rate, the Muslim group may have become equal to or even larger than the Christian group.

The Maronites are Christians who "originally held the monothelete doctrine that Christ had two Natures but one Will." In the twelfth century, they abandoned this doctrine and affiliated with the Roman Catholic church, although they continued to practice the Syriac liturgy.[14] Politically, the Maronites "stand adamantly for unconditional independence and against the inclusion of Lebanon in any Arab or Syrian federation or union." [15] The Sunnite Muslims consider themselves faithful to the original tenets of Islam. Politically, they are inclined toward closer relations with the Arab countries and do not oppose the inclusion of Lebanon in some kind of an Arab political unity.

13. J. C. Hurewitz, "Lebanese Democracy in Its International Setting," *The Middle East Journal*, XVII, 5 (1963), 488.
14. Leila M. T. Meo, *Lebanon: Improbable Nation* (Bloomington: Indiana University Press, 1965), p. 229.
15. H. B. Sharabi, *Government and Politics of the Middle East in the Twentieth Century* (Princeton: Van Nostrand, 1962), p. 135.

In addition to the Maronites and the Sunnites, the Lebanese population includes Shi'ites, Druzes, Greek Orthodox, Greek Catholics, Syrian Catholics, Protestants, Armenian Gregorian, Armenian Catholics, Syrian Orthodox, and other smaller groups. Of these religious groups, the Greek Orthodox, the Druzes, and the Shi'ites rank next in importance to the Maronites and the Sunnites.

The Greek Orthodox separated from the Roman Catholic church in the eleventh century. In Syria and Lebanon, they use Arabic in their liturgy. The Druzes became a distinct religious group in eleventh-century Egypt. It is considered to be a "heretic Muslim sect." The Shi'ites, mentioned earlier, separated from the Sunnite Muslims in the seventh century. In Lebanon they are commonly known as the Metawilis. Politically, these three groups are inclined to support Lebanese independence without disrupting Lebanon's Arab regional identity: they would maintain Lebanon as an independent country but they would cooperate with the Arab countries.

The sectarian structure of Lebanese political life [16] is old and is not the product of entirely local conditions. In the formal sense, it goes back to 1861, when Mount Lebanon became an autonomous political entity under Ottoman suzerainty. Unofficially, the structure was developed many years before. In the 1840's and 1850's, the Ottoman sultan encouraged sectarian rivalries to induce the Lebanese to give up their traditional autonomy and submit to a stronger Ottoman control. This traditional autonomy had, in a sense, been forced upon the Ottoman sultans by the European powers, who courted the religious minorities to gain influence in the Middle East. France identified herself with Maronite interests, while Russia and Britain backed the Greek Orthodox Christians and the Druzes, respectively. In the 1850's, Druze-Maronite relations were so strained that they culminated, in 1860, in a religious war known as the "massacre." The causes of the war were not purely external; local conditions, mostly economic, also contributed.

During the mandate, France continued the sectarianism of Lebanon. She believed that the "confessional" (i.e., religious) structure of the country contributed to effective French control, and she invested the religious courts with authority over the personal status of the Lebanese. By 1941, when Lebanon became independent, the sectarian system was already well established.

In 1943, Christian and Muslim leaders worked out an informal agreement, known as the National Pact, by which political power was distributed among the religious sects. The Christians were assured of a majority of the seats in Parliament, and they were also to nominate the president.

16. For greater details, see Ralph E. Crow, "Religious Sectarianism in the Lebanese Political System," *Journal of Politics*, XXIV, 3 (1962), 489–520.

The Muslims were conceded a monopoly over the prime ministership of the government. The pact also produced a great compromise between the two major religious groups: The Christians abandoned the idea of a Lebanon isolated from the Arab World and accepted a Lebanese independence with cooperation with the Arab countries, and the Muslims abandoned the idea of union with the Arab countries in return for the same thing.

In practice, the arrangements in the pact were as follows. The Maronites controlled the presidency, the Sunnite Muslims the prime ministership, and the Shi'ite Muslims the presidency of the Chamber of Deputies. (An exception took place in 1947 when a Greek Orthodox was elected to the Chamber's presidency.) Representation of the other religious groups in the Cabinet was also recognized.

In the Chamber of Deputies, representation of the sects was in accordance with a specific formula. There were to be six Christian members to every five non-Christians. This is why the Chamber's total membership is always fixed in multiples of eleven. It is now ninety-nine.

The distribution of power among the religious sects in this manner has no basis in Lebanese constitutional law, but the terms of the National Pact have become a well-established constitutional custom. The pact has been responsible for the relative stability of the Lebanese political system, and it has been the strongest guarantee of Lebanese independence. As we shall see later, the violation of the spirit of the pact was one of the reasons for the Lebanese civil war of 1958.

THE POWER STRUCTURE: THE ELITE

Under the Turks, power in Mount Lebanon was "distributed among a number of autonomous hereditary aristocratic chiefs subordinate in certain political aspects to a common overlord." [17] The patriarchal character of the government still persisted at the time of World War II, and the traditional aristocratic families still exercised substantial influence over the government. Economic differences had lessened, however, and Lebanon had "very little abject poverty and very few rich people." [18]

Today the traditional pattern of influence remains dominant, but to a lesser degree than before. Owing to purely economic reasons, the social structure of society has changed, but the change has not been altogether good. Although poverty in Lebanon is still less evident than in the past,

17. Illiya F. Harik, "The Iqta System in Lebanon: A Comparative Political View," *The Middle East Journal*, XIX, 4 (1965), 405.
18. Charles Issawi, "Economic Development and Liberalism in Lebanon," *The Middle East Journal*, XVIII, 3 (1964), 287.

and a Lebanese middle class has grown in numbers and wealth, the rich have become richer, and a "sharp increase in the degree of inequality" has become obvious since 1945.[19]

According to a recent study,[20] the landlords—the traditional aristocratic class of Lebanon—had the largest representation in the Parliaments between 1943 and 1953, but in 1960 and 1964 the professionals became the largest group. Despite this evidence of change in the composition of Parliament, the Chamber of Deputies nevertheless "remains a most exclusive club," partly because "the very poor are still represented by the very rich." [21]

The study referred to above explains this dilemma in terms of financial obstacles in elections. To be able to run at all in a parliamentary election, a prospective candidate must pay a $1,000 registration fee which is forfeited if the candidate receives less than 20 per cent of the vote. In addition, the study shows that in 1960 the cost of a candidate's electoral campaign ranged between $6,600 and $266,000. For a small country like Lebanon, such costs can be a real hindrance to the progress of democracy.

There is no doubt that the Lebanese political system is oligarchic. As mentioned earlier, 134 individuals occupied all of the 333 Cabinet positions available between 1926 and 1963. In Parliament, deputies tend to perpetuate themselves in office. In the seven Parliaments between 1943 and 1964, "nearly one-third of the seats available have been occupied by fourteen per cent of all the deputies elected to those seven parliaments." [22]

Despite these handicaps, the people of Lebanon have shown some interest in the electoral process in recent years. In 1943, voters constituted a mere 12 per cent of the total population; in 1964 they were 32 per cent. Woman suffrage, introduced in 1953, was partly responsible for the increase.[23] What is less encouraging is that the urban areas—mainly the capital—are not as integrated into the political system as are the rural areas and that the increase in the ratio of voters to population is not an indication that the Lebanese system has become more democratic. Of course, the 1958 civil war demonstrated the delicacy of the balance of power in Lebanon.

---

19. Issawi, *The Middle East Journal,* p. 287.
20. Michael C. Hudson, "The Electoral Process and Political Development in Lebanon," *The Middle East Journal,* XX, 2 (1966), 179.
21. Hudson, *The Middle East Journal,* p. 179.
22. Hudson, *The Middle East Journal,* p. 176.
23. Hudson, *The Middle East Journal,* pp. 174–75.

THE POWER STRUCTURE: POLITICAL PARTIES

In Lebanon, political parties have little influence on the outcome of elections. The feudal-sectarian elements of political power are so strong that they have been able to limit party influence. Nevertheless, parties do play an important role. First, some of them have kept a close watch on the traditionalist political leaders, thereby forcing these leaders to unite in a time of crisis. By attempting to woo the masses of people to their side, they have forced the traditionalist leaders to pay some attention to the demands of the people. Thus, had there been no political parties in Lebanon, the traditionalist leaders would have been less responsive to popular demands for political participation and more rigid in the use of political authority. Lebanese political parties have been an important factor in changing the traditionalist leader from a feudal lord to a modern political "boss."

Secondly, political parties, mainly the doctrinal parties, have influence outside the government. Some of them, like the Syrian Social Nationalist party (P.P.S.) and the Communist party, have strong organizations, and their appeal, though limited, is politically significant. Their effectiveness cannot be measured by their numerical size; it is their militancy that makes them important. Sometimes, their activity threatens the life of a government and, more important, the country's sovereign existence. For instance, if the abortive coup of 1961, instigated by the P.P.S., had been successful, it would eventually have brought about the political merger of Lebanon and Syria.

The most important Lebanese doctrinal party is the Syrian Social Nationalist party. It was the first genuine party—having an organization, a program, and a comprehensive ideology—established in any part of the Fertile Crescent. It was founded by Antun Saadeh, a Lebanese intellectual who spent part of his life in Latin America as an immigrant. Well read in political and social literature, Saadeh attempted to formulate a political and social philosophy to suit a Middle Eastern environment. He saw in the geographic environment of "natural Syria" the necessary elements for constructing a national identity to include all of the people of that environment.

Accordingly, Saadeh believed in Syrian rather than Lebanese nationalism. He advocated the unification of Lebanon, present-day Syria, the old Palestine (without Israel), Iraq, Jordan, Kuwait, and Cyprus, these countries being parts of "natural Syria." He realized the difficulties of uniting all these political divisions, but he had great faith in the political and economic potential of such unity.

Saadeh's party was highly organized. It maintained a militia and was prepared to take over the responsibility of government, and its membership included a number of individuals with outstanding qualifications for governmental service. In 1949, it instigated a revolution that failed, and Saadeh was executed. In 1961, it attempted a coup but failed again, mainly because of bad strategy and because the government knew about its plans well in advance.

Although the party's plans for the unification of the "Syrian" states seem to synthesize successfully two diametrically opposed situations—the political *status quo* and the idea of an all-encompassing Arab unity—they have not been politically possible. One reason is the opposition to the party's nonsectarian philosophy, which it derived from many organized and informal groups. In Lebanon, the political *status quo* is sectarian, and it naturally resists the party's nonsectarian approach to politics. Thus the party is opposed by Muslims as well as Christians, especially by those whose influence is based on the support of the religious groups. For obvious reasons, Arab nationalists and the Communist elements consider the P.P.S. their greatest enemy.

The party has organizations in Syria, Jordan, Kuwait, and Iraq. Before the Arab-Israeli war of 1967, Nasser's appeal in these countries diminished the influence of the P.P.S. Since the war, the party has tried unsuccessfully to rejuvenate its organization. Most of its leaders have been in prison since the attempted coup in 1961. In any case, no leader of Saadeh's capability has emerged.

A second party, of a different kind, is the Phalanges (Kata'ib) party. It was established in 1937 as a youth movement but after independence, it became a party with an organization and a program. The leader of the Phalanges possesses virtually absolute authority over the members, and the party maintains a paramilitary force.

The Phalanges believes in the sovereign independence of Lebanon. It considers the country to be a complete geographic and historical entity and the people of Lebanon to constitute a nation. Consequently, the party opposes the incorporation of Lebanon into any Arab or Syrian unity. Although the party's official doctrine is secular, it is identified with the Maronite community. In fact, the party's emphasis on Lebanese independence and its negative attitude toward the Arab world are largely motivated by its desire to keep Lebanon a Christian country dominated by the Maronites. The party also implicitly believes in the excellence and superiority of the Lebanese.

The Muslim counterpart of the Phalanges is the Najjadah party, which also has a military organization. The Najjadah, however, does not oppose Pan-Arabism so long as Lebanese autonomy is respected. Since the unification of the Arab states would require the disavowal of localism, provincialism, and particularism, the party discourages such parochial political attachments. The Syrian Nationalist party and the other political groups that oppose Lebanon's independence also tend to discourage fragmented loyalties.

The Progressive Socialist party was founded in 1949 by Kemal Jumblat, a Druze landlord who served in Parliament between 1943 and 1949. The party's program is based upon a Socialist theory intellectually inferior to most European Socialist theories, from which it was derived. After its foundation, the party succeeded in attracting some attention in cultural and intellectual circles, but politically its influence was no greater than its leader's influence. In fact, its political strength comes from the support of the Druzes and their loyalty to Jumblat and his feudal family.

Of course, like all other Middle Eastern countries, Lebanon has a Communist party, which does not differ from its counterparts elsewhere. It is directed from Moscow, subscribes to Marxist theories, and follows the policies formulated by the Soviet state. In Lebanon, the party operates secretly because it is legally proscribed. However, it has made effective use of front organizations to infiltrate unions, clubs, and educational and cultural institutions.

Lebanon has other parties, but they are basically groupings made up of personal followings of some traditional leaders; they support the *status quo,* which is sectarian and feudal. Among these are the Constitutional Bloc and the National Bloc, both of which were founded in 1934 by two former presidents, Bishara al-Khouri and Emile Edde. There is also the National Liberal party, which was founded in 1958 by Camille Chamoun, also a former president. These parties are more successful in elections than the parties which are mostly doctrinal. Their success, however, is limited and is due to the traditionalism of the power structure and the modernism of the party concept.

FOREIGN POLICY

The National Pact, referred to earlier, provides the general framework for Lebanon's foreign policy. It assumed that Lebanese independence could be preserved only if the Christian population refrained from looking to the Western powers—specifically to France—for protection and if the Muslim Lebanese abandoned their dream of union with Syria and the Arab countries. Since the pact also provided the sectarian formula for governing Lebanon, an intimate relationship developed between Lebanon's international policy and her domestic sectarian structure. Consequently, any change in the domestic formula was bound to affect the foreign policy. The opposite is also true.

For Lebanon to continue to be an independent state, its foreign policy must always be neutral. This, of course, does not mean that the Christians have abandoned their desire to identify themselves with the West in the international struggle or that the Muslims have ceased to sympathize with the idea of an Arab unity. It simply means that neither side can act to substantiate its desire or sympathy without jeopardizing independence. Consequently, Lebanon occasionally suffers from the two conflicting desires. From the time of independence (1941) until 1956, Lebanon adhered to the policy of neutrality. While it refused to align with either camp in the international struggle, it pursued a friendly policy toward the Western powers. This was acceptable to the Muslim population. At the same time, while it resisted attempts to merge with Syria, it pursued a friendly policy with the Arab countries. And this was acceptable to the Christian population. Thus in 1948, it joined the Arab League in the war against Israel. In 1950, it adhered to the Arab security pact espoused by the Arab League. (Lebanon has been a member of the league since its inception in 1945.) Finally, in 1955, Lebanon refused to join the Baghdad Pact but continued to maintain friendly relations with both Egypt and Iraq.

It was in 1956 that the government of President Chamoun began to move away from the policy of neutrality, thereby altering the formula prescribed by the National Pact of 1943 and jeopardizing the traditional domestic political balance. In 1956—the year of the Suez crisis—Lebanon refused to sever diplomatic relations with Britain and France. This aroused the Muslim communities in Lebanon who understood the pact to mean no union with the Arab states but cooperation with these states on matters of common interest. Had France, Britain, and Israel been successful in their military effort, the results would have been detrimental to all the Arab countries. Lebanese Muslims, therefore, expected the government to join the other Arab countries in denouncing the invaders.

And when in April 1957, the Chamoun government decided to endorse the Eisenhower Doctrine, it became clear that the traditional policy of neutrality had been broken and that Lebanon had aligned itself with the United States. Tension ran high, particularly among the Sunnite Muslims. Some Christian elements also resented the Chamoun policy because they feared it would disrupt the balance established by the pact and cause a political upheaval. Tension was intensified by the parliamentary elections held in June 1957, in which the government's slate of candidates acquired a large majority in the Chamber of Deputies. The opposition, under the name of the United National Bloc, received only a few seats, and it charged the Chamoun government with manipulating the electoral process to its own advantage. Soon a rumor spread that Chamoun intended to have the Constitution amended to be able to succeed himself when his term of office ended in 1958.

Street riots, mainly in Tripoli and Beirut, threatened to spread into an all-out insurrection. The danger became evident in May 1958, after a reshuffle in the Cabinet which removed the critics of Chamoun's pro-Western policy. The civil war took on a religious tone, with Chamoun's support coming from the Maronites, the opposition mostly from Muslims, and the Druzes divided between government and opposition.

The Muslims had contributed their share to the causes of the civil war. Chamoun's violation of the spirit of the pact was a reaction to Muslim enthusiam for Arab unity which became evident after the Suez crisis and reached its climax in February 1958, when Syria and Egypt became united in the United Arab Republic. Many Muslim leaders began openly to advocate union with the U.A.R. They demanded the taking of an official and accurate census, for they believed the Muslims had become a majority in Lebanon (a belief that is probably correct).

Chamoun charged that the United Arab Republic was instigating the riots, which had already developed into a large-scale civil war. A group of United Nations observers were sent to Lebanon to investigate the charge and found no evidence to substantiate it.

By July 1958, there were signs that the revolutionaries might succeed in bringing Lebanon into the Nasser camp. The Lebanese army had taken a neutral position in the civil war, and the government was defended mainly by the militia of the Syrian Social Nationalist party, which was well organized and well trained. This party, as mentioned earlier, opposed Arab nationalism, but it became involved in the war not to safeguard Lebanese independence or to save Chamoun's government, but to put a halt to Nasser's penetration of the Fertile Crescent, the area in which their own Syrian unity was to be established.

When on July 14, 1958, a successful military coup took place in Iraq, possibility of a nationalist takeover in Lebanon and Jordan increased. Chamoun then asked the United States to intervene, and the United States responded by sending troops. By July 20, there were no less than ten thousand United States troops in the Beirut area, and it was only a matter of time until the civil war would end. Chamoun was allowed to complete his term. In September, Lebanon elected a new president, General Fuad Shihab, who as chief of staff had taken a neutral position in the war, thereby becoming acceptable to both Christians and Muslims. The civil war had come to an end.

THE ECONOMY

With very limited mineral and other resources, Lebanon cannot sustain a sizable industry. However, by Middle Eastern standards, its manufacturing industries are highly developed. Although recent statistical data about the country's economic position are not available, in 1962 there were some 5,000 industrial establishments in Lebanon employing about 21,000 people.

In addition to the lack of raw materials, the shortage of fuel and electric power has inhibited industrialization. However, it is hoped that the impact of this problem will be considerably lessened when the Litani River Project is completed. The project is designed to increase Lebanon's electrical power by about four times. It will also increase the irrigated area of Lebanon by 50,000 acres.

Industry in Lebanon owes its existence to private initiative and private enterprise. The government has only minimal involvement in economic activity, in spite of the fact that state activity expanded after Lebanese independence. Indirect assistance to industry has been provided by low tax rates on profit. And tax evasion is very common in Lebanon.

Lebanon's ability to feed its inhabitants is also limited. Over 50 per cent of the land area comprises mountains, swamps, and desert; only 23 per cent is cultivated. Wheat and flour have to be imported. Nevertheless, the Lebanese have tried to improve their situation by shifting to the production of high-value products (mainly for export) like fruits and poultry, and by increasing the cultivated area through terracing mountain slopes and providing additional irrigation.

Without adequate industry or agriculture, one would expect Lebanon to be a poor country. Yet it has the highest per capita income in the Arab world and surpasses the other Arab countries in many aspects of economic and cultural life. Indeed, many economic experts are puzzled by Lebanon's outstanding achievements in the economic field.[24]

Economists, however, point to the ingenuity of the Lebanese people in explaining the surprising prosperity of Lebanon. The Lebanese have historically attempted to overcome their economic obstacles by concentrating on commerce, and in this area of economic activity they have a long record of excellence, traceable to their Phoenician ancestors. Beirut, the capital, has become the distributing center of the Middle East, aided by the fact that it is a free port. Although Lebanon has an adverse balance of visible trade, the problem has been made less troublesome by Lebanon's highly important transit trade, which is many times greater than the value of its domestic exports. Syrian, Jordanian, and Iraqi transit trade passes through Beirut.

Lebanese have been ingenious in making their country a suitable place for business and financial transactions. With the exception of an occasional crisis, the political climate in Lebanon—the best in the Middle East—

24. Issawi, *The Middle East Journal*, XVIII, 291.

encourages foreign business activity. Many foreign firms doing business in the Arab countries prefer to locate their regional offices in Lebanon. Of course, the civil war of 1958 hurt the Lebanese economy; but by 1961 the situation had returned to normal and Lebanon resumed its role as the trading and financial center of the eastern Mediterranean. Today over twenty-five foreign banks operate in the Beirut area in addition to the more than thirty-five local banks.

The political climate is reinforced by Lebanon's ideal resort weather, which has made it attractive to tourists. In 1965 more than 600,000 people visited Lebanon. To encourage tourism, Lebanon has built luxurious hotels, excellent night clubs, good restaurants, and other facilities intended for the comfort and entertainment of tourists. Furthermore, it has built a modern international airport, equipped to accommodate the largest and most modern airliners. In 1965, 35,462 aircraft and 1,205,867 passengers used the airport.

The United Nations no longer considers Lebanon to be an underdeveloped country. Thus the Arab country least likely to advance economically, because of its limited natural resources, is now the most advanced. Lebanon has indeed set an example of how native ingenuity can surmount natural handicaps.

CHAPTER 13

SYRIA

HISTORICALLY, the name Syria has included those territories of the Levant which correspond to modern Syria, Lebanon, Palestine (Israel), Jordan, and parts of Arabia. Its history has been affected by three important geographical factors: its location at the main trade routes between Europe, Mesopotamia, and India; its varied topography which has prevented the establishment of its political unity; and the encroaching desert which has influenced its culture and the ethnic composition of its population.

Syria's contribution to mankind is outstanding. Its "civilization has been a going concern since the fourth millennium before Christ. The early culture of Europe was but a pale reflection of this civilization of the eastern Mediterranean." [1] The Phoenicians, who as we mentioned, invented the alphabet, inhabited the west (mostly Lebanon); in its southern part (Palestine), Judaism and Christianity originated. The third of the great monotheistic religions, Islam, also left traces in that part of Syria. "Had the people rendered no other service," said historian Philip K. Hitti, "this would have been enough to mark them out among the greatest benefactors of history." [2]

THE HISTORICAL BACKGROUND

From the earliest times, Syria was the favorite target of great conquerors, and foreign powers have held it for most of its history. In the early periods, these included Hittites, Egyptians, Assyrians, Babylonians, and Persians. In 333–332 B.C. Alexander the Great conquered it; but his descendants held it for only a few years, when they were succeeded by the Seleucids in 312. The Seleucids became known as the Kings of Syria. Their rule, however, extended only to some parts of ancient Syria. In the first century B.C. Syria was invaded by the Armenians under Tigranes and

1. Philip K. Hitti, *Syria: A Short History* (New York: The Macmillan Company, 1959), p. 4.
2. Hitti, *Syria,* p. 2.

then by the Parthians. The Romans under Pompey had conquered it by 63 B.C. They borrowed the Syrian gods, and they later adopted Christianity, born in its southern part, Palestine.

When the Roman Empire divided into the Western and Byzantine empires, Syria became part of the latter and remained under a lax Byzantine rule until conquered by the Arabs in 633–36. The impact of the new conquerors upon the region was great: they gave it the Arabic language and the Islamic religion. (It was during Arab rule that the bonds between Muslim Syria and Christian Lebanon were strained.) Damascus became the center of the Arab empire during the Umayyad rule (661–750). Arab dominance of Syria was disrupted in the eleventh century when the Crusaders entered Syria and established new political divisons. Saladin (1137–93), the Ayyubite sultan of Egypt, expelled the Crusaders, but his rule was short, and in the thirteenth century Syria came under the Mamelukes of Egypt. Later in the same century the Mongols invaded the territory several times, and in 1300 they destroyed most of Damascus. Three years later, however, they were defeated by the Mamelukes, who continued to dominate Syria until 1516, when the Ottoman Turks succeeded them.

Under Ottoman rule (1516–1918), the people of Syria enjoyed a measure of autonomy. The new ruler respected their language, and they in turn respected his authority and gave the Ottomans their loyalty. The Ottomans were Muslim, and until the second half of the nineteenth century, Syrians cared more about their Islamic identity than their Arabic identity.

After 1864, however, as the Ottoman system became centralized and as Turkish replaced Arabic as the official language of the Arab provinces, a national consciousness began to appear. Irritated by the depreciation of their language, Arabs formed secret societies and demanded local autonomy. Some even joined Turkish organizations (like the Young Turks and the Society of Union and Progress) whose purpose was the establishment of constitutional government. Even at this stage, Arabs were not interested in independence, but only in reforming the Ottoman Empire. And in this respect they were not alone, for many Turks also desired reform.

In 1909, the Young Turks captured Ottoman power, but they were a great disappointment to the people of Syria and to the Arabic-speaking population. Instead of reforming the Empire, they stressed the supremacy of the Turks and began to Turkify the population and the system. This, of course, strengthened national feelings among the Arabs, who began to organize separatist movements. Although until 1918 Arab nationalism was a child of rich landlords and middle-class intelligentsia,[3] it was not a mass movement.

3. George Haddad, *Fifty Years of Modern Syria and Lebanon* (Beirut: Dar-al-Hyat, 1950), p. 39.

Until World War I the Arabs had hesitated to take up arms against the Turks, their co-religionists. But during the war, Jamal Pasha, known to the Arabs as "the executioner," was appointed commander-in-chief of the Ottoman armies in Syria. He purged Arab leaders and earned Arab hatred for Ottoman rule: Arab notables from Damascus, Beirut, Aleppo, Jerusalem, and many other Syrian towns were executed for alleged treason. Jamal had had experience in this kind of work; a few years earlier, he had been one of the organizers of the massacre of the Armenians—one of history's most savage acts.

The Allied powers lost no time in taking advantage of Arab dissatisfaction with the Turks. They encouraged Husain I, the sharif of Mecca, to lead an armed rebellion, making ambiguous promises which Husain understood to include Arab independence and freedom. As we saw in chapter twelve, Britain and France later divided Syria between themselves. Like Lebanon, modern Syria became a French territory to be governed by the mandate agreement that was confirmed by the League of Nations in 1923.

SYRIA UNDER THE FRENCH MANDATE

The Syrian people, who had hoped to gain independence as a reward for fighting on the side of the Allied powers, were extremely disappointed to see their country fall under French rule. On March 8, 1920, a Syrian congress met in Damascus and declared its rejection of the mandate. It proclaimed Husain's son, Faisal, king of "natural Syria," which included Lebanon, Palestine, and Jordan. Of course, the French did not accept the arrangement, and they used force to enter Damascus and establish political control.[4]

Thereafter, the French applied the principle of "divide and rule," which resulted in the dismemberment of Syria. In 1920 Lebanon became a separate political entity, also under French control; it included traditionally Muslim areas, like Tripoli, within its boundaries. Southern Syria went to the British. The remaining portions of Syria were grouped into four states: Jebel Druze, Damascus, Aleppo, and Latakia. In 1925, the French merged Aleppo and Damascus into the state of Syria, but in 1939 they were again given separate administrative autonomy and were not reintegrated into Syria until 1942. Finally, and in violation of the mandate agreement, France gave the Syrian Sanjak of Alexandretta, in the northwest, to Turkey. The Sanjak had a large Turkish minority, but the Arabs were in the majority. France's decision was motivated by her desire to induce Turkey to side with the Allies in World War II.

The Syrians never forgave France for partitioning their country, and in

4. For further details see Zein N. Zein, *The Struggle for Arab Independence* (Beirut: Khayyat's, 1960).

1925 they revolted, led by the Druzes. (France had an easier time governing Lebanon, where the traditional Maronite support was helpful.) The revolution spread out to include all Syrians regardless of their religious background, and it was two years before the French were able to crush it, by bombing Damascus, the capital.

Syria benefited very little from the French mandate. Like Lebanon, she gained no experience in self-rule. Until 1930, the country was without a constitution, a violation of the mandate agreement, which required the promulgation of a constitutional document within three years. Moreover, when the French high commissioner instituted a constitution in May 1930, he did so without consulting native "authorities" as required by the mandate. Nor were there any economic improvements, for both the French and the Syrians were more interested in politics than economics. The French did try to improve education and communication, but they achieved very little in two decades of rule.

In 1938, Syria was put under martial law. Although World War II was somewhat beneficial to Syria economically, the political situation did not improve. When France fell under German military control, the French commissioner in Syria declared his loyalty to the Vichy regime, and Syria was to await the end of the war hoping she could then gain her independence.

The war did not have to end for Syria to gain her independence. On June 8, 1941, British and Free French troops entered the country with the objective of liberating her from Axis domination. On the same day, the French commander of the Levant force declared his intention to proclaim the independence of Syria. The formal proclamation was issued on September 16, and Britain gave it her blessing.

Unfortunately, the declared independence was more fiction than fact. The French, whose troops were still in Syria, did not transfer governmental authority to the Syrians until 1943, and even then they insisted on a new treaty which would give them a privileged position. When the Syrians rejected the proposal, France brought in additional troops, and in May 1945, Damascus was once more bombarded by French artillery and aircraft. Only British intervention and world opinion, expressed by the delegates assembled in San Francisco to prepare the United Nations Charter, were able to save Syria. On April 12, 1945 France and Syria became members of the United Nations. On April 17, 1946 French troops evacuated Syria.

THE POWER STRUGGLE: THE MILITARY

Between 1946 and 1949, Syria was led by a group of conservative nationalists whose political education was primarily French and Ottoman and whose political experience was limited to opposing and resisting foreign domination and interference. Once in power, they proved incapable of governing the country, and it was soon evident that more efficient leadership was needed. The Arab-Israeli war of 1948 further exposed the ineptness of the conservatives, so that at the beginning of 1949, a political vacuum existed.

Unfortunately, there was not a single political group in Syria capable of filling the vacuum. The more progressive political parties were not yet strong enough to assume governmental responsibilities, and consequently the army took over the government in March 1949.

This takeover initiated a new era of army involvement in Syrian political life. Between 1949 and 1958, when Syria merged with Egypt in the United Arab Republic, five coups d'état took place. The first was led by Colonel Husni al-Za'im, but his regime lasted only five months. Its failure was due mainly to Za'im's pro-French and pro-Egypt inclinations, his clumsy attempts to develop a cult of personality, and his betrayal of Antun Saadeh, the leader of the Syrian social nationalists whom he surrendered to the Lebanese authorities.

The second coup d'état, led by Colonel Sami Hinnawi, a conservative and pro-Iraqi officer, was also short-lived. Hinnawi, a puppet of the old conservative politicians, tried to help them regain influence and was overthrown in December 1949 by a coalition of army officers under Colonel Adib Shishakli and politicians led by the Socialist leader Akram Hourani. This third coup introduced the longest one-man regime in Syria's postwar history. Colonel Shishakli became the strong man, although he remained in the background, and in December 1951, he engineered still another coup and got rid of the civilian government he had helped to establish. This fourth coup established a military dictatorship with Shishakli temporarily running the government from behind the scenes. In July 1953, a new constitution went into effect, and Shishakli was elected president of the republic.

Shishakli's long tenure did not result from any outstanding political ideas or reforming spirit.[5] The length of his rule is explained by the fact that Syrian agriculture prospered during this time and by the fact that he was able to unite the army behind him at least in the first two years of his rule. His predecessors had neglected the army, whereas Shishakli tried to modernize it. Also unlike his predecessors, he saw the need for a political organization to establish contact with the masses of the people and created the Arab Liberation Movement for that purpose. This party ran candidates in the parliamentary elections of July 1953, winning seventy-two of eighty-

5. Patrick Seale, *The Struggle for Syria, A Study of Post-War Arab Politics 1945–1958* (London: Oxford University Press, 1965), p. 130.

two seats, thereby giving the regime a façade of legitimacy and democracy.

But even a Shishakli had to fall, for the Syrians are politically unstable, not because of their nature, but because ever since the partitioning of their country, their goals and aspirations have been greater than their economic and military capabilities. The resulting disappointment and frustration has fostered instability.

In Syria's fifth postwar coup, Shishakli was brought down by army units in the northern cities. These units, aroused by politicians like former President Hashim al-Atasi and Akram Hourani, received assistance from the Druzes, who had suffered under the Shishakli regime. It is also possible that Iraq, angered by Shishakli's pro-Egypt policy, extended financial aid to the insurgents. Although Damascus was not affected by these developments in the north, Shishakli would have had to risk civil war to stay in power. He preferred to leave the country, and his regime came to an end in February 1954.

After the coup, the country gradually returned to the old political order. Shukri al-Kuwatly, who was president before the first coup, returned to the presidency in August 1955. In the following two years, Syria's international and domestic positions deteriorated: the Baghdad Pact (1955) and the Suez crisis (1956) were important factors in Syria's drift toward an anti-Western foreign policy. Internally, there was an alignment between the Communists and the Arab nationalists—an alignment which threatened to subvert the al-Kuwatly regime. By the end of 1957 the Arab nationalists saw the dangerous implications of this alliance and decided that the only alternative to Communist takeover was merger of Syria with Nasser's Egypt. The result was the establishment of the United Arab Republic in February 1958.

THE POWER STRUGGLE: POLITICAL PARTIES

Unlike the political parties of Lebanon, whose role is usually limited to nongovernmental political activity, Syrian parties, like the Syrian army, try to capture power and control government. In fact, they often try to control the army to assure their control of the government.

Syria has had a number of traditionalist parties like the People's (al-Shaab) party and the National (al-Watani) party, both going back to the mandate period. These parties, however, became more or less obsolete after the first military coup of 1949, and in recent years it is the doctrinal parties that have become important. True, the traditionalist parties became temporarily active after the downfall of Shishakli and also after the dissolution of the United Arab Republic in 1961, but they could no longer attract the masses of the people.

The doctrinal parties are the Syrian Social Nationalist party (P.P.S.), the Communist party, and the Baath party. The doctrines of the three are radically different. The P.P.S. believes in Syrian nationalism and political unity for the Fertile Crescent; the Baathists believe in Arab nationalism and an Arab unity; and the Communists believe in the well-known Marxist concept of an international socialist order. Although Communist ideology is antinationalist, for tactical reasons the Communists have pursued nationalistic policies, which have enabled them to increase their influence. Their leader, Khalid Bukdash, was among the prominent leaders of the post-Shishakli period, and his star looms on the political horizon whenever Soviet influence in Syria increases.

The Baath party is Socialist, but its socialism differs from the Marxist type in that it does not accept the theory of the class struggle and in that it is concerned with the Arab World only.[6] Furthermore, the socialism of the Baath party is intellectually inferior to that of Marxism and to some of the well-known Socialist theories of Europe. The program of the party is extremely ambitious: it aims at the establishment of a single Arab state to include all of the Arab countries. In practice, the party has been a failure in the sense that it has contributed very little to the Arab unification process. Although it was among the groups which in 1958 favored unity with Egypt, it was also among the groups which in 1961 caused the separation of the two countries. Thus, like Nasser, the Baath party made Arab unity conditional upon the power structure prevalent in the Arab countries. It failed to give absolute priority to the principle of Arab unity.

The party's political fortunes began to rise in 1954, just before the overthrow of the Shishakli regime, when Akram Hourani merged his Arab Socialist party with the Baath. Prior to the merger, the Baath party lacked effective and attractive leadership, for its founder, Michael Aflaq, who was interested in ideological matters, did not have the qualities of a dynamic politician. His first lieutenant, Salah Bitar, was even less qualified. It was Hourani, a practical politician rather than an ideological leader, who provided the party with the flexibility it lacked.

There was, however, one main obstacle before the Baath party in its reach toward power. The Syrian Social Nationalist party opposed it on every political front. Even in the Syrian army, the P.P.S. organized against the Baath as well as for its own fortune. For a brief period, the P.P.S. had

6. For more details on the Baath party see Kamel S. Abu Jaber, *The Arab Ba'th Socialist Party: History, Ideology, and Organization* (Syracuse: Syracuse University Press, 1966).

a strong ally in Shishakli, who was a member of the party; but when Shishakli began to pursue a pro-Egypt policy, he formed his own party. The struggle between the Baath and the P.P.S. continued until 1955, when a member of the P.P.S. assassinated Colonel Adnan Maliki, a Baath supporter. It was the P.P.S.'s biggest mistake. The government arrested many of its leaders and purged the army of its followers. After that, the Baath had very little difficulty moving toward a position of power.

During Syria's partnership with Egypt (1958–61), two Baath leaders, Hourani and Bitar, held the position of vice-president. When the partnership was dissolved, the Baath party was openly anti-Nasser, but it continued to advocate Arab unity and in May 1962 called for a federal union with Egypt. The federalist principle was injected to limit Nasser's control over Syria. But the Syrian government, which was not yet under Baathist control, resented the party's propaganda attacks on it and limited its activity.

But Baathist propaganda and organization were very effective. On February 8, 1963, the party toppled the Kassem regime in Iraq, and a month later it overthrew the Syrian government in a military coup headed by Major-General Atasi. With the party now in control of both Arab countries, the possibility of uniting them seemed strong. However, the Baath party itself became divided on the general question of Arab unity. Some Baathists opposed merging with Egypt; others favored it strongly. Furthermore, in November 1963, a coup d'état in Iraq swept away the Baathist regime, so that hope for unity with either Iraq or Egypt was destroyed.

Intraparty factional rivalries continued. In October 1964, General Amin Hafiz replaced Bitar as prime minister, in addition to being head of state, a position he had held since July 1963. Hafiz became the strong man of Syria. Although he was a Baathist, his regime was less ideological than that of Bitar and Aflaq. But in spite of Hafiz' forceful rule, party extremists continued to challenge the official leadership, which still included Aflaq, Bitar, and Hafiz (but not Hourani, who was expelled from the party in 1961). And in February 1966, they were able to engineer a successful coup d'état, which brought to power a collective leadership consisting of General Salah Jedid as chief of staff, Nuri Atasi as head of state, and Yusuf Zeayen as prime minister. Accusing Aflaq, Bitar, and Hafiz of betraying Baathist principles, the collective leadership began a career which verged on totalitarianism. Domestically and internationally, the new Baathist regime pursued extremist policies. In 1967, it attempted to challenge Nasser's leadership of the Arab world, and as a result it precipitated the Aqaba crisis, which led to the Arab-Israeli war in June 1967. Syria is the most determined of Israel's Arab enemies. Although defeated along with Egypt and Jordan in the 1967 war, Syria was already preparing for another war in the first months of 1968. Consequently, it moved further to the left in its international posture. Internally, it tightened control over society and accepted the Communist party of Syria as its political ally.

THE POWER STRUGGLE: SOCIAL DIVISION

The majority of Syria's population is Sunnite Muslim, but as in Lebanon, there is a great degree of social diversity. Earlier in this chapter we saw how France fragmented Syrian society along racial, ethnic, and religious lines, and exploited these divisions for her own benefit. In the end this policy failed, but it has left its marks on Syria's recent history. Let us, therefore, identify the minorities of Syria and comment on their political roles.[7]

The most important minority is the Druzes, whose brethren in Lebanon we have mentioned. They are concentrated in the southeast in an area known as Jebel (mountain) Druze. The Druzes are a warlike people, with a long history of rebellion against any external authority that attempted to interfere in their community life. In 1925, they revolted against the French, and their revolution developed into a national resistance movement which included all Syrians regardless of religious or ethnic background. And in 1954, they led the revolt against the Shishakli regime and were punished severely by the dictator. In 1964, a Druze revenged his people by assassinating Shishakli in Brazil, where he had been living since 1960. Thus, the Druzes have shown a strong desire for political autonomy. Within the community, however, their organization is feudal. The well-known Atrash family heads the community and has long represented it on the national political scene.

Although the Druzes have played an important role in Syrian politics, being a political force every Syrian regime must recognize and respect, they have not sought a separate sovereign existence. As long as they are free to manage their own local affairs, they are content to be part of Syria, and they identify themselves with the Arab national movement. Occasionally, however, they have influenced the national power structure.

Next to the Druzes in importance are the Alawis. These people inhabit the Latakia region in northwestern Syria, where they constitute a majority. At the beginning of the mandate period, the French established the state of Latakia in recognition of their minority status. But the Alawis, like the Druzes, have had no persistent desire to separate from the rest of Syria. They also identify themselves with the Arab nationalist movement.

The Alawis constitute a division of Shi'ite Muslims. They have a distinctive subculture, which over the years they have tried to preserve. The Alawi

7. A brief but useful analysis of Syrian minorities is found in Don Peretz' *The Middle East Today* (New York: Holt, Rinehart & Winston, 1965), pp. 342–52.

region, which is mountainous, has enabled them to live in semi-isolation from the rest of Syria, and this has been a factor in the continuation of their local identity. It must be stressed, however, that the Alawis have not envisaged a political identity separate from that of the whole country, although they are important in the power structure of Syria.

Other minorities in Syria include the various Christian sects and the non-Arabic-speaking groups. Most Arabic-speaking Christians are fully assimilated into the Arab way of life. The veteran politician Faris al-Khuri, who has been prime minister more than once, is a Christian. But the non-Arabic-speaking groups have not been so assimilated. The Armenians, for instance, who are located largely in the Aleppo area, have kept their own language, customs, and traditions.

More important, however, are the Kurds, who number about a quarter of a million and live mostly in the Jezira region. Although the Syrian Kurds have not shown the same separatist political inclinations as their brethren in Iraq, Turkey, and Iran, they have been susceptible to external political influences. In 1936, they insisted on political autonomy and better representation in the government. A year later, they revolted, but the revolt was quelled by the French, who used the occasion to argue against Arab demands for the establishment of a single government for all of Syria. After Syria gained independence, however, the Kurds began to enter the mainstream of political life. Today, their role in national politics is more regional than ethnic.

Although the Syrian minorities do not threaten the country's political unity, they do place some limitations on that unity. Political centralization is resisted, and efforts to modernize the country usually come into conflict with different but established customs and traditions. Furthermore, social division is complicated by the fact that it has a direct relationship with regional division. If the minorities did not live in specific geographical regions, their influence would not have been so divisive.

THE ECONOMY

Syria's basic and traditional occupation is agriculture, although the majority of the people live in urban areas. Manufacturing is relatively new, but has already become important. Its contribution to the national income may have reached half the contribution of agriculture in 1966.[8]

In many ways, Syria's economic future appears better than that of many of its Arab neighbors, especially Jordan and Lebanon. Unlike Egypt, Syrian agriculture does not depend on one crop. Unlike Lebanon, there is

8. For more details on Syria's economy see *The Middle East and North Africa, 1966–67* (London: Europa Publications, 1966), pp. 631–38.

more land available for cultivation—over one-third of the total land area. Although presently only about one-seventh of the land area is cultivated, Syria is making plans to exploit the remaining cultivable land.

The most outstanding progress made in agriculture has been the large-scale production of cotton. This was stimulated by the high price of cotton after World War II and by the dissatisfaction of foreign manufacturers with Egyptian cotton in the 1950's. Cotton was one of the few agricultural products that received strong governmental attention and encouragement: in fact, this was Shishakli's major contribution to economic improvement. In recent years, raw cotton has become an important export item.

Other agricultural products, some of them exportable, include wheat, which Jordan and Lebanon usually buy. Of course, climate as well as political conditions have a great impact upon the value of Syria's exports, which are mainly agricultural products.

Another factor that has affected Syrian agriculture is the government's socialistic program, introduced in 1961 and strengthened in 1965 and 1968. In 1961, the economic dislocation resulting from the government's nationalization program was one of the reasons for the dissolution of the United Arab Republic. Agricultural policy is also a factor in domestic politics. Land reforms introduced in 1958 and thereafter have angered Syria's landed aristocracy, which had been in power before the first military coup in 1949. Occasionally, this group attempts to regain political influence, thereby threatening the continuity of economic policy.

There are limitations upon industrial progress, owing to a scarcity of minerals of commercial value and other raw materials. However, these limitations have not prevented the development of certain types of manufacturing industries, and in the 1950's oil was discovered in commercial quantities in the northwest. For several years, foreign companies solicited oil concessions, but the government procrastinated until 1964, when it decided to grant concessions to a government-owned agency, the General Petroleum Authority.

Syria receives transit dues from two international pipelines which cross her territory. One of these connects the oil installations at Kirkuk in Iraq to a point near the Syrian city of Homs, where the line branches northwest to Banias in Syria and southwest to Tripoli in Lebanon. The second line connects ARAMCO's installations in Saudi Arabia with Sidon in Lebanon, crossing one hundred miles of Syrian territory. Occasionally, the two pipelines create political problems between Syria on the one hand and Iraq, Saudi Arabia, and Lebanon on the other. For example, Syria closed the two lines after the Arab-Israeli war of 1967 to keep the oil from Western markets, specifically from countries sympathetic to Israel.

As mentioned earlier, Syria's economic future is promising. However, political instability has long been a major obstacle to effective planning. Each new regime has brought a new economic approach and a different economic philosophy, and no one regime has lasted long enough to effect its plan. Syrian socialism, introduced by Nasser in 1961 and continued by the Baathist regime, requires even greater political stability than a free economy. Being government-controlled, the economic program is naturally sensitive to governmental change. Furthermore, instability has made it difficult for the government to acquire the knowhow needed to implement its plans. What knowhow Syria does possess is private, and this makes it vital that the government have the cooperation of qualified private citizens. The instability of Syrian politics has made such cooperation extremely difficult.

Military priorities have also affected development. The Arab desire to fight Israel has been given first priority in governmental planning, and this has prevented effective development resources. The problem of priorities, however, is now common to Israel, Egypt, Iraq, and Jordan; and in all of these countries economic development has been overshadowed by defense requirements.

FOREIGN AFFAIRS

Three elements have characterized Syria's international relations since World War II: her anti-Western inclination; her desire to achieve an Arab political unity; and her partnership with the Soviet Union—a partnership that has become a source of discomfort to the United States and her allies in Europe and the Middle East. It is important to remember that Syria did not become pro-Soviet until she was unable to resolve her differences with the West. And she did not become very closely identified with the Communist bloc until she began to feel frustrated and disappointed with the failure of her Arab unity policy.

Syria and the West. The partition of Syria by Britain and France after World War I, the support given by the Western countries to the Zionist movement between the two world wars, and the creation of the State of Israel in 1948 were all factors in the anti-Western attitudes of Syrians, which in the 1950's and 1960's took the form of active opposition to Western influence in the Arab Middle East.

In the view of Syrian leaders, the Western powers, first France and Britain, and then the United States, consistently ignored Arab interests and aspirations. The United States, they argue, has supported Israel and ignored Arab rights and interests because of domestic Jewish influence. Furthermore, Syrians believe that the United States wants Arab friendship only to use it against the Soviet Union and to stop Communist influence in the Middle East. This policy, they argue, assumes that the Soviet Union and communism must not only be inimical to United States interests but also to the interests of the Arabs and everyone else. They believe that such assumptions are erroneous if not ridiculous, since their first enemy is Israel. The Soviet Union had little contact with the Arab Middle East before World War II. It was, according to the Syrians, the Western powers which had a long history of domination in the Arab world. Why, then, should they suspect or fear the Soviet Union? Would it not make more sense to eye the West with suspicion and doubt?

This Syrian argument, although it seems logical, ignores the real objectives of communism, which are definitely imperialistic. However, some aspects of Syria's anti-Western inclinations and policies are understandable. The Syrian people were exploited by Western occupying nations, and Western countries pursued a policy of political fragmentation in the Fertile Crescent—one which paid slight attention to the economic well-being and social unity of the area.

Syria's anti-Western policy was not formulated until the establishment of the Baghdad Pact in 1955. Before then, anti-Westernism was no more than an attitude, a state of mind. In 1955, however, Syria joined Egypt in attacking the pact, and in October 1955 the two countries signed a military agreement providing for the creation of a joint command. In 1956, Syria's anti-Westernism was intensified by the Suez crisis: the government declared a state of emergency, and troops stopped the flow of oil to the Mediterranean by damaging the pipelines on Syrian territory. And when the Eisenhower Doctrine was announced early in 1957, the Syrian government refused to talk to a personal emissary of President Eisenhower and declared that it would resist the enforcement of the doctrine, which it viewed as designed to disrupt Arab unity. American intervention in the Lebanese civil war the following year convinced Syria that the United States was determined to preserve the political *status quo* in the Arab Middle East and that the United States had become opposed to the aims of the Arab nationalist movement. The passage of time saw a continuing deterioration of Syrian-United States relations. In 1967, the tension between the two countries was climaxed by the Arab-Israeli war: Syria was angered by what she considered an American-Israeli conspiracy aiming at the destruction of Arab nationalism and the expansion of Israeli territory. As a result of the war, relations between Syria and the United States reached their lowest point, and the year 1969 showed no hope of early improvement. It is quite possible that the West has permanently lost its influence in Syria.

Syria and the Arab World. Syria has always been the center of the Arab nationalist movement. In the latter part of the nineteenth century, this movement received its inspiration from the literary works of Lebanese Christian writers and journalists. Early in the twentieth century, the movement took political form, and it culminated in the Arab revolt of 1916. Although Husain I of the Hijaz was the leader of the revolt, it was the Syrian Arab nationalists who organized it and inspired it. From 1916 until World War II, Syrian Arab nationalists were active in opposing the mandate systems of France and Britain, not only in Syria but also in Palestine and Iraq. Their main goal was the independence of the Fertile Crescent countries.

After the war, many of the Arab countries became independent, either in fact, as in the case of Syria, or in name, as in the case of Jordan, Egypt, and Iraq. In response to these developments, the Arab nationalists of Syria gradually began to emphasize the need for the political unification of the Arab countries. They also continued to resist foreign interference in the Arab countries. This, of course, irritated the pro-Western regimes in Iraq and Jordan. Until 1958, when the Iraqi monarch was toppled, both Iraq and Jordan attempted on occasion to instigate revolutions and military coups in Syria. They wanted a Syrian government which would stop anti-Hashimite propaganda and pursue a more conciliatory policy toward themselves. In some instances, they desired the absorption of Syria by their states. King Abdullah of Jordan, for example, entertained the idea of a "Greater Syria" under Hashimite rule. And Iraq under Nuri Said and the crown prince was also involved in bringing about the merger of Syria with Iraq.

Arab rivalries involving Syria were sharpened by the rise of Nasser in Egypt. In 1955 and after, Nasser's image in the Arab world was strong, and Egypt became the leader of the nationalist Arab forces. The conservative forces included mainly the monarchical and pro-Western states. Syria aligned herself with Egypt, and although she continued to be the spiritual leader of the Arab unity movement, actual leadership was provided by Nasser. In 1958, the two countries merged; what had been a political alliance became a political partnership.

We have mentioned the United Arab Republic several times in previous pages. In 1961, the United Arab Republic came to an end, and with the break the rivalries between Syria and Egypt began. After 1963, the Baath party led the opposition to Nasser's leadership to the Arab world. Then, for a brief period, Iraq entertained the idea of unity with Syria. Neither Iraq nor Syria excluded the possibility of partnership with Egypt. In fact, a plan for federating the three countries was agreed upon in 1963. Soon, however, continued rivalries between the Baath party and Nasser destroyed hope for the implementation of the agreement.

In the next three years, the Baath party was busy with its internal problems; rivalries among its factions disrupted any efforts toward Arab unity. In Iraq, the regime became exceedingly anti-Baath and pro-Egypt. The problem of Arab unity remained.

Of course, Arab-Israeli feuds played a significant role in all of these developments. Although all the Arab countries opposed the State of Israel, their opposition varied in intensity and form. Syria took the strongest stand, advocating the use of force to destroy Israel. In 1967, the Baathist regime in Syria began an anti-Nasser campaign, accusing him of being "soft" on Israel. Perhaps in an effort to reassert his leadership in the Arab world, Nasser in May 1967 decided to blockade the Gulf of Aqaba. The resulting Arab defeat culminated in an extremist Arab policy on the part of Syria, whose president refused to attend the Arab Summit Conference meeting in Khartoum in September 1967. The Syrian government wanted the other Arab states to organize guerrilla warfare against Israel. Nasser took the position that such a war was impractical because it could not bring any substantial benefits to the Arabs. Since then, Syria has closed her doors to the outside world and has been determined to have another war with Israel.

Syria and the Soviet Union. In reacting to Western imperialism, Arab nationalism became characterized by negativism: protest was one of its functions. When it became difficult for it to limit Western political influence in the area (exemplified by the Baghdad Pact and the Suez crisis) it turned to the Soviet Union for support. Egyptian leadership cooperated with the Soviet state, although not with the Egyptian Communist party. In Syria, the cooperation went beyond the relations of governments and included relations between the Baath party and the Syrian Communist party. This is one of the reasons that, of all the Arab countries, Syria is the most vulnerable to Communist subversion.

But Arab nationalism has a positive element also. It desires to unite the Arab countries under one state. In pursuing this objective, Syria was unsuccessful, and her frustration has made her more anti-Western. The disappointment has been so great that Syria began to develop what one might call suicidal tendencies—a policy of extremism in which she acts out of anger and frustration rather than out of national interest and rational planning. And the more frustrated Syria becomes through failing to accomplish national goals (Arab unity, the destruction of Israel, and the assertion of Arab independence), the closer she is to becoming a Communist regime. Of course, United States commitments to the State of Israel have made it difficult for the United States to lessen Syria's dependence upon the Soviet Union. Consequently, Syria's drift to the left continues, and her vulnerability increases.

Syria's relations with the Soviet Union have gone through two stages of cooperative efforts. The growth of Soviet influence in Syria between 1954 and 1957 was caused by Syria's reaction to the Baghdad Pact, the Suez crisis, and the Eisenhower Doctrine—a reaction which was manifested by

Syria's opposition to Western interference and influence in Arab affairs. During that period, Syria accepted Soviet arms, recognized the Communist regime in China, and signed a number of trade agreements with the Soviet Union and other Communist countries. Economically, Syria became exceedingly dependent on the Communist bloc. In October 1957, she concluded a twelve-year economic and technical-aid pact with the Soviet Union. By the end of the year, the United States and Turkey had become alarmed at the growth of Communist influence in Syria, and Turkey had concentrated her troops on the Syrian border. An international crisis would have developed had it not been for Syria's decision to merge with Egypt in the United Arab Republic. Nasser, as the head of the new state, took measures to limit Communist influence in Syria. He banned the Communist party, although he continued to cooperate with the Soviet Union.

The second stage began after the coup d'état of February 1966, which brought the extremists in the Baath party to power. Khalid Bukdash, the secretary-general of the Syrian Communist party, returned to Damascus, the capital, in April 1966. He had been residing in eastern Europe since 1958, when Syria and Egypt were merged. His return marked a second era of cooperation between communism and Arab nationalism.

This time, however, the cooperation was of a slightly different nature than that between 1954 and 1957. The Arab-Israeli war of 1967 caused Syria to move further to the left. It compelled her to rely more on Soviet technicians and weaponry to prepare for another clash with Israel. The implications for the West and for both Syria and the Soviet Union were great. In the first few months of 1968, there were indications that Syria's determination to go to war with Israel was unchangeable. On the other hand, the Soviet Union seemed apprehensive, for although the Soviet Union sided with Syria against Israel, she did not want a war which might damage Soviet prestige as did the June 1967 war.

There was also the question regarding the real intentions of the Soviet Union. Was the Soviet Union really serious about helping Syria destroy Israel? If so, was she prepared to go to war to achieve such objective? If not, did she hope to benefit from another Syrian defeat? These questions remain unanswered, and only the future can provide the answer. In the meantime, Syria is not free of the danger of communism.

CONCLUSION

Syria is the political center of the Arab national movement and embodies both the ideals and the weaknesses of that movement. Proud of her heritage, Syria always yearns to return to her glorious past. Frustrated by the numerous problems which prevented her from attaining her goals, she has become politically unstable. Her politics is bitter and turbulent, and her future is uncertain. In short, Syria is like a mother who has lost her children: while she searches in desperation she is afraid of dying before she can see them.

Because Syria is preoccupied with the problems of Israel and of Arab unity, she pays little attention to her economic and social welfare. She is so anxious to attain her goals she has forgotten herself. Although this might seem an abstraction, the description, nevertheless, fits Syria's condition. Consequently, one might say Syria is sacrificing her own happiness to attain her two goals: the elimination of Israel and the establishment of an Arab union. To the Western man Syria is "sick," to many Arabs she is the embodiment of "Arab virtues."

Syria's dilemma lies in not being able to realize that the means are very often just as important as the goals. In the case of Syria, the goals are unattainable without the correct means, which should include political stability and economic power.

Whether Syria will perish in the heat created by her restlessness or be able to achieve her ambitious goals remains to be seen. We can be sure of one thing, however: whatever happens to her will have an impact upon the Arab world. The Arab national movement will perish if Syria perishes. If Syria succeeds, the Arab world will be a different world.

BIBLIOGRAPHY

General

Antonius, George, *The Arab Awakening* (New York, London: Hamish Hamilton, 1938).

Asad, Muhammad, *The Principles of State and Government in Islam* (Berkeley, California: University of California Press, 1961).

Atiyah, Edward, *The Arabs* (London: Penguin Books, 1955).

Badeau, John S., *The American Approach to the Arab World* (New York: Harper & Row, 1968).

Berger, Morroe, *The Arab World Today* (Garden City, New York: Doubleday, 1962).

Berger, Rabbi Elmer, *Who Knows Better Must Say So!* (New York: American Council for Judaism, 1955).

Bonné, Alfred, *The Economic Development of the Middle East* (London: Kegan Paul, Trench, Trubner and Co., 1945).

Bonné, Alfred, *State and Economics in the Middle East: A Society in Transition,* rev. ed. (London: Routledge & Kegan Paul, 1955).

Boutros-Ghali, B.Y., *The Arab League, 1945–1955,* International Conciliation, no. 498. (New York: Carnegie Endowment for International Peace, 1955).

Brooks, Michael, *Oil and Foreign Policy* (London: Lawrence & Wishart, 1949).

Bullard, Sir Reader, *Britain and the Middle East* (New York: Longmans, Green, 1963).

Bustani, Emile, *March Arabesque* (London: Robert Hale, 1961).

Campbell, John C., *Defense of the Middle East,* 2nd ed. (New York: Frederick A. Praeger, 1960).

Cumming, Henry H., *Franco-British Rivalry in the Post-War Near East* (New York: Oxford University Press, 1938).

Davis, Helen Miller, ed., *Constitutions, Electoral Laws, Treaties of States in the Near and Middle East,* 2nd ed. (Durham, North Carolina: Duke University Press, 1953).

Edmonds, C.J., *Kurds, Turks, and Arabs* (London: Oxford University Press, 1957).

Ellis, Harry B., *Challenge in the Middle East* (New York: Ronald Press, 1960).

Ellis, Harry B., *Heritage of the Desert: The Arabs and the Middle East* (New York: Ronald Press, 1956).

Faris, N.A., and Husayn, M.T., *The Crescent in Crisis: An Interpretive Study of the Modern Arab World* (Lawrence, Kansas: University of Kansas Press, 1955).

322 BIBLIOGRAPHY

Fisher, Sydney N., *The Middle East: A History* (New York: Alfred A. Knopf, 1968).

Fisher, Sydney N., ed., *The Military in the Middle East: Problems in Society and Government* (Columbus, Ohio: Ohio State University Press, 1963).

Fisher, Sydney N., ed., *Social Forces in the Middle East* (Ithaca, New York: Cornell University Press, 1955).

Frye, Richard N., ed., *The Near East and the Great Powers* (Cambridge, Massachusetts: Harvard University Press, 1951).

Gibb, Hamilton A.R., *Mohammedanism, An Historical Survey* (New York: Oxford University Press, 1962).

Guillaume, Alfred, *The Life of Muhammad* (London: Oxford University Press, 1955).

Haddad, George Meri, *Revolutions and Military Rule in the Middle East* (New York: Robert Speller & Sons, 1965).

Halpern, Manfred, *The Politics of Social Change in the Middle East and North Africa* (Princeton, New Jersey: Princeton University Press, 1963).

Hitti, Philip K., *The Arabs: A Short History* (Princeton, New Jersey: Princeton University Press, 1956).

Hitti, Philip K., *Makers of Arab History* (New York: St. Martin's Press, 1968).

Hoskins, Halford L., *The Middle East Oil and United States Foreign Policy* (Washington, D.C.: Library of Congress, 1950).

Hoskins, Halford L., *The Middle East: A Problem Area in World Politics* (New York: Macmillan, 1954).

Hourani, Albert H., *Minorities in the Arab World* (New York: Oxford University Press, 1947).

Hurewitz, J.C., ed., *Diplomacy in the Near and Middle East, A Documentary Record,* 2 v. (Princeton, New Jersey: Van Nostrand, 1956).

Hurewitz, J.C., *Middle East Dilemmas* (New York: Harper & Brothers, 1953).

Ionides, Michael, *Divide and Lose: The Arab Revolt, 1955–1958* (London: Geoffrey Bles, 1960).

Izzeddin, Nejla, *The Arab World: Past, Present, and Future* (Chicago: Regnery, 1953).

Karpat, Kemal H., *Political and Social Thought in the Contemporary Middle East* (New York: Frederick A. Praeger, 1968).

Kedourie, Elie, *England and the Middle East* (London: Bowes and Bowes, 1956).

Kerr, Malcolm H., *The Middle East Conflict* (New York: Foreign Policy Association, 1968).

Kirk, George E., *Contemporary Arab Politics* (New York: Frederick A. Praeger, 1961).

Kirk, George E., *The Middle East in the War* (London: Royal Institute of International Affairs, 1953).

Kirk, George E., *The Middle East, 1945–1950* (New York: Oxford University Press, 1954).

Kirk, George E., *A Short History of the Middle East: From the Rise of Islam to Modern Times,* rev. ed. (New York: Frederick A. Praeger, 1955).

Laqueur, Walter Z., *Communism and Nationalism in the Middle East* (New York: Frederick A. Praeger, 1956).

Laqueur, Walter Z., ed., *The Middle East in Transition* (London: Routledge & Kegan Paul, 1958).

Laqueur, Walter Z., *The Soviet Union and the Middle East* (London: Routledge & Kegan Paul, 1959).

Lawrence, T.E., *Seven Pillars of Wisdom* (New York: Doubleday, 1947).

Lenczowski, George, *The Middle East in World Affairs*, 3rd ed. (Ithaca, New York: Cornell University Press, 1962).

Lenczowski, George, *Oil and State in the Middle East* (Ithaca, New York: Cornell University Press, 1960).

Lerner, Daniel, and Peusner, Lucille W., *The Passing of Traditional Society: Modernizing the Middle East* (Glencoe, Illinois: Free Press, 1958).

Lewis, Bernard, *The Middle East and the West* (Bloomington, Indiana: Indiana University Press, 1964).

Lilienthal, Alfred M., *There Goes the Middle East*, 3rd ed. (New York: Devin-Adair, 1960).

Longrigg, Stephen H., *Oil in the Middle East*, 3rd ed. (New York: Oxford University Press, 1967).

Marlowe, John, *Arab Nationalism and British Imperialism* (New York: Frederick A. Praeger, 1961).

Monroe, Elizabeth, *Britain's Moment in the Middle East* (Baltimore, Maryland: Johns Hopkins Press, 1963).

Nolte, Richard H., ed., *The Modern Middle East* (New York: Atherton Press, 1963).

Nuseibeh, Hazem Zaki, *The Ideas of Arab Nationalism* (Ithaca, New York: Cornell University Press, 1956).

Peretz, Don, *The Middle East Today* (New York: Holt, Rinehart & Winston, 1963).

Roosevelt, Kermit, *Arabs, Oil and History: The Story of the Middle East* (New York: Harper & Brothers, 1949).

Royal Institute of International Affairs, *British Interests in the Mediterranean and Middle East* (London: Oxford University Press, 1958).

Sayegh, Fayez A., *Arab Unity: Hope and Fulfillment* (New York: Devin-Adair, 1958).

Sharabi, Hisham B., *Governments and Politics of the Middle East in the Twentieth Century* (Princeton, New Jersey: Van Nostrand, 1962).

Sharabi, Hisham B., *Nationalism and Revolution in the Arab World* (Princeton, New Jersey: Van Nostrand, 1966).

Shwadran, Benjamin, *The Middle East: Oil and the Great Powers* (New York: Frederick A. Praeger, 1955).

Smith, Wilfred C., *Islam in Modern History* (Princeton, New Jersey: Princeton University Press, 1957).

Spector, Ivar, *The Soviet Union and the Muslim World, 1917–1958* (Seattle, Washington: University of Washington Press, 1959).

Spencer, William, *Political Evolution in the Middle East* (New York: J.B. Lippincott, 1962).

Von Grunebaum, Gustave E., *Modern Islam: The Search for Cultural Identity* (Berkeley, California: University of California Press, 1962).

Yale, William, *The Near East: A Modern History* (Ann Arbor, Michigan: University of Michigan Press, 1968).

Zeine, Zeine N., *The Struggle for Arab Independence* (Beirut, Lebanon: Khayat, 1960).

Egypt

Abdel Malek, Anouar, *Egypt: Military Society* (New York: Random House, 1968).

Ahmed, Jamal Mohammed, *The Intellectual Origins of Egyptian Nationalism* (New York: Oxford University Press, 1960).

Barawy, Rashed, *The Military Coup in Egypt: An Analytical Study* (Cairo: Renaissance Book Shop, 1952).

Barker, A.J., *Suez: The Seven Day War* (New York: Frederick A. Praeger, 1965).

Berger, Morroe, *Bureaucracy and Society in Modern Egypt: A Study of the Higher Civil Service* (Princeton, New Jersey: Princeton University Press, 1957).

Bloomfield, L.M., *Egypt, Israel, and the Gulf of Aqaba in International Law* (Toronto: Carswell, 1957).

Carnegie Endowment for International Peace, *Egypt and the United Nations* (New York: Manhattan, 1957).

Childers, Erskine B., *The Road to Suez: A Study of Western-Arab Relations* (London: MacGibbon & Kee, 1962).

Cromer, Evelyn B., First Earl of, *Modern Egypt* (New York: Macmillan, 1968).

Epstein, Leon D., *British Politics in the Suez Crisis* (Urbana, Illinois: University of Illinois Press, 1964).

Finer, Herman, *Dulles over Suez: The Theory and Practice of His Diplomacy* (Chicago: Quadrangle Books, 1964).

Harris, George L., ed., *Egypt* (New Haven, Connecticut: Human Relations Area Files, 1957).

Holt, P.M., *Egypt and the Fertile Crescent* (London: Longmans, Green, 1966).

Holt, P.M., *Political and Social Change in Modern Egypt* (New York: Oxford University Press, 1967).

Husaini, Ishak Musa, *The Moslem Brethren* (Beirut, Lebanon: Khayat, 1956).

Issawi, Charles, *Egypt at Mid-Century: An Economic Survey* (New York: Oxford University Press, 1954).

Issawi, Charles, *Egypt in Revolution: An Economic Analysis* (New York: Oxford University Press, 1965).

Kardouche, G.S., *The U.A.R. in Development* (New York: Frederick A. Praeger, 1967).

Kerr, Malcolm H., *Egypt Under Nasser* (New York: Foreign Policy Association, 1963).

Lacouture, Jean and Simonne, *Egypt in Transition* (London: Methuen, 1958).

Lauterpacht, E., ed., *The Suez Canal Settlement* (New York: Frederick A. Praeger, 1960).

Little, Tom, *Modern Egypt* (New York: Frederick A. Praeger, 1967).

Longgood, William F., *The Suez Story: Key to the Middle East* (New York: Greenberg, 1957).

Marlowe, John, *A History of Modern Egypt and Anglo-Egyptian Relations, 1800–1953* (London: Cresset Press; New York: Frederick A. Praeger, 1954).

Mead, Donald C., *Growth and Structural Change in the Egyptian Economy* (Homewood, Illinois: Richard D. Irwin, 1967).

Nasser, Gamal Abdel, *Egypt's Liberation: The Philosophy of the Revolutions* (Washington, D.C.: Public Affairs Press, 1955).

Neguib, Mohammed, *Egypt's Destiny* (London: Victor Gollancz; New York: Doubleday, 1955).

Nutting, Anthony, *No End of a Lesson: The Story of Suez* (London: Constable, 1967).

Robertson Terence, *Crisis: The Inside Story of the Suez Conspiracy* (New York: Atheneum, 1965).

Royal Institute of International Affairs, *Great Britain and Egypt, 1914–1951* (London, 1952).

Saad, G.S., *Egyptian Agrarian Reform, 1952–1962* (New York: Oxford University Press, 1966).

Sadat, Col. Anwar El., *Revolt on the Nile* (London: Allen Wingate, 1957).

Safran, Nadav, *Egypt in Search of Political Community: An Analysis of the Intellectual and Political Evolution of Egypt, 1804–1952* (Cambridge, Massachusetts: Harvard University Press, 1961).

Schonfield, Hugh J., *The Suez Canal in World Affairs* (London: Constellation Books, 1952).

Shaw, Stanford J., *Ottoman Egypt in the Eighteenth Century* (Cambridge, Massachusetts: Harvard University Press, 1962).

Stevens, Georgiana G., *Egypt, Yesterday and Today* (New York: Holt, Rinehart & Winston, 1963).

Thomas, Hugh, *The Suez Affair* (London: Weidenfeld and Nicolson, 1967).

Tignor, R.L., *Modernization and British Colonial Rule in Egypt, 1882–1914* (Princeton, New Jersey: Princeton University Press, 1966).

Vatikiotis, P.J., *The Egyptian Army in Politics: Pattern for New Nations?* (Bloomington, Indiana: Indiana University Press, 1961).

Vatikiotis, P.J., *A Modern History of Egypt* (New York: Frederick A. Praeger, 1966).

Waterfield, Gordon, *Egypt* (London: Thames and Hudson, 1967).

Wheelock, Keith, *Nasser's New Egypt: A Critical Analysis* (New York: Frederick A. Praeger, 1960).

Wynn, Wilton, *Nasser of Egypt: The Search for Dignity* (Cambridge, Massachusetts: Arlington Books, 1959).

Zayid, Mahmud Yusuf, *Egypt's Struggle for Independence* (Beirut, Lebanon: Khayat, 1965).

Iran

Avery, Peter, *Modern Iran* (London: Ernest Benn, 1965).

Baldwin, George B., *Planning and Development in Iran* (Baltimore, Maryland: Johns Hopkins Press, 1967).

Banani, Amin, *The Modernization of Iran, 1921–1941* (Stanford, California: Stanford University Press, 1961).

Browne, Edward G., *The Persian Revolution of 1905–1909* (London: Frank Cass, 1966).

Cottam, R.W., *Nationalism in Iran* (Pittsburgh, Pennsylvania: University of Pittsburgh Press, 1964).

Eagleton, William, *The Kurdish Republic of 1946* (London, New York: Oxford University Press, 1963).

Elwell-Sutton, Lawrence P., *Persian Oil: A Study in Power Politics* (London: Lawrence Wishart, 1955).

Fatemi, Nasrollah S., *Diplomatic History of Persia, 1917–1923: Anglo-Russian Power Politics in Iran* (New York: R.F. Moore, 1952).

Fatemi, Nasrollah S., *Oil Diplomacy: Powderkeg in Iran* (New York: Whittier Books, 1954).

Ford, Alan W., *The Anglo-Iranian Oil Dispute of 1951–1952* (Berkeley, California: University of California Press, 1954).

Frye, Richard N., *Iran* (New York: Henry Holt, 1953).

Haas, William S., *Iran* (New York: Columbia University Press, 1946).

Hamzari, A.H., *Persia and the Powers: An Account of Diplomatic Relations, 1941–1946* (London, New York: Hutchinson, 1946).

Jacobs, Norman, *The Sociology of Development: Iran As an Asian Case Study* (New York: Frederick A. Praeger, 1966).

Lenczowski, George, *Russia and the West In Iran, 1918–1948* (Ithaca, New York: Cornell University Press, 1949).

Marlowe, John, *Iran, a Short Political Guide* (New York: Frederick A. Praeger, 1963).

Millspaugh, Arthur C., *Americans in Persia* (Washington, D.C.: Brookings Institution, 1946).

Mohammed Reza Shah Pahlavi, *Mission For My Country* (New York: McGraw-Hill, 1961).

Ramazani, Rouhollah K., *The Foreign Policy of Iran, A Developing Nation in World Affairs, 1500–1941* (Charlottesville, Virginia: University of Virginia Press, 1966).

Ramazani, Rouhollah K., *The Northern Tier: Afghanistan, Iran and Turkey* (Princeton, New Jersey: Van Nostrand, 1966).

Shuster, William M., *The Strangling of Persia* (New York: Century, 1912).

Skrine, Sir Clarmont P., *World War Two in Iran* (London: Constable, 1962).

Sykes, Sir Percy M., *A History of Persia*, 2 v. (London: Macmillan, 1930).

Thomas, Lewis V., and Frye, Richard N., *The United States and Turkey and Iran* (Cambridge, Massachusetts: Harvard University Press, 1951).

Upton, Joseph M., *The History of Modern Iran: An Interpretation* (Cambridge, Massachusetts; Harvard University Press, 1960).

Van Wagenen, Richard W., *The Iranian Case, 1946* (New York: Carnegie Endowment for International Peace, 1952).

Vreeland, Herbert Harold, ed., *Iran* (New Haven, Connecticut: Human Relations Area Files, 1957).

Warne, William E., *Mission for Peace: Point Four in Iran* (Indianapolis, Indiana: Bobbs-Merrill, 1956).

Wilber, Donald N., *Iran: Oasis of Stability in the Middle East?* (New York: Foreign Policy Association, 1959).

Wilber, Donald N., *Iran: Past and Present*, 6th ed. (Princeton, New Jersey: Princeton University Press, 1967).

Iraq

Alnasrawi, Abbas, *Financing Economic Development in Iraq: The Role of Oil in a Middle Eastern Economy* (New York: Frederick A. Praeger, 1967).

Arfa, Hassan, *The Kurds* (London, New York: Oxford University Press, 1966).

Birdwood, Lord, *Nuri as-Said: A Study in Arab Leadership* (London: Cassell, 1959).

Burne, Alfred H., *Mesopotamia: The Last Phase* (Aldershot: Cale, 1936).

Caractacus (pseud.), *Revolution in Iraq* (London: Victor Gollancz, 1958).

Erskine, Beatrice (Strong), *King Faisal of Iraq* (London: Hutchinson, 1933).

Foster, Henry A., *The Making of Modern Iraq* (Norman, Oklahoma: University of Oklahoma Press, 1935).

Gallman, W.J., *Iraq Under General Nuri* (Baltimore, Maryland: Johns Hopkins Press, 1964).

Haldane, Sir Aylmer L., *The Insurrection in Mesopotamia, 1920* (London: William Blackwood & Sons, 1922).

Harris, George L., and others, *Iraq* (New Haven, Connecticut: Human Relations Area Files Press, 1958).

Ireland, Philip W., *Iraq: A Study in Political Development* (London: Jonathan Cape, 1937).

Khadduri Majid, *Independent Iraq from 1932 to 1958* (London: Oxford University Press, 1960).

Langley, Kathleen M., *The Industrialization of Iraq* (Cambridge, Massachusetts: Harvard University Press, 1961).

Lloyd, Seton, *Iraq* (New York: Oxford University Press, 1944).

Longrigg, Stephen H., *Iraq, 1900 to 1950: A Political, Social, and Economic History* (London: Oxford University Press, 1953).

Longrigg, Stephen H., and Stoakes, Frank, *Iraq* (London: Ernest Benn, 1958).

Main, Ernest, *Iraq from Mandate to Independence* (London: George Allen and Unwin, 1935).

Marayati, Abid A. al-, *A Diplomatic History of Modern Iraq* (New York: Robert Speller, 1961).

Qubain, Fahim, *The Reconstruction of Iraq, 1950–1957* (New York: Frederick A. Praeger, 1958).

Schwadran, Benjamin, *The Power Struggle in Iraq* (New York: Council for Middle Eastern Affairs Press, 1960).

Stewart, Desmond, and Haylock, John, *New Babylon: A Portrait of Iraq* (London: William Collins Sons, 1956).

Wilson, Sir Arnold T., *Loyalties: Mesopotamia, 1914–1917* (London: Oxford University Press, 1930).

Wilson, Sir Arnold T., *Mesopotamia, 1917–1920: A Clash of Loyalties* (London: Oxford University Press, 1931).

Israel

Arian, Alan, *Ideological Change in Israel* (Cleveland, Ohio: Press of Case Western Reserve University, 1968).

Badi, Joseph, *The Government of the State of Israel: A Critical Account of its Parliament, Executive, and Judiciary* (New York: Twayne Publishers, 1963).

Balfour, Arthur J., *Speeches on Zionism* (London: Arrowsmith, 1928).

Barbour, Neville, *Palestine: Star or Crescent?* (New York: Odyssey Press, 1947).

Ben-Gurion, David, *Rebirth and Destiny of Israel* (New York: Philosophical Library, 1953).

Ben-Gurion, David, *Israel: Years of Challenge* (New York: Holt, Rinehart & Winston, 1963).

Bentwich, Norman, *Israel* (New York: McGraw-Hill, 1953).

Bentwich, Norman, *Israel Resurgent* (New York: Frederick A. Praeger, 1960).

Berger, Elmer, *Judaism or Jewish Nationalism: The Alternative to Zionism* (New York: Twayne Publishers, 1957).

Bernadotte, Folke, *To Jerusalem* (London: Hodder and Stoughton, 1951).

Bernstein, Marver H., *The Politics of Israel: The First Decade of Statehood* (Princeton, New Jersey: Princeton University Press, 1957).

Bilby, Kenneth W., *New Star in the Near East* (Garden City, New York: Doubleday, 1950).

Brandeis, Louis D., *Brandeis on Zionism* (Washington, D.C.: Zionist Organization of America, 1942).

Carnegie Endowment for International Peace, *Israel and the United Nations* (New York: Manhattan, 1956).

Churchill, Randolph Spencer, *The Six Day War* (Boston: Houghton Mifflin, 1967).

Dickson, Mora, *Israeli Interlude* (London: Dennis Dobson, 1966).

Dunner, Joseph, *The Republic of Israel* (New York: Whittlesey House, 1950).

Edelman, Maurice, *Ben Gurion: A Political Biography* (London: Hodder and Stoughton, 1964).

Ellis, Harry B., *Israel and the Middle East* (New York: Ronald Press, 1957).

Elston, D. R., *Israel: The Making of a Nation* (London, New York: Oxford University Press, 1963).

Eytan, Walter, *The First Ten Years: A Diplomatic History of Israel* (New York: Simon and Schuster, 1958).

Friedrich, Carl J., *American Policy toward Palestine* (Washington, D.C.: Public Affairs Press, 1944).

Halpern, Ben, *The Idea of the Jewish State* (Cambridge, Massachusetts: Harvard University Press, 1961).

Henriques, Robert, *One Hundred Hours to Suez: An Account of Israel's Campaign in the Sinai Peninsula* (London: William Collins Sons, 1957).

Herzl, Theodor, *The Jewish State* (New York: Scopus, 1943).

Horowitz, David, *State in Making* (New York: Alfred A. Knopf, 1953).

Hurewitz, J. C., *The Struggle for Palestine* (New York: W. W. Norton, 1950).

Hutchinson, E. H., *Violent Truce* (New York: Devin-Adair, 1956).

Kimche, Jon and David, *A Clash of Destinies: The Arab-Jewish War and the Founding of the State of Israel* (New York: Frederick A. Praeger, 1960).

Kraines, Oscar, *Government and Politics in Israel* (Boston: Houghton Mifflin, 1961).

Laqueur, Walter Z., *The Road to Jerusalem: the Origins of the Arab-Israeli Conflict, 1967* (New York: Macmillan, 1968).

Laufer, Leopold, *Israel and the Developing Countries: New Approaches to Cooperation* (New York: Twentieth Century Fund, 1967).

Lehrman, Hali, *Israel: The Beginning and Tomorrow* (New York: William Sloan, 1951).

Leonard, L. Larry, *The United Nations and Palestine* (New York: Carnegie Foundation for International Peace, 1949).

Lilienthal, Alfred, *What Price Israel* (Chicago: Regnery, 1953).

Lowenthal, Marvin, ed. and trans., *Diaries of Theodor Herzl* (New York: Grosset and Dunlap, 1965).

Nussbaum, Elizabeth, *Israel* (London: Oxford University Press, 1968).

O'Ballance, Edgar, *The Arab-Israeli War, 1948* (New York: Frederick A. Praeger, 1957).

O'Ballance, Edgar, *The Sinai Campaign, 1956* (London: Faber and Faber, 1959).

Patai, Raphael, *Israel Between East and West* (Philadelphia: Jewish Publication Society of America, 1953).

Pearlman, Lt. Col. Moshe, *The Army of Israel* (New York: Philosophical Library, 1950).

Peretz, Don, *Israel and the Palestine Arabs* (Washington, D.C.: Middle East Institute, 1958).

Polk, William R., Stamler, David M., and Asfour, Edmund, *Backdrop to Tragedy: The Struggle for Palestine* (Boston: Beacon Press, 1957).

Rackman, Emanuel, *Israel's Emerging Constitution, 1948–1951* (New York: Columbia University Press, 1955).

Rubner, Alex, *The Economy of Israel* (New York: Frederick A. Praeger, 1960).

Safarn, Nadav, *The United States and Israel* (Cambridge, Massachusetts: Harvard University Press, 1963).

Sakran, Frank C., *Palestine Dilemma: Arab Rights versus Zionist Aspirations* (Washington, D.C.: Public Affairs Press, 1948).

Sayegh, Fayez A., *The Palestine Refugees* (Washington, D.C.: Amara Press, 1952).

Seligman, Lester G., *Leadership in a New Nation: Political Development in Israel* (New York: Atherton Press, 1964).

Spiro, Milford, *Kibbutz: Venture into Utopia* (Cambridge, Massachusetts: Harvard University Press, 1956).

Stock, Ernest, *Israel on the Road to Sinai, 1949–1956* (Ithaca, New York: Cornell University Press, 1967).

Weizmann, Chaim, *Trial and Error: The Autobiograph of Chaim Weizmann* (New York: Harper & Brothers, 1949).

Jordan

Abdullah, King of Jordan, *My Memoirs Completed,* translated by Harold Glidden (Washington, D.C.: American Council of Learned Societies, 1954).

Dearden, Ann, *Jordan* (London: Robert Hale, 1958).

Glubb, Sir John Bagot, *A Soldier with the Arabs* (New York: Harper & Brothers, 1957).

Glubb, Sir John Bagot, *The Story of the Arab Legion* (London: Hodder and Stoughton, 1948).

Glubb, Sir John Bagot, *Syria, Lebanon, Jordan* (London: Thames and Hudson, 1967).

Graves, Philip, ed., *Memoirs of King Abdullah of Transjordan* (New York: Philosophical Library, 1950).

Harris, George L., ed., *Jordan: Its People, Its Society, Its Culture* (New Haven, Connecticut: Human Relations Area Files Press, 1958).

Hussein, King of Jordan, *Uneasy Lies Ahead* (New York: Bernard Geis Associates, 1962).

International Bank for Reconstruction and Development, *The Economic Development of Jordan* (Baltimore, Maryland: The Johns Hopkins Press, 1957).

Kirkbride, Alec S., *A Crackle of Thorns: Experiences in the Middle East* (London: John Murray, 1956).

Lias, Godfrey, *Glubb's Legion* (London: Evans Brothers, 1956).

Morris, James, *The Hashemite Kings* (New York: Pantheon Books, 1959).

Patai, Raphael, *The Kingdom of Jordan* (Princeton, New Jersey: Princeton University Press, 1958).

Peake, Frederick G., *History and Tribes of Jordan* (Coral Gables, Florida: University of Miami Press, 1958).

Shwadran, Benjamin, *Jordan: A State of Tension* (New York: Council for Middle Eastern Affairs, 1959).

Sparrow, Gerald, *Modern Jordan* (London: George Allen and Unwin, 1961).

Toukan, Baha Uddin, *A Short History of Trans-Jordan* (London: Luzac, 1945).

Vatakiotis, Panayiotis J., *Politics and the Military in Jordan: A Study of the Arab Legion, 1921–1957* (London: Frank Cass, 1967).

Young, Peter, *Bedouin Command: With the Arab Legion, 1953–1956* (London: William Kimber, 1956).

Syria and Lebanon

Asfour, Edmund Y., *Syria: Development and Monetary Policy* (Cambridge, Massachusetts: Harvard University Press, 1959).

Fedden, Henry Romilly, *Syria and Lebanon*, 3rd ed. (London: John Murray, 1965).

Haddad, George, *Fifty Years of Modern Syria and Lebanon* (Beirut, Lebanon: Dar al-Hayat, 1950).

Hitti, Philip K., *History of Syria* (New York: Macmillan, 1951).

Hitti, Philip K., *Lebanon in History from the Earliest Times to the Present* New York: St. Martin's Press, 1967).

Hourani, Albert H., *Syria and Lebanon: A Political Essay* (London: Oxford University Press, 1946).

International Bank for Reconstruction and Development, *The Economic Development of Syria* (Baltimore, Maryland: The Johns Hopkins Press, 1955).

Longrigg, Stephen H., *Syria and Lebanon under French Mandate* (London: Oxford University Press, 1958).

Meo, Leila M., *Lebanon, Improbable Nation: A Study in Political Development* (Bloomington, Indiana: University of Indiana Press, 1965).

Pearse, Richard, *Three Years in the Levant* (London: Macmillan, 1949).

Puryear, Vernon J., *France and the Levant* (Berkeley, California: University of California Press, 1968).

Qubain, Fahim I., *Crisis in Lebanon* (Washington, D.C.: Middle East Institute, 1961).

Salibi, Kemal Suleiman, *The Modern History of Lebanon* (London: Weidenfeld & Nicolson, 1965).

Seale, Patrick, *The Struggle for Syria: A Study of Post-war Arab Politics, 1945–1958* (London, New York: Oxford University Press, 1965).

Stewart, Desmond, *Turmoil in Beirut* (London: Allan Wingate, 1958).

Suleiman, Michael W., *Political Parties in Lebanon: The Challenge of a Fragmented Political Culture* (Ithaca, New York: Cornell University Press, 1967).

Thayer, Charles W., *Diplomat* (New York: Harper & Brothers, 1959).

Torrey, Gordon H., *Syrian Politics and the Military, 1945–1958* (Columbus, Ohio: Ohio University Press, 1964).

Ziadeh, Nicola, *Syria and Lebanon* (London: Ernest Benn, 1957).

Turkey

Alderson, Anthony Dolphin, *The Structure of the Ottoman Dynasty* (Oxford: Clarendon Press, 1956).

Armstrong, Harold C., *Grey Wolf, Mustafa Kemal: An Intimate Study of a Dictator* (New York: Putnam, 1961).

Berkes, Niyazi, *The Development of Secularism in Turkey* (Montreal: McGill University Press, 1964).

Berkes, Niyazi, ed., *Turkish Nationalism and Western Civilization: Selected Essays of Ziya Gökalp* (New York: Columbia University Press, 1951).

Bisbee, Eleanor, *The New Turks: Pioneers of the Republic, 1920–1950* (Philadelphia: University of Pennsylvania Press, 1951).

Carnegie Endowment for International Peace, *Turkey and the UN* (New York: Manhattan, 1961).

Ekrem, Selma, *Turkey: Old and New* (New York: Charles Scribner's Sons, 1947).

Eliot, Sir Charles Norton Edgecumbe, *Turkey in Europe* (London: Frank Cass, 1965).

Eren, Nuri, *Turkey Today and Tomorrow: An Experiment in Westernization* (New York: Frederick A. Praeger, 1963).

Frey, Frederick W., *The Turkish Political Elite* (Cambridge, Massachusetts: M.I.T. Press, 1965).

Heyd, Uriel, *Foundations of Turkish Nationalism: The Life and Teachings of Ziya Gökalp* (London: Harvill Press, 1950).

Hostler, Charles Warren, *Turkism and the Soviets* (London: George Allen and Unwin, 1957).

Howard, Harry N., *The Partition of Turkey* (Norman, Oklahoma: University of Oklahoma Press, 1931).

Johnson, Walter, *Turbulent Era: A Diplomatic Record of Forty Years, 1904–1945* (Boston, Massachusetts: Houghton Mifflin, 1952).

Karpat, Kemal H., *Turkey's Politics: The Transition to a Multiparty System* (Princeton, New Jersey: Princeton University Press, 1959).

Kilic, Altemur, *Turkey and the World* (Washington, D.C.: Public Affairs Press, 1959).

Kinross, Patrick Balfour, Lord, *Within the Taurus* (London: John Murray, 1955).

Kral, August Ritter von, *Kemâl Atatürk's Land: The Evolution of Modern Turkey* (London: King, 1938).

Lewis, Bernard, *The Emergence of Modern Turkey* (London: Oxford University Press, 1961).

Lewis, Geoffrey, *Turkey*, 3rd ed. (New York: Frederick A. Praeger, 1965).

Lingeman, E.R. *Turkey: Economic and Commercial Conditions in Turkey* (London: H.M. Stationery Office, 1948).

Luke, Sir Henry Charles Joseph, *The Making of Modern Turkey* (London: Macmillan, 1936).

Mango, Andrew, *Turkey* (London: Thames and Hudson, 1968).

Mardin, Serif, *The Genesis of Young Ottoman Thought: A Study in the Modernization of Turkish Political Ideas* (Princeton, New Jersey: Princeton University Press, 1962).

Price, Morgan Philips, *A History of Turkey, from Empire to Republic* (London: Hillary; New York: Macmillan, 1961).

Ramsaur, Ernest E., *The Young Turks: Prelude to the Revolution of 1908* (Princeton, New Jersey: Princeton University Press, 1957).

Robinson, Richard D., *The First Turkish Republic: A Case Study in National Development* (Cambridge, Massachusetts: Harvard University Press, 1963).

Spencer, William, *The Land and People of Turkey* (Philadelphia: J. B. Lippincott Co., 1964).

Thornburg, Max, Spry, George, and Soule, George, *Turkey: An Economic Appraisal* (New York: Twentieth Century Fund, 1949).

Toynbee, Arnold J., *The Western Question in Greece and Turkey* (London: Constable, 1922).

Ward, Barbara, *Turkey* (New York: Oxford University Press, 1942).

Webster, Donald E., *Turkey of Atatürk* (Philadelphia: American Academy of Political and Social Science, 1939).

Weiker, Walter F., *The Turkish Revolution, 1960–1961: Aspects of Military Politics* (Washington, D.C.: Brookings Institution, 1963).

Yalman, Ahmed Emin, *Turkey in My Time* (Norman, Oklahoma: University of Oklahoma Press, 1956).

Zenkovsky, Serge A., *Pan-Turkism and Islam in Russia* (Cambridge, Massachusetts: Harvard University Press, 1960).

INDEX

335